Smoking and Society

Toward a More Balanced Assessment

Edited by
Robert D. Tollison
George Mason University

Lexington Books
D.C. Heath and Company/Lexington, Massachusetts/Toronto

Library of Congress Cataloging in Publication Data
Main entry under title:

Smoking and society.

Includes index.
1. Smoking—Social aspects—Addresses, essays, lectures. 2. Tobacco—Economic aspects—Addresses, essays, lectures. 3. Tobacco—Physiological effect—Addresses, essays, lectures. 4. Smoking—Government policy—Addresses, essays, lectures. I. Tollison, Robert D.
HV5735.S66   1985   362.2′ 9   85-18070
ISBN 0-669-11603-3 (alk. paper)

5D, 85%

Published simultaneously in Canada
Printed in the United States of America
Casebound International Standard Book Number: 0-669-11603-3
Library of Congress Catalog Card Number: 85-18070

The paper used in this publication meets the minimum requirements of American National Standard for Information Sciences—Permanence of Paper for Printed Library Materials, ANSI Z39.48-1984.
∞

Contents

List of Figures   vii

List of Tables   ix

Preface   xiii

Part I   Introduction   1

1. Smoking: Toward a More Balanced Assessment   3
   Robert D. Tollison

Part II   Smoking: The Context of the Individual   15

2. Smoking and Health   17
   Hans J. Eysenck

3. Psychological Determinants of Smoking Behavior   89
   Charles D. Spielberger

Part III   Smoking: The Context of Society   135

4. Health Issues Relating to "Passive" Smoking   137
   Domingo M. Aviado, M.D.

5. The Social Role of Smoking   167
   Sherwin J. Feinhandler

6. Smoking, Human Rights, and Civil Liberties   189
   Douglas J. Den Uyl

7. Smokers versus Nonsmokers   217
  William F. Shughart II and Robert D. Tollison

8. A Sociological View of the Antismoking Phenomenon   225
  Peter L. Berger

Part IV   Smoking: The Context of the Economy   241

9. The Economic Contribution of the Tobacco Industry to
   the Aggregate Economy   243
   H. Peter Gray and Ingo Walter

10. Smoking and Market Failure   271
   Stephen C. Littlechild

11. The Incidence of Taxes on Tobacco   285
   James M. Savarese and William F. Shughart II

12. Tobacco Advertising in a Free Society   309
   J.J. Boddewyn

Part V   Final Perspective   333

13. Politics and Meddlesome Preferences   335
   James M. Buchanan

14. Concluding Remarks   343
   Robert D. Tollison

Author Index   347

Subject Index   357

About the Contributors   365

About the Editor   369

List of Figures

2–1. Cigarette Consumption and Number of Deaths per Million in Various Countries 22

2–2. Smoking as Related to Rate of Nondiagnosis of Lung Cancer during Life, and Search Rate for Diagnostic Tests 28

2–3. Rate of Smoking and Relative Risks of Lung Cancer in British and Japanese Samples 34

2–4. Alternative View of Smoking-Lung Cancer Correlations, Involving Genetic Factors 50

2–5. Personality Traits Characteristic of P (Psychoticism) 54

2–6. Personality Traits Characteristic of E (Extraversion) 55

2–7. Personality Traits Characteristic of N (Neuroticism) 56

2–8. Relationships between Personality and Cancer, and Possible Endocrine and Stress Intermediaries 68

9–1. Pro-Forma Activity-Impact Analysis 244

9–2. Tax Revenues and Tax Rates: I 263

9–3. Tax Revenues and Tax Rates: II 263

11–1. Effects of Excise Tax on the Market for Cigarettes 287

List of Tables

2–1. Expected and Observed Deaths from Various Causes, and Mortality Ratios   19

2–2. Personality and Smoking as Related to Deaths from Various Causes   58

2–3. Heidelberg Prospective Study   69

3–1. Rank Order, Means, and Standard Deviations of Factors Reported by Male and Female College Students to Influence Them to Begin Smoking   106

3–2. Rank Order, Means, and Standard Deviations of Factors Reported by Male and Female College Students to Influence Them to Continue Smoking   107

3–3. Means, Standard Deviations, and Rank Order of the Ratings of Female and Male Current, Occasional, and Ex-Smokers of the Reasons That Influenced Them to Continue Smoking   108

3–4. Factor Analysis of the Preliminary Smoking Motivation Questionnaire   116

3–5. Factor Analysis of the Smoking Motivation Questionnaire   118

3–6. Item Loadings for the SMQ Anxiety and Anger Smoking Motivation Factors, and Item Remainder Correlations and Alpha Coefficients of the Subscales for Assessing These Factors   120

3–7. Means, Standard Deviations, and Intercorrelations among the SMQ Factor Scores   122

3–8. Correlations of the SMQ and the EPQ Extraversion, Neuroticism, and Psychoticism Scales   123

3–9. Correlations of the SMQ with the STPI Trait Anger, Anxiety, and Curiosity Scale   124

3–10. Correlations of Daily Cigarette Smoking with the Smoking Motivation Factors and the EPQ and STPI Scores of Current and Ex-Smokers   125

4–1. Carbon Monoxide and Blood Carboxyhemoglobin Levels of Subjects in Controlled Chambers or Nonventilated Rooms   142

4–2. Indoor and Outdoor Carbon Monoxide Levels: Mean or Range   144

7–1. State Laws Restricting Smoking   218

9–1. Direct Impact of Tobacco Core Sector on National Employment and Compensation, 1983   253

9–2. The Impact of the U.S. Tobacco Industry: Selected Economic Indicators, 1983   254

9–3. Direct Impact of Tobacco Core Sector   255

9–4. Persons Engaged in the Tobacco Industry in the European Economic Community, Portugal, and Spain, 1982   256

9–5. Full-time Equivalents (FTEs) in the Tobacco Industry in the European Economic Community, Portugal, and Spain, 1982   257

9–6. Summary of Pretax Personal Incomes Attributable to the Tobacco Industry in the European Economic Community, Portugal, and Spain, 1982   257

9–7. Summary Tax Revenues Raised in Association with the Tobacco Industry, 1982   258

9–8. Economic Impact of the Tobacco Industry on Malaysia   259

9–9. The Tobacco Industry in Zimbabwe: Selected Employment Effects   260

9–10. Cigarette Industry Significance in the Argentine Economy, 1983   261

11–1. Number of Present Regular Smokers by Age and Family Income, and as a Percentage of Total Regular Smokers   291

11–2. U.S. Population by Age and Family Income, and as a Percentage of Total Population over 17 Years   292

11–3. Number of Present Regular Smokers by Age and Education, and as a Percentage of Total Regular Smokers   293

11–4. U.S. Population by Age and Education Level, and as a Percentage of Total Population over 17 Years   294

11–5. Effective Tax Rates on Tobacco Products, 1976   296

11–6. Elasticity of Real Cigarette Tax Collections with Respect to Real Personal Income, by State, 1976–1981   298

11–7. Excise Tax Rates for Two-Person Households by Disposable Income Class, The Netherlands, 1974   301

11–8. Excise Tax Rates by Income Decile for Three Countries   302

11–9. Elasticities of Excise Taxes with Respect to Disposable Income, Selected Goods, United Kingdom, 1977   303

12–1. Sales of Filter Cigarettes in Countries with and without Advertising Bans   315

12–2. Penetration of Low Tar (0–15 mgs tar) Cigarettes in Countries with and without Advertising Bans   316

Preface

Robert D. Tollison

T his book is the outgrowth of a workshop on smoking and society held in New York City in the Summer of 1984. The purpose of the workshop was to bring together a group of concerned scholars to address the conventional wisdom about smoking from various perspectives—economic, social, health, and so on. Our efforts have been fruitful. We acknowledge the assistance and support of representatives of a number of tobacco companies in our efforts.

Part I
Introduction

1
Smoking: Toward a More Balanced Assessment

Robert D. Tollison

The issue which this book analyzes is smoking, and the reasons for this choice are simple: the production and consumption of tobacco products is presently the subject of much discussion and debate, and proposals abound to increase the presence of government in this area through such means as <u>increased regulation and taxes</u>. By analyzing the case that is made for restricting smoking, we can learn several useful things. We can learn about the methods of those who call for increased regulation of smoking, and we can determine how strong their case is. The public debate about smoking has been remarkably one-sided. The scientific and intellectual case against smoking is taken generally as a settled matter. It is assumed that scientists and scholars have examined the issues carefully and concluded unanimously that smoking has no redeeming virtues. Indeed, most members of the antismoking movement see increased regulation of smoking as a second-best policy; their goal is to have it banned altogether.

The basic point of this volume is that this view of the debate about smoking is simply not the case. No matter how one approaches the issue—as a scientific problem about smoking and health, as an economic debate about the costs and benefits of smoking, <u>as a sociological or cultural phenomenon, as a political or public policy analysis, or as a philosophical problem about,</u> for example, personal freedom—there is a serious and useful scholarly case to be made that the conventional wisdom about smoking behavior is either wrong, unproven, built upon faulty analysis, or pushed well beyond the point of common sense. Area by area, issue by issue, this volume seeks to bring this basic point home to the reader.

The average reader, even one who smokes, will no doubt find this a bold claim. With this in mind the purposes of this introductory essay are simple. First, I want to set the tone for the volume by discussing, albeit briefly, the idea of balance in the approach to an issue such as smoking. There is another side to the smoking issue, and it is time that it had a fair hearing and a fair chance to influence public policy. Second, I offer the reader a brief preview of the volume. In general, my goal is to cast the net widely and to bring together the work of a group of serious intellectuals and scientists to address the wide range of issues that have been raised about smoking. The volume will offer a decidedly different point of view about these issues, presented in a literate, scholarly, scientific manner.

The Need for Balance

A simple lesson of economics is that one can have too much or too little of a good thing. Too much ice cream gives us a tummy ache, too little leaves our appetite unsatisfied. The same point applies to government policy toward consumer protection—there can be too much as well as too little protection. Another way of saying the same thing is to point out that consumer protection is not free; it comes at the expense of other things that we want. Additional consumer protection must be compared to its additional cost, and this is where the critical idea of balance enters. There is an optimal or best amount of protection where its additional cost equals its additional benefit.

By contrast, much government action in the area of consumer protection seems to be based on the idea that any additional protection is worth its cost, or, indeed, that costs are irrelevant to the consideration of consumer protection issues. Additional regulation seems to be desired if it provides any benefits at all. In this sense, regulators have chosen to ignore the dictates of cost-benefit analysis and to seek a standard of absolute rather than cost-effective protection.

Absolute consumer protection defies common sense. Trains could be made absolutely safe for occupants by limiting their speed to ten miles per hour. To allow trains to go faster is to say that it is worth accepting some reduction in protection (an increase in the risk of derailment) because the benefits (faster travel) are worth bearing the additional risk. A sensible approach to protection represents the purchase of an amount of protection up to the point that the value placed on additional protection is equal to the cost of that protection.

Protection is valuable, but is also costly. If the value of additional protection is more than its cost, more protection should be provided. If the cost of additional protection exceeds its value, the amount of protection should be reduced. The point that is sought is the point of balance, that is, where the extra costs and extra benefits of protection are equal. One can drive fast or slow to get to grandmother's. The faster one drives, the more valuable is the time that is saved for visiting grandmother relative to the increased risk of an accident. In such ways, individuals make cost-benefit decisions daily that reflect this trade-off between protection and risk.

It should be kept in mind that this concept of an optimal amount of protection is intended as a way of thinking about consumer protection rather than as a precise calculation from cost-benefit analysis. While the latter may be desirable, it is probably not feasible in any particular policy application. The relevance of the concept of optimal regulation in practice pertains to the mental calculus of regulators. Regulators should be held to at least a rough accounting of the costs and benefits of their decisions, and in cases where appropriate calculations and commonsense judgment suggest that the cost of an action exceeds its benefit, they should feel compelled to cease and desist, like a naughty corporation, in their pursuit of additional regulation.

In essence, then, the cost-benefit perspective means that public policy makers should seek balance in their approach to consumer protection issues. This applies to public policy toward smoking, just as it does to public policy toward other consumer protection issues. Yet it is precisely this sort of balance that is missing in the debate over smoking and its role in society. For example, as a general matter, we know that it is improper to speak of costs without also speaking of benefits. Yet the various studies of the alleged costs attributed to smoking typically neglect the benefit side of the account. At most, the benefits are said to inhere in the tax revenues collected by the government from the taxation of tobacco products. But what about the benefits to the users of tobacco? We observe people willingly purchasing and using these products. The price of these products reflects the value of the resources used to produce them, and we therefore know that, at a minimum, users obtain benefits from tobacco products equal to their expenditures on these items. Thus, because of the failure to consider the benefits to users, the standard economic studies of smoking are seriously biased and one-sided.

The point is general. The omission of benefits from cost-benefit studies of smoking is just a small example of the degree to which the debate about smoking has proceeded in unbalanced terms. The purpose of this volume is to restore balance to the debate and, in so doing, to provide a rational framework for the discussion of smoking as a public issue.

A Preview of the Volume

Before turning to a summary of the volume, it should be stressed that smoking is not a local issue confined to the United States or, for that matter, to the developed countries of the world. Although the push by various antismoking groups for additional regulatory measures against smoking is, perhaps, stronger in the developed countries, pressures are also being brought to bear on less developed countries to copy the more stringent smoking regulations of the advanced countries. Smoking is an international issue. Since most of the authors in the volume are based in the United States, a good part of their discussions and analysis reflect their familiarity with U.S. examples and data. Nonetheless, some effort has been made in virtually every paper to stress the international dimension of smoking issues, and this important point should not be forgotten as the reader makes his or her way through the various points made in each paper.

In his wide-ranging and fascinating chapter, Hans J. Eysenck carefully examines the scientific and statistical credibility of the "received view" (or conventional wisdom) of the impact of smoking on health: that smoking *causes* lung cancer, coronary heart disease, and other medical problems. The statistical association between smoking and certain types of health problems is well known, and many adherents of the received view take the position that association is equal to causation. Eysenck examines the claim of causation in light of the work of statisticians, epidemiologists, and oncologists to determine what scientific validity exists for such a claim. His conclusion, in brief, is that the claim that smoking causes health problems, especially lung cancer and coronary heart disease, is unproven and rests on very shaky data and statistical procedures. Eysenck's indictment of the conventional wisdom about smoking and health is lengthy and substantial. He discusses problems in the data used by researchers at length. Indeed, he stresses that the data base used to establish the correlation between smoking and health is significantly flawed by problems of self-selection and by the use of death certificates rather than autopsy results to establish the cause of death. He goes on to argue that even if the data base is accepted, the received view on smoking and health has serious holes in it. For example, if the received view is accepted, a given amount of smoking would appear to lead to quite different effects measured in health terms in different countries. Eysenck's interest in these matters is purely scientific, and the clues that he gathers through his critical analysis of the conventional wisdom are directed to the elaboration of an alternative hypothesis about smoking and health. He feels that there is sufficient basis to pursue a constitutional explanation of smoking which seems to be more in accord with the available evidence than the conventional wisdom. Such an approach suggests that some individuals may have a constitutional predisposition to certain diseases such as lung cancer and coronary heart disease, and that part of this behavior pattern may involve a predisposition to smoke. This hypothesis, especially when combined with work on personality and stress, argues that smoking is not a causal factor in disease formation. It is, rather, an effect of a certain constitutional predisposition. Eysenck stresses that while the conventional wisdom about smoking and health is unproven, so too is the constitutional hypothesis. His point, however, is well taken. There is enough evidence at hand to suggest the potential scientific benefits from additional work along the lines of the constitutional model.

Charles D. Spielberger pursues the question of why people smoke from the perspective of psychological theory and evidence in his chapter. He establishes first that psychological theory suggests clearly the importance of investigating the role of motivational and emotional factors as determinants of smoking behavior. In particular, he compares and contrasts the behavioral theories offered by Eysenck and Tomkins. Looking to the evidence on motivational and emotional factors, Spielberger reports several interesting findings. First, there appears to be a strong positive relationship between the smoking behavior of parents and children. A similar relationship appears to hold between older siblings and peers with respect to influencing adolescents to initiate smoking behavior. Second, the evidence on smoking and personality suggests clearly that smoking is linked to certain personality traits, particularly extraversion and antisocial tendencies. Third, Spielberger reports the results of a study of the smoking habits of 424 U.S. college students. He found that the initiation of smoking was related strongly to such factors as personal enjoyment, the influence of peers who smoked, and the reduction of tension. In no case was the influence of media advertising an important influence on smoking behavior. Thus, both psychological theory and evidence suggest that the smoking decision is a complex, personal process that as yet is only partially understood. Moreover, to the extent that it is understood, it seems to be related to factors such as family history, personality type, personal enjoyment, stress reduction, and peer group experience—that is, to the stuff that is part and parcel of everyday life.

Increasing public attention is being given to questions related to the possible effects of environmental tobacco smoke on the health of non-smokers. In recent years, a number of articles have appeared in the scientific literature on the claimed health effects of so-called "passive smoking." "Public" or "passive" smoking refers to the exposure of nonsmokers to environmental tobacco smoke. The alleged health effects of passive smoking (which range from eye irritation to lung cancer) are relied upon by those who support public smoking restrictions. In his chapter Domingo M. Aviado reviews the scientific literature relating to environmental tobacco smoke and health. He concludes that there is no substantial evidence to support the view that exposure to environmental tobacco smoke presents a significant health hazard to the nonsmoker. More particularly, he reports that: (1) carbon monoxide in experimental settings and public places, which may be partly due to environmental tobacco smoke, is generally within air quality standards for workplaces; (2) tobacco smoke has not been shown to be allergenic in humans; and (3) there is no substantial scientific evidence to support the proposition that environmental tobacco smoke leads to respiratory illness or disease in nonsmokers. Aviado suggests that the environmental tobacco smoke issue may well find its roots in psychological considerations rather than in the domain of adverse health effects. He points out, however, that his focus on psychosocial factors and their possible role in eliciting reactions to environmental tobacco smoke is not meant to ignore the fact that environmental tobacco smoke can, under certain conditions, be annoying to the normal nonsmoker. Nevertheless, Aviado states that it is difficult to explain scientifically why certain nonsmokers react so violently to the presence of environmental tobacco smoke. He suggests that the reasons for such emotional reactions may be elucidated by additional research and investigation.

In his chapter, Sherwin J. Feinhandler poses an alternative approach to explaining smoking behavior which differs from strictly physiological or psychological theories. He argues that smoking should be evaluated in terms of its social or cultural role. In other words, Feinhandler seeks to learn why individuals smoke by observing smoking as it occurs in the daily lives of smokers. The results of his research in this respect are quite interesting. He finds, for example, that smoking serves a number of social functions, including exchange, affect management, group definition, and boundary mediation. Through observational studies of smokers, Feinhandler is able to categorize the functions of smoking behavior as personal, social, or ordering. The personal function refers to such matters as the expression of a specific self-image. One might think of the use of smoking by actors in a movie who are seeking to communicate a certain type of image. The social function of smoking refers to such activities as group definition where smoking may reconfirm a relationship among members of a group. The ordering function of smoking refers to the use of tobacco in such activities as concentrating and filling empty time. Feinhandler's basic hypothesis, therefore, is that smoking is culturally rather than physiologically or psychologically determined and that it is in the fulfillment of its social functions that the explanation and understanding of smoking behavior is to be found.

Douglas J. Den Uyl brings the philosopher's perspective to the smoking issue. He analyzes public policy toward smoking, in particular the Smoking Pollution Control Ordinance passed in San Francisco and the political philosophy exhibited by the World Health Organization, from the standpoint of certain basic individual rights found in the concept of personal liberty. In this approach, liberty is seen as a basic moral right of all persons and a fundamental purpose of the state is to protect the individual against unwarranted intrusions into his or her personal liberty. Looking at public policy in terms of its impact on basic rights contrasts with the approach of legal paternalism, which argues that individuals are not always the best judges of their interests and the state is somehow justified in informing and shaping individual behavior on these grounds. Den Uyl argues that the basic rights approach is much more germane to the case of smoking than legal paternalism. Government paternalism fails in this case because the use of tobacco products is a voluntary decision and the alleged risks associated with their consumption are well known to consumers. Moreover, if done in a considerate way, smoking does not interfere with the welfare of others in a dramatic fashion. Applying this argument, Den Uyl finds that the San Francisco ordinance is a clear violation of individual liberty and that, as such, it is an unwarranted extension of the power of government. He argues from a property-rights perspective that the owners of private firms have sufficient incentive to provide the type of environments that workers and customers want. In other words, Den Uyl argues for freedom of the private marketplace to arbitrate the relationship between smokers and nonsmokers. When there is no private ownership of property, such as in the case of a public building, for example, Den Uyl admits that his approach offers ambiguous answers to the smoking issue. He stresses, however, that smokers' rights are not to be set equal to zero in this case; rather, some way of working out a balanced approach to smoking versus nonsmoking must be found for such cases. In sum, Den Uyl argues that it is a basic mistake to politicize the smoking issue and to use it as a stalking horse to attack personal liberties. Instead he argues for the respect of individual freedom and for allowing the private marketplace to control any problems that smoking causes in personal manners and behavior. Den Uyl applies the same analysis to the political philosophy espoused by the World Health Organization with respect to smoking, and finds that this philosophy is rife with elements of paternalism, social engineering, and crude utilitarianism.

Chapter seven, "Smokers versus Nonsmokers," by William F. Shughart II and Robert D. Tollison, and chapter eleven, "The Incidence of Taxes on Tobacco," by James M. Savarese and William F. Shughart II tackle the issue of public smoking with the aid of economic analysis. As noted above, it is claimed by some that public smoking can cause adverse health effects in nonsmokers. A typical economic analysis would treat these alleged health effects, as well as any annoyance that might result from environmental tobacco smoke, as social costs borne by nonsmokers. This analysis, however, ignores the incentives of market participants (restaurant and bar owners and employers, for example) to take account of such possible effects. In chapter seven we contend that the social costs of public smoking are equal to zero, and hence, that there is no case for government intervention in these areas. San Francisco–type ordinances to regulate public smoking have no basis in principle. Where, then, does the pressure for these inefficient laws come from? We argue that these laws and regulatory programs are best explained as schemes whereby nonsmokers benefit at the expense of smokers. If smoking is banned in the workplace, for example, who wins and who loses? Clearly, smokers lose. They are denied the option of smoking at work, and to the extent that this action negatively affects their productivity, they will be less competitive in the job market relative to nonsmokers. This is only one example, but the point is general. Public smoking regulation is a scheme, not to increase economic efficiency, but to increase the wealth of nonsmokers at the expense of smokers.

Peter Berger, in his sociological analysis of the antismoking movement, takes what might be called an up-front approach to his subject. He readily admits his own stake in the issue (he is a smoker, for example), and with the reader so warned, he launches into his analysis. He begins by pointing out the vested interests of the two sides of the smoking issue. The concerns of the tobacco industry are well known and simple; the industry has a clear economic stake in public policy toward smoking. The politics of the antismoking movement are less well known and less analyzed, and it is to these that Berger turns his considerable skills as a sociologist. He identifies two types of antismoking interest groups. First, there is the antismoking *movement,* which is characterized by groups such as ASH (Action on Smoking and Health) and GASP (Group Against Smokers' Pollution) in the United States. These groups exhibit a fervent ideological interest in the single issue of eradicating smoking from the world. The movement is populated by members of the upper middle class, and is located primarily in Western advanced societies (although the World Health Organization has internationalized the smoking issue). Based on charisma and voluntarism, such groups do not normally last for long without the support of government. Thus, the second group in the movement identified by Berger is the antismoking *bureaucracy* in government. In the United States, for example, the Office on Smoking and Health represents the antismoking bureaucracy in the federal government. This part of the movement is entrenched in government and acts like any other bureaucratic agent—cautious and primarily interested in bureaucratic survival. The positions of both sides of the antismoking movement are the same. There is strong opposition to smoking in any form, and the scientific case against smoking is considered definitive and not open to debate. The attitude of the movement toward smokers is paternalistic—smokers simply do not know what is good for them. Finally, Berger applies his analysis to the behavior of the movement at the Fourth and Fifth World Conference on Smoking and Health held in Stockholm and Winnipeg, respectively, in 1979 and 1983. The 1979 Conference focused on the scientific debate; the 1983 Conference sounded the theme that the scientific debate is over, and the problem now is how to reduce and ultimately to eradicate smoking. As Berger sees it, the antismoking movement faces two fundamental problems. It is a middle-class phenomenon directed at changing the habits of the working class, and resistance by the working class is to be expected. Moreover, the movement must overcome the general antipathy that has evolved in recent years to government regulation of any sort.

H. Peter Gray and Ingo Walter assess the contribution of the tobacco industry to various economies around the world in chapter nine. Their approach to this problem falls into several analytical categories. First, they stress that in order to measure the economic impact of anything, one must first address the issue, "with respect to what?" In this case, they take the perspective that the institution one wants to address is government, which determines the conditions under which the industry operates. To do so requires the specification of an objective function for government, consisting of its various economic and social targets. These targets are a function of the prevailing political environment in a country, and will obviously differ across countries. Gray and Walter stress that government objective functions in the case of tobacco differ markedly for three types of countries—developed, industrializing, and less developed. Second, with the relevant objective function in hand, the next task is the technical one of impact estimation, involving both quantitative and qualitative measures. Quantitative estimates focus on the output and employment effects of the industry, both direct and indirect, using input–output analysis. In this respect, the tobacco industry in general contributes about 1 to 2 percent of manufactured output in industrialized countries. In tobacco-growing countries, which encompass many industrializing and less developed economies, the contribution of the industry is considerably larger. A second quantitative measure of the contribution of the industry is its fiscal contribution to government. The impact of tobacco varies greatly across countries in this regard. For example, tobacco taxes in Brazil constitute 10.7 percent of national tax revenue, in West Germany they constitute 7.3 percent, and in Japan they constitute only 1.5 percent. In general, however, tobacco taxes represent an important revenue source to governments in almost all countries. Finally, Gray and Walter assess the more subjective impact of the tobacco industry on the dynamic aspects of an economy, that is, on the process of economic growth. In this area, the industry has made significant contributions to capital formation, improvement in labor skills and motivation, and so forth. However measured and approached, the central theme of this paper is that the tobacco industry is an important, indeed vital, part of the economies of many countries around the world.

Stephen C. Littlechild examines the case for regulating smoking based on the economic concept of "market failure." A market failure arises when private economic activity is somehow flawed or imperfect. A market failure thus sets the stage for government intervention. Whether government is able to correct the market failure in a cost-effective manner requires to be ascertained. Clearly, no one desires a situation in which government intervention to correct a market imperfection makes things worse. Two types of market failure have been claimed in the case of smoking. First, it is claimed that smokers do not realize the health risks of smoking. In other words, smokers supposedly have imperfect information regarding the possible effects of smoking on their health. Littlechild observes that government has done a great deal to inform smokers of the possible risks of smoking. There is abundant dissemination of information and public awareness of the pros and cons of this issue. There is no obvious additional role for government to play in this area. The second alleged market failure is that smokers impose certain types of costs on nonsmokers. As Aviado shows, there is no convincing evidence that smoking represents a health hazard to nonsmokers. Where smoking poses a nuisance to nonsmokers, this is already taken into account by the forces of the marketplace. There is little or nothing that government can do to improve upon these situations, insofar as there is no relevant market failure to correct.

Littlechild also examines the argument that smokers impose costs on non-smokers through their "overuse" of health care facilities. This argument will not stand close examination. Where health care costs are privately financed, as through private health insurance, no such problem arises. Each person pays for his or her own expenses through insurance policies or through direct payments for medical care. With socialized medicine, there is no compelling reason to single out smokers for special tax treatment. Indeed, if nonsmokers live longer than smokers for reasons unrelated to smoking, it is entirely possible that they draw more heavily on socialized health care resources than do smokers. Littlechild's argument in a nutshell, then, is that arguments based on imperfect information and market failure offer no convincing basis for additional regulation of smoking.

Smoking is a heavily taxed activity, and economic theory offers a methodology for evaluating the consequences of taxing tobacco consumption. In chapter eleven, James M. Savarese and William F. Shughart II apply this methodology to recent data on income levels and smoking behavior to derive conclusions about the impact of the tax on smoking on the economy. Their argument is straightforward and replicates the well known result that most consumption excise taxes are regressive in nature—that is, the poorer members of the society pay more of the tax. In applying the classical theory of tax incidence to the tobacco excise tax, Savarese and Shughart point out that the tax falls especially heavily on consumers in this case because they are relatively less sensitive to price changes (producers and tobacco farmers also pay a portion of the tax, as does society in general through the lower economic efficiency caused by the tax). With respect to the consumers who pay the tobacco tax, Savarese and Shughart next ask if the tax is fair in the normative sense of tax theory. That is, is the burden of the tax borne equally by all taxpayers or is it concentrated on a particular category of consumers? In addressing this question empirically, the authors apply the concept of horizontal equity, which suggests that the cigarette tax is equitable if tax payments represent the same proportion of income for low- and high-income consumers. Savarese and Shughart apply this criterion to a variety of data sets from the United States and for several other countries. They find that smokers tend to have a lower income than the average citizen, and thus that the application of an excise tax to tobacco products is strongly regressive—the poor pay a larger proportion of their income in tobacco taxes than do those who are better off. Moreover, this result holds across virtually every country in which tobacco is taxed. Taxes on smoking fall most heavily on those individuals at the lower end of the income distribution; this is the central result produced by Savarese and Shughart. In the sense of horizontal equity, therefore, the tax on smoking is not fair.

J.J. Boddewyn examines the role of tobacco advertising in a free society. His argument addresses three basic issues. First, he stresses the important but limited role of advertising in a free market system. Not only is advertising only one of many factors influencing consumer decisions, but it is probably not a very key factor. Tobacco advertising, for example, seems to be more a consequence of consumer decisions to smoke than a cause, and econometric evidence suggests that such advertising does not expand the total demand for cigarettes. Moreover, bans on advertising tend to do more harm than good, causing the spread of product innovation to be impeded. Second, Boddewyn argues that government's ability to regulate tobacco advertising is, or should be, limited. Governments have limited regulatory resources, and the mass of public opinion in most Western countries today is running against the further encroachment of government regulation over the private sector. In addition, advertising is accorded limited constitutional protection in the United States. Third, Boddewyn argues that the attack on tobacco advertising has serious implications for a free society that go beyond the issue of smoking per se. For example, where does one draw the line with respect to the advertising of so-called "objectionable" products—at tobacco, at alcohol, at tea, coffee, salt, eggs, red meat? The danger of such a trend is self-evident. In sum, Boddewyn offers a strong brief for the view that tobacco advertising is not the reason that people smoke and that restrictions on such advertising carry serious implications for the producers and consumers of other products in a free economy.

In the final substantive essay of the volume, James M. Buchanan makes a compelling argument that a huge dose of commonsense is needed in approaching public policy toward smoking. His message is simply about the wisdom of individuals respecting one another's preferences. Some may feel strongly about restricting smoking behavior, others about open air burning of leaves, others about carrying guns, and still others about other issues. If we *each* seek to restrict the specific activities of others which offend us, we *all* end up worse off as a result. "Politics and Meddlesome Preferences" is a powerful brief for the wisdom of mutual self-respect and tolerance in governing the relationships among a free people when it comes to issues such as smoking.

At the end of the volume I have added some brief concluding remarks in which I summarize the main points of the analysis. Here I also present my thought that the agenda of the antismoking movement may well extend beyond the idea of restricting smoking to restricting other forms of behavior. If we do not draw the line somewhere, such as at smoking, we may very well have to endure not simply an *over*regulated, but a *totally* regulated society.

Conclusion

Since the point of view we offer about smoking in this book departs from the conventional wisdom so significantly, we would be foolish not to expect to arouse some debate and controversy. In this regard we hope to receive a fair

hearing and to contribute useful and informative insights to the public dia-
logue about smoking. What we hope to avoid is the form of intellectual Lud-
dism practiced by some opponents of smoking, that is, the view that the case
against smoking is proven, the debate is over, and nothing more remains to
be said. This book is written in the spirit that the debate is far from over,
there is much that we do not know, and that the case against smoking is unproven. Nonetheless, it is hard to have a viable debate if the opposition persists in an ostrich-like posture of ignoring facts and hypotheses. None of this
is by way of asking our readers and critics to be easy on us; we think that we
have strong grounds on which to debate. What we do request is what is
perhaps far harder to deliver in this case—an open mind.

Part II
Smoking: The Context
of the Individual

2
Smoking and Health

Hans J. Eysenck

In the philosophy of science, it became commonplace in the early 1920s for philosophers to construe scientific theories as axiomatic calculi which are given a partial observational interpretation by means of correspondence rules. This analysis has been commonly referred to as the *received view of theories* (Putnam, 1962; Suppe, 1974) and between the 1920s and 1950 this view, sometimes also called *logical positivism* or *the Vienna School*, was employed or tacitly assumed by almost all philosophers of science. In the 1950s the received view began to be subjected to critical attacks challenging its very conception of theories and scientific knowledge; these attacks were so successful that by the late 1960s a general consensus had been reached among philosophers and scientists that it was inadequate as a review of scientific theory. As Suppe (1974) has pointed out, the received view is now totally rejected, but no proposed alternative analysis or theory enjoys widespread acceptance. A similar position seems to be developing in the field of smoking, considered as a hazard to health and the cause of lung cancer, coronary heart disease, and many other medical disorders. This view has been widely publicized in reports by the Surgeon General of the United States, and by the Royal College of Physicians in the United Kingdom, but it has come under increasing scrutiny and many criticisms of it have been voiced by eminent statisticians, epidemiologists and oncologists. These have caused considerable doubt about the validity of the received view, but although alternative theories have been suggested, none has been widely accepted.

The suggestion of a statistical association between smoking and cancer goes back over fifty years. Lombard and Doering (1928) in the United States, and Muller (1939) and Schairer and Schoeniger (1943) in Germany noted that smokers constituted a higher percentage of lung cancer patients than they did of controls. In 1950 the retrospective studies on smoking habits of lung cancer patients and controls by Schrek et al. (1950), Mills and Porter (1950), Levin et al. (1950), and Wynder and Graham (1950) produced evidence of the consistent association between smoking and cancer of the lung, a conclusion more firmly established by the better controlled studies of Doll and

Hill (1952) in the United Kingdom and Hammond and Horn (1958) in the United States. Doll and Peto (1976) reported on general mortality among smokers as compared with controls, and the U.S. Surgeon General's reports of 1964, 1971, 1972, 1973, 1982, and the Reports of the Royal College of Physicians (1971, 1983) have summarized an enormous amount of material collected subsequent to these early studies.

⌐According to the latest reports of the U.S. Surgeon General (1982), cancer was responsible for approximately 412,000 deaths in the United States; the report estimated that in 1982 there would be 430,000 deaths due to cancer: 233,000 among men and 197,000 among women. It claimed that 22%–38% of these deaths can be attributed to smoking, and therefore are, potentially, "avoidable" if smoking did not exist in human behavior. The report clearly suggests a *causal* interpretation of the *statistical* association between smoking and lung and other cancers, and it is this interpretation of the data which has been criticized by many experts, such as Berkson (1958), Berkson and Elveback (1960), Burch (1976, 1978abc, 1983), Fisher (1958abc), Katz (1969), Mainland and Herrera (1956), Oeser (1979), Sterling (1973), Yerushalmy (1962, 1966). The purpose of this chapter is to examine the claims made by the supporters of the received view in light of the criticisms made by leading statisticians, epidemiologists and oncologists, and to attempt to decide to what extent the claims made for this view are scientifically acceptable. In a later section of this chapter, an attempt will also be made to consider facts and data not accommodated by the received view, such as the relationship between personality and cancer and between stress and cancer. We will also examine some alternative theories. Lastly, we will consider similar data in relation to coronary heart disease, which is also often claimed to be statistically and causally related to smoking. The evidence here has been equally subject to criticism, and this will be reviewed in some detail. Here, too, there may be alternative theories which explain many of the facts not covered by the received view.

The theory that smoking plays a *causal* role in the etiology of cancer, coronary heart disease and various other disorders has given rise to speculation about the number of lives that could be saved if smoking could be prevented. Burch (1978) quotes studies by Higginson and Doll, claiming that we should be able to reduce the incidence of cancer "by at least 80%–90%" if cigarette smoking could be eliminated, and the U.S. Surgeon General's Report (1982) states that "it is estimated that 85% of lung cancer cases are due to cigarette smoking," and that consequently "85% of lung cancer mortalities could have been avoided if individuals never took up smoking." In a speech on January 11, 1978, the Secretary of the Department of Health, Education and Welfare in the United States, Joseph Califano, stated that in 1977, smoking caused 220,000 deaths from heart disease, 78,000 from lung cancer, and 22,000 from other cancers, including bladder cancer, for a total of 320,000 deaths. One month later, Secretary Califano attributed to cigarette smoking 15,000 deaths from chronic bronchitis and emphysema, 125,000 from heart disease, and 100,000 from cancer, and stated this total to be "more than 320,000." No source was given for any of these figures, and no explanation given for why chronic bronchitis and emphysema were included in the February total but not in the January one. He also failed to explain how his estimate of smoking accounts for 40% of all cancer deaths yearly, double that suggested by the American Cancer Society.

In a similar vein, Dr. David Owen, former Minister of Health and Social Services in the United Kingdom, stated that 50,000 deaths in the United Kingdom were due to smoking, and could have been prevented by people stopping smoking. Such figures are extrapolations from epidemiological figures to be examined presently, and have no scientific meaning of any kind. It will be our task to look at the uncertain foundations on which such estimates are based, and to see whether they have any validity or are entirely speculative. Essentially, all such speculations are based on figures like those given in table 2–1. These figures purport to demonstrate that smokers of a given age

Table 2–1
Expected and Observed Deaths from Various Causes, and Mortality Ratios

	Expected	Observed	D	Mortality Ratio
Cancer of the lung	170	1,833	1,657	10.8
Bronchitis and emphysema	90	546	456	6.1
Cancer of the larynx	14	75	61	5.4
Cancer of the oral cavity	37	152	115	4.1
Cancer of the oesophagus	34	113	79	3.4
Stomach and duodenal ulcers	105	294	189	2.8
Other circulatory diseases	254	649	395	2.6
Cirrhosis of liver	169	379	210	2.2
Cancer of bladder	112	216	104	1.9
Coronary artery disease	6,431	11,177	4,746	1.7
Other heart diseases	526	868	342	1.7
Hypertensive heart disease	409	631	222	1.5
General arteriosclerosis	211	310	99	1.5
Cancer of kidney	79	120	41	1.5
All other cancer	1,061	1,524	463	1.4
Cancer of the stomach	285	413	128	1.4
Influenza, pneumonia	303	415	112	1.4
All other causes	1,509	1,946	437	1.3
Cerebral vascular lesions	1,462	1,844	382	1.3
Cancer of prostate	253	318	65	1.3
Accidents, suicides, violence	1,063	1,310	247	1.2
Nephritis	156	173	17	1.1
Rheumatic heart disease	291	309	18	1.1
Cancer of rectum	208	213	5	1.0

Source: From Royal College of Physicians Report on Smoking and Health, 1971.

and sex die more frequently of a given disease than nonsmokers. The difference can be expressed as a "mortality ratio" (age-standardized mortality rate, or SMR), indicating the proportion of smokers to nonsmokers who are certified as having died of a particular disease. The heading "Observed" refers to actual deaths in the population under study; "Expected" refers to deaths among nonsmokers. Column D gives the absolute difference between the first two columns; thus 4,746 more people who smoked died of coronary heart disease in the United States than a comparable group of nonsmokers out of a total of 100,000 people. The column headed "Mortality Ratio" gives the ratio Observed/Expected; in the case of lung cancer, this is 10.8, indicating that almost eleven times as many smokers died of this disease than did a comparable group of nonsmokers. It will be seen that there are a large number of different diseases with mortality ratios above 1, indicating the possibility that smoking may have increased the chances of a given individual succumbing to these diseases.

The table shows that the mortality ratio for cancer of the lung is the highest in the whole table, but for coronary heart disease the absolute difference between the two columns of "Expected" and "Observed" deaths is the largest. This is of course due to the fact that far more people die of coronary artery disease than of lung cancer. Because these two types of disease have usually been singled out as being the most relevant to the received view, I have concentrated in this chapter on evidence relating to cancer of the lung and coronary heart disease.

Three points should be made here before any detailed discussion of the results in this table. In the first place, the mortality ratios differ considerably from one population to another, and those in table 2–1 are only given as an example to illustrate what happened in a particular year in the United States. Figures for different populations, at different times, would give quite different results; this point will be discussed in much more detail later on. The second point to be noted is that mortality ratios for smoking may be below 1 as well as above, thus apparently indicating a beneficent effect of smoking if we use the same method or argument as that which has been used by the supporters of the received view. Thus Kahn (1966) found a mortality ratio of 0.90 for cancer of the rectum. Hammond (1966) found mortality ratios of 0.78 and 0.66 respectively for colorectal cancer in women who smoked or smoked heavily; for males, the mortality ratios were just over 1. Choi, Schumann and Gullen (1970) found a negative correlation of primary central nervous system neoplasms with cigarette smoking; they found a similar negative association between such neoplasms and alcohol consumption. Another disease in which negative correlations have been found consistently is Parkinson's disease. Kahn (1966) has reported a mortality ratio of 0.26; Hammond (1966) one of 0.81 for an older group, while Nefzger et al. (1968) found that among 138 patients with Parkinson's disease, only 70% had ever smoked, compared with 84% of 166 controls. The differences in smoking habits were established before the onset of the disease, and hence the negative correlation was not brought about by the disease itself. Kessler (1972) found similar results, as did Westlund (1970) in Norway. Other diseases, such as trigeminal neuralgia (Rothman & Monson, 1973) and diabetes (Hirayama, 1972) can also be mentioned here.

It is not suggested that these figures indicate a beneficial effect of smoking, just as we would maintain that the positive mortality ratio in table 2–1 does not necessarily indicate a nefarious effect of smoking; the problem of inferring causation from correlation is a much more complex one than that.

A third point to be mentioned is that even if smoking were a cause of cancer (assuming for the moment that it is meaningful to talk about single causes in relation to such a complex disease as cancer), then it clearly is neither a *necessary* nor a *sufficient* cause. For Caucasian groups at least, only one out of ten heavy smokers dies of lung cancer. Hence, smoking is clearly not a sufficient cause. Of ten people who die of lung cancer, one is a non-smoker; hence smoking clearly is not a necessary cause. Arguments about causation are difficult enough at the best of times, but when a given alleged cause is neither necessary nor sufficient, the argument clearly becomes very complex indeed.

Mortality ratios such as those given in table 2–1 refer to the position in a particular country at a particular time. An additional argument used by the adherents of the received view is illustrated in figure 2–1 which shows the relationship between the crude male death rate for lung cancer in 1950 (on the ordinate) and per capita consumption of cigarettes in 1930 in various countries; the time difference of 20 years is used because it is believed that smoking affects health only after a lengthy period of use. The actual correlation in this sample of countries is 0.73 ± 0.30; other investigators using other samples have found quite different correlations, which are insignificant. As we shall see, international comparisons of this kind are subject to additional sources of error to those based on a single country, and are even less reliable.

In considering such data as these, it should be borne in mind that there are many similar statistics linking disease with external variables where a direct causal relationship is often difficult to support. One example is the close correlation between meat consumption and intestinal cancer over 22 countries, which is closer than that shown in figure 2–1 (Eysenck, 1980, p. 20). Another example is the correlation between ischaemic heart disease and daily milk consumption (r = .75 over 43 countries), and a correlation of .75 between consumption of refined sugar and ischaemic heart disease, also over 43 countries. Sugar is also implicated in breast cancer, a close correlation being reported across 20 countries (Monitor, 1983; Seely & Horrabin, 1983).

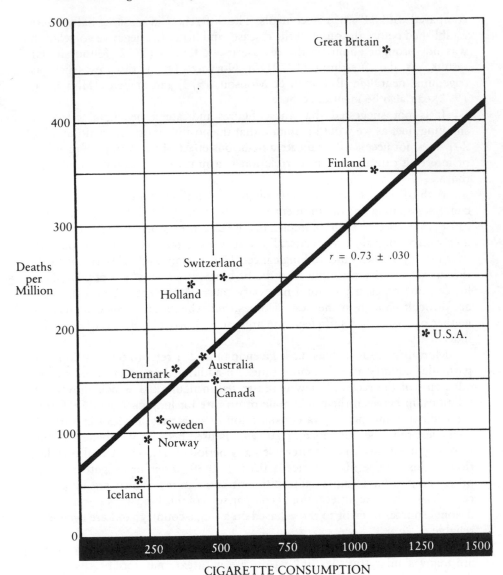

Source: Royal College of Physicians Report on Smoking and Health, 1971.

Figure 2–1. Cigarette Consumption and Number of Deaths per Million in Various Countries

Of the making of statistics, truly, there is no end. Following through the kind of argument on which the received view is based, we may consider how many lives would be saved if we gave up eating meat, drinking milk, and using sugar!

A third argument for the received view relies on the fact that when mortality rates are examined by birth cohorts, it can be seen that most male and female cohorts, with increasing smoking prevalence, also have increasing age-specific mortality rates. In other words, over time there appears to be a correlation between the amount of smoking and prevalence of lung cancer. Correlations over time are of course particularly susceptible to erroneous causal interpretations; over the periods of time considered, there was not only an increase in smoking, but equally in car ownership, number of ballpoint pens sold, number of telephones per unit of population, and so forth; these show correlations with the increase in lung cancer equally as well as the observed correlations with cigarette smoking. This argument will be examined in more detail later on.

The fourth major argument, on which more and more reliance is being placed, is the fact that lung cancer mortality ratios are apparently lower in groups of people who have given up smoking than groups who have continued to smoke. A table (Table 10) in the Surgeon General's report (1982) shows the results in four major studies, by number of years stopped smoking, and the overall effect is certainly apparent in these figures. There are some obvious oddities about this table: the mortality ratios for people who have stopped smoking for 1–4 years appear to be greater than those for current smokers! However, this is not the major argument used to discount these figures; the significance of the demonstration is based on the hypothesis that continued smokers and ex-smokers, at a time when the latter give up smoking, are similar or identical from the point of view of health, and this hypothesis has been decisively disproved, as we shall see. Here, as elsewhere, self-selection makes the simple application of statistical methods invalid (Yerushalmy, 1962).

The Reliability of the Data

It is epidemiological studies following one of these four paradigms that bear practically the whole burden of the argument in favor of the received view. Much effort has been spent in finding animal models which might be used to support this view, but, as the U.S. Surgeon General's Report (1982, p. 89) makes clear, "the useful animal model for the experimental study of oral carcinogenesis has not been found. Cigarette smoke and cigarette smoke condensates generally fail to produce malignancies when applied to the oral cavities of mice, rabbits or hamsters. Mechanical factors, such as secretion of saliva, interfere with the retention of carcinogenic agents." This being so, it becomes necessary to consider the logic of the epidemiological argument, and to see what causal relations might be active in the statistical associations disclosed. Yerushalmy (1966) has discussed the issue in some detail, as has Burch

(1983); we will refer to the major points only briefly as the lines of the argument are reasonably clear. The main positions on this issue were already adumbrated in the first report by the Surgeon General in the series on Smoking and Health (1964), and in Brownlee's (1965) critical review in the *Journal of the American Statistical Association*, where the latter argued that the Surgeon General's Committee had not established the case for causality between smoking and lung cancer. Brownlee did not argue that the causal hypothesis had been *falsified*; he argued that it was not possible at that stage to reach definitive conclusions because, among other things, the genetic hypothesis had not been disproved. In the latest Surgeon General's Report (1982, p. 16), it is argued that "once artifactual association has been ruled out, it is then necessary to determine whether the association is an indirect or direct (causal) one." As Burch (1983, p. 82) points out, "this key step at the early stage of the argument is incomplete and incorrect. Our choice is not of the either/or kind; 'indirect' and 'direct' associations are not mutually exclusive." Burch also points out that another possibility has been overlooked. Given the existence of a genuine association between the habit (H) of smoking and the subsequent incidence of a particular cancer (C), we are obliged by the rules of scientific inference to consider all the following possibilities.

1. H causes C. This of course is in essence the received view. It is always tempting to interpret the observed statistical association in these terms, but alternatives must be considered.

2. An aspect of the smoking habit other than smoking might provide the causal agent. Burch gives as an example that the means of ignition, and not the combustion of the tobacco might, in principle, be the cause of the effective carcinogens. Murray (1964) has actually argued for this particular causal relation, and published figures showing a closer relation between value and number of lighters sold, on the one hand, and deaths from lung cancer, on the other, than between cigarette smoking and lung cancer. The particular examples may be unlikely agents, but the possibility of some such agent being responsible must be examined.

3. A correlate of H causes C. There are several candidates here for the role of causal agent. Stress, to take one example, has been shown to be a possible cause of cancer, and there is evidence that stress causes people to smoke. Drinking, criminal behavior, and womanizing are all associated with smoking; these and other factors increase what Pearl (1928) called the "rate of living," and this may be responsible for C.

4. C, or an associated precondition, causes H. Burch has called this the "converse causal" hypothesis. In other words, factors associated with C, or conditions predisposing to C, might cause a person to take up or maintain the smoking habit.

5. Some other factor causes, or predisposes to, both H and C. This is Fisher's constitutional hypothesis. As Fisher argued, one or more genetic factors predispose to H; one or more genetic factors predispose to C; the association between H and C then arises at the genetic level.

6. These various causal hypotheses are, of course, not mutually exclusive, and any combination might be needed to account for the observed associations. This is particularly true of the main hypotheses considered in the past, that is, (1) and (5). As Burch (1983, p. 822) points out, "If any 'evaluation' of an association is to be truly 'comprehensive', the relative contributions of (the various hypothetical causes), together with their respective confidence limits, would have to be assessed. No such assessments have appeared in the Surgeon General's reports."

If genetic factors are at all important, and the evidence indicates clearly that they are (Eysenck, 1980), then all arguments from correlations are subject to the obvious criticism that self-selection plays an important part, vitiating the observed relationships to an unknown extent. It is well known that the application of statistical criteria of significance demands a process of randomization, and such randomization is conspicuously missing in the data usually produced to support the received view. There are, of course, ways of getting around the tech¬ical difficulties in the way of randomization in connection with smoking and disease, as demonstrated, for instance, by Rose and Hamilton (1978) and Rose et al. (1982), but these have not been explored by the authors of the Surgeon General's reports, or those of the Royal College of Physicians.

The conclusions that can be drawn from a statistical study of epidemiological data are, of course, dependent not only on the logic of the experimental design and the quality of statistical analysis, but even more crucially on the quality of the actual data collected. If the data themselves are highly unreliable, and in particular when they are biased, erroneous conclusions may be drawn, even though methodology and statistical analysis appear impeccable. The data on which the received view is based are almost always diagnoses made by a physician and recorded on the death certificate; the questions raised in this section deal with the reliability of such data. It is noteworthy that data of this kind have been used in all the official reports by the Surgeon General and the College of Physicians, without seriously dealing with the very high level of misdiagnosis that seems to be prevalent; neither has there been any discussion of the possibility of bias, which appears to be a very real danger in these fields.

There has been a good deal of criticism of the use of statistics derived from diagnoses on death certificates; they have been generally considered as inaccurate and unreliable (Abramson et al., 1971; Beadenkopf et al., 1963; Briggs, 1975; Wells, 1923; Willis, 1967). Surveys by Britton (1974), Cameron et al.

(1977), Gruver and Freis (1957), Hartveit (1979), Heasman and Lipworth (1966), and Waldron and Vickerstaff (1977) have given ample support to these criticisms. Britton (1974), for instance, found that the reported frequency of disagreements between clinical and autopsy diagnoses ranges from 6% to 65%! If we regard autopsies as completely reliable criteria (an assumption which, as we shall see, is not entirely true), then clearly the amount of inaccuracy in diagnoses is unacceptable for serious statistical work.

Some quotations may give a rough idea of the consensus in this area. Bauer and Robbins (1972, p. 1474) state that "our study indicates that accurate clinical diagnoses of cancer are as much a problem today as they were a half-century ago." Abramson, Sacks, and Cabana (1971, p. 430) state that "the death certificate data had marked limitations as an indication of the presence of myocardial infarction, cerebrovascular disease, pulmonary embolisms or infarctions. . . . They gave a fairly accurate indication of the presence of malignant neoplasms but not of the specific sites or categories of neoplasms." And Britton (1974, p. 208) concluded that "autopsies earlier did and still do reveal a considerable number of errors in clinical diagnoses. . . . There is no convincing sign that the rate of errors had diminished over the years." So much for the accuracy of the data on which the received view is based.

As an example of the most carefully planned and conducted work in this field, let us consider the study by Cameron and McGoogan (1981). They reported a prospective study of 1,152 hospital autopsies, comparing these with death certification in each case. They were merely concerned with the *major* disease leading to death as indicated by the physician filling in the death certificate. They found that the main clinical diagnosis was confirmed in 703 out of the 1,152 cases, or in 61%, leaving an error of 39%. This figure is not far removed from that observed by Britton (1974) in Sweden, where he found, in a careful, clinically controlled assessment, that main clinical diagnoses were confirmed in 57% of cases, leaving an error of 43%. Heasman and Lipworth (1966) and Waldron and Vickerstaff (1977) reported confirmed diagnoses in only 45% and 47.5% respectively, leaving error rates of 55% and 52.5% It is small surprise that Cameron and McGoogan (1981, p. 281) come to the conclusion that: "In our experience, statistics from death certificates are so inaccurate that they are not suitable for use in research or planning." If this be true, then clearly all the statistical work supporting the received view is based on extremely uncertain foundations.

One other item of interest emerged from the Cameron and McGoogan study: a marked increase in the proportion of diagnostic discrepancies with increasing age of the subjects. Below the age of 45 years, diagnoses were correct in 78%, but thereafter they fell off in a step-like manner with each succeeding decade until, over 75 years, fewer than half were confirmed. This has particular relevance to the incidence of lung cancer, as this of course occurs mainly in older men and women.

It is of interest to look specifically at data for neoplasms and for coronary heart disease diagnoses, as errors in these are of special relevance to the topic of this chapter. Cancer of the bronchus/lung was correctly diagnosed in 88 cases and wrongly diagnosed in 61 cases; thus the error rate is about the same as for all diseases. Bauer and Robbins (1972) looked at autopsies on 2,734 cancer patients, and found that 26% had clinically undiagnosed cancer; in a further 14% the condition was incompletely diagnosed, that is, cancer was suspected but its primary site was not known or was wrongly identified. Cameron and McGoogan conclude their comments on neoplasms by stating, "Carcinoma of bronchus was the most common neoplasm in our series and provided the largest group of misdiagnoses" (p. 294).

Turning now to cardiorespiratory conditions, we find for acute myocardiac infarct an agreement on 198 cases, and a disagreement on 109 cases— again an unacceptable level of error of diagnoses. Cerebrovascular disease scored an agreement in 129 cases and disagreement in 118 cases, with an error rate of almost 50%. "The most common problem of differential diagnosis appeared to be in distinguishing it from cardiovascular disease," Cameron and McGoogan stated (p. 293). Hartveit (1979), Heasman and Lipworth (1967), and Kagan et al. (1966) also found a large amount of overdiagnosis and underdiagnosis of cerebrovascular disease.

Where diagnoses are as unreliable as they have been found to be in the case of lung cancer and coronary heart disease, we must be particularly concerned about the phenomenon of "detection bias," that is, the tendency of the physician to diagnose "smoking-related diseases" in smokers rather than in nonsmokers. Feinstein and Wells (1974) have published data to show that such detection bias is a reality, and might easily lead to false conclusions in the absence of careful necropsy examination of the causes of death. Detection bias undoubtedly contributes part of the high mortality ratios for lung cancer recorded in table 2–1, and should be carefully excluded in any study purporting to have scientific validity.

Feinstein and Wells (1974) looked at 654 patients who were diagnosed after necropsy as having died of lung cancer. In this series, they studied the relationship between the rate of nondiagnosis during life and the amount of antecedent cigarette smoking. In patients whose history of cigarette smoking was unknown, this nondiagnosis rate was 37%. The rate of nondiagnosis then portrays a distinctive downward gradient, falling from 38% undetected among the non-cigarette smokers, to 20% among the light smokers, 14% in the moderate, and 10% and 11% respectively in the heavy and extreme smokers. These data are shown in diagrammatic form in figure 2–2. "The data therefore suggested that the more patients smoke, the more likely they were to have the lung cancer detected during life," stated Feinstein and Wells (1974, p. 185).

Feinstein and Wells also investigated how this premortem detection gradient was related to the intensity of diagnostic examinations received during

Rate of nondiagnosis
(lung cancer) during life

Search rate in ordering
sputum pap smears

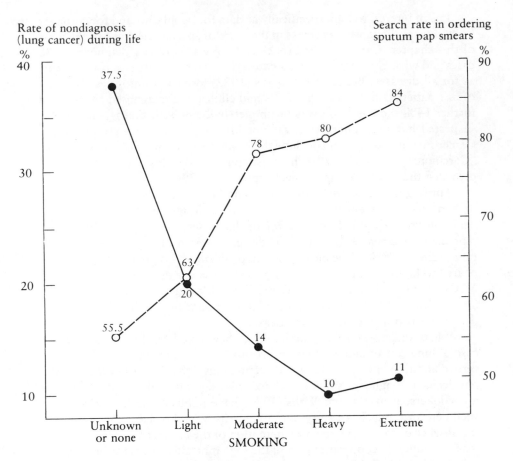

Figure 2–2. Smoking as Related to Rate of Nondiagnosis of Lung Cancer during Life, and Search Rate for Diagnostic Tests

life by patients in their entire series, which included 677 cases which were diagnosed during life but received no necropsy. They used for this purpose the Papanicolaou cytologic examination (or pap smear) of the sputum. Since this test had not been obtained by all of their patients, its solicitation might have been affected by diverse factors, including the patient's smoking history. They therefore examined the pap smear research rate, and the results are also shown in figure 2–2. The test was requested more frequently in smokers than in nonsmokers. Statistical tests showed that the trend was very highly significant. Detection bias was consequently found to be distinctly related to the amount of cigarette smoking.

There is no space to go into the other analyses done by Feinstein and Wells, which tend to support the general conclusion that "cigarette smoking may contribute more to the diagnosis of lung cancer than it does to producing the disease itself" (p. 184), and they go on to say: "It seems important to recall that in epidemiologic surveys of causes of disease, the investigators get data about the occurrence of diagnoses not the occurrence of diseases, and that the rates of diagnosis may be affected by bias in the way that doctors order and deploy the available diagnostic technology" (p. 184). Taken together with the general unreliability of diagnoses of lung cancer, these findings make it doubly improbable that the observed diagnostic data which furnish the foundations for epidemiological studies can be taken seriously by scientific investigators. More research is urgently required on the actual unreliability of diagnoses, as well as on "detection bias"; if reliable data on these two points were available, then possibly statistical corrections might be made to the published data on the relationship between smoking and lung cancer. Without such data, all conclusions are clearly based on very unfirm foundations indeed.

What light do these considerations throw on the problem of the apparent rapid rise in lung cancer over the years? This is copiously illustrated in the report of the Surgeon General, together with the rise, 20 years previous, of cigarette consumption; it will be remembered that this temporal correlation is one of the major arguments put forward by epidemiologists in favor of the received view. At the same time this apparent rise presents great difficulties for those who, like Burch (1976) and Deser (1979), argue in favor of theories of the conception and development of carcinomas which are based on genetic hypotheses and largely disregard the role of external carcinogens. It is quite implausible to argue that there have been genetic changes of such a size and nature as to cause such manifold increases in the occurrence of lung cancer, and consequently the argument for the causal effects of environmental changes, air pollution and cigarette smoking, for example, must be taken seriously. An alternative suggestion is that the increase in deaths diagnosed as lung cancer has been due to improvements in diagnostic techniques, and is therefore more apparent than real. This argument has been put forward by Rigdon and Kirchoff (1953), who concluded that claims of genuine increase in the frequency of lung cancer were "open to question." Willis (1967, p. 187), after an extensive review of the literature, concluded: "It is not possible either to affirm or to deny that there has been a real increase." Similarly, Feinstein (1974) concluded his historical discussion by stating that diagnostic changes have played the most important role in the increase in death rate from lung cancer. Burch (1976) cites much evidence to support this view.

It seems certain that in the first years of the century lung cancer was considerably underdiagnosed. Sehrt (1904) described 178 cases of lung cancer discovered at necropsy, only six of which had been recognized during life. If we take this ratio of 172 failures to diagnose lung cancer as compared with six successful diagnoses of lung cancer, and argue that with our modern techniques all or most of the 178 cases of lung cancer would have been so diagnosed, then it seems quite reasonable to assume that much if not all of the apparent increase in deaths from lung cancer may have been due to improvements in diagnostic techniques.

The evidence suggests that at present there is a considerable overdiagnosis of lung cancer, and the question arises: What causes false-positive diagnoses? Rosenblatt (1969) has suggested that in the post-1930 period, false-positive clinical diagnoses of lung cancer have often been reported due to metastases in the lung from primary locations at many different sites. He too believed that the very great increase in recorded lung cancer deaths over the past 30 years was not due to an extrinsic carcinogen but resulted from the use of new diagnostic techniques, in particular, radiology, bronchoscopy, sputum examination, and surgery. He further suggested that the great interest in lung cancer stimulated by the theory that it might be due to smoking had produced a tendency to overdiagnose this particular disorder, and Smithers (1953) discovered that even specialists in thoracic diseases were guilty of a large proportion of false-positive diagnoses from 1944 to 1950.

Rosenblatt et al. (1971a,b) supported this argument by showing that at the doctors' hospital in New York, *clinical* diagnosis of lung cancer was over twice as frequent as diagnosis following necropsy. Carcinoma of the lung was the only neoplasm to be greatly overdiagnosed clinically, and in which no unsuspected cases were found at necropsy. Primary lung cancer had been simulated by pulmonary metastases from carcinoma of the pancreas, kidney, stomach, breast and thyroid, and by malignant melanoma. Burch (1976) makes the interesting comment: "It is of great interest that the 5.5% of lung cancers found in this recent New York necropsy series of malignancy is *lower* than a proportion found amongst several necropsy series from Austria, Germany and the U.S. published at the end of the 19th and beginning of the 20th century. In five subseries in which necropsy findings were the main basis of diagnosis, lung cancer diagnosis ranged from 8.3% to 11.5% of all cancers." This finding must throw doubt on the alleged increase in lung cancer.

The problem of metastasis to the lung being erroneously diagnosed as lung cancer is emphasized by a study reported by Burch (1978c). He found that a total of 747 primary lung cancers was recorded in a large-scale postmortem study of the anatomical distribution of metastases in Swedish cancer cases, but some 2,079 metastases to the lung from primary sites outside the lung! Burch gives many further instances, and it is difficult not to agree with him when he concludes: "There can be no doubt . . . that diagnostic artefacts have contributed massively to the secular increases in recorded death rates from lung cancer. . . . The beginning of the century was characterized by a severe under-diagnosis, especially above the age of 40 years" (p. 458).

We have assumed in this section that autopsies will normally constitute a completely reliable criterion. However, it is fairly optimistic to imagine that diagnoses, even when based on autopsies, can be relied upon to give a true picture of the actual condition of the patient which caused death. In a recent editorial (1971) in the *Annals of Thoracic Surgery*, it was pointed out that: "The most experienced pathologists often disagree on classification of these tumours, and differential criteria are poorly defined." Large bodies of data are available to indicate that the reliability of medical diagnosis using pathological material relevant to respiratory diseases is well below what would be regarded as acceptable in psychological tests (see Kern et al., 1968; McCarthy and Widmer, 1974; Reid and Rose, 1964; Stebbings, 1971; Thurlbeck et al., 1968; Wilson and Burke, 1957; Yesner, 1973; and Yesner et al., 1965, 1973).

Autopsies, while greatly superior to death-bed diagnoses, are obviously still unreliable in that different experts have different views. Such unreliability makes validity suspect, although it would be difficult to give a numerical assessment of the degree of unreliability or the lack of validity in these data.

The difficulties introduced by errors in the certification of the cause of death make it desirable to study trends in *overall* mortality, rather than mortality due to specific diseases. Doll and Peto (1976) conducted a large-scale study of this kind and concluded that "much of the excess mortality in cigarette smokers could be attributed with certainty to the habit." Burch (p. 1534) (1978c) examined this conclusion and carried out a large-scale statistical analysis of smoking and mortality in England and Wales from 1950 to 1976, calculating percentage changes in sex- and age-specific death rate for all causes of death in England and Wales, by three-year periods. These changes in death rates were compared with corresponding trends and sex- and age-specific "constant tar" and "current" cigarette consumption in the United Kingdom. He concluded that: "No obvious cause-and-effect relation can be discerned" (p. 87). As he points out, the main problem is to explain the fairly consistent *decrease* in death rates in both sexes and all age groups during periods when cigarette consumption was either rising or falling. "The trends failed to support the hypothesis that smoking influenced mortality," he states (p. 87). Altogether he concluded that "This paper has shown that secular trends in overall mortality in England and Wales give no consistent indication that they were appreciably influenced by changes in cigarette consumption . . . on scientific grounds there can be little doubt that the conclusions drawn by the Royal College of Physicians (1971), Doll and Peto (1976), and the Surgeon General of the United States (1979) about the lethality of smoking are precipitate and unwarranted" (p. 102). These conclusions are supported by findings from monozygotic and dizygotic twins discordant for smoking (Cederlof et al., 1977); unfortunately, the number of subjects in this study is too small to permit definitive conclusions. Nevertheless, the evidence appears to be definitely in favor of a "not proven" vote as far as the lethal action of smoking on health in general is concerned.

We have dwelt at some length on the issue of the reliability and validity of the raw data on which all statistical and epidemiological calculations must be based, because if these data are wanting, then no firm conclusions can possibly be based on them. It would be possible to break off the whole discussion at this point and declare that the lack of reliability and validity of the data makes it doubtful whether the observed relationships, if they exist at all, are anywhere near as strong as they are supposed to be. It is thus impossible to make a definitive choice between the different causal theories enumerated in the first section. However, it may be worthwhile to look in more detail at the epidemiological evidence, to see whether even if the data are admitted as being at least to some extent reliable and valid, the argument for the received view may not still be found to be lacking in logical consistency and factual support. To this task we will turn in the next section.

Epidemiological Criteria for Causality

The attribution of causality on the basis of correlational data requires a definition of the idea of cause. The U.S. Surgeon General (1982) defines the notion of "cause" as follows: "The notion of a significant, effectual relationship between an agent and an associated disorder or disease in the host" (p. 16–17). Later on we read that: "The causal significance of an association is a matter of judgement that goes beyond any statement of statistical probability" (p. 17). Burch (1983) considers this emphasis on *judgment*, here and in other parts of the report, as disturbing. As he points out, subjective methods in science should be allowed as little scope as possible.

The report gives five explicit criteria for evaluating causal significance (p. 17):

1. The consistency of the association.
2. The strength of the association.
3. The specificity of the association.
4. The temporal relationship of the association.
5. The coherence of the association.

These criteria have remained unchanged in the 18 years since the first Surgeon General's report appeared, and their application to the association between smoking and lung cancer will now be discussed.

The Consistency of the Association

The definition of consistency given by the report (1982) is: "This criterion implies that diverse methods of approach in the study of an association will provide similar conclusions" (p. 17). Also: "Replication assures that the association is not likely to be an artefact due to bias in the study methodology or subject selection, and that it is not indirect due to confounding variables such as diet, occupation, or genetics" (p. 17). It is interesting to look at the relative risk ratios (smokers vs. non-smokers) for lung cancer mortality in certified retrospective studies published over the period 1939–1970 given in Table 4 (p. 35) of the report. For males, the observed ratios range from 1.2 to 36.0, and for females from 0.2 to 5.3. Similar data are reported in Table 5 (p. 36), giving mortality ratios found in eight prospective studies; these range from 3.76 to 14.2 in males and from 2.03 to 5.0 in females.

Figure 2–3 shows a comparison between relative risks of lung cancer in smokers, differing in rate of smoking, as compared to nonsmokers, for a Caucasian and a Japanese male sample (Burch, 1984b, p. 151). The difference is too large to suggest "consistency of association." In addition, Burch has demonstrated a very significant contrast in the *forms* of the two dose-response relationships; this presents an even more formidable challenge for the received view. Burch (1983, p. 823) comments that: "With ratios showing a range, overall, of more than two orders of magnitude, it is not self-evident that any acceptable criterion of consistency has been satisfied. The Committee would appear to have been faced with a choice of either abandoning the causal interpretation, or of explaining away this enormous diversity." The report fails to do this; instead it claims that: "Regardless of the method, these studies have consistently found an association between smoking and lung cancer" (p. 34). In fact even this statement is untrue; the table gives two examples of relative risk ratios less than unity, that is, negative associations; it is difficult to see how such data can satisfy a criterion based on consistency of association.

Strength of the Association

It is almost impossible to consider "strength" and "consistency" in isolation and separate from each other, but the Surgeon General's Report argues that: "The relative risk ratio measures the strength of an association and provides an evaluation of the importance of that factor in the production of a disease" (p. 17). This statement contravenes the logic of epidemiological inquiry and takes for granted that which is to be proved. The risk ratio only provides an evaluation of the importance of a factor in the production of a disease *once its causal effect has been proved*—it cannot be used by itself to prove the causal relationship. Nevertheless, the strength of the association, if found to differ from one population to another, may provide interesting evidence in favor of a genetic, and opposed to a causal, inference. On the hypothesis of the universal causal effect of smoking on lung cancer, similar or identical risk ratios should be found, say, in Oriental and Caucasian populations. This, however, is not so.

Roughly speaking, as will be seen from Table 5 of the report (p. 36), mortality ratios in seven predominantly Caucasian populations cluster around

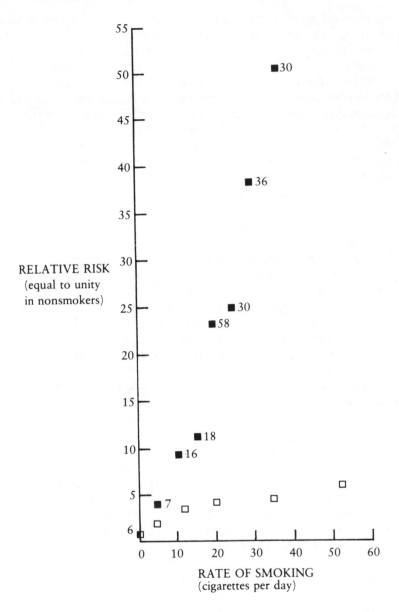

Figure 2–3. Rate of Smoking and Relative Risks of Lung Cancer in British and Japanese Samples

an average mortality rate of about ten, ranging from 7.0 to 14.2. Compared to this we have a value for Japan of 3.8; for Chinese residents in Singapore of 3.8 (MacLennan et al., 1977); in Northern Thailand the value was 1.6 (not significantly different from unity) (Simarak et al., 1977); from mainland China the risk ratio of 1.57 has been reported by Henderson (1979). For women, the incidence of lung cancer in the Chinese in Hong Kong gives a relative risk of only 1.74 (Chan et al., 1979). For women of Hawaiian, Japanese and Chinese origin, Hinds et al. (1981) found relative risks of 10.5, 4.9 and 1.8 respectively, thus aligning the Hawaiian women with the Caucasian mortality ratios, and contrasting them with the Japanese and Chinese women studied. It is difficult to account for these very large differences in mortality ratios between Caucasians and Oriental groups in terms of the received view; it is much more natural to appeal to genetic causes in this context. (See also figure 2–3.)

In this connection, it is relevant to cite the important work of Belcher (1971) on world-wide differences in the sex-ratio of bronchial carcinoma. The ratio of men affected as compared to women affected varies widely in different parts of the world and in people of different racial origin in the same part of the world. In Nigeria, for instance, the incidence is actually higher among the women than among the men, whereas in Holland it is 13.5 to 1 in favor of the men! There is no relationship between the sex ratio and the total tobacco consumption in different countries, nor is the different age structure of the different populations responsible. Belcher concludes "that there is a genetic factor in the aetiology of bronchial carcinoma" (p. 220).

Under the heading of "Strength of the Association," the report states that: "Important to the strength, as well as to the coherence of the association, is the presence of the dose-response phenomenon in which a positive gradient between degree of exposure to the agent and incidence or mortality rates of the disease can be demonstrated (p. 17)." Such a dose-response relationship would also be predicted from the genetic hypothesis, as Burch (1983, p. 826) points out:

> To take the simplest postulates, smokers can be divided into two categories, social and habituated. Social smokers tend to be light smokers and could quit readily; habituated, genetically-predisposed smokers, tend to be heavy smokers. Hence, in any group of light smokers, social smokers will predominate and the association with lung cancer will be relatively weak; in any group of heavy smokers, habituated, genetically-predisposed smokers will predominate and the association with lung cancer will be strong. An apparent 'dose-response' relation will be observed.

The causal hypothesis, in its pure form, would predict the same response from the same "dose" in different populations; the genetic hypothesis, which assumes that the association between smoking and lung cancer depends on the strength of the associations between patients presenting genotypes, rather than on smoking levels, would predict some correlation, though not necessarily a very high one, between national mortality and national smoking levels. As we have seen in figure 2–1, the observed relationship between national mortality from lung cancer and national cigarette consumption is not very strong. As an example of discordance, we may take the age-standardized mortality from lung cancer in Finnish men in 1960–61, which was about double that in U.S. white males, whereas cigarette consumption in 1950 in Finland was about half that in the United States (Burch, 1976). There are many other anomalies of this kind, as the perusal of the report will show; Burch (1983, p. 826) has pointed out: "The pure causal hypothesis might, by this test alone, appear to be untenable. The existence of the weak correlation between national rates of mortality and smoking is consistent with the causal component but it is also consistent with the pure constitutional hypothesis and no causal action."

Passey (1962) has thrown doubt on the existence of a proper dose-response relationship within a given population. As he points out: "Nowhere has it been claimed that the heavy smoker is stricken with cancer earlier than the light smoker. If lung cancer in smokers is the result of direct carcinogenic action, one would certainly expect this to happen; for experiment has shown beyond question that a potent carcinogen induces tumours early" (p. 110). Passey next examines the smoking history of 499 men with lung cancer, grouping the cases according to the number of cigarettes smoked. He gives a table which shows "that the amount smoked makes no appreciable difference to the mean age at which the person first reported to the clinic. The light smoker is afflicted with lung cancer at the same age as a heavy smoker. This is a surprising observation. The mean age at which smoking was started was 17; the average amount smoked daily was 23 cigarettes; the mean age at which the patient presented at the clinic was 57 years . . . the mean smoking period was some 40 years" (p. 109). Nor was it true, as might be said, that the youngest of these patients with lung cancer might have smoked particularly heavily, and that the eldest had survived because they were specially moderate smokers: "The amount smoked daily by old and young is not dissimilar. Yet the oldest patient had smoked for some 50 years longer than the youngest patient—this represents well over a quarter of a million more cigarettes. These figures suggest that there is no relation between the amount smoked daily and the age of onset of lung cancer" (p. 111. See also Herrold, 1972).

Pike and Doll (1965) replicated Passey's findings from their sample of British doctors. They concluded that: "Neither the amount smoked nor the age of starting made any substantial difference to the (period) average age of onset of the disease" (p. 667), and these conclusions were also found valid for the "life-span" average under the conditions in which lung cancer is produced in man.

Last but not least in discussing the strength of the association, we must consider the paradox presented by mortality ratios as related to degree of inhalation. On the received view it would be expected that inhalation would give much higher mortality ratios, for equal amounts smoked, than would lack of inhalation. Fisher (1959) analyzed retrospective data of disease by daily rate of smoking and inhalation status, and found that within a given range of smoking, inhalers had a paradoxically *lower* risk of lung cancer than noninhalers. Doll and Peto (1976), in a twenty-year follow-up of British male doctors, standardized for age and amount smoked (in nine groups) and found overall that the risk of lung cancer in inhalers was 84% of that of noninhalers. A thorough discussion of the evidence is given by Eysenck (1980).

The latest study along these lines (Higgenbottam et al., 1982), reporting on 18,403 male civil servants, found that "lung cancer rates were higher overall for (non-inhalers), particularly in heavy smokers" (p. 113). They attempt an ex posteriori explanation, but this is highly speculative and has no basis in empirical studies. Furthermore, it would not allow us to predict that coronary deaths were more common among inhalers, as also found by Higgenbottam. The facts as they stand are clearly an embarrassing anomaly for adherents of the received view, and difficult to reconcile with it. The absence of the anticipated relationship between inhalation and lung cancer must, as Fisher already pointed out in his original paper, be a severe blow to the received view, but remarkably little effort seems to have been made to accommodate the finding and attempt to explain it along causal lines.

Specificity of the Association

The Surgeon General's report states that: "Specificity implies that a causal agent invariably leads to a single specific disease, an event rarely observed" (p. 18). This notion, which seems to be based on Koch's postulate, does not seem very relevant, and the report itself makes it clear that specificity is not to be regarded as an important consideration. "In summary, despite the fact that the demonstration of specificity in an association makes the causal hypothesis more acceptable, lack of specificity does not negate such an hypothesis, since many biologic and epidemiologic aspects of the association must be considered" (p. 19). To find positive mortality ratios, although rather low ones, with many different types of cancer does not detract from the possibility that smoking causes lung cancer. It is possible that one or more components of cigarette smoke act as a fairly general carcinogen with a wide distribution through the body, or that smoking affects the immune system and renders it less effective.

More difficult for the received view, however, is the existence of negative associations between smoking and disease. These negative relationships (with colorectal cancer and Parkinson's disease, for instance) have already been noted, and will not here be discussed. They do present a problem which proponents of the received view have been reluctant to tackle.

Temporal Relationship of the Association

We have already dealt with a major point made by the adherents of the received view, namely that: "The chief reason for rejecting the genetic hypothesis is its inability to account for the enormous rise in death rates from lung cancer in the past half century" (Royal College of Physicians, 1971, p. 53). This "enormous rise" may be largely or even entirely fictitious, and due to better methods of ascertainment of the disease. Until better figures are available, little can be said about the true increase in lung cancer, if any, over this period.

The best statistics to use in considering the suggestion, contained in table 2–1, that smoking is responsible to some degree for many different types of cancer, is of course total mortality from cancer. This statistic has the advantage, for reasons already given, of being much more reliable than mortality rates for specific cancers. If, indeed, there is a tendency for smoking to promote cancer, then the marked increase in smoking over the past fifty years should show a corresponding increase in the death rates for cancer. Is this so? There has certainly been a marked increase in the number of deaths from cancer and in the proportion of total deaths due to cancer, but this increase is entirely accounted for by the increase in age which has taken place at the same time in the populations in question. Now cancer is a disease of old age, and hence the increase in longevity has produced a disproportionate increase in cancers. When corrected for differential age distributions, however, this increase *vanishes completely*. On this basis there is no evidence that there has been an increase in the death rate from cancer corresponding to the increase in smoking. This statistic alone should convince us that the alleged saving of hundreds of thousands of lives if only people would stop smoking is mythology rather than extrapolation from reliable data along meaningful scientific venues. The evidence has been examined in great detail by Oeser (1979), Koeppe (1980), and Koeppe et al. (1977). The data have also been examined by Burch (1976), with similar results.

There has been an apparent *relative* increase of cancer of the lung, mainly in men, and cancer of the uterus, entirely in women of course. It seems likely, as we have pointed out, that the former increase is largely if not entirely due to errors in diagnosis, in particular detection bias. The latter, as Koeppe et al. (1977) have suggested, may be due to the earlier menarche in girls, which makes their effective sexual age greater now than it would have been fifty years ago; this hypothesis is of course speculative but sounds reasonable. The figures quoted by these authors certainly give little support to the view that many lives could be saved by the cessation of smoking, or that many lives have been lost in the past fifty years because of smoking, through cancer.

The report of the U.S. Surgeon General makes rather a different case. "The criterion of temporal relationship requires that exposure to the suspect aetiologic factor precedes the disease. Temporality is more difficult to establish for diseases with long latency periods, such as cancer" (p. 19). The report goes on to point out that: "One study examined the relationship between *per capita* tobacco consumption in 1930 and many lung cancer deaths in 1950 in 11 different countries. There was a strong positive correlation between tobacco consumption in 1930 and many lung cancer deaths in 1950 in 11 different countries . . . there was a strong positive correlation between tobacco consumption in 1930 and lung cancer death rates in 1950" (p. 40). Figure 9 in the report (p. 43) graphs the data and shows the correlation of 0.73 ± 0.30; it is clear there are many grave anomalies in this table. Thus Great Britain, where about 10% fewer cigarettes were smoked than in the United States in 1930, had in 1950 a death rate from lung cancer about 2.5 times as large. Attempts can, of course, be made to explain away such anomalies, but they are too large to be easily accounted for in terms of such factors as different smoking habits, for example.

Of particular interest is the temporary relationship observed in the differential patterns for males and females. In the United Kingdom there occurred a sharp increase in cigarette consumption by women about thirty years after that which occurred in males. However, Burch (1976, 1983) has shown that: "When rise in recorded mortality from lung cancer is studied in detail, it is seen that the temporal pattern of increments, from one five-year period to the next, is remarkably synchronous in the two sexes from the beginning of the century to 1955 and then from 1965 onwards. It follows that the main causes of the recorded increases in both sexes were also synchronous in both sexes and therefore could not have been cigarette smoking" (1983, p. 828). Thus what is claimed to be one of the strongest proofs for the received view turns out, on detailed examination, to be a strong argument against that view.

We must conclude that the study of the temporary relationship of the association between cigarette smoking and cancer is vitiated by the poor quality of the data, but as far as that goes it does not offer any support for the received view.

The Coherence of the Association

The report defines the relevance of this criterion by saying that: "In order to establish the coherence of the specific association, other possible explanations for the association must be systematically considered and excluded or taken into account" (p. 20). Unfortunately, the report does little in the way of examining or taking into account "other explanations," particularly the genetic or constitutional one. In this section we will examine some of the evidence that is relevant to this problem of "coherence." We have already examined the dose-response relationship and the question of sex differences in the incidence of lung cancer, finding in both cases that the coherence claimed by the report is in fact nonexistent. No more need be said here on these points.

However, one very important argument relevant to consistency, and said to be in favor of the received view, is the apparent decline in lung cancer mortality with duration of cessation of smoking (Report, Table 2). As already pointed out, subjects were self-selected in all of these studies and it is widely recognized that no valid conclusions regarding causality can be drawn from studies of self-selected populations only. It is now quite clear that this is a crucial factor making it impossible to compare ex-smokers and continuing smokers with the aim of establishing the causal link between smoking and disease. Friedman et al. (1979) have shown that ex-smokers and continuing smokers are already very different from the point of view of health at the time that the ex-smokers give up smoking, and Eysenck (1980) has shown that with respect to personality, ex-smokers are more like nonsmokers than they are like continuing smokers. Thus the necessary conditions for the paradigm is not fulfilled, namely that ex-smokers and continuing smokers should be similar or identical from the point of view of personality and health at the time that ex-smokers give up smoking. Thus, no interpretation along causal lines can be made of the differential mortality rate of ex-smokers and continuing smokers.

From a general point of view, the study of the Multiple Risk Factor Intervention Trial Research Group (1982) is an example of the type of study of groups which are not self-selected, but include a measure of randomization. In this randomized primary prevention trial to test the effect of a multifactor intervention program on mortality from coronary heart disease, 12,866 high-risk men aged 35–57 years were randomly assigned *either* to a special intervention program consisting of drug care treatment for hypertension, counseling for cigarette smoking, and dietary advice for lowering blood cholesterol levels, *or* to the usual resources of health care in the community. An average follow-up period of 7 years showed that risk factor levels declined in both groups, but to a significantly greater degree for the experimental group. Mortality from coronary heart disease was 17.9 deaths per thousand in the experimental group and 19.3 deaths per thousand in the control group, a statistically nonsignificant difference. Total mortality rates were 41.2 per thousand in the experimental group and 40.4 per thousand in the control group, that is, mortality was greater in the experimental than in the control group. Thus, the effect of lowering significantly the consumption of cigarettes (as well as significantly lowering blood cholesterol levels and also lowering blood pressure) was practically nonexistent; the slightly greater mortality rate for the experimental group can hardly be taken seriously. The results as far as coronary heart disease are concerned will be discussed again later on; the overall mortality rate, however, is important because it includes cancers, and should have declined as a consequence of the lower levels of cigarette consumption in the experimental group. This is important in view of the statement, made in the U.S. Surgeon General's Report (1982, p. 5), that "Cigarette smokers have overall mortality rates substantially greater than those of non-smokers," and that it would be expected that giving up cigarette smoking would reduce these overall mortality rates. Apparently this is not so overall, and, as other studies have shown, it is not so with respect to cancers specifically.

One last word must be said about the multiple risk factor intervention trial. The reasons advanced after the fact to explain away the disappointing results (see Oliver, 1982), if they are to be taken seriously, suggest that the large group of specialists who planned this 115 million dollar trial were incompetent to a degree that seems hardly credible. Attempts to salvage isolated positive findings from the overall negative result goes counter to the spirit of statistical inquiry; individual comparisons, taken by themselves, cannot be subjected to the usual statistical calculus of probabilities, as they constitute a selected one or two out of a more numerous number of comparisons made.

It should be noted that other trials, such as the continuing World Health Organization European Trial, which comprises 63,733 men aged 40–59 in 44 parent factories in Britain, Belgium, Italy, Poland, and Spain (World Health Organization European Collaborative Group, 1982) also makes depressing reading in that changes were smaller than expected and not completely consistent or sustained. The authors found that, despite an estimated fall of 14% in coronary heart disease risk in the whole group and of 24% in the high-risk sub-group after 4 years, no equivalent fall in incidence of coronary heart disease might be shown even in a study of this size. Similarly, in the North Jarelia project (Puska et al., 1979), an overall mean net reduction of 17% in men and of 12% in women occurred 5 years after inception with regard to cigarette smoking, blood pressure, and plasma cholesterol concentrations in the intervention community, compared with the control community, but here also there was no reduction in mortality from coronary heart disease. Only the small-scale Oslo study (Hjermann et al., 1981) succeeded in showing a reduction in the incidence of coronary heart disease with cessation of smoking and dietary intervention to lower lipid concentrations in non-hypertensive men in high-risk categories. Overall, the outlook is not promising, although better-designed, better-controlled and longer-continued studies might alter the outlook. All one can say is that attempts to prove the influence of cigarette smoking as a causal factor in disease by means of trials avoiding the obvious error of self-selection have not on the whole been successful.

The studies so far mentioned have all dealt in the main with coronary heart disease, and it might be thought that the results might not apply to lung cancer. There is, however, the report by Rose et al. (1982) of a ten-year follow-up study of middle-aged male smokers at high risk of cardiorespiratory disease who were allocated randomly to an intervention or a normal care group. The intensive advice given to the first group was successful in reducing the average consumption of cigarettes by just over one half in this group. In the normal care group of 731 men, 25 cases of lung cancer were reported; in the intervention group of 714, there were 22 comparable cases—a nonsignificant difference. Data for all deaths in these groups are free from diagnostic error, and are hence the most reliable: 17.2% in the intervention group died compared with 17.5% in the normal care group, giving a negligible and statistically nonsignificant difference. Thus, this study gives results similar to the other intervention studies using randomized groups—*a failure to detect any effect of giving up smoking.* Curiously, Rose et al. found at a significant level of $p < 0.003$ that the intervention group subjects had a much higher rate of "all cancers other than lung cancer" than the nonintervention group subjects (p. 106); whether this result can be replicated is, of course, another matter, particularly since there are difficulties in assigning a valid probability value to an a posteriori hypothesis. Burch (1983) comments that, for all these studies, the results for total mortality are entirely in line with the analysis of temporal trends of sex- and age-specific mortality from all causes in the whole of England and Wales (Burch, 1983), which "failed to detect any causal influence of cigarette smoking when consumption was rising and no prophylactic influence when consumption was falling" (p. 832).

The last point raised by the report deals with the correspondence of lung cancer mortality among different populations with different tobacco consumption (Lyon, et al., 1980, pp. 48–50); the main point made is that Mormons and Californian Seventh Day Adventists, that is, nonsmoking groups, have a low incidence of lung cancer. The membership of such groups, of course, involves self-selection, or descent from self-selection progenitors, but even overlooking this obvious point, the results present difficulties for the received view, as Enstrom (1980) concluded after a careful examination of the evidence. According to the pure causal hypothesis, Mormons, who refrain from smoking in accordance with the dictates of their religion, should have an incidence of lung cancer the same as that which is found in comparable nonsmokers of the general population. Lyon et al. (1980) compared the incidence in Mormons with that in non-Mormons (smokers and nonsmokers) in Utah over the period 1967–75, finding an age-adjusted incidence of lung cancer in male Mormons of 46% of that in male non-Mormons; for females the incidence was 44%. Comparing the Mormons with nonsmokers only, it would appear that, on the basis of the received view, the incidence of lung cancer in male Mormons is at least twice that expected for a population of nonsmokers who are not Mormons. "On the constitutional hypothesis, the Mormon population—involving selection—comprises a mixture of never-smoking and smoking genotypes with, among males at least, a relatively high proportion of the former" (Burch, 1983, p. 832). The cancer mortality patterns in Mormons are "not clearly explained by their smoking habits" (Enstrom, 1980).

It would be possible to pursue many minor points which figure in the reports of the U.S. Surgeon General, or the Royal College of Physicians in the United Kingdom, but such detailed discussion seems inappropriate as the major points dealt with here give quite a clear picture; other points are discussed by Burch (1983) and Eysenck (1980). We may conclude that as far as lung cancer is concerned (and many of the arguments apply equally well to coronary disease), the data on which all analyses are based are unreliable and extremely faulty; it is doubtful whether any firm conclusions can be based on them. When we look at the five epidemiological criteria for causation adopted by the U.S. Surgeon General's Report, and consider the evidence in detail, we find that the evidence is not conclusive for any of them, and in many cases it is directly contradictory to the claims of the received view. Most of the work is marred by self-selection of cases, and by the failure of the report's authors to take this factor into account. Alternative theories are hardly considered, particularly the constitutional or genetic hypothesis. Although there is much evidence in its favor, this hypothesis has never been compared with the causal hypothesis for the purposes of determining which is more in accord with the actual facts. The results certainly do not *disprove* the possibility that smoking may cause lung cancer, and other cancers as well; the evidence equally certainly does not establish that it does so. It will be clear that we cannot agree with the conclusion in the report (Surgeon General, 1982) that: "Cigarette smoking is the major cause of lung cancer in the United States" (p. 62), or that smoking is responsible for 85% of lung cancer mortality (p. 63). These conclusions do not follow from the evidence, and indeed are contradicted by much of the evidence. We still have to decide whether the received view is true, in whole or in part; whether the genetic hypothesis (to be treated in more detail in a later section) is true; whether both hypotheses are complementary, and act together to produce lung cancer; or whether any of the other alternative hypotheses considered in an earlier section may also play a part. One cannot help but feel that the quality of the research might have been better had there been a clear recognition of the importance of alternative hypotheses, and less determination to prove that the received view could account for all the facts.

Epidemiology and Coronary Heart Disease

For coronary heart disease, as for lung cancer, the received view appears to be that the relationship between smoking and coronary heart disease is not only statistical, but also causal (Working Party of the Royal College of Physicians, 1976). As an editorial in the *British Medical Journal* (1979) states: "Today's main killing diseases are due to the way we live. Each year in Britain cancer kills over 120,000 people, and many of these cancers are known to be due to environmental factors. Cigarette smoking causes not only 30,000 deaths from lung cancer but even more from coronary heart disease." We have already considered the evidence for this view with respect to lung cancer; with respect to coronary heart disease also the received view has been doubted by a number of critics (see, for example, Burch, 1978, 1980; Seltzer, 1970, 1975; Thomas, 1968; Werko, 1976).

Much of what has been said in the previous sections applies here too, particularly the unreliability of the data on which conclusions are based and the self-selection of cases. The failure of intervention trials has been particularly noticeable in the case of coronary heart disease; this subject has been dealt with in detail in the last section. Many authors, while on the whole conceding some causal role to smoking, have been cautious in their advocacy for two major reasons. First, the mortality ratio for coronary heart disease is much lower than that for lung cancer; compared to 10.8 for lung cancer, the mortality ratio for coronary heart disease is only 1.7. If it has been found difficult to prove the causal efficacy of smoking as far as lung cancer is concerned, clearly it would be much more difficult in regard to coronary heart disease.

Second and equally important is the fact that, while smoking has been, if not the only, certainly the major alleged causal factor for lung cancer, there are several other probably more important causal factors for coronary heart disease, such as hypercholesterolaemia and hypertension. Thus not only is the correlation between smoking and disease much lower in coronary heart disease, but smoking is only one of three (and possibly many more) factors supposed to have a causal effect on coronary heart disease. Here too the constitutional alternative has seldom been considered, but presents a powerful challenge—all the more powerful because the alleged causal effects of smoking are so much weaker than in the case of lung cancer and are clearly not the only external factors relevant to coronary heart disease, even if smoking should be found to be so relevant.

The possible importance of the relationship between smoking and coronary heart disease (CHD) lies of course in the fact that although the mortality ratio for heart disease is much lower than that for lung cancer, the numbers involved are much larger. Coronary heart disease is now the leading cause of death in many countries, and in Britain, for instance, the numbers of deaths attributed to it have been rising steadily over the past forty years. Most authorities agree that a *statistical* association between smoking and heart disease exists; the crucial question again is whether or not there is a *causal* relation. In 1964 the U.S. Surgeon General's report concluded that: "It is not clear that the association has causal significance" (p. 64). The 1977 report of the Royal College of Physicians, here as always more ready to jump to possibly unjustified conclusions, decided that "the association between smoking and heart disease is largely one of cause and effect" (p. 84). The evidence, as we shall see, does not support this conclusion.

There is little question that constitutional factors are important. Seltzer (1975) took three methods of quantifying pulmonary function: forced vital capacity, forced expiratory volume in one second, and expiratory flow. His population consisted of 65,086 white, black and Oriental cigarette smokers and nonsmokers, 20–79 years of age. Important ratio distinctions between smokers and nonsmokers were found with respect to the three measures of pulmonary function used. For the white group, larger mean pulmonary function values were found among nonsmokers in comparison with cigarette smokers in virtually every age group and for both sexes. For blacks and Orientals, however, no such differences between smokers and nonsmokers were noted! The virtual absence of appreciable differences between smokers and nonsmokers in pulmonary function values for blacks and Orientals, in contrast to those of whites, could not be explained by the analysis of data related to amount of smoking, duration of smoking, and inhalation of cigarette smoke. Similarly, no explanations were readily available for the lack of significant differences in mean pulmonary function values between smokers who inhale and those who do not. These data indicate clearly that generalizations which leave out constitutional, racial and other important genetic factors can have no meaning in this very complex field.

This conclusion is supported by the results of a very large-scale study of Japanese men living in Japan, Hawaii and California (Kagan et al., 1975; Marmot et al., 1975; Rhoades et al., 1978; Stemmermann et al., 1976; Syme et al., 1975; Winkelstein et al., 1975; Worth et al., 1975). In these studies it was shown that among men of Japanese ancestry, there is a gradient of CHD mortality, increasing from Japan to Hawaii to California, although the rates of smoking of these men are not substantially different. Findings in these papers are too detailed to discuss here, but what is demonstrated is the complex intermingling of race and environmental influences in the causation of coronary heart disease.

While there is an overall mortality ratio of about 1.7 for coronary heart disease, the results differ according to the particular diagnosis. Angina pectoris, for instance, has given rise to very contradictory results; thus in one large-scale study it was found that those who smoked 20 or more cigarettes per day had a *lower* morbidity ratio than non-cigarette smokers, giving rise to the conclusion that the risk of angina pectoris as a sole initial manifestation of CHD appears to be unrelated to the tobacco habit. Other studies give similar results (Seltzer, 1968). Cederlof et al. (1969), in a study of morbidity among monozygotic twins from Sweden, found a similar frequency of angina pectoris among smokers and nonsmokers, a finding also exonerating smoking as a causal factor in this disease. As Seltzer (1968) points out: "Uncomplicated angina pectoris comprises about 20% of all manifestations of CHD in men; elimination of such cases would mean elimination of a significant segment of CHD cases from consideration of being related to the tobacco habit" (p. 197).

The effects of age present curious anomalies. Seltzer (1975) has computed age-standardized CHD rates and mortality ratios from data available in four major prospective cohort investigations of smoking and health, and found that the data examined gave consistent results. For elderly men, there were no appreciable excess risks of CHD mortality or morbidity among cigarette smokers compared to ex-cigarette smokers and non-cigarette smokers. "For elderly women, the CHD rate seemed lower in continuing cigarette smokers than in ex-cigarette smokers . . . among elderly people, the risk of CHD is essentially the same with persistence of cigarette smoking as its cessation" (p. 168). Thus even the statistical association breaks down over the age of 64 or thereabouts.

Dose-response relations provide another difficulty, as pointed out by Seltzer (1968). As he argues:

> Significantly, the majority of the new studies show inversion of consistencies in the gradient of mortality or morbidity with average number of cigarettes smoked daily. While it is true that in virtually all these instances, those who smoke the most cigarettes give consistently higher CHD and myocardiac infarction rates than those who smoke the least, the consistency of the gradient is broken down as between the group which smokes the least and the intermediate group, with intermediate rates the same or lower than the rates of the group which smokes the least . . . the new data, which has many inconsistencies and inversions in the "rising gradient," indicate that this whole subject is not as clear-cut as it appeared at first blush (p. 195).

These inversions have been found in countries where there exists a statistical relationship; it must be added, however, that in a multinational study, Keys (1962) found *no association at all* between cigarette smoking and CHD in Finland, the Netherlands, Yugoslavia, Italy, Greece and Japan! Thus even the statistical relationship, however inconsistent, is confined only to some countries.

We have already noted in the case of lung cancer that there appears to be an absence of association between duration of heavy cigarette smoking and risk of disease; the same is found for myocardial infarction. Seltzer (1968, p. 198) summarizes three studies, concluding that: "It is notable that while duration of cigarette smoking is considered an important factor in connection with lung cancer mortality, the new evidence in the 1964 report points to an exoneration of this important element with respect to CHD. The evidence would appear to be consistent with the conclusion of the authors of the combined Albany and Framingham study that it is not any cumulative effect of inhaling cigarette smoking which precipitates myocardial infarction and death from CHD." The authors of the Framingham heart study suggested that coronary heart disease is only *acutely* connected with cigarette smoking, and not *chronically*, acting by the triggering of a lethal arrhythmia or thrombosis in subjects predisposed by an already compromised coronary circulation. If this were indeed true, then the effects of smoking would be limited solely to those persons with already diseased circulations; such a conclusion would seem to suggest that cigarette smoking is without deleterious effect on those with a normal, healthy coronary apparatus.

As in the case of lung cancer, inhalation gives contradictory and puzzling data in relation to CHD. Doll and Hill (1964, p. 1408) found that: "Only small and statistically insignificant differences were observed in coronary disease without hypertension," but in Hammond's (1966) prospective study there was a tendency for CHD death rate to increase with the degree of inhalation. It is difficult to account for these differences.

Data for ex-smokers are even more puzzling. The Surgeon General's report (1964) pointed out that "Men who stop smoking have a lower death rate from coronary disease than those who continue," but Seltzer's (1968) extensive review of later data showed that while ex-smokers are at times intermediate between smokers and nonsmokers with respect to CHD mortality, they may also appear significantly safer than nonsmokers in other reports. No final conclusions can be drawn on the basis of existing data. Evidence on the effects of cigar smoking and pipe smoking have indicated that there is no statistical relationship between CHD and these forms of smoking. Doll and Hill (1964, p. 1409) concluded that: "Pipe or cigar smokers gave a lower death rate than the group of non-smokers." In the Dorn study of U.S. veterans, the mortality ratios of persons who smoked cigars or a pipe were virtually the same as those of nonsmokers. The Hammond (1966) study of American men show that the pipe smokers on the whole had a lower CHD death rate than nonsmokers, while the cigar smokers tended to have a slightly higher rate than the nonsmokers. These studies thus present a considerable anomaly since nicotine in the tobacco smoke is regarded by many as the agent responsible for the effects on coronary heart disease. Carbon monoxide is often suggested as the most likely agent to be responsible, but the evidence here was based largely on Astrup's studies on rabbits, which he himself was unable to replicate.

An additional problem not considered by the received view is the fact that, in distinction with lung cancer, mortality ratios for CHD are high at 40–49 years (up to 5.5 for heavy smokers), but decrease with advancing age, approaching or going below unity at 70–79 years (Hammond and Garfinkel, 1969). As Burch (1980) has pointed out, this finding goes counter to a dose-response relationship expected by the received view. If smoking for 20 years is very predictive of fatal heart attacks, one might expect on this basis that smoking for 30, 40 or 50 years would be increasingly, rather than less, dangerous. A genetic hypothesis, on the other hand, has no difficulties with such findings (Burch, 1984).

For lung cancer, Doll (1971) has proposed a theory which predicts that the age-specific incidence in smokers would rise much more steeply with age than that in nonsmokers. Thus, his theory predicts that mortality ratios should rise from about 3.4 at 40 years to 25 at 80 years. This prediction is falsified by observations showing that mortality ratios remain effectively consistent with age (Hammond, 1972; Burch, 1978c). Here too a genetic hypothesis is consistent with the data (Burch, 1984).

These are epidemiological studies; investigations of a more medical kind have looked at the pathological, clinical and experimental evidence. After a careful review of the evidence, Seltzer (1970, p. 190) concluded that:

> The chronic effect of cigarette smoking is not clear and is inconsistent with other information. As far as acute effects are concerned, a series of physiological mechanisms have been advanced whereby cigarette smoking could trigger myocardial oxygen deficits of a critical degree in the presence of impaired coronary circulation due to CHD. This hypothesis has not been reasonably substantiated. Some of the evidence is provocative, but in many instances the hypothesized mechanisms are inadequately documented or are not documented at all.

He goes on to say that the statistical association between cigarette smoking and CHD still remains to be explained, stating that:

> An explanation may lie in a constitutional and genetic predisposition both for cigarette smoking and CHD. The genetic factor in the aetiology of CHD is well accepted and there is a growing body of evidence that smokers are different from non-smokers in a large variety of biological ways and behaviour patterns, including 'style of life'. If smokers show a greater tendency towards heart disease than non-smokers because they are different kinds of people than non-smokers—more vulnerable constitutional types—this could explain the comparatively low degree of association (mortality ratio 1.7) of excess heart disease among cigarette smokers.

Indeed, the latest and most satisfactory study of the relation between smoking and coronary artery disease (Vlietstra et al., 1982) found "no positive correlation (indeed, in some subgroups, a negative correlation) . . . between the arteriographic measures of disease and the cigarette smoking history" (p. 208). Thus, severity of coronary artery disease appears to be unconnected with smoking, at least in this large group of 15,298 patients carefully examined by means of arteriography. The authors suggest that perhaps some factors, such as smoking, may only influence onset and not further development of the disease, but such dissociation appears unlikely. We must include this study and its outcome among the many anomalies which beset the received view in relation to coronary heart disease.

A last point to be made concerns the surprising decline of cardiovascular mortalities in Switzerland from 1951 to 1976 (Guberan, 1979), in spite of *increasing* smoking by women and roughly stationary smoking rates in men. There was also a 20% rise in consumption of animal fats; yet age-standardized death rates for all diseases of the circulatory system decreased by 22% in males and by 43% in females. These results are difficult to assimilate for adherents of the received view.

This review of the association between cigarette smoking and CHD has been much shorter than our review of the evidence concerning lung cancer because much of the evidence reviewed on the latter disease is also relevant to the consideration of the former. The conclusions that we reached are very similar in both cases, namely, that while there is suggestive evidence, it is far from conclusive as far as the causal role of cigarette smoking is concerned. Alternative hypotheses have not been disproved, and no decisive evidence has been offered to explain the suggested causal effects of cigarette smoking. It is unfortunate that the alternative theories, particularly the constitutional and genetic hypothesis, have not been stated in a properly testable form. It is not sufficient simply to appeal to constitutional and genetic factors; more specific hypotheses have to be stated regarding their mode of action, and, in particular, indications made concerning how these hypotheses can be empirically tested. It is the absence of a testable and clearly stated alternative hypothesis that has been more responsible than anything else for the widespread belief in the received view and the disregard by experimentalists of alternative hypotheses. It is to consideration of such an alternative hypothesis, and the evidence supporting it, that we must now turn.

The Constitutional Hypothesis

Sir Ronald Fisher (1958,b,c) is often credited with having given rise to the constitutional or genetic hypothesis to account for the association between smoking and lung cancer, but this is not strictly speaking correct. What Fisher put forward was not a theory or a scientific hypothesis in the usual sense, but merely a view that an alternative explanation of the association not involving direct causation might be possible. Fisher's "hypothesis" is too broad and indefinite to be testable or falsifiable, and before being considered scentifically meaningful and acceptable, it must be formulated in such a manner that suitable experiments can be carried out which would either support or falsify the theory.

An attempt to do this has been made by the author (Eysenck, 1984), but it must be admitted that while there are a number of facts to support this view, it should still be regarded as somewhat speculative. The reason for this is the dearth of data relevant to the hypothesis, due perhaps to the fact that practically all research money and research effort has gone into attempts to support the received view, and very little into attempts to support an alternative (or perhaps supplementary) view.

Figure 2–4 illustrates the general character of the theory here discussed. The dotted line (8) signifies the correlation (r_{SL}) between smoking and lung cancer; it is dotted rather than solid to suggest that the correlation may not be based on any direct causation. The sold lines in the figure suggest (1) that

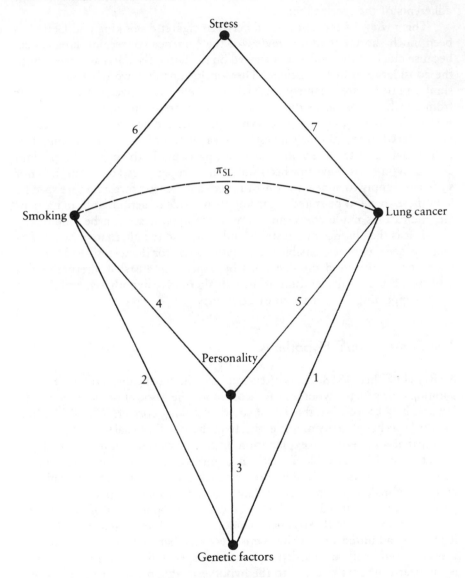

Figure 2–4. Alternative View of Smoking-Lung Cancer Correlations, Involving Genetic Factors

genetic factors play a large part of the causation of lung cancer and (2) that genetic factors play a large part of the causation of smoking; it is suggested that these factors are likely to overlap. It is also suggested (3) that genetic factors are very influential in determining individual differences in personality, and that these differences in turn are related (4) to smoking and (5) to lung cancer. It is further suggested that (6) stress is related to smoking and (7) to lung cancer; it will also be argued that personality is related to stress.

The theory is quite specific with respect to the particular variables involved in smoking and lung cancer, and the evidence along these lines is perhaps the most impressive as far as the general theory is concerned. It will be shown that there is evidence in favor of all the relationships indicated by solid lines in figure 2–4, although the strength of the evidence, and its interpretation, differs from one set of relations to another. The demonstration that the relationships here postulated exist in fact is a necessary but not a sufficient condition for explaining the smoking and lung cancer relationship along non-causal lines; the relations would have to be quantified in a fairly precise manner to make possible some form of path analysis in order to exclude the causal hypothesis contained in the received view. Such precision is impossible at the moment, but if future research took seriously the possibilities of the constitutional model, then in due course we might be able to argue the case on a quantitative basis. At the moment the theory is merely suggestive, but it does have a firm foundation on a number of facts which are impossible to explain on the basis of the received view, and hence constitute anomalies within that view which would have to be explained before the received view could be accepted, even if the contradictions within that view explored in the preceding sections could be overcome.

Let us first consider the determination of lung cancer (as well as other types of cancer and of coronary heart disease) by genetic factors. It is not suggested, of course, that genetic factors by themselves are sufficient to cause lung cancer (or coronary heart disease); it is merely suggested that they play an important part in predisposing certain types of persons to develop these particular diseases. As the evidence is quite well known, and hardly in doubt, we will not discuss it in detail, but merely list some of the publications which may be consulted to support the view that genetic factors are important in these disorders. As far as coronary heart disease is concerned, we may refer to the work of Burch (1979), Cederlof et al. (1969), Faine (1974), Gertler and White (1954), Harvald and Hauge (1963), Hrubec et al. (1976), Lundman (1966), Rose (1964), Slack and Evans (1966), and Thomas and Cohen (1955).

As far as cancer is concerned, there is a good general review by Lynch (1977) and, with respect to lung cancer specifically, I recommend the work of Tokuhata (1964), and Tokuhata and Lilienfield (1963a,b) which would seem to establish a firm genetic basis for lung cancer. Other more general sources that might be consulted with advantage are: Albert and Child (1977), Anderson (1978), Cinader (1975), Cohen et al. (1977), Feingold (1978), Harris

(1980), Harvald and Hauge (1963), Heston (1976), Jackson (1978), Knudson (1973), Kohl et al. (1977), Litwin (1978), Lynch et al. (1981, 1982), Marks (1981), Mulvihill (1976), Schneider (1981), and Strong (1977).

The action of genetic factors in the case of cancer is often misunderstood (Lynch et al., 1982). It seems likely that most human cancers are not caused by conventional mutagens, but are more likely to be the result of genetic transpositions. It is clearly important to discover what classes of external agents or features of cellular behavior raise the frequency of such transpositions (Cairns, 1981). It is interesting to note that conventional mutagens often appear to have no effect. As Cairns says, "it may not be a simple matter to devise a general assay for the factors that drive the carcinogenic transpositions" (p. 357).

Regarding the influence of genetic factors on smoking behavior, there is a long list of studies comparing monozygotic (MZ) and dizygotic (DZ) twins (see Fisher, 1958a,b,c; Shields, 1962; Todd and Mason, 1959; Friberg et al., 1959; Conteno and Chiarelli, 1962; Hamtoft and Lindhardt, 1956; and Cederlof et al., 1977). These studies universally find a greater concordance among MZ than among DZ twins. The work of Eysenck (1980) deals with much larger samples of MZ and DZ twins than previous studies, and in addition uses the latest model-fitting methods of genetic analysis; they also make use of data gathered from adopted children and from intrafamilial analyses. The general conclusion from their work was that while the *origin* of the smoking habit was not much influenced by genetic factors, but rather was due to peer pressure, the *maintenance* of the smoking habit was strongly influenced by genetic factors. The picture that emerges from these analyses is much more complex than this, of course, but these complexities are of no particular interest in the development of our theme, and will therefore not be detailed here.

The determination of personality by genetic factors has been discussed in great detail by Fulker (1981), and again no attempt will be made to discuss the evidence in detail. As he shows, the major dimensions of personality, and extraversion and neuroticism in particular, are strongly determined by genetic factors, to the extent of approximately two-thirds of the total "true" variance. The picture differs from that presented by the determination of intelligence by genetic factors since nonadditive genetic variance (dominance, assortative mating) plays a highly significant part in determining intelligence, while these nonadditive genetic factors are absent in relation to personality. Furthermore, whereas between-family environmental factors are about twice as important as within-family environmental factors for intelligence, between-family environmental factors seem to play little if any part for personality. In any case, there can be no doubt that genetic factors play a vitally important part in determining individual differences in personality. It is thus clearly possible that some of the genetic influences that link smoking with lung cancer may be mediated through personality, and in order to support this view, we must find evidence to prove that personality is related to smoking and also to lung cancer.

There is now a great deal of evidence to support the view that personality is related to smoking (Eysenck, 1980), and it has been shown that all the major personality dimensions (extraversion, neuroticism, psychoticism) are correlated with smoking. Furthermore, there is evidence to indicate that certain causal hypotheses about motivational factors related to personality, and leading to smoking, are implicated. The evidence here is so strong and unanimous that little needs to be said in order to support the view that the link between smoking and personality is essentially in line with the facts (Eysenck, 1980).

The importance of psychological factors as indicative of risks for lung cancer is brought out well by Horne and Picard (1979), who find that a set of personality and stress ratings predicted diagnosis at least as well as did smoking history. This conclusion should be viewed in light of the evidence concerning detection bias discussed earlier; this bias would artificially increase the relationship between diagnosis and smoking history, but would leave psychological factors unaffected.

The relationship between personality and lung cancer is crucial to the particular type of constitutional hypothesis here advocated, and will be dealt with in greater detail than some of the other relationships shown in figure 2–4. It is important to emphasize from the beginning that the relationships between personality and lung cancer (and coronary heart disease) are predicated on a system of personality description which is very different from the psychoanalytic one which has frequently been associated with the analysis of psychosomatic diseases. The difficulties of dealing with psychoanalytic hypotheses are well-known; these are not clearly enough defined to be testable, and such personality measures as are used are normally of the projective type, and hence neither reliable nor valid. The dimensions of personality here used are the outcome of many large-scale studies of objective data, statistically analyzed in many different countries (Royce and Powell, 1983; Eysenck and Eysenck, 1985). Essentially, this system is based on correlational studies isolating individual traits and then analyzing correlations between these traits to define the major dimensions of personality. These major dimensions are three in number, and have been variously named by different authors; for our purpose we shall refer to them as P (Psychoticism), E (Extraversion) and N (Neuroticism). Figures 2–5, 2–6, and 2–7 show the various traits constituting these major dimensions of personality. All three dimensions have been shown to be positively correlated with smoking (Eysenck, 1980).

The same is true of the involvement of personality and cancer. Certain predictions arise from the early and relatively unscientific observational studies conducted ever since Galen in the second century A.D. formulated the view that cancer and certain other diseases were related to personality. Briefly, the

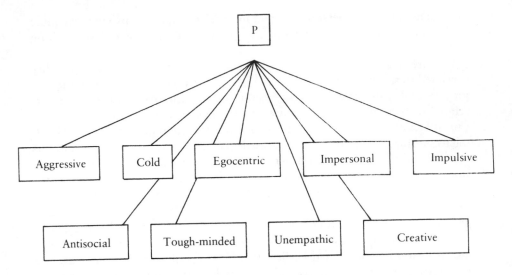

Figure 2–5. Personality Traits Characteristic of P (Psychoticism)

hypothesis concerning lung cancer (and possibly other cancers as well) is that these develop more readily in extraverted than introverted persons, stable rather than emotionally unstable or neurotic persons, and in normal rather than in persons tending towards psychoticism and psychosis. In other words, abnormality, whether neurotic or psychotic, appears to be in some way a *protection* against lung cancer, a view which may be intuitively difficult to accept, but for which there is now a good deal of evidence, as we shall see. As far as coronary heart disease is concerned, the hypotheses go in the opposite direction, if anything; coronary heart disease is expected to be related to neuroticism rather than stability, psychoticism rather than normality, and introversion rather than extraversion, although different types of coronary heart disease may show different relationships as far as extraversion–introversion is concerned.

The so-called psychosocial views of disease usually couple together two other different factors, stress and personality, in the origin of disease. LeShan (1959) cites a number of physicians' reports that consistently pointed to an association between severe emotional traumas and subsequent onset of cancer, with particular reference to grief, mental depression, deep anxiety, deferred hope, and disappointment. In addition to such experienced stress, however, there were various conceptualizations involving ego-defense mechanisms, and theories were advanced that the onset and development of malignancies were associated with general emotional inhibition (Kissen, 1963a,b) and excessive use of repressive and denying defenses (Bahnson and Bahnson, 1964). A review of some of the earlier work on these hypotheses is given by

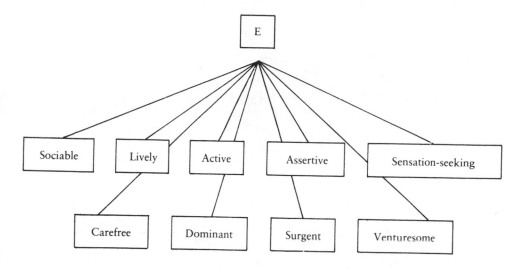

Figure 2–6. Personality Traits Characteristic of E (Extraversion)

Dattore et al. (1980). As they point out, much of this work is suggestive rather than conclusive (Brown, 1960; Abse et al., 1974; Perria and Pierce, 1959).

The literature of concern to us begins as a study by Kissen and Eysenck (1962) in which 116 male lung cancer patients and 123 noncancer controls were tested, both groups being patients at surgical and medical chest units tested *before* diagnosis. It was found that the control group had much higher N scores than the cancer group, regardless of psychosomatic involvement, although it was found that psychosomatic groups, both cancer and control, had somewhat higher neuroticism scores than did the nonpsychosomatic group. Extraversion only discriminated between cancer and control patients among those who *also* had psychosomatic disorders, where the cancer group was considerably more extraverted than the control group. Kissen followed up this early work in a series of further studies (1963a, 1963b, 1964a, 1964b, 1967, 1968; Kissen and Rowe, 1969) in which he found additional support for the *negative* relationship between cancer and neuroticism. He concluded that very low scorers on N have about a 6 to 1 possibility of developing lung cancer as compared with very high scorers.

The work of Kissen and Eysenck was followed up by Berndt et al. (1980), who studied patients and controls with particular reference to breast cancer or bronchial carcinoma, using very large groups of both patients and controls. He found in all these groups that cancer patients had neuroticism scores significantly *lower* than the controls, thus finding results essentially identical with those of the Kissen and Eysenck study. (Eysenck, 1981, pointed

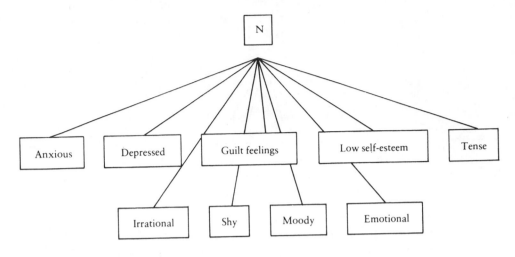

Figure 2–7. Personality Traits Characteristic of N (Neuroticism)

out some statisical errors in Berndt's analyses; his paper should be consulted in conjunction with the original one by Berndt.) It should also be noted that Berndt and his colleagues did not find any significant differences for extraversion.

Hagnell (1966), using a special Swedish concept of personality which has, however, been shown to be related to extraversion, reported on the results of an epidemiological survey of the 2,515 inhabitants of two adjacent rural parishes in the south of Sweden. During a ten-year follow-up he observed that a significantly higher proportion of women who had developed cancer had been originally rated as extraverted. Hagnell was not concerned with lung cancer as such, but with many different kinds of cancer. The argument was further strengthened by a study published by Coppen and Metcalfe (1963); they too found that the cancer group (again containing several different types of cancers) had significantly higher extraversion scores than two control groups used. They did not find significant differences for neuroticism.

Greer and Morris (1975) reported another interesting replication of the Kissen and Eysenck study, but used breast cancer cases instead of lung cancer cases. A consecutive series of 160 women at a hospital for breast tumor biopsy was studied by means of detailed structured interviews and standard tests, with both interviews and tests being conducted on the day before exploratory operation without provisional knowledge of the diagnosis. The principal finding was the significant association between the diagnosis of breast cancer and the behavior pattern, persisting throughout adult life, of abnormal relief of emotion. "This abnormality was, in most cases, extreme suppression of other feelings. Extreme expression of emotions, though much less common, also occurred in a higher proportion of cancer patients than controls" (Greer and Morris, p. 147). Greer and Morris found no correlation with extraversion. In a later paper, Morris et al. (1981) again found that mean N scores were significantly lower for cancer patients as compared with the control group (see also Greer, 1979).

Abse et al. (1974) carried out interview studies of 59 male patients, 31 of whom were later diagnosed as having lung cancer. It is difficult to summarize the results, since these are expressed rather loosely in nonstandard terminology, but on the whole the personality of cancer patients seemed to reveal less emotional reactivity than that of the controls.

A recent study by Dattore et al. (1980) gives more positive results, with the cancer group, as compared with the control group, showing more repression and less report of deep depression, as well as less hysterical reaction. These results are in line with the Kissen and Eysenck report, but the results from a study by Watson and Schuld (1977) seem to go in a different direction, showing no differentiation between cancer patients and controls. However, in this study the population consisted of subjects all of whom had psychiatric diagnoses at the time of testing, and hence would not be comparable with the normal population studied by all other researchers.

Blumberg et al. (1954) studied two groups of cancer patients matched for age, intelligence, and stage of cancer, administering the MMPI (Minnesota Multiphasic Personality Inventory) following initial treatment. Those dying in less than two years, as compared with those dying after more than six years, had higher depression scores and lower neurotic outlet scores, as well as very low acting-out scores at the time of the first assessment.

Blohmke et al. (in press) have reported another study comparing lung cancer patients with noncancer controls on a large scale. The most important difference between the groups was "lack of nervousness," characterizing cancer patients, followed by "positive social conformity" and "no external control"; these are all in the direction predicted from the Kissen and Eysenck study. Two further differences were in the direction of greater extraversion for cancer patients; they showed more changes in the conditions of life, and had more subjective complaints.

In another study, Butler et al. (1982), using the Cattell 16PF scale (see Glossary), concluded that: "The research study supports the general hypothesis that cancer patients are homogeneous in measurable personality patterning, and show different personality correlates from normal population. The data suggests that the samples were not similar to other mean profiles, such as cardiac patients or psychosomatic samples" (p. 20). It is difficult to see whether this study agrees with the Kissen and Eysenck results in detail, since the subscales of the 16PF are difficult to interpret psychologically (Eysenck and Eysenck, 1985). Several other more indirect studies of the general hypothesis are found in Eysenck (1980), but will not be considered here.

Retrospective studies have obvious difficulties in interpretation, and hence a prospective study by Grossarth-Maticek et al. (in press) is of particular interest. They studied 1,353 inhabitants of a Yugoslav town, of whom 619 died between 1966 and 1976. The general method of selection was to choose the oldest person in every second house in order to obtain a sample with a high mortality rate. However, where preliminary questioning indicated a personal high psychosomatic risk of disease (25% of the sample) in a household member other than the oldest, this person was selected instead. Subjects who were in a moribund state, or who had ever had cancer, heart disease, stroke, diabetes or certain dangerous diseases like multiple sclerosis, chronic nephritis with decompensated heart insufficiency, or who had acute tuberculosis were not included in the study.

The main features of the inquiry relate to the influence of smoking, and the influence of a personality variable, measured by means of a questionnaire, which the authors call "rationality and antiemotionality" (R/A). The main outcome of this comparison is indicated in table 2–2, showing Chi^2 for smoking and personality. Some variables were subdivided into three groups, the smoking group, for example, was divided into nonsmokers, people smoking 1 to 20 cigarettes a day, and people smoking 21 or more cigarettes a day. The personality variable R/A was divided into groups scoring 0, 1 to 9, or 10 and above. The table shows clearly that as far as lung cancer is concerned, personality was considerably more important than smoking; this is even more obvious for other cancers, and for ischaemic heart disease and stroke. For all causes of death, personality is clearly much more important than smoking, which has a significance level of only 0.05.

The data are truly remarkable: 158 of the 166 cancer deaths, and all 38 of the lung cancer deaths occurred in those who scored about 10 on the personality inventory, and no cancer deaths at all occurred in those who scored 0 compared with an expected number of 23. As the authors also point out, "Cancer incidence was some 40 times higher in those who answered positively to 10 or 11 of the questions for R/A . . . than for the remaining subjects who answered positively to about 3 questions on the average." The

Table 2–2
Personality and Smoking as Related to Deaths from Various Causes

Cause of Death	Smoking χ^2	Personality χ^2
Lung cancer	68.8	84.1
Other cancer	10.7	211.2
Ischaemic heart disease	3.4	70.4
Stroke	− 5.5	39.7
Other causes	− 6.1	− 0.2
All causes	4.9	232

Source: From Grossarth-Maticek, R., et al., 1985.

results of this study are even more impressive than those found by Kissen and Eysenck; furthermore, since it is a prospective study, it is inevitably less subject to criticism than the retrospective studies of Kissen. It is difficult to dismiss personality variables as important correlates of lung cancer and coronary heart disease in view of these results. (Other relevant papers by Grossarth-Maticek and his colleagues are listed in the Bibliography.)

Of particular interest in this connection is the fact that, based on his measurement of the typical personality of the cancer-prone and CHD-prone person, Grossarth-Maticek and his colleagues were able to devise methods of behavior therapy which, when applied to groups of subjects at danger from one or the other disease, proved of great prophylactic value. In other words, by altering these subjects' behavior and cognitive appraisals of their situation, they could be prevented from contracting these diseases at anything like the rate shown by comparable control groups. Similarly, using the same techniques of behavior therapy based on his personality description and diagnosis, Grossarth-Maticek could significantly *prolong* the lives of sufferers from incurable cancer, to a degree equaling that achieved by chemotherapy. (A combination of the two methods proved even better.) A summary of the evidence is given in Eysenck (in press), with full references. These results leave little doubt about the *causal* relation between personality and disease.

Only one further paper will be discussed, because of its great importance to the theory under investigation. In this paper, Rae and McCall (1973) attempted to demonstrate that an association between cancer and personality could be discovered on an international scale. National extraversion and anxiety levels in eight advanced countries, and statistics of the number of cigarettes smoked per adult per annum in these countries were correlated with the mortality rates per 100,000 of the population due to lung cancer (males and females separately), and in cancer of the cervix.

Rank order correlations were then calculated between national personality levels and cancer mortality rates. There was a highly significant correlation between extraversion and male lung cancer (0.66) and between extraversion and female lung cancer (0.72). Corresponding correlations for cigarette consumption and lung cancer for males and females were quite insignificant (0.07). For cancer of the cervix, the correlation with extraversion was again significant (0.64), whereas for cigarette consumption it was insignificant (0.45). Correlations between anxiety and lung cancer were negative in both sexes (-0.52 and -0.71). This is an interesting replication on an international scale of the findings of Kissen and Eysenck of lower mean N score for lung cancer cases as compared with controls, and the general tendency for extraversion to be found correlated with lung and other types of cancer.

Regarding psychoticism, no data exist in which this questionnaire has been related to lung cancer. However, there is ample evidence relating cancer to psychosis in a negative direction. Bahnson and Bahnson (1964a) considered "cancer as an alternative to psychosis," and their evidence (Bahnson and Bahnson, 1964b) supports this view. Rassidakis et al. (1971, 1972, 1973a,b, c,d) showed that mentally ill populations, especially patients with schizophrenia, seem to be at relatively low risk for cancer. They found that the percentage of mental patients who died from cancer was considerably lower than that of the general population: 15% of deaths were caused by malignant neoplasms in the general population compared with 4.9% among the mentally ill. Other randomly selected causes of death showed no appreciable differences. In England and Wales about 20% of deaths were caused by neoplasms compared with 6.9% of deaths in mentally ill populations; for Scotland the figures are 17% and 5% respectively (Eysenck, 1980).

Schizophrenic patients seem to be more resistant to neoplasms than patients with other forms of mental disease. Many other studies from the United States, the Soviet Union, and other countries are cited by Eysenck (1980); all of them support the view that schizophrenics and other functional psychotics tend to suffer from lung cancer and other types of cancer less frequently than do nonpsychotic patients and normals. Some possible reasons for this are discussed by Levi and Waxman (1975), but at the moment all these hypotheses are still highly speculative.

We must now turn to a consideration of the relationship between personality and coronary heart disease. It will be remembered that our hypothesis states that the personality of patients likely to develop coronary heart disease would be quite the opposite to that of people liable to develop lung cancer or other types of cancer. Good evidence for this is provided by the work of Caroline Thomas (Thomas, 1968; Thomas and Cohen, 1955; Thomas and Duszynski, 1974; Thomas and Greenstreet, 1973); her studies are concerned both with cancer and heart disease. Between 1946 and 1964 she collected data on 1,337 medical students at Johns Hopkins University, recording complete physical examinations, psychological profiles, and family histories. These students were followed up through 1974; by that time there had been 43 cases of cancer and 14 heart attacks. It was found that cancers tended to develop in people who were generally quiet, nonaggressive, and emotionally contained. Such persons scored low on tests of anxiety, anger, and depression. The picture is very much like that found by Kissen and Eysenck. Coronary victims, on the other hand, scored higher on depression, anxiety, and nervous tension. They tended to suffer from insomnia and were often tired in the morning. This still-ongoing study (Thomas, 1976) provides excellent evidence of the prospective kind to link personality with disease, even though some of the tests used (like the Rorschach) have little validity or reliability; fortunately, the information on which these conclusions are based is predominantly derived from more secure foundations (see also Thomas and Greenstreet, 1973; and Thomas and Duszynski, 1974). It is also relevant that Thomas et al. (1955) found that anxiety was the most important variable in a discriminatory analysis based on parental history of coronary heart disease; this agreed with later findings by Thomas (1968). Among early authors, Dunbar (1943), Miles et al. (1954), and Ostfeld et al. (1964) also found evidence for the important role of anxiety in coronary heart disease.

More recently, work by Blumenthal et al. (1979), Rime and Bonami (1979) and Pleszewski (1977) has found evidence for similar personality correlates of coronary heart disease already predicted many years ago by Osler (1910). To these may be added high levels of hostility (Barefoot et al., 1983 and Williams et al., 1984). Hostility being one of the components of the P scale, we can see that the evidence is fairly conclusive both for P and N. There were positive correlations with coronary heart disease just as there were negative correlations with lung cancer.

The relationship with extraversion–introversion is less clear. Studies like that by Van Dijl (1979) suggest a correlation between myocardial infarction and sociability, that is, extraversion, and similar results have been reported by Bendien and Groen (1963). Other studies of coronary heart disease, however, suggest that this finding may be peculiar to myocardial infarction, and that angina pectoris, hypertension and tachycardia may be related to introversion, although all these forms of coronary heart disease are positively related to neuroticism. A survey of the evidence, with original material, is given by Floderus (1974). It remains to discuss the well-known hypothesis linking Type A behavior (Rosenman and Chesney, 1980) with coronary heart disease. The very large literature on this topic has been reviewed by Steptoe (1981) and Price (1982), and will not be reviewed again here. The main reason for this reluctance to describe this large body of work is that it has been shown (see Eysenck and Fulker, 1983) that Type A behavior is really a mixture of neuroticism and extraversion, with the contribution of the former predominant. Thus insofar as there is a true relationship between coronary heart disease and Type A behavior, the evidence relating to Type A behavior merely strengthens the evidence suggesting the relationship between coronary heart disease and neuroticism, and possibly extraversion.

Myrtek (1983) has recently published an experimental investigation and a literature survey of Type A theories and investigations which confirms our view concerning this typology. He concludes that it proved impossible to confirm deductions from Type A theory, regardless of the criterion used (interview or questionnaire). Myrtek believes that the concept is in process of dissolution, and in any case constitutes little more than a revival of the ancient Eppinger and Hess theory of Vagotomia vs. Sympatheticotomia (Eppinger, 1917), a theory which Myrtek considers more likely to generate useful empirical research than the Type A modification. He also rightly criticizes the tendency of adherents of the Type A typology to concentrate on positive results and disregard the more numerous negative ones. Altogether, the concept played a useful part in convincing the medical profession that psychological factors might be important in CHD, but this propaganda war having been won, we must now abandon faith in a clearly defective theory and advance towards a more meaningful and better established one.

Clearly, all this extensive literature on the relationship between personality and disease does not lend itself to overly simplistic summary. Different investigators have studied different populations, using different systems of measurement and different methods of ascertainment; results are seldom directly comparable, and differences have been reported for one age group which do not necessarily extend to other age groups. The question of whether there is a single cancer personality, or a single coronary heart disease personality, or whether different personalities correspond to different types of cancer or CHD, has not been answered in a satisfactory manner. Much work remains to be done, but the impression of this large amount of research that remains is certainly that there do exist relationships between personality and disease, and that these go in opposite directions for cancer, on the one hand, and coronary heart disease on the other. At this stage of the research it would not be wise to draw any further conclusions (Eysenck, forthcoming).

We must now turn to the problem of stress as related to smoking and lung cancer. There is much evidence (Eysenck, 1973, 1980) to indicate that smoking is often resorted to as a consequence of boredom or stress; while in small quantities nicotine increases cortical arousal (relieves boredom), in larger quantities it has a sedative, tranquilizing effect, reducing tension and anxiety produced by stress. The relationship of stress and disease, in our case lung cancer and coronary heart disease, has been studied as part of the larger plan of psychosomatic investigation (Cooper, 1983; Cooper and Payne, 1980; Dohrenwend and Dohrenwend, 1974, 1981; Eliot, 1974; Society for Psychosomatic Research, 1959; Tache et al., 1979). However, there has been much criticism of the methodology used and the conclusions reached (Kasl, 1983; Miller, 1981; Schroeder and Costa, in press), and causal mechanisms, while much investigated, are still in doubt (see Borysenko and Borysenko, 1982; Frankenhaeuser, 1980; Gray et al., 1981; Locke, 1982; Sterling and Eyer, 1981; Williams, 1983). Other studies have considered the relationship between stress and personality (Duckitt and Broll, 1982; Linn et al., 1981), showing that extraverts are significantly more tolerant of recent life changes than introverts, and that anxiety has contradictory effects.

The relationship between stress and cancer has been reviewed recently by Bammer and Newberry (1981) and Sklar and Anisman (1981). The work of DeChambre (1981) indicates immunological involvement: if immunological attack on tumor cells is weakened by psychosocial stress, less cell lysis will occur. Riley et al. (1981) have come to a similar conclusion in their studies of psychoneuro-immunologic factors in neoplasia. They conclude their survey by saying that: "Some of the biological consequences of emotional or anxiety stress result in adverse influences upon identifiable elements of the mouse immune system" (p. 183) (see also Fox and Newberry, 1984).

Bammer (1981) reviews evidence to show that stress can increase metastasis in animals, and there is also some evidence that this is true for humans. This can happen either by the physical action of the stressor, or by stress-induced impairment of immune function. Unfortunately, there are many contradictory results, and Sklar and Anisman (1979, 1981) conclude from their review of the evidence that: "Although many animal tumour systems have been shown to be responsive to stress, the animal studies have used such a variety of procedures that drawing general conclusions is difficult. It is suggested that much of the diversity in animals' stress-cancer findings can be explained by differences between studies in the stressors and background environmental conditions employed" (1981, p. 403).

In relation to the development of cancer in humans, retrospective studies have shown that life stress events frequently precede the appearance of forms of neoplasia (Bahnson and Bahnson, 1964a,b; Greene, 1966; Horne and Picard, 1979; Jacobs and Charles, 1980). Greene and Swisher (1969) succeeded in eliminating genetic factors by looking at leukemia in monozygotic twins discordant for the illness, and found that psychological stress was an important feature in the origins of this disease. Reviews by Bloom et al. (1978) and Fox (1978) give a good survey of the literature. One of the stressors most frequently studied has been loss of spouse, and here again there are a number of studies (Bloom et al., 1978; Greene, 1966; LeShan, 1966; Lombard and Potter, 1950; Ernster et al., 1979) showing that cancer appeared in higher than expected frequency among such individuals. Retrospective studies, of course, are exposed to many difficulties (Fox, 1974; Sklar and Anisman, 1981), but the findings are remarkably uniform in suggesting the importance of stress in the causation of cancer.

These findings make the negative relationship between neuroticism and psychoticism on the one hand, and lung cancer on the other, appear rather paradoxical. Emotional instability and neuroticism, and, even more, psychoticism and psychotic breakdown, certainly impose stress on the organism, and hence should be positively instead of negatively correlated with lung cancer. The answer to this problem may lie, as Eysenck (1983a,b; 1984) has suggested, in the difference between *acute* and *chronic* stress. There is evidence (Sklar and Anisman, 1981) that these different types of stress have opposite effects on the occurrence of carcinomas.

Enhancement of tumour development has usually been reported in studies using acute, uncontrollable physical stress, chronic social stress, or stimulating housing conditions. Chronic uncontrollable physical stresses tended to be associated with tumour inhibition. There is considerable correspondence between brain neurochemical responses to stress and cancer development under stress. Stress increases the synthesis and utilisation of compounds such as norepinephrene and if synthesis does not keep pace with utilisation, brain depletion is observed. Brain neurochemical activity in cancer development has been shown to respond similarly to the difference between acute and chronic stress, to the availability of coping responses, and in some cases to social conditions [p. 404].

They also found that there was evidence for changes in immune functioning under stress which corresponds to neurochemical, hormonal and tumor development effects. The neural systems affected by stress are involved in hormone increase and immune reactions. It is thus possible that the chronic stress imposed by mental disorders and emotional instability may have a *preventive* rather than a *causative* effect as far as lung cancer is concerned, and that this makes sense of apparently paradoxical findings.

Specific studies demonstrating the inhibiting effect of chronic stress are summarized by Eysenck (1984), who found not only that there is good evidence for the inhibitory effects of chronic stress on tumor induction but also that while acute stress may exacerbate metastasis, chronic stress inhibits metastasis.

This "innoculation hypothesis" (Eysenck, 1983b) does not explain the correlation between extraversion and lung cancer (and possibly other cancers as well). Here the answer may lie in the fact that it is now apparent that the immune reaction can be conditioned along Pavlovian lines (Ader, 1981; Ader and Cohen, 1975; Rogers et al., 1976; Wayner et al., 1978; Cohen et al., 1979). These conditioning studies utilized the taste aversion paradigm (Garcia et al., 1974; Riley and Clarke, 1977). In recent studies, Bovbjerg et al., (1982) extended these experiments to include cellular responses in demonstrating the importance of conditioning for the manipulation of the immune response. All these studies demonstrate the possibility of the *suppression* of the immune reactions by Pavlovian conditioning, but they also suggest the possibility of *strengthening* the immune reaction along similar lines. Indeed, in everyday life immunosuppression is much less likely to occur than immunoenhancement, possibly through chronic stress reactions as pointed out before. If this were so, then clearly introverts, who form conditioned responses more quickly and more strongly than extraverts (Eysenck, 1967, 1981a), will benefit from this and be more likely to acquire the strengthened immune reaction. Thus the reasons for the greater susceptibility of extraverts to neoplasias may be their failure to acquire conditioned immune reactions as regularly and as strongly as do introverts; this would account for the observed correlation between cancer and extraversion.

It should be noted that the postulated effects of conditioning might also affect the negative correlation between neuroticism and lung cancer. Under certain specified conditions, strong emotions also facilitate the conditioning process, and hence anxiety and neuroticism can be found positively correlated with conditioning (Spence and Spence, 1966). Thus the conditioning mechanism may also mediate a better conditioning of the immune reaction in high N scorers, particularly as the strong degree of emotion necessary for producing these effects is more likely to be found under conditions of environmental stress.

It may be possible to posit an even more specific and fundamental theory to explain the personality–cancer relationship and the importance of stress in mitigating cancer or protecting against it.* In defensive responses to threat, the psychological, neuroendocrinological and immunological systems are intimately interconnected. Fluctuations in immunity may be influenced by neuropeptides, as is now well documented, though by no means well understood (Fox and Newberry, 1984). The assumption of the present working hypothesis is that *the same neuropeptides which alter levels of immunity may also simultaneously be altering levels of neuroticism and introversion.*

One of the outstanding characteristics of neuroticism is its persistence. Within a learning-theory framework, neurotics do not follow the reinforcement contingencies—in short, their behavior does not readily extinguish when it is no longer reinforced (Eysenck, 1982). For instance, while there is good evidence that phobias arise from conditioning experience (Ost and Hugdahl, 1983) and while it is possible to account for the associative selectivity of phobias to only certain kinds of "prepared" stimuli (Öhman et al., 1975, 1976), the perplexing issue is why phobics do not spontaneously extinguish their fears after everyday, nonreinforced exposures to phobic stimuli. This capacity of phobic stimuli to extinguish very slowly and possibly increase in excitatory strength when they are presented alone has been called the incubation of fear by Eysenck (1979).

Individual differences in the neuroendocrine system may be an important determinant of when incubation effects will occur. Adrenocorticotrophic hormone (ACTH) reliably produces a striking increase in resistance to extinction in animals which is not dependent upon species or particular training procedures; moreover, this occurs after endogenous or exogenous increases in ACTH in a dose-dependent fashion and is not a result of tropic properties (de Wied and Jolles, 1982). These anxiogenic properties of ACTH (Britton and Britton, 1981; Britton et al., 1982) have been experimentally demonstrated to mediate the incubation process; nonreinforced exposure to fear cues with concomitant high levels of ACTH not only retards extinction but can also produce a large, permanent increase in excitatory strength (Concannon et al., 1980a,b; Bohus, 1974). The opposite effect (the facilitation of extinction) occurs after injections of corticosterone (Bohus et al., 1982).

In the human literature there are hints that these effects of neuropeptides may be a robust explanation of the persistence of anxiety-related disorders. Plasma levels of beta-endorphin covary perfectly with ACTH (Jacquet, 1978), and CSF levels of endorphins are highly correlated (.67) with neuroticism as

---

*This theory has been jointly elaborated by the writer and Dr. M. Kelly, whose assistance in writing this section is gratefully acknowledged.

measured on the Eysenck Personality Questionnaire (Post et al., 1984). One major negative feedback mechanism for controlling excessive ACTH secretion is the rise in cortisol (Jones et al., 1982), thus it is of considerable interest that an increase in plasma cortisol does not occur when phobic patients are made intensely afraid during in vivo forced exposure to the stimuli they fear (Curtis et al., 1976, 1978). Elevations in ACTH but not cortisol are physiologically possible. There is now good physiological evidence to challenge the classical hypothesis that elevations in ACTH and cortisol are necessarily always tightly linked together (Fehm et al., 1984). ACTH has also been implicated in obsessive-compulsive disorders. When the opiate antagonist naloxone was recently infused into two obsessive patients, this exacerbated their condition (Insel and Pickar, 1983). As preparations which give rise to opiate-related analgesia have an inhibitory effect on the excitatory properties of ACTH, and as naloxone increases the excitatory properties of ACTH (Volavka et al., 1983; Taylor et al., 1983; Smock and Fields, 1981), this pilot study again suggests that ACTH may play an important role in the persistence of neurotic behavior.

The oversecretion of ACTH in depression is now well documented by dexamethasone-resistance studies (Yerevanian et al., 1983; Kalin et al., 1982; Reus et al., 1982) but unlike the above phobic patients observed by Curtis, depressives are more apt to have concomitant high levels of cortisol secretion. As elevations of corticosteroids are frequently correlated with immunosuppression, this may explain why all studies have not shown a positive relationship between immunity from cancer and measures of neuroticism: different studies may have to varying degrees sampled neurotic populations with high levels of ACTH-cortisol or high ACTH but low cortisol. The hypercortisolism in depressives would account for the correlation between loss of significant personal relationship and immunosuppression which is frequently found (Jemmott and Locke, 1984; Sklar and Anisman, 1981). This also explains the strong correlation between hopelessness and cancer in the Yugoslavian study by Grossarth-Maticek (in press).

Thus far ties between neuropeptides and forms of neurotic behavior and between different neurotic behaviors and immuno-enhancement have been suggested. The intriguing question is whether a similar link can be made between immunity from cancer and the same neuropeptides. Immuno-enhancing properties of ACTH and the endogenous opioid peptides are sometimes reported, but contradictory findings have also been reported (Greenberg et al., 1984). The direct effects of these peptides (and other pituitary hormones) must (and can) be experimentally separated from their tropic properties (de Wied et al., 1984). One assumption of the present project is that these simple effects and contradictory findings can only be understood in the context of interactions with other processes and factors, such as individual differences.

The effects of changes in levels of these peptides must also interface with the complex relationship between stress and cancer. For instance, as already shown, in the animal psycho-immunological literature it has been shown that acute stress by inescapable shock produces a decline in resistance to cancer; however, there may be a reversal of this immunosuppression if the stress is protracted (Sklar and Anisman, 1979; Monjan and Collector, 1977). As it has been shown that endogenous opiates are involved in these reactions to acute stress (MacLennan et al., 1982), the effect of protracted stress can possibly be explained by development of tolerance to endogenous opiates. This form of tolerance has been reliably observed (Christie and Chresher, 1982; Christie et al., 1982). One consequence of this may be a concomitant hypocortisolism to stress-induced elevations in ACTH. Recently it has been shown that infusions of ACTH (1-24) into a group of healthy volunteers resulted in the predicted rise in cortisol, but this did not occur in a group of methadone addicts (Dackis et al., 1982; Pullman et al., 1983). Hence, this hypothesis about tolerance to endogenous opiates and hypocortisolism is not without some empirical support. Physiologically this might occur by the suppression of ACTH by endogenous opiates with the consequent atrophy of the adrenal gland. Quite consistent with this hypothesis is the finding that when nutritional factors are controlled for, heroin addicts show immuno-enhancement (Heathcote and Taylor, 1981).

There are reasons for thinking that neuropeptide fragments of pituitary hormones may have potential as immuno-enhancing agents, but there is also reason to believe that this will be achieved only in the context of individual differences. To illustrate, Franklin and Broadhurst (1979) found that the behavioral effects of providing rats with the acute stress of inescapable shocks interacted with the genotype of the animals. In a similar learned-helplessness experiment with humans, Tiggeman (1982) found an interaction with the introversion–extraversion dimension of personality. Breier et al. (1979) have found that differences on this personality dimension determine whether ACTH (4-10) will have excitatory or inhibitory effects on heart rate in a stress situation. Pain-insensitive subjects find shocks more painful after naloxone administration while pain-sensitive subjects find the shock to be less painful (Almond, 1977). Thus, in investigating the direct effect of peptides or other factors in immuno-enhancement, it is to be expected that individual differences and genetic factors will play a major role (Eysenck, 1980, 1983b; Barchas and Sullivan, 1982; Horwitz and Dubek, 1983). Figure 2–8 illustrates the general features of the model.

The putative role of tolerance to opiates in the above model must accommodate the increasing evidence of potent associative learning factors in the development of tolerance (Shapiro et al., 1983; O'Brien et al., 1977; Walter and Riccio, 1983). It is now apparent that all the laws of associative learning will be

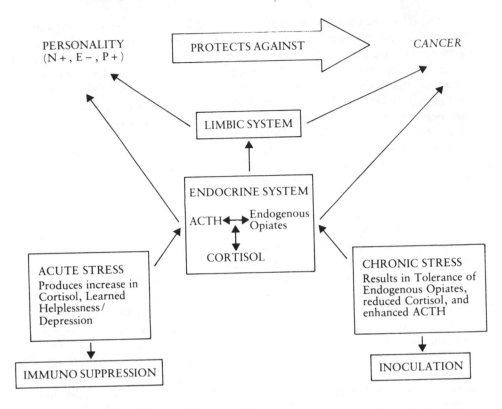

Figure 2–8. Relationships between Personality and Cancer, and Possible Endocrine and Stress Intermediaries

applicable to this phenomenon (Mackintosh, 1974). Undoubtedly, the learning involved will also be biologically constrained (Shettleworth, 1972; LoLordo, 1979; Hinde and Stevenson-Hinde, 1973; Seligman and Hager, 1972). The conditioned immuno-modulation which has been demonstrated is relatively small and transient (Ader and Cohen, 1981). This is undoubtedly not unlike the early days of avoidance conditioning before it was understood that the limitations on defensive conditioning need to be understood in the broader context of the causation of defensive behavior itself (Bolles, 1970; Grossen and Kelley, 1972; Bolles and Fansellow, 1980). Such an analysis should be particularly applicable to interactions between different defensive systems (behavioral, immunological and neuro-endocrine). If such associative tolerance in conjunction with individual differences in neuro-endocrine functioning and direct behavioral conditioning can account for the development of different types of neurotic disorders and concomitant changes in immunity, it should be possible to produce a neurobehavioral technology of cancer inoculation. The success of behavioral therapy during the last twenty years suggests that this promise can be met, and Grossarth-Maticek et al. (1982b) have given impressive evidence of the possible value of behavior therapy in relation to cancer.

Table 2–3 shows the results of Grossarth-Maticek's (unpublished) Heidelberg prospective study, in which behavior therapy was used prophylactically on 91 high cancer-risk and 82 high CHD risk subjects, who were randomly divided into control and therapy groups. Therapy was addressed to a change in personality and behavior found previously to be correlated with cancer or CHD respectively. Highly significant effects were obtained for these therapeutic efforts.

Similar success was obtained in using behavior therapy to prolong life in terminally ill women with cancer of the breast. Behavior therapy was as successful in prolonging life as was chemotherapy; both together were more successful than either alone, and least successful was a regime employing neither. The combined action was more successful than a simple addition of the effects of each by itself.

In summary, sustained stress may give rise to increased immunity from cancer and an enhanced proclivity to certain anxiety-related disorders. The neuroendocrine characteristics common to both conditions may be acquired tolerance in the endogenous opiate system and sustained high levels of ACTH produced by hypocortisolism. Other work suggests that the effects of stress and neuropeptides will interact with individual differences.

For coronary heart disease, the positive correlation with emotional instability and neuroticism does not present the paradoxical effects noted for lung cancer, although here also, while there are many speculations regarding causal mechanisms, the final word has not yet been spoken. We can only conclude that while the relations depicted in figure 2–4 are probably de-

Table 2–3
Heidelberg Prospective Study

	Living	Died of Risk Factor	Died of Other Causes	Total
Cancer Risk Groups				
Control Group	25	12	9	46
Therapy Group	40	0	5	45
Total	65	12	14	91
CHD Risk Groups				
Control Group	20	14	5	39
Therapy Group	34	3	6	43
Total	54	17	11	82

Source: Grossarth-Maticek, et al., Psychosomatic factors in the process of cancerogenesis: The Heidelberg Prospective Study. Paper presented at Hamburg World Congress of Psychosomatic Medicine. Unpublished report. 1983.

scriptively in line with the facts, causal relations are difficult to explain, although hypotheses exist which have some factual support. The reason for this lack of clear-cut evidence, as already pointed out, is the failure of grant-giving bodies to support work on the constitutional model, and the consequent lack of experimental studies along these lines. Thus the alternative to the received view cannot be regarded as being any more firmly established than the received view itself; all we can conclude at the moment is that no final answers are known, that there are two alternative theories in the field, neither of which can be said to explain all the facts, and both of which are clearly beset by many anomalous findings. We will not follow the adherents of the received view in attempting to achieve the premature crystalization of spurious orthodoxies; the assumption that a truth is already known, or that no alternative theories exist, most powerfully prevents scientists from undertaking the research needed to increase our knowledge and put our theories on a firmer footing.

We may thus conclude that the received view—that smoking causes lung cancer and coronary heart disease and is responsible for the major portion of the deaths that occur from these two causes—has not been proven correct by existing research, but has encountered so many anomalies and difficulties, and is based on such insecure foundations (largely due to the lack of reliability of the data, and the incautious use of statistics based on these data) that the only possible conclusion is a verdict of "not proven." On the other hand, the constitutional view, particularly when integrated with work on personality and stress, can successfully account for some facts, although it also is weak with respect to causal mechanisms. The position thus clearly remains one of doubt and questioning; either theory might be right, both theories might be right and complement each other, or possibly both theories in the present form might be wrong. This may be a pessimistic conclusion to draw from such a large amount of research, but it is the only conclusion that is scientifically admissible at the present time.

References

Abramson, J.H., Sacks, U.I., Cabana, E. 1971. Death certificate data as an indication of the presence of certain common diseases at death. *Journal of Chronic Diseases* 14, 417–431.

Abse, D.W., Wilkins, M.M., Castle, R.C., Buxton, W.D., Demars, J.P., Brown, R.S. & Kirschner, L.G. 1974. Personality and behavioural characteristics of lung cancer patients. *Journal of Psychosomatic Research* 18, 101–113.

Ader, R. (ed.), 1981. Psychoneuroimmunology. New York: Academic Press.

Ader, R. & Cohen, N. 1975. Behaviourally conditioned immunosuppression. *Psychosomatic Medicine* 37, 333–340.

Ader, R. & Cohen, N. 1981. Conditioned immuno-pharmacologic responses. In R. Ader (ed.), *Psycho-immunology*. Academic Press.

Albert, S. & Child, M. 1977. Familial cancer in the general population. *Cancer* 40, 1674–1679.

Almond, J.W. 1977. Naloxone alters pain perception and somatosensory evoked potentials in normal subjects. *Nature* 270, 620–621.

Anderson, D.E. 1978. Familial cancer and cancer families. *Seminars in Oncology* 5, 11–16.

Bahnson, C.B. & Bahnson, M.B. 1964a. Cancer as an alternative to psychosis. In D.M. Kissen & L.C. LeShan (eds.), *Psychosomatic aspects of neoplastic disease*. Philadelphia: Lippincott.

Bahnson, C.B. & Bahnson, M.B. 1964b. Denial and repression of primitive impulses and of disturbing emotions in patients with malignant neoplasms. In D.M. Kissen & L.C. LeShan (eds.), *Psychosomatic aspects of neoplastic disease*. Philadelphia: Lippincott.

Bammer, K. 1981. Stress, spread and cancer. In K. Bammer & B.H. Newberry, *Stress and cancer*. Toronto: C.J. Hogrefe.

Bammer, K. & Newberry, B.H. 1981. *Stress and cancer*. Toronto: C.J. Hogrefe.

Barchas, J.D. & Sullivan, S. 1982. Opioid peptides as neuroregulators: Potential areas for the study of genetic-behavioural mechanisms. *Behaviour Genetics* 12, 69–91.

Barefoot, J.C., Dahlstrom, W.B. & Williams, R.B. 1983. Hostility, CHD incidence, and total mortality: A 25-year follow-up study of 253 physicians. *Psychosomatic Medicine* 45, 59–63.

Bauer, F.W. & Robbins, S.L. 1972. An autopsy study of cancer patients. *Journal of the American Medical Association* 227, 1431–1474.

Beadenkopf, W.G., Abrams, M., Daoud, A. & Marks, R.U. 1963. An assessment of certain medical aspects of death certificate data for epidemiologic study of arteriosclerotic heart disease. *Journal of Chronic Diseases* 16, 249–262.

Belcher, J.R. 1971. World-wide differences in the sex ratio of bronchial carcinoma. *British Journal of the Diseases of the Chest* 65, 205–221.

Bendien, J. & Groen, J. 1963. A psychological–statistical study of neuroticism and extraversion in patients with myocardial infarction. *Journal of Psychosomatic Research* 7, 11–14.

Berkson, J. 1958. Smoking and lung cancer: Some observations on two recent reports. *Journal of the American Statistical Association* 53, 28–38.

Berkson, J. & Elveback, L. 1960. Competing exponential risks, with particular reference to the study of smoking and lung cancer. *Journal of the American Statistical Association* 291, 415–428.

Berndt, H., Gunther, H. & Rohte, G. 1980. Personlichkeits struktur nach Eysenck bei Kranken mit Brustdrusen—und Bronchialkrebs und Diagnoseverzogerung durch den Patienten. *Archiv fur Geschuulstfurschung* 50, 359–368.

Blohmke, M., Englehardt, B. & Stelzer, D. In press. Psychosocial factors and smoking as risk factors in lung carcinoma. *Journal of Psychosomatic Research*.

Bloom, B.L., Asher, J.J. & White, S.W. 1978. Marital disruption as a stressor: A review and analysis. *Psychological Bulletin* 85, 867–894.

Blumberg, E.M., West, P.M. & Ellis, F.W. 1954. A possible relationship between psychological factors and human cancer. *Psychosomatic Medicine* 16, 277–286.

Blumenthal, J.A., Thompson, L.W., Williams, B.R. & Kong, Y. 1979. Anxiety-proneness and coronary heart disease. *Journal of Psychosomatic Research* 23, 17–21.

Bohus, B. 1974. Pituitary-adrenal hormones and the forced extinction of a passive avoidance response in the rat. *Brain Research* 66, 366–367.

Bohus, B., de Kloet, E.R. & Veldhuis, H.D. 1982. Adrenal steroids and behavioral adaptation: Relationship to brain corticosteroid receptors. D. Ganten & D. Pfaff (eds.), *Adrenal actions on brain.* New York: Springer-Verlag.

Bolles, R.C. 1970. Species-specific defensive reactions and avoidance learning. *Psychological Review* 77, 32–48.

Bolles, R.C. & Fanselow, M.S. 1980. A perceptual-defensive-recuperative model of fear and pain. *The Behavioral and Brain Sciences* 3, 291–323.

Borysenko, U. & Borysenko, J. 1982. Stress, behaviour, and immunity: Animal models and mediating mechanisms. *General Hospital Psychiatry* 4, 59–67.

Bovbjerg, D., Ader, R. & Cohen, N. 1982. Behaviorally conditioned suppression of a graft-versus-host response. *Proceedings of the National Academy of Sciences* 79, 583–585.

Breier, C., Kain, H. & Konzett, H. 1979. Personality dependent effects of the ACTH 4-10 fragment on test performances and on concomitant autonomic reactions. *Psychopharmacology* 65, 239–246.

Briggs, R.L. 1975. Quality of death certificate diagnosis as compared with autopsy findings. *Arizona Medicine* 32, 617–624.

Britton, D.R. & Britton, K.T. 1981. A sensitive open field measure of anxiolytic drug activity. *Pharmacology, Biochemistry and Behavior* 15, 577–582.

Britton, D.R., Koob, G.F., River, J. & Vale, W. 1982. Intraventricular corticotropin-releasing factor enhances behavioral effects of novelty. *Life Sciences* 31, 363–367.

Britton, M. 1974. Diagnostic errors discovered at autopsy. *Acta Medica Scandinavia* 196, 203–210.

Britton, M. 1974. Clinical diagnostics: experience from 383 autopsied cases. *Acta Medica Scandinavia* 196, 211–219.

Brown, F. 1960. The relationship between cancer and personality. *Annals of the New York Academy of Science* 125, 865-875.

Brownlee, K.A. 1965. A review of "Smoking and Health." *Journal of the American Statistical Association* 60, 722–739.

Burch, P.R.J. 1976. *The biology of cancer: A new approach.* Lancaster: Medical and Technical Publishers.

Burch, P.R.J. 1978a. Are 90% of cancers preventable? *IRCS Journal of Medical Science* 6, 353–356.

Burch, P.R.J. 1978b. Coronary heart disease: Risk factors and ageing. *Gerontology* 24, 123–155.

Burch, P.R.J. 1978c. Smoking and lung cancer: The problem of inferring cause. *Journal of the Royal Statistical Society* 141, 437–477.

Burch, P.R.J. 1979. Coronary disease: Risk factors, age, and time. *American Heart Journal* 97, 415–419.

Burch, P.R.J. 1980. Review: Ischaemic heart disease: Epidemiology, risk factors and cause. *Cardiovascular Research* 14, 307–338.

Burch, P.R.J. 1982. Cigarette smoking and lung cancer: A continuing controversy. *Medical Hypotheses* 9, 293–306.

Burch, P.R.J. 1983. The Surgeon-General's "epidemiologic criteria for causality": A critique. *Journal of Chronic Diseases* 36, 821–836.

Burch, P.R.J. Smoking and health. 1985. In press. In S. Modgil and C. Modgil (eds.) *Hans Eysenck: Consensus and Controversy.*

Burch, P.R.J. 1984. The Surgeon-General's "epidemiologic criteria for causality": A reply to Filienfeld. *Journal of Chronic Diseases* 37, 148–156.

Butler, J., Regelson, W., Lawlis, G.F. & Bristow, O.V. 1982. Personality profile comparison between cancer patients and other disease groups. *Multivariate Experimental Clinical Research* 6, 15–21.

Cairns, J. 1981. The origin of human cancers. *Nature* 289, 353–357.

Cameron, M. & McGoogan, E. 1981. A prospective study of 1152 hospital autopsies. Part 1: Inaccuracies in death certification. *Journal of Pathology* 133, 273–283.

Cameron, H.M. & McGoogan, E. 1981. A prospective study of 1152 hospital autopsies: II. Analysis of inaccuracies in clinical diagnoses and their significance. *Journal of Pathology* 134, 285–300.

Cameron, H.M., McGoogan, E., Clarke, J. & Wilson, B.A. 1977. Trends in hospital necropsy rates: Scotland, 1961–1974. *British Medical Journal* 1, 1577–1579.

Cederlof, R., Friberg, L. & Hrubec, Z. 1969. Cardiovascular and respiratory symptoms in relation to tobacco smoking. *Archives of Environmental Health* 18, 934–940.

Cederlof, R., Friberg, L. & Lundman, T. 1977. The interaction of smoking, environment and heredity and their implications for disease etiology. *Acta Medica Scandinavia* Supplement 612.

Chan, W.C., Colbourne, M.J., Fung, S.C. & Ho, H.C. 1979. Bronchial cancer in Hong Kong, 1976–1977. *British Journal of Cancer* 39, 182–192.

Choi, N.W., Schumann, L.M., and Gullen, W.H. 1970. Epidemiology of primary central nervous system neoplasms. Part 2: Case-control study. *American Journal of Epidemiology* 91, 467–485.

Christie, M.J. & Chesher, G.B. 1982. Physical dependence on physiologically released endogenous opiates. *Life Sciences* 30, 1173–1177.

Christie, M.J., Trisdikoon, P. & Chesher, G.B. 1982. Tolerance and cross tolerance with morphine resulting from physiological release of endogenous opiates. *Life Sciences* 31, 839–845.

Cinader, B. 1975. Individuality in disease and therapy. *CMA Journal* 113, 11–14.

Cohen, S. 1980. After-effects of stress on human performance and social behaviour: A review of research and theory. *Psychological Bulletin* 88, 82–108.

Cohen, B.H., Diamond, E.L., Graves, C.G., Kreiss, O., Levy, D.A., Menkes, H.A., Permutt, S., Omaskey, S. & Tockman, M.S. 1977. A common familial component in lung cancer and chronic obstructive pulmonary disease. *Lancet* 2, 523–526.

Cohen, N., Ader, R., Green, N. & Bovbjerg, D. 1979. Conditioned suppression of a thymus-independent antibody response. *Psychosomatic Medicine* 41, 487–491.

Concannon, J.T., Riccio, D.C., Maloney, R. & McKelvey, J. 1980a. ACTH mediation of learned fear: Blockade by naloxone and naltrexone. *Physiology and Behavior* 25, 977–979.

Concannon, J.T., Riccio, D.C. & McKelvey, J. 1980b. Pavlovian conditioning of fear based upon hormonal mediation of prior aversive experience. *Animal Learning and Behavior* 8, 75–80.

Conteno, F. & Chiarelli, B. 1962. Study of the inheritance of some daily life habits. *Heredity* 17, 347–359.

Cooper, C.L. (ed.). 1983. *Stress Research*, London: John Wiley.

Cooper, C.L. & Payne, R. (eds.). 1980. *Current concerns in occupational stress*. Chichester: J. Wiley.

Coppen, A. & Metcalfe, M. 1963. Cancer and extraversion. *British Medical Journal* July, 18–19.

Crabbe, J.C., Allen, R.G., Gantte, N.D., Young, A.K. & Stack, J. 1981. Strain differences in pituitary B-endorphin and ACTH content in inbred mice. *Brain Research* 219, 219–223.

Curtis, G.C., Buxton, M., Lippman, D., Nesse, R. & Wright, J. 1976. "Flooding in vivo" during the circadian phase of minimal cortisol secretion: Anxiety and therapeutic success without adrenal cortical activation. *Biological Psychiatry* 11, 101–107.

Curtis, G.C., Nesse, R., Buxton, M. & Lippman, D. 1978. Anxiety and plasma cortisol at the crest of the circadian cycle; Reappraisal of a classical hypothesis. *Psychosomatic Medicine* 40, 368–370.

Dackis, C.A., Gurpegui, M., Pottash, A.L.C. & Gold, M.S. 1982. Methadone induced hypoadrenalism. *Lancet* 2, 1167.

Dattore, P.J., Shautz, F.C. & Coyne, L. 1980. Premorbid personality differentiation of cancer and non-cancer groups: A test of the hypothesis of cancer proneness. *Journal of Counselling and Clinical Psychology* 48, 388–394.

DeChambre, R.F. 1981. Psychosocial stress and cancer in mice. In K. Bammer & B.H. Newberry (eds.), *Stress and Cancer*. Toronto: C.J. Hogrefe.

de Wied, D. & Jolles, J. 1982. Neuropeptides derived from propiocortin: behavioural, physiological and neurochemical effects. *Physiological Reviews* 62, 976–1060.

de Wied, D., Gafforio, Van Ree, J.M. & de Jong, W. 1984. Central target for behavioural effects of vasopressin neuropeptides. *Nature* 308, 276–278.

Dijl, H. 1979. Myocardial infarction patients and sociability. *Journal of Psychosomatic Research* 23, 3–6.

Dohrenwend, B.S. & Dohrenwend, B.P. 1974. *Stressful life events: Their nature and effects*. New York: Wiley.

Dohrenwend, B.S. & Dohrenwend, B.P. (eds.). 1981. *Stressful life events and their contexts*. New York: Provdist.

Doll, R. 1971. The age distribution of cancer: Implications for models of carcinogenesis. *Journal of the Royal Statistical Society* 134, 133–166.

Doll, R. & Hill, A.B. 1952. A study of the aetiology of carcinoma of the lung. *British Medical Journal* 2, 1271–1286.

Doll, R. & Hill, A.B. 1964. Mortality in relation to smoking: Ten years' observations of British doctors. *British Medical Journal* 1, 1399–1410; 1460–1467.

Doll, R. & Peto, R. 1976. Mortality in relation to smoking: 20 years' observations on male British doctors. *British Medical Journal* 2, 1525–1536.

Duckitt, J. & Broll, T. 1982. Personality factors as moderators of the psychological impact of life stress. *South African Journal of Psychology* 12, 76–80.

Dunbar, F. 1943. *Psychosomatic diagnosis*. New York: Hoeber.

Editorial. 1979. Medical charities and prevention. *British Medical Journal* 2, 1616.

Eliot, R.S. 1974. *Stress and the heart*. New York: Future Publishing Company.

Enstrom, J.E. 1980. Cancer mortality among Mormons in California during 1968–1975. *Journal of the National Cancer Institute* 65, 1073–1082.

Eppinger, H. 1917. *Vagotomia*. New York: Nervous and Mental Diseases Monograph No. 20.

Ernster, V.L., Sacks, S.T., Selvin, S. & Petrakis, N.L. 1979. Cancer incidence by marital status: U.S. Third National Cancer Survey. *Journal of the National Cancer Institute* 63, 567–585.

Eysenck, H.J. 1965. Smoking, Health and Personality. London: Weidenfeld & Nicolson.

Eysenck, H.J. 1967. *The biological basis of personality*. Springfield: C.C. Thomas.

Eysenck, H.J. 1973. Personality and the maintenance of the smoking habit. In W.L. Dunn (ed.), *Smoking behaviour: Motives and incentives*. New York: Wiley.

Eysenck, H.J. 1979. The conditioning model of neurosis. *The Behavioral and Brain Sciences* 2, 155–199.

Eysenck, H.J. 1980. *The causes and effects of smoking*. London: Maurice Temple Smith; Los Angeles: Sage.

Eysenck, H.J. (ed.). 1981a. *A model for personality*. New York: Springer.

Eysenck, H.J. 1981b. Personality and cancer: some comments on a paper by H. Berndt. *Archiv fur Geschwuhlstforschung* 51, 442–443.

Eysenck, H.J. 1982. Neobehavioristic (S-R) Theory. In G.T. Wilson & C.M. Franks, *Contemporary behavior therapy*. London: Guilford Press.

Eysenck, H.J. 1983a. Psychopharmacology and personality. In W. Janke (ed.), *Response variability to psychotropic drugs*. New York: Pergamon.

Eysenck, H.J. 1983b. Stress, disease, and personality: The "innoculation effect." In C.L. Cooper (ed.), *Stress Research*. London: John Wiley.

Eysenck, H.J. 1984. Personality, stress and lung cancer. In S. Rachman (ed.), *Contributions to Medical Psychology* (Vol. 3). London: Pergamon.

Eysenck, H.J. Forthcoming. Personality, cancer and cardiovascular disease: Causal analysis. *Personality and Individual Differences*.

Eysenck, H.J. & Eysenck, M.W. 1985. *Personality and Individual Differences*. New York: Plenum.

Eysenck, H.J. & Fulker, D.W. 1983. The components of type of behaviour and its genetic determinants. *Personality and Individual Differences* 4, 499–505.

Faine, D. 1974. Ischaemic heart disease in death discordant twins: A study of 205 male and female pairs. *Acta Medica Scandinavia* Supplement 588, 1–129.

Fehm, H.L., Klein, E. & Voight, K.H. 1984. Evidence for extra-pituitary mechanisms mediating the morning peak of plasma cortisol in man. *Journal of Clinical Endocrinology and Metabolism* 58, 410–414.

Feingold, J. 1978. Genetique et cancers humains: Methodologe d'stude. *Bulletin du Cancer* 65, 73–77.

Feinstein, A.R. & Wells, C.K. 1974. Cigarette smoking and lung cancer: The problem of "detection bias" in epidemiologic rates of disease. *Transactions of the Association of American Physicians* 87, 180–185.

Fisher, R.A. 1958a. Cigarettes, cancer, and statistics. *Centennial Review of the Arts and Sciences* (Vol. 2). Michigan: State Universities.

Fisher, R.A. 1958b. Lung cancer and cigarettes. *Nature* 182, 108.

Fisher, R.A. 1958c. Cancer and smoking. *Nature* 182, 596.

Fisher, R.A. 1959. *Smoking, the cancer controversy*. Edinburgh: Oliver and Boyd.

Floderus, B. 1974. Psycho-social factors in relation to coronary heart disease and associated risk factors. *Nordisk Hygienisk Tidskrift* Supplement 6.

Fox, B.H. & Newbery, B.H. 1984. *Impact of psychoendocrine systems in cancer and immunity*. New York: Hogrefe.

Frankenhaeuser, M. 1980. Psychological aspects of life stress. In S. Levine & H. Ursiu (eds.), *Coping and Health*. New York: Plenum.

Franklin, R.V. & Broadhurst, P.L. 1979. Emotionality in selectively bred strains of rats. *Behavior Research and Therapy* 17, 349–354.

Friberg, L., Kay, L., Dencker, S.J. & Joneson, E. 1959. Smoking habits of monozygotic and dizygotic twins. *British Medical Journal* 1, 1090–1092.

Friedman, G.D., Siegelaub, A.B., Dales, L.G. & Seltzer, C.C. 1979. Characteristics predictive of coronary heart disease in ex-smokers before they stopped smoking: Comparison with persistent smokers and non-smokers. *Journal of Chronic Diseases* 32, 175–190.

Fulker. D. 1981. The genetic and environmental architecture of psychoticism, entraversion and neuroticism. M.H. Eysenck (ed.), *A Model for Personalities*. New York: Springer.

Garcia, J., Hankins, W.G. & Rusiniak, K.W. 1974. Behavioural regulation of the milieu interne in man and rat. *Science* 185, 824–831.

Gertler, M.G. & White, P.D. 1954. *Coronary heart disease in young adults*. Cambridge: Harvard University Press.

Gray, J., Davis, N. & Owen, S. 1981. Stress tolerance: Possible neural mechanisms. In M.L. Christie & P.G. Mellett (eds), *Foundations of Psychosomatics*. New York: J. Wiley.

Greenberg, A.H., Dyck, D.G. & Sandler, L.S. 1984. Opponent processes, neurohormones and natural resistance. In B.H. Fox & B.H. Newberry (eds.), *Impact of psychoendocrine systems in cancer and immunity*. New York: C.J. Hogrefe.

Greene, W.A. 1966. The psychosocial setting of the development of leukemia and lymphoma. *Annals of the New York Academy of Sciences* 125, 794–801.

Greene, W.A. & Swisher, S.N. 1969. Psychological and somatic variables associated with the development and course of monozygotic twins discordant for leukemia. *Annals of the New York Academy of Sciences* 164, 394–408.

Greer, S. 1979. Psychological enquiry: A contribution to cancer research. *Psychological Medicine* 9, 81–89.

Greer, S. & Morris, T. 1975. Psychological attributes of women who develop breast cancer: A controlled study. *Journal of Psychosomatic Medicine* 19, 147–153.

Grossarth-Maticek, R. 1980. Synergic effects of cigarette smoking, systolic blood pressure, and psychosocial risk factors for lung cancer, cardiac infarct and apoplexi cereboi. *Psychotherapy and Psychosomatics* 34, 267–272.

Grossarth-Maticek, R., Bastiaans, J. & Kanasir, D.T. 1985. Psychosocial factors as strong predictors of mortality from cancer, ischaemic heart disease and stroke: The Yugoslav Prospective Study. *Journal of Psychosomatic Research* 29, 167–176.

Grossarth-Maticek, R., Bastiaans, J., Schmidt, P. & Vetter, H. 1983. Psychosomatic factors in the process of cancerogenesis: The Heidelberg Prospective Study. Paper presented at Hamburg World Congress of Psychosomatic Medicine.

Grossarth-Maticek, R., Frentzel-Beyme, R. & Becker, V. 1984. Cancer risk associated with life events and conflict resolution. *Cancer Detection and Prevention* 7, 201–209.

Grossarth-Maticek, R., Kanasir, D.T., Schmidt, P. & Vetter, H. 1982a. Psychosocial and organic variables for lung cancer, cardiac infarct and apoplexy. Paper presented at XIV European Conference on Psychosomatic Research.

Grossarth-Maticek, R., Kanasir, D.T., Schmidt, P. & Vetter, H. 1982b. Psychosomatic factors in the process of cancerogenesis. *Psychotherapy and Psychosomatics* 38, 284–302.

Grossarth-Maticek, R., Kanasir, D.T., Schmidt, P. & Vetter, H. 1985. Psychosocial and organic variables as predictors of lung cancer, cardiac infarct and apoplexy: Some differential predictors. *Personality and Individual Differences* 6, 313–321.

Grossarth-Maticek, R., Kanasir, D.T., Vetter, H. & Schmidt, P. 1983. Psychosomatic factors involved in the process of cancerogenesis. *Psychotherapy and Psychosomatics* 40, 191–210.

Grossarth-Maticek, R., Siegrist, J. & Vetter, H. 1982. Interpersonal repression as a predictor of cancer. *Social Science and Medicine* 16, 493–498.

Grossen, N.E. & Kelley, M.J. 1972. Species-specific behaviour and the acquisition of behaviour in rats. *Journal of Comparative and Physiological Psychology* 81, 306–311.

Gruver, R.H. & Freis, E.D. 1957. A study of diagnostic error. *Annals of Internal Medicine* 47, 108–120.

Guberan, E. 1979. Surprising decline of cardiovascular mortality in Switzerland: 1951–1976. *Journal of Epidemiology and Community Health* 33, 114–120.

Hagnell, O. 1966. The premorbid personality of persons who develop cancer in a total population. *Annals of the New York Academy of Science* 125, 846–855.

Hammond, E.C. 1966. Smoking in relation to death rates of one million men and women. *National Cancer Institute Monograph* 19, 127–204.

Hammond, E.C. 1972. Smoking habits and air pollution in relation to lung cancer. In D.K. Lee (ed.), *Environmental factors in respiratory diseases.* New York: Academic Press.

Hammond, E.C. & Garfinkel, L. 1969. Coronary heart disease, stroke, and aortic aneurysm: Factors in the etiology. *Archives of Environmental Health* 19, 167–182.

Hammond, E.C. & Horn, D. 1958. Smoking and death rates—report on forty-four months of follow-up on 187,783 men. Part 1: Total mortality. *Journal of the American Medical Association* 166, 1159–1172.

Hamtoft, H. & Lindhardt, M. 1956. Tobacco consumption in Denmark. Part 2. *Danish Medical Bulletin* 3, 150.

Harris, C.C. 1980. Individual differences in cancer susceptibility. *Annals of Internal Medicine* 92, 809–825.

Hartveit, F. 1979. Autopsy findings in cases with a clinically uncertain diagnosis. *Journal of Pathology* 129, 111–119.

Harvald, B. & Hauge, M. 1963. Hereditary factors elucidated by twin studies. In J.V. Weel, M.V. Shaw & W.J. Schull (eds.), *Genetics and the epidemiology of chronic diseases.* Washington: Public Health Service.

Heasman, M.A. & Lipworth, L. 1966. *Accuracy of certification of cause of deaths.* London: H.M.S.O.

Heathcote, J. & Taylor, K.B. 1981. Immunity and nutrition in heroin addicts. *Drug and Alcohol Dependence* 8, 245–255.

Horne, R.L. & Picard, R.S. 1979. Psychosocial risk factors for lung cancer. *Psychosomatic Medicine* 41, 503–514.

Horwitz, G.P. & Dudek, B.C. 1983. Behavioral pharmacogenetics. In J.L. Fuller & E.C. Simmel (eds.), *Behavior Genetics*. London: Lawrence Erlbaum.

Hrubec, Z., Cederlof, R. & Friberg, L. 1976. Background of angina pectoris: Social and environmental factors in relation to smoking. *American Journal of Epidemiology* 103, 16–29.

Insel, T.R. & Pickar, D. 1983. Naloxone administration in obsessive-compulsive disorders: Report of two cases. *American Journal of Psychiatry* 140, 1219–1220.

Jackson, L.G. 1978. Chromosomes and cancers: Current aspects. *Seminars in Oncology* 5, 3–10.

Jacobs, T.J. & Charles, E. 1980. Life events and the occurrence of cancer in children. *Psychosomatic Medicine* 42, 11–24.

Jacquet, Y.F. 1978. Opiate effects after adrenocorticotropin or B-endorphin injection in the periaqueductal gray matter of rats. *Science* 201, 1032–1034.

Jemmott, J.B. & Locke, S.E. 1984. Psychosocial factors, immunologic mediation and human susceptibility to infectious disease: How much do we know? *Psychological Bulletin* 95, 78–108.

Jones, M.T., Gillham, B., Greenstein, B.D., Beckford, V. & Holme, M.C. 1982. Feedback actions of adrenal steroids. In D. Ganten and D. Pfaff (eds.), *Adrenal actions on brain*. New York: Springer-Verlag.

Kagan, A., Katsuki, S., Sternley, N. & Vanecek, R. 1967. Reliability of death certificate data on vascular lesions affecting the central nervous system. *Bulletin of the World Health Organization* 37, 477–483.

Kagan, A., Gordon, T., Rhoads, G. & Schiffman, J.C. 1975. Some factors related to coronary heart disease incidence in Honolulu Japanese men: The Honolulu Heart Study. *International Journal of Epidemiology* 4, 271–279.

Kahn, H.A. 1966. The Dorn study of smoking and mortality among U.S. veterans: Report on eight and one-half years observation. *National Cancer Institute Monograph* 19, 1–125.

Kalin, N.H., Weiler, S.J. & Shelton, S.E. 1982. Plasma ACTH and cortisol concentrations before and after dexamethasone. *Psychiatry Research* 7, 1982.

Kasl, S.V. 1983. Pursuing the links between stressful life experiences and disease: A time for reappraisal. In C.L. Cooper (ed.), *Stress Research*. New York: J. Wiley.

Katz, L. 1969. *Statement to the committee on cigarette labelling and advertising.* Washington: Committee on Interstate and Foreign Commerce.

Kern, W.H., Jones, J.C. & Chapman, V.D. 1968. Pathology of bronchogenic carcinoma in long term survivors. *Cancer* 21, 772–780.

Kessler, I.I. 1972. Epidemiological studies of Parkinson's disease. Part 3: A community based survey. *American Journal of Epidemiology* 96, 242–254.

Keys, A. 1962. Diet and coronary heart disease throughout the world. *Cardiological Practice* 13, 225–244.

Kissen, D.M. 1963a. Personality characteristics in males conducive to lung cancer. *British Journal of Medical Psychology* 36, 27–36.

Kissen, D.M. 1963b. Aspects of personality of men with lung cancer. *Acta Psychotherapeutica* 11, 200–210.

Kissen, D.M. 1964a. Relationship between lung cancer, cigarette smoking, inhalation, and personality. *British Journal of Medical Psychology* 37, 203–216.

Kissen, D.M. 1964b. Lung cancer, inhalation, and personality. In D.M. Kissen & L.L. LeShan (eds.), *Aspects of neoplastic disease*. London: Pitman.

Kissen, D.M. 1967. Psychological factors, personality, and lung cancer in men aged 55–64. *British Journal of Medical Psychology* 40, 29–34.

Kissen, D.M. 1968. Some methodological problems in clinical psychosomatic research with special reference to chest disease. *Psychosomatic Medicine* 30, 324–335.

Kissen, D.M. & Eysenck, H.J. 1962. Personality in male lung cancer patients. *Journal of Psychosomatic Research* 6, 123–137.

Kissen, D.M. & Rowe, L.G. 1969. Steroid excretion patterns and personality in lung cancer. *Annals of the New York Academy of Sciences* 164, 476–482.

Knudson, A.G. 1973. Genetics and etiology of human cancer. In H. Harris & K. Hirschhorn (eds.), *Advances in Human Genetics*. New York: Plenum.

Koeppe, P. 1980. Uberlegungen zur Krebsstatistik und—epidemiologie. *Biologische Medizin* 3, 99–110.

Koeppe, P., Oeser, H. & Rach, K. 1977. Increased cancer mortality rate = increased risk of cancer? *Scandinavia* 1, 8–10.

Kohl, F., Rudiger, H.W. & Wichert, P. 1977. Genetik und Bronchial Karzinom. *Praxis der Pneumologie* 31, 503–504.

Kopp, M.S. & Koranyi, L. 1982. Autonomic and psychologic correlates in hypertension and duodenal ulcer. *Pavlovian Journal of Biological Science* 9, 178–187.

Kouri, R.E. (ed.). 1980. *Genetic differences in chemical carcinogenesis*. Boca Raton, Florida: CRC Press.

LeShan, L.C. 1959. Psychological states as factors in the development of malignant disease. A critical review. *Journal of the National Cancer Institute* 22, 1–18.

LeShan, L.C. 1966. An emotional life-history pattern associated with neoplastic disease: *Annals of the New York Academy of Science* 125, 780–793.

Levi, R.N. & Waxman, S. 1975. Schizophrenia, epilepsy, cancer, methionine, and foliate metabolism. Pathogenesis of schizophrenia. *Lancet*, 5 July, 11–13.

Levin, M.I., Goldstein, H. & Gerhardt, P.R. 1950. Cancer and tobacco smoking: A preliminary report. *Journal of the American Medical Association* 143, 336–338.

Linn, B.S., Linn, M.W. & Jensen, J. 1981. Anxiety and immune responsiveness. *Psychological Reports* 49, 969–970.

Litwin, S.D. (ed.). 1978. *Genetic determinants of pulmonary disease*. New York: Marcel Dekker.

Locke, S.E. 1982. Stress, adaptation, and immunity. *General Hospital Psychiatry* 4, 49–58.

LoLordo, V.M. 1979. Constraints on learning. In M.E. Bitterman, V.M. LoLordo, J.B. Overmier & M.E. Rasotte (eds.) *Animal learning: Survey and analysis*. London: Plenum Press.

Lombard, H.I. & Doering, C.R. 1928, 1978. Classics in oncology. Cancer studies in Massachusetts, Part 2: Habits, characteristics and environment of individuals with and without cancer. *New England Journal of Medicine* 198, 411–417.

Lombard, H.L. & Potter, E.A. 1950. Epidemiological aspects of cancer of the cervix: Hereditary and environmental factors. *Cancer* 3, 960–968.

Lundman, T. 1966. Smoking in relation to coronary heart disease and lung function in twins. *Acta Medica Scandinavia* 180, Supplement 455.

Lynch, H.T. 1977. Pulmonary disease: Defence mechanisms and populations at risk. In M.A. Clark (ed.), *Proceedings of Tobacco and Health Research Institute Symposium*. Kentucky: University of Kentucky.

Lynch, H.T., Fain, P.R., Albano, W., Black, L. & Shouka, M. 1981. *Genetic/epidemiological findings in a study of smoking associated tumours*. Washington, D.C.: American Association for Cancer Research Publications.

Lynch, H.T., Fain, P.R., Albano, W., Ruma, T., Black, L. & Lynch, J. 1982. Genetic/epidemiological findings in a study of smoking-associated tumours. *Cancer Genetics and Cytogenetics* 6, 163–169.

Lyon, J.L., Gardner, J.W. & West, D.W. 1980. Cancer incidence in Mormons and non-Mormons in Utah during 1967–75. *Journal of the National Cancer Institute* 65, 1063–1071.

McCarthy, E.G. & Widmer, G.W. 1974. Effects of screening by consultants on recommended elective surgical procedures. *The New England Journal of Medicine* 291, 1331–1335.

Mackintosh, N.J. 1974. *The psychology of animal learning*. London: Academic Press.

MacLennan, R., da Costa, J., Day, N.E., Law, C.H., Ng, Y.K. & Shanmugaratnam, K. 1977. Risk factors for lung cancer in Singapore Chinese, a population with high female incidence rates. *International Journal of Cancer* 20, 854–860.

MacLennan, J.A., Drugan, R.C., Hyson, R.L. & Maier, S.F. 1982. Corticosterone—a critical factor in an opioid form of stress-induced analgesia. *Science* 215, 1530–1532.

Mainland, D. & Herrera, L. 1956. The risk of biased selection in forward going surveys with non-professional interviewers. *Journal of Chronic Disease* 4, 240–244.

Marks, D.A. 1981. Genetic predisposition to cancer. *Surgery* 90, 132–136.

Marmot, M.G., Syme, S.L., Kagan, A., Kato, H., Cohen, J.B. & Belsky, J. 1975. Prevalence of coronary and hypertensive heart disease and associate risk factors. *American Journal of Epidemiology* 102, 514–525.

Miles, H.H., Waldvogel, S., Barrahee, E.C. & Cobb, S. 1954. Psychosomatic study of 46 young men with coronary artery disease. *Psychosomatic Medicine* 16, 455–462.

Miller, S.M. 1981. Predictability and human stress: Toward a clarification of evidence and theory. *Advances in Experimental Social Psychology* 14, 203–255.

Mills, C.A. & Porter, M.Y. 1950. Tobacco smoking habits and cancer of the mouth and respiratory system. *Cancer Research* 10, 539–542.

Monjan, A.A. & Collector, M.I. 1977. Stress-induced modulation of immune response. *Science* 196, 307–308.

Monitor, S. 1983. Sugary foods may promote breast cancer. *New Scientist* 10 March, 648.

Moore, J.E. 1983. Arginine vasopressin enhances tolerance. *Pharmacology, Biochemistry and Behavior* 19, 561–656.

Mooris, T., Greer, S., Pettingale, K.W. & Watson, M. 1981. Patterns of expression of anger and their psychological correlates in women with breast cancer. *Journal of Psychosomatic Research* 25, 111–117.

Muller, F.H. 1939. Tabakuiss brauch und Lungencarcinoma. *Zeitschrift fur Krebsforschung* 49, 57–84.

Multiple Risk Factor Intervention Trial Research Group. 1982. Multiple risk factor intervention trial. *Journal of the American Medical Association* 248, 1465–1477.

Mulvihill, J.J. 1976. Genetic factors in pulmonary neoplasms. *Birth Defects* 12, 99–111.

Murray, I.D. 1964. Possible relationships between smoking and lung cancer. *Analog* 15, 83–85.

Myrtek, M. 1983. *Typ-A-Verhalten.* Munich: Minerva.

Nefzger, M.D., Quadsfasel, F.A. & Karl, V.C. 1968. A retrospective study of smoking in Parkinson's disease. *American Journal of Epidemiology* 88, 149–158.

Newell, D.Z. 1962. Errors in the interpretation of errors in epidemiology. *American Journal of Public Health* 52, 1925–1928.

O'Brien, C.P., Testa, T., O'Brien, T.J., Brady, J.P. & Wells, B. 1977. Conditioned narcotic withdrawal in humans. *Science* 195, 1000–1002.

Oeser, H. 1979. *Krebs: Schicksal oder Verschulden?* Stuttgart: G. Thieme.

Ohman, A., Eriksson, A. & Olofsson, C. 1975. One-trial learning and superior resistance to extinction of autonomic responses conditioned to potentially phobic stimuli. *Journal of Comparative and Physiological Psychology* 88, 619–627.

Ohman, A., Frederickson, M., Hugdahl, K. & Rimmo, P. 1976. The premise of equipotentiality in human conditioning: Conditioned electrodermal responses to potentially phobic stimuli. *Journal of Experimental Psychology: General* 105, 313–337.

Ohma, A. 1980. Fear relevance, autonomic conditioning and phobias. In P.O. Sjoden & S. Bates (eds.), *Trends in behavior therapy.* New York: Academic Press.

Oliver, M.F. 1982. Does control of risk factors prevent coronary heart disease? *British Medical Journal* 285, 1065–1066.

Osler, W. 1910. The Lumleian lectures on angina pectoris. *Lancet* 1, 839–845.

Ost, L. & Hugdahl, K. 1983. Acquisition of agoraphobia mode of onset and anxiety response patterns. *Behaviour Research and Therapy* 21, 623–631.

Ostfeld, A.M., Lebovitz, B.Z., Shekelle, R.B. & Paul, O. 1964. A prospective study of the relationship between personality and coronary heart disease. *Journal of Chronic Disease* 17, 265–272.

Passey, R.D. 1962. Some problems of lung cancer. *Lancet* 11, 107–112.

Passey, R.D., Blackmore, M., Warbrick-Smith, D., & Jones, R. 1971. Smoking risks of different tobaccos. *British Medical Journal* 4, 198–201.

Pearl, R. 1928. *The rate of living.* New York: Knopf.

Perria, G.U. & Pierce, I.R. 1959. Psychosomatic aspects of cancer: A review. *Psychosomatic Medicine* 21, 397–421.

Pike, M.C. & Doll, R. 1965. Age at onset of lung cancer: Significance in relation to effect of smoking. *Lancet* March, 665–668.

Pleszewski, Z. 1977. *Funkcjonowanie Emocjonalne Pacjentow Przed I Po Zawale Serca.* Dozuan: Uniwersytet lm. Adama Mickiewicza W Poznanius.

Post, R.M., Pickar, D., Ballenger, J.C., Naber, D. & Rubinow, D.R. 1984. Endogenous opiates in cerebrospinal fluid: Relationship to mood and anxiety. In R.M. Post & J.C. Ballenger (eds.), *Neurobiology of Mood Disorders.* London: Williams and Wilkins.

Price, V.A. 1982. *Type A behaviour pattern.* London: Academic Press.

Pullman, P.T., Watson, F.E., Seow, S.S.W. & Rappaport, W. 1983. Methadone-induced hypoadrenalism. *Lancet* 1, 1167.

Puska, P., Tuomilehito, J. & Saloney, J. 1979. Changes in coronary risk factors during a comprehensive five-year community programme to control cardiovascular disease. *British Medical Journal* 2, 1173–1178.

Putnam, H. 1962. What theories are not. In E. Nagel, P. Snypes & A. Tarski (eds.), *Logic, Methodology, and Philosophy of Science.* Stanford: Stanford University Press.

Rae, G. & McCall, J. 1973. Some international comparisons of cancer mortality rates and personality: A brief note. *The Journal of Psychology* 85, 87–88.

Rassidakis, N.C., Kelepouris, M. & Fox, S. 1971. Malignant neoplasms as a cause of death among psychiatric patients, I. *International Mental Health Research Newsletter* 13, 3–6.

Rassidakis, N.C., Kelepouris, M., Goulis, K. & Karaiossefidis, K. 1972. Malignant neoplasms as a cause of death among psychiatric patients, II. *International Mental Health Research Newsletter* 14, 3–6.

Rassidakis, N.C., Erotokristow, A., Validou, M. & Collaron, T. 1973a. Anxiety, schizophrenia and carcinogenesis. *International Mental Health Research Newsletter* 15, 3–6.

Rassidakis, N.C., Erotokristow, A., Validou, M. & Collaron, T. 1973b. Schizophrenia, psychosomatic illness and malignancy. *International Mental Health Research Newsletter* 15, 3–6.

Rassidakis, N.C., Erotokristow, A., Validou, M. & Collaron, T. 1973c. Malignant neoplasms as a cause of death among psychiatric patients, III. *International Mental Health Research Newsletter* 15, 3–6.

Rassidakis, N.C., Grotoerton, A. & Validou, M. 1973d. An essay on the study of the aetiology and pathogenesis of schizophrenia, the psychosomatic illnesses, diabetes mellitus, and cancer. *International Mental Health Research Newsletter* 15, 3–8.

Reid, D.D., & Rose, G.A. 1964. Assessing the comparability of mortality statistics. *British Medical Journal* 2, 1437–1439.

Reif, A.E. 1981. Effect of cigarette smoking on susceptibility to lung cancer. *Oncology* 38, 76–85.

Reus, V.I., Joseph, M.S. & Dallman, M.F. 1982. ACTH levels after the dexamethasone suppression test in depression. *New England Journal of Medicine* 306, 238–242.

Rhoads, G.G., Balckwelder, W.C., Stemmermann, G., Hayashi, T. & Kagan, A. 1978. Coronary risk factors and autopsy findings in Japanese–American men. *Laboratory Investigation* 38, 304–311.

Rigdon, R.H. & Kirchoff, H. 1953. Smoking and cancer of the lung—Let's review the facts. *Texas Reports on Biology and Medicine* 11, 715–727.

Riley, A.L. & Clarke, C.M. 1977. Conditioning and food selection. In L.M. Baker, M.R. Best & M. Domjan (eds.), *Learning mechanisms in food selection*. Waco, Texas: Baylor University Press.

Riley, V., Fitsmaurice, M.A. & Spackman, D.H. 1982. Psychoneuroimmunologic factors in neoplasia: Studies in animals. In R. Ader (ed.), *Psychoneuroimmunology*. New York: Academic Press.

Rime, B. & Bonami, M. 1979. Overt and covert personality traits associated with coronary heart disease. *British Journal of Medical Psychology* 52, 77–84.

Rogers, M.P., Reich, T.B., Strom, T.B. & Carpenter, T.B. 1976. Behaviourally conditioned immunosuppression: Replication of a recent study. *Psychosomatic Medicine* 38, 447–452.

Rose, G. 1964. Familial patterns in ischaemic heart disease. *British Journal of Preventive and Social Medicine* 18, 75–83.

Rose, G. 1977. Ischaemic heart disease. *Journal of Medical Genetics* 14, 330–331.

Rose, G. & Hamilton, P.J.S. 1978. A randomised controlled trial of the effect on middle aged men of advice to stop smoking. *Journal of Epidemiology and Community Health* 32, 275–281.

Rose, G., Hamilton, P.J.S., Colvell, L. & Shipley, M.J. 1982. A randomized controlled trial of anti-smoking advice: 10-year results. *Journal of Epidemiology and Community Health* 36, 102–108.

Rosenblatt, M.B. 1969. The increase in lung cancer: Epidemic or artifact? *Medical Counterpoint* 1, 29–39.

Rosenblatt, M.B. 1974. Lung cancer and smoking—The evidence reassessed. *New Scientist*, May, 332.

Rosenblatt, M.B., Teng, P.K., Kerpe, S. & Beck, I. 1971a. Causes of death in 1000 consecutive autopsies. *New York State Journal of Medicine* 71, 2189–2193.

Rosenblatt, M.B., Teng, P.K., Kerpe, S., & Beck, I. 1971b. Prevalence of lung cancer: Disparity between clinical and autopsy certification. *Medical Counterpoint* 3, 53–59.

Rosenman, R.H. & Chesney, M. 1980. The relationship of type A behaviour patterns to coronary heart disease. *Activitas Nervosa Superior* 22, 1–46.

Rothman, K.J. & Monson, R.R. 1973. Epidemiology of trigeminal neuralgia. *Journal of Chronic Disease* 26, 3–12.

Royal College of Physicians. 1971. *Smoking and health now*. London: Pitman.

Royal College of Physicians, 1977. *Smoking and health now*. London: Pitman.

Royal College of Physicians. 1983. *Smoking and health now*. London: Pitman.

Royce, J.R. & Powell, A. 1983. *Theory of personality and individual differences: Factors, systems and processes*. Englewood Cliffs: Prentice-Hall.

Schairer, E. & Schoeniger, E. 1943. Lungenkrebs und Tabakverbrauch. *Zeitschrift fur Krebsforscung* 54, 261–269.

Schneider, N.R. 1981. The relationship of genetic predisposition to cancer and age of onset of disease in a general population and cancer patients. Unpublished Ph.D. thesis, Cornell University.

Schonfield, J. 1975. Psychological and life-experience differences between Israeli women with benign and cancerous breast lesions. *Journal of Psychosomatic Research* 19, 229–234.

Schrek, R., Baker, A., Ballard, G.P. & Dolgoff, S. 1950. Tobacco smoking as an etiologic factor in disease. Part 1: Cancer. *Cancer Research* 10, 49–58.

Schroeder, D.H. & Costa, P.T. In press. The influence of life event stress on physical illness: Substantive effects or methodological flaws?

Seely, S. & Horrabin, D.F. 1983. Diet and breast cancer: The possible connection with sugar consumption. *Medical Hypotheses* 11, 319–327.

Segall, J. 1973. Is milk a coronary hazard? *British Journal of Preventive and Social Medicine* 31, 81–85.

Sehrt, E. 1904. *Beitrage zur kenntnis des primaren lungencarcinoma.* Leipzig: George.

Seligman, M.E.P. & Hager, J.L. 1972. Biological boundaries of learning. New York: Appleton-Century-Crofts.

Seltzer, C.C. 1968. An evaluation of the effect of smoking on coronary heart disease. *The Journal of the American Medical Association* 203, 193–200.

Seltzer, C.C. 1970. The effect of cigarette smoking on coronary heart disease. *Archives of Environment and Health* 25, 187–191.

Seltzer, C.C. 1975. Smoking and cardiovascular disease. *American Heart Journal* 90, 125–176.

Shapiro, N.R., Dudek, B.C. & Rosellini, R.A. 1983. The role of associative factors in tolerance to the hypothermic effects of morphine in mice. *Pharmacology, Biochemistry and Behavior* 19, 327–333.

Shettleworth, S.J. 1972. Constraints on learning. In D.S. Lehrman, R.A. Hinde & E. Shaw (eds.), *Advances in the study of behaviour* (Vol. 4). New York: Academic Press.

Shields, J. 1962. *Monozygotic twins.* Oxford: Oxford University Press.

Simarak, S., de Jong, U.W., Breslow, N., Dahl, C.J., Ruckphaopunt, K., Scheelings, P. & MacLennan, R. 1977. Cancer of the oral cavity, pharynx/larynx and lung in North Thailand: Case control study and analysis of cigar smoke. *British Journal of Cancer* 36, 130–140.

Sklar, L.S. & Anisman, H. 1979. Stress and coping factors influence tumour growth. *Science* 205, 513–515.

Sklar, L.S. & Anisman, H. 1981. Stress and cancer. *Psychological Bulletin* 89, 396–406.

Slack, J. & Evans, K.A. 1966. The increased risk of death from ischaemic heart disease in first degree relatives of 121 men and 96 women with ischaemic heart disease. *Journal of Medical Genetics* 3, 239–257.

Smithers, D.W. 1953. Facts and fancies about cancer of the lung. *British Medical Journal* 1, 1235–1239.

Smock, T. & Fields, H.L. 1981. ACTH (1-24) blocks opiate-induced analgesia in rats. *Brain Research* 212, 202–206.

Society for Psychosomatic Research. 1959. *The nature of stress disorder.* London: Hutchinson.

Spence, J.T. & Spence, K.W. 1966. The motivational components of manifest anxiety: Drive and drive stimuli. In C.D. Spielberger (ed.), *Anxiety and Behaviour.* London: Academic Press.

Stebbings, J.H. 1971. Chronic respiratory disease among non-smokers in Hagerstown, Maryland. Part II: Problems in the estimation of pulmonary function values in epidemiological surveys. *Environmental Research* 4, 163–192.

Stemmermann, G.A., Steer, A., Rhoads, G., Lee, K., Hayashi, T., Nakashima, T. & Keehn, R. 1976. A comparative pathology study of myocardial lesions and atherosclerosis in Japanese men living in Hiroshima, Japan, and Honolulu, Hawaii. *Laboratory Investigations* 34, 592–600.

Steptoe, A. 1981. *Psychological factors in cardiovascular disease*. London: Academic Press.

Sterling, P. & Eyer, J. 1981. Biological basis of stress-related mortality. *Social Science and Medicine* 15, 3–42.

Sterling, T.D. 1973. The statistician vis-à-vis issues of public health. *The American Statistician* 27, 212–217.

Strong, L.C. 1977. Genetic etiology of cancer. *Cancer Monograph* 40(1), 438–444.

Suppe, F. (ed.). 1974. *The structure of scientific theories*. Urbana, Ill.: University of Illinois Press.

Syme, S.L., Marmot, M.G., Kagan, A., Kato, H. & Rhoads, G. 1975. Epidemiological studies of coronary heart disease and stroke in Japanese men living in Japan, Hawaii, and California: Introduction. *American Journal of Epidemiology* 102, 477–480.

Tache, D., Selye, M. & Day, S.B. 1979. *Cancer, stress and death*. New York: Plenum.

Taylor, T., Dluhy, R.G. & Williams, G.H. 1983. Beta endorphin and cortisol in normal human subjects. *Endocrinology* 112, 41A.

Thomas, C.B. 1968. On cigarette smoking, coronary heart disease, and the genetic hypothesis. *Johns Hopkins Medical Journal* 122, 69–76.

Thomas, C.B. 1976. Procession of preventive disease and death. *Annals of Internal Medicine* 85, 653–658.

Thomas, C.B. & Cohen, B.H. 1955. The familial occurrence of hypertension and coronary artery disease, with observations concerning obesity and diabetes. *Annals of Internal Medicine* 42, 90–96.

Thomas, C.B. & Duszynski, K.R. 1974. Closeness to parents and the family constellation in a prospective study of five disease states. *The Johns Hopkins Medical Journal* 134, 251–270.

Thomas, C.B. & Greenstreet, R.L. 1973. Psychobiological characteristics in youth as predictors of five disease states. *The Johns Hopkins Medical Journal* 132, 16–43.

Thurlbeck, W.M., Anderson, A.E., Jarvis, M., Mitchell, R.S., Pratt, P., Restrepo, G., Ryan, S.F. & Vincent, T. 1968. A cooperative study of certain measurements of emphysema. *Thorax* 23, 217–228.

Tiggeman, M., Winfefield, A.H. & Brebner, J. 1982. The role of extraversion in the development of learned helplessness. *Personality and Individual Differences* 3, 27–34.

Todd, G.F. & Mason, J.I. 1959. Concordance of smoking habits in monozygotic and dizygotic twins. *Heredity* 13, 417–444.

Tokuhata, G.K. 1964. Familial factors in human lung cancer and smoking. *American Journal of Public Health* 54, 24–32.

Tokuhata, G.K. & Lilienfeld, A.M. 1963a. Familial aggregation of lung cancer among hospital patients. *Washington Public Health Reports* 78, 277–283.

Tokuhata, G.K. & Lilienfeld, A.M. 1963b. Familial aggregation of lung cancer in humans. *Journal of the National Cancer Institute* 30, 289–312.

U.S. Surgeon-General. 1964. *Smoking and Health*. Washington: U.S. Department of Health, Education and Welfare.

U.S. Surgeon-General. 1971. *Health consequences of smoking*. Washington: U.S. Department of Health, Education and Welfare.

U.S. Surgeon-General. 1972. *Health consequences of smoking*. Washington: U.S. Department of Health, Education and Welfare.

U.S. Surgeon-General. 1973. *Health consequences of smoking*. Washington: U.S. Department of Health, Education and Welfare.

U.S. Surgeon-General. 1979. *Health consequences of smoking*. Washington: U.S. Department of Health, Education and Welfare.

U.S. Surgeon-General. 1982. *The health consequences of smoking—Cancer*. Rockville, Md.: U.S. Department of Health and Human Services.

Van Dijl 1979. Myocardial infarction patients and variability. *Journal of Psychosomatic Research* 23, 3–6.

Vlietstra, R.E., Kroumal, R.A., Frye, R.L., Seth, A.K., Tristani, F.E. & Ill, T.K. 1982. Factors affecting the extent and severity of coronary artery disease in patients enrolled in the coronary artery surgery study. *Arteriosclerosis* 2, 208–215.

Volavka, J., Bauman, J., Pevnick, J., Reker, D., James, B. & Cho, D. 1980. Short-term hormonal effects of naloxone in man. *Psychoendocrinology* 5, 225–234.

Waldron, H.A. & Vickerstaff, L. 1977. *Intimations of quality*. Oxford: Nuffield Provincial Hospitals Trust.

Walter, T.A. & Riccio, D.C. 1983. Overshadowing effects in the stimulus control of morphine analgesia tolerance. *Behavioural Neuroscience* 97, 658–662.

Watson, C.G. & Schuld, D. 1977. Psychosomatic factors in the etiology of neoplasms. *Journal of Counselling and Clinical Psychology* 45, 455–461.

Wayner, E.A., Flannery, G.R., Singer, G. 1978. Effects of taste aversion conditioning on the primary antibody response to sheep red blood cells and Brucella abortus in the albino rat. *Physiology and Behaviour* 21, 995–1006.

Wells, H.G. 1923. Relation of clinical to necropsy diagnosis in cancer and value of existing cancer statistics. *Journal of the American Medical Association* 80, 737–740.

Werko, L. 1976. Risk factors and coronary heart disease—fact or fancy? *American Heart Journal* 91, 87–98.

Westlund, K. 1970. Distribution and mortality time trend of multiple sclerosis and some other diseases in Norway. *Acta Neurologica Scandanavia* 46, 455–483.

Williams, R.B. 1983. Neuroendocrine response patterns and stress: Biobehavioural mechanisms of disease. In R.B. Williams (ed.), *Perspectives on behavioural medicine: Neuroendocrine control and behaviour*. New York: Academic Press.

Williams, R.B., Barefoot, J.C. & Shekelle, R.B. 1984. The health consequences of hostility. In M.A. Chesney, S.E. Goldstan & R.H. Roseman (eds.), *Anger, hostility and behavioural medicine*. New York: Hemisphere/McGraw-Hill.

Willis, R.A. 1967. *Pathology of tumours*, (4th ed.). London: Butterworth.

Wilson, E.B. & Burke, M.H. 1957. Some statistical observations as a cooperative study of human pulmonary pathology. *Proceedings of the National Academy of Sciences* 43, 1073–1078.

Wimer, R.E., Norman, R. & Eleftheriow, B.E. 1974. Serotonin levels in hippocampus: Striking variations associated with mouse strain and treatment. *Brain Research* 63, 397, 401.

Winkelstein, W., Kagan, A., Kato, H. & Sacks, S.T. 1975. Blood pressure distributions. *American Journal of Epidemiology* 102, 502–513.

Working Party of the Royal College of Physicians of London and the British Cardiac Society. 1976. The care of the patient with coronary heart disease. *Journal of the Royal College of Physicians* 10, 213–275.

World Health Organization European Collaborative Group. 1982. Multifactorial trial in the prevention of coronary heart disease. Part 2: Risk factor change at two and four years. *European Heart Journal* 3, 184–190.

Worth, R.M., Kato, H., Rhoads, G.G., Kagan, A. & Syme, S.L. 1975. Mortality. *American Journal of Epidemiology* 102, 481–490.

Wynder, E.L. & Graham, E.A. 1950. Tobacco smoking as a possible etiologic factor in bronchiogenic carcinoma: A study of six hundred and eighty-four proved cases. *Journal of the American Medical Association* 143, 329–336.

Yerevanian, B.I., Woolf, P.D. & Iker, H.D. 1983. Plasma ACTH levels in depression before and after recovery: Relationship to dexamethasone suppression test. *Psychiatry Research* 10, 175–181.

Yerushalmy, J. 1962. Statistical consideration and evaluation of epidemiological incidence. In G. James & T. Rosenthal (eds.), *Tobacco and health*. Springfield: C.C. Thomas.

Yerushalmy, J. 1966. On inferring causality from observed associations. In F.J. Ingelpinger, A.S. Relman & M. Finland (eds.), *Controversy in internal medicine*. London: W.B. Saunder.

Yesner, R. 1973. Observer variability and reliability in lung cancer diagnosis. *Cancer Chemotherapy Reports* 4, 55–57.

Yesner, R., Geostl, B. & Anerbach, O. 1965. Application of the World Health Organisation classification of lung carcinoma to biopsy material. *The Annals of Thoracic Surgery* 1, 33–49.

Yesner, R., Selfman, N.A. & Feinstein, A.R. 1973. A reappraisal of histopathology in lung cancer and correlation of all types with antecedent cigarette smoking. *American Review of Respiratory Disease* 107, 790–797.

Glossary

ACTH. Adrenocorticotrophic hormone; secreted by pituitary gland and stimulating adrenal cortex.

Assortative mating. Like marrying like.

Autopsy. Necropsy, postmortem inspection.

Cattell 16PF scale. Personality inventory giving 16 scores for different personality traits.

Constitutional factors. Causal influences present at birth, but not necessarily genetic.

Detection bias. Bias introduced into medical diagnosis through preconceived ideas.

Dominance (of genes). Characters finding expression over recessive genes.

Dose-response relationship. Increase in response to drug with increase in dosage.

DZ twins. Dizygotic twins; fraternal twins.

Epidemiology. Study of prevalence of diseases in different communities.

Genetic factors. Causal influences indicative of hereditary effects.

Immunology. Protection against infectious diseases.

Incubation. Incrementation of conditioned fear responses after presentation of conditioned stimulus without reinforcement.

Metastasis. Spreading of neoplasms from one site to another.

MMPI. Minnesota Multiphasic Personality Inventory. Widely used but rather primitive questionnaire.

Mortality ratio. Age-standardized mortality rate of smokers, as compared with nonsmokers.

MZ twins. Monozygotic twins; identical twins.

Pavlovian conditioning. Formation of association between S (stimulus) and R (responses) through contiguity.

Peptide. Chemical compound with two or more amino acids linked in linear sequence with elimination of water molecules.

Recessive (of genes). Characters only finding expression when paired with another recessive gene.

Stress. Life events which cause strain (depression, unhappiness, anxiety, etc.).

Variance. Index of distribution of a trait; square of standard deviation.

3

Psychological Determinants of Smoking Behavior

Charles D. Spielberger

S moking is certainly a widespread and highly-persistent habit. On the basis of large-scale national surveys, it is currently estimated that more than 50 million Americans smoke, constituting approximately one-third of the adult population (Evans et al., 1979; National Clearing House, 1966). Although the overall percentage of smokers in the United States has declined in recent years, there has been a notable increase in smoking among females in their teens and early twenties (National Clearing House, 1966; Spielberger et al., 1983). A significant trend has also been observed for children to engage in "experimental smoking" at an earlier age (Evans, 1976).

How can we account for the prevalence and persistence of the smoking habit? In the preceding chapter, Eysenck reviews and evaluates laboratory and epidemiological investigations of relationships between genetic-constitutional factors, individual differences in personality, and smoking behavior. He also examines evidence bearing on the contribution of genetic-personality factors to the etiology of degenerative medical disorders such as cancer and heart disease. In challenging the simplistic environmental theory that smoking causes disease, Eysenck contends that genetics and personality contribute to the persistence of the smoking habit, and that genetically-determined individual differences in personality interact with environmental stress to account for the known facts with regard to observed associations of smoking and illness.

In the chapter that follows, Feinhandler examines medical, psychological, and sociocultural explanations of smoking behavior. Citing historical and contemporary evidence of the symbolic, psychosocial and cultural functions of smoking, he concludes that the prevailing medical and psychological models do not provide an adequate explanation of tobacco use because they are too narrow and limited in terms of the variables that are considered.

I am greatly indebted to Dr. Gerard Jacobs, Mr. Timothy Worden, Mr. William Kearns, and Ms. Virginia Berch for their assistance in the analyses of the data reported in this paper and in the preparation of this manuscript.

According to Feinhandler, explanations of smoking as addictive behavior, or as a strongly learned habit, fail to take into account numerous psychosocial and cultural factors that are known to be associated with the initiation, prevalence and persistence of smoking in various societies.

The impressive evidence and compelling arguments marshalled by Feinhandler and Eysenck leave little doubt that sociocultural and genetic-personality factors are significant determinants of smoking behavior. But the interpretations of smoking set forth by Eysenck and Feinhandler do not provide a comprehensive answer to the question, Why do people smoke? because they do not adequately specify the nature of the internal emotional states and motivational processes that maintain the smoking habit. The present chapter reviews research findings that are more directly relevant to the influence of these emotional-motivational processes and other psychological factors on smoking behavior. Three specific types of evidence are considered: (1) the effects of family smoking habits on smoking behavior; (2) the relationship between personality traits and smoking; and (3) the nature of the emotional and motivational states and processes that maintain the smoking habit. Prior to examining this evidence, the influential models of smoking behavior that have been proposed by Hans J. Eysenck (1965, 1973, 1980) and Silvan S. Tomkins (1966, 1968) are briefly considered.

Psychological Models of Smoking Behavior

Researchers generally agree that it is essential to distinguish between the factors that influence people to take up smoking and those that contribute to the persistence of smoking behavior once the habit has been established (Matarazzo and Saslow, 1960; Evans et al., 1979). In investigations of the initiation of smoking, current smokers and persons who previously smoked and have given up the habit (ex-smokers) are generally grouped together, and these groups are compared with individuals who have never smoked. In identifying factors that contribute to the maintenance of smoking behavior, current smokers and ex-smokers must be considered as separate groups. Among smokers, it is also important to distinguish between individuals who currently smoke from time-to-time, but not every day (occasional smokers), and persons who smoke one or more cigarettes every day.

Social influence variables, such as peer-group pressures and parental smoking habits, have been repeatedly identified with the initiation of smoking (Evans et al., 1979; Leventhal and Cleary, 1980; Matarazzo and Matarazzo, 1965; National Institute of Education, 1979). Research findings with regard to the factors that maintain the smoking habit are typically less consistent and more difficult to interpret. For example, Russell and his colleagues (1971a, 1971b; Russell et al., 1974) consider smoking to be a "dependence disorder," in which the maintenance of the smoking habit " . . . is due largely to dependence on the pharmacological effects of nicotine" (1971a, p. 330). In contrast, the models of smoking behavior proposed by Eysenck and Tomkins that are described below emphasize the role of genetic, personality, and motivational factors in the maintenance of the smoking habit. Over the past two decades, the Eysenck and Tomkins models have stimulated and guided much of the research on the psychological determinants of smoking.

Eysenck's Diathesis-Stress Model

Consistent with the research literature, Eysenck's model attributes the initiation of smoking primarily to environmental factors, for example, peer group pressures and adult modeling behavior. To explain the prevalence and persistence of smoking behavior, Eysenck (1965, 1973, 1980) proposes a Diathesis-Stress model, which assumes that genetic, personality, motivational-emotional, physiological, and situational factors all contribute to maintaining the smoking habit. According to this model, individual differences in personality associated with genetic predispositions (diathesis) interact with environmental factors to produce the motivational and reinforcement conditions that are conducive to smoking. Boredom and emotional stress are postulated as the two major internal motivational states that stimulate smoking. The model further assumes that these internal states are directly modified by the ingestion of nicotine, which acts on the nervous system to reinforce smoking behavior.

Extraversion, neuroticism, and psychoticism, the three principal dimensions in Eysenck's (1952, 1967, 1981) theory of personality, are presumed to have different effects on smoking behavior. (For conceptual definitions of these personality dimensions, see Eysenck, chapter 2, figures 2–5, 2–6, and 2–7, this volume.) Persons high in extraversion or neuroticism would be expected to smoke more than introverts and emotionally stable persons because of the neurophysiological processes associated with these personality traits.

Extraverts are known to show less cortical arousal than introverts and to be more susceptible to boredom. Therefore, according to Eysenck's Diathesis-Stress model, extraverts would be expected to smoke more in situations lacking in stimulation in order to increase cortical arousal to a more optimal level. Eysenck also theorizes that social factors may reinforce the smoking behavior of extraverts because of their motivation to emulate the practices of their peers. Anxious, neurotic persons have labile autonomic nervous systems and high levels of cortical arousal, and are thus genetically disposed to respond with more intense emotional reactions to environmental stress than emotionally stable persons. Therefore, persons high in neuroticism would be expected to smoke more in stressful situations in which they feel nervous or overstimulated in order to reduce tension and associated cortical arousal.

Given the fact that men tend to be more extraverted and women more introverted, it follows from Eysenck's model that men will smoke more often from boredom than women, and this has been found to be the case. Since women tend to be higher in neuroticism than men, Eysenck's model predicts that women would be more likely to smoke under conditions in which they feel nervous or emotionally upset, and this too has been confirmed. It also follows that extraverted men are more likely to smoke when they are bored than introverted men, and that the smoking behavior of neurotic women will increase in stressful circumstances that evoke intense emotional reactions.

In a recent extension of his model, Eysenck postulates a positive relationship between psychoticism and smoking behavior. Individuals with high psychoticism scores are "tough-minded" and more likely to engage in aggressive, impulsive, and antisocial-rebellious behavior than persons with low scores on this dimension. For persons high in psychoticism, smoking brings social reinforcement from peers for this nonconforming, rebellious behavior. Although there are important gender differences in psychoticism, Eysenck's theory predicts that both males and females who are high on this dimension— delinquents and criminals, for example—are more likely to smoke than individuals low in psychoticism, and this prediction has been confirmed.

According to Eysenck's model, nicotine is the active agent that links individual differences in personality with smoking behavior, but the dose-response relationship between nicotine consumption and cortical arousal is complex. It has been demonstrated in animal studies that nicotine can both increase and reduce the level of cortical arousal (Armitage et al., 1969). The fact that nicotine has both stimulating and sedative pharmacological effects is basic to Eysenck's theory of smoking. Small amounts of nicotine provide stimulation that increases cortical arousal and relieves boredom, whereas larger quantities relieve tension and anxiety by reducing autonomic (sympathetic) nervous system activity. Thus, males and extraverts exposed to boredom-producing situations are more likely to smoke because nicotine provides pleasurable stimulation, whereas females and persons high in neuroticism smoke because of the tension-reducing effects of nicotine.

Predictions from Eysenck's Diathesis-Stress model regarding the interactive effects of personality, situational stress, and nicotine on smoking behavior are supported by substantial evidence from laboratory studies. The relationships posited by Eysenck's model with regard to the interactive influence of personality, social and situational factors on smoking behavior are more speculative at the present time, but recent empirical findings have generally been consistent with predictions derived from his model.

Tomkin's Affect Control Model

Tomkins's (1966, 1968; Ikard and Tomkins, 1973) Affect Control model of smoking behavior is derived from his comprehensive theory of emotion. Affects are defined as innate psychobiological mechanisms that motivate human behavior when they are activated. Eight primary affects are postulated by Tomkins; three are positive in tone (excitement, enjoyment, surprise) and five are negative (distress, anger, fear, shame, and contempt). The potential to experience these primary affects is assumed to be an inherent part of human nature. The stimuli that activate an affect can be either innate or learned.

According to Tomkins's model, human beings are intrinsically motivated to maximize positive affective experience and to minimize negative affects. Any behavior capable of readily evoking positive affect or reducing negative affect will be consistently reinforced, and hence more likely to be repeated. Since smoking behavior has both stimulating and tension reducing effects, it follows from Tomkins's theory that smoking is likely to develop into a strong, persistent, and pervasive habit because of its critical role in the management of affect.

Within the context of his Affect Control model, Tomkins distinguishes four general types of smoking behavior: (1) Positive affect smoking; (2) Negative affect smoking; (3) Addictive smoking; and (4) Habitual smoking. Positive affect smokers generally smoke when they feel good, and may never smoke while experiencing negative affect. Two subtypes of positive affect smoking are identified: (a) Smoking that stimulates the positive affect of excitement by increasing arousal to a more optimal level; and (b) smoking for relaxation that enhances the positive affect of enjoyment. The pleasurable stimulation (excitement) of smoking, which gives the smoker a "lift," occurs most often in situations characterized by low levels of arousal associated with boredom. Smoking to enhance relaxation and enjoyment typically occurs under pleasant circumstances, such as following a meal or during a coffee break.

In negative affect or sedative smoking, according to Tomkins's theory, an individual smokes to reduce unpleasant feelings of distress, anger, fear, shame, contempt, or any combination of these primary affects. Since negative affect smokers smoke primarily to reduce unpleasant feelings, they may not smoke at all under pleasant circumstances. In contrast to positive and negative affect smokers, the addictive type smoker smokes both to stimulate positive affect and to reduce negative affect. Moreover, according to Tomkins's theory, addictive smokers are keenly aware whenever they are *not* smoking, and this awareness of not-smoking invariably evokes negative affect. For the habitual smoker, according to Tomkins's theory, smoking has become an automatic habit. Although habitual smokers may have originally smoked to enhance positive affect, reduce negative affect, or both, affect is no longer associated with smoking. Consequently, the habitual smoker does not miss a cigarette if one is not available, and thus differs greatly from the addictive smoker who is presumed to suffer when deprived of cigarettes.

Tomkins and his colleagues (Ikard et al., 1969; Ikard and Tomkins, 1973) developed a smoking behavior questionnaire to differentiate the four types of smokers specified in Tomkins's model. This questionnaire, generally referred to in the literature as the Horn-Waingrow Smoker Survey, was administered to a national probability sample of more than 2,000 adult smokers (Ikard et al., 1969). The respondents were instructed to indicate whether each of 23 specific smoking behaviors (for example, "When I feel uncomfortable or upset about something, I light up a cigarette) was "always," "frequently," "occasionally," "seldom," or "never" typical of their own experience and/or behavior. Based on a factor analysis of the questionnaire responses, six smoking motivation factors were identified and given the following names: Negative affect reduction, Addictive, Habitual, Pleasurable relaxation, Stimulation, and Sensorimotor manipulation.

Ikard et al. also administered the Horn-Waingrow Smoker Survey to college students and participants in a smoking withdrawal program. Factor analyses of the responses of these samples resulted in essentially the same six smoking motivation factors that were identified in the national probability sample. Moreover, the individual questionnaire items had similar loadings in these samples as in the original sample.

The first three smoking motivation factors identified by Ikard et al. correspond quite well with three of the four smoking types specified in Tomkins's model. Representative items with high loadings on these factors are: (1) Negative affect reduction—"When I feel 'blue' or want to take my mind off cares and worries, I smoke cigarettes"; (2) Addictive—"I get a real gnawing hunger for a cigarette when I haven't smoked for awhile"; and (3) Habitual—"I smoke cigarettes automatically without even being aware of it." The three remaining factors appear to reflect different aspects of what Tomkins collectively referred to as positive affect smoking. Representative items with high loadings on these positive affect factors are: (4) Pleasurable relaxation—"Smoking cigarettes is pleasant and relaxing"; (5) Stimulation—"I smoke cigarettes to stimulate me, to perk myself up"; and (6) Sensorimotor manipulation—"Part of the enjoyment of smoking a cigarette comes from the steps I take to light up."

Separate subscales were derived by Ikard et al. (1969) for each of the six smoking motivation factors; each subscale consisted of two to four items with the highest loadings on a particular factor. The correlation of .58 between the Negative affect reduction and Addictive subscales, and correlations of .38 and .42, respectively, between these subscales and the Habitual subscale, indicate that these three factors were not independent. Somewhat smaller but significant correlations were also found between the Addictive subscale and the three positive affect subscales. Males scored significantly higher than females on the Habitual and Addictive subscales, whereas females had higher scores on the Negative affect reduction subscale. The average number of cigarettes smoked per day was positively and significantly correlated with scores on the Habitual, Addictive and Negative affect reduction subscales.

Although the findings reported by Ikard et al. provide support for Tomkins's Affect Control model, the pattern of correlations among the six subscales would seem to indicate that most smokers smoke both to stimulate positive affect and to reduce negative affect. Moreover, the magnitude of these correlations suggest that so-called habitual and addictive smoking are more strongly associated with reducing negative affect than with enhancing positive affect. Contrary to Tomkins's theory, which asserts that there is no affect associated with habitual smoking, the Habitual smoking subscale correlated positively and significantly with the Negative affect reduction subscale, and was negatively correlated with two of the three positive affect subscales (Stimulation, Sensorimotor Manipulation). Thus, it would seem that automatic habitual smoking contributes to the management of both positive and negative affect.

Additional support for Tomkins's Affect Control model has been reported by McKennell (1970), Coan (1973), Russell et al. (1974), Costa et al. (1980), and Stanaway and Watson (1980). Moreover, Costa et al. have shown that the six smoking motivation factors identified by Ikard et al. were relatively stable over a period of three years. A "Psychosocial Smoking" factor that was not included in Tomkins's model has been consistently reported by McKennell (1970), Russell et al. (1974), and Stanaway and Watson (1980). This factor has been defined as smoking to create a socially desirable image of importance that fosters feelings of social confidence. Costa and McCrae (1981) have also reported a social confidence factor. These psychosocial and social confidence factors appear to reflect some of the sociocultural and symbolic reasons for smoking that are described by Feinhandler in the following chapter.

The research literature provides substantial support for the Tomkins and Eysenck models, but the results of recent studies are not completely consistent with either theory. While the contribution of smoking to the management of affect appears to be well established, research findings indicate that the four types of smokers posited by Tomkins are not independent, nor do Tomkins's smoking categories encompass the psychosocial variables observed by Feinhandler to be important in maintaining the smoking habit. Some of the personality, motivational, and emotional factors recognized by Eysenck and Tomkins as important determinants of smoking behavior are considered in greater detail in later sections of this chapter. Relationships between family smoking habits and the initiation and maintenance of smoking behavior, considered important by Eysenck but largely neglected by Tomkins, are reviewed next, along with recent research findings that endeavor to clarify these relationships.

Family Smoking Habits as Determinants of Smoking Behavior

Positive relationships between the smoking habits of parents and the smoking behavior of their children have been reported in a number of studies (for example,

Banks et al., 1978; Borland and Rudolph, 1975; Clausen, 1968; Horn et al., 1959; Merki et al., 1970; Palmer, 1970; Salber and MacMahon, 1961; Spielberger et al., 1983), but the degree to which these relationships reflect environmental and/or constitutional-genetic influences is unclear (Eysenck, 1980). Leventhal and Cleary (1980) contend that the modeling behaviors of both peers and parents are important sources of environmental influence in cigarette smoking. They further suggest that older siblings may be even more important than other peers in stimulating adolescents to initiate smoking.

Consistent with this view, Banks et al. (1978) observed that high school students whose siblings smoked were more likely to be smokers themselves, but Laoye et al. (1972), in a study of the maintenance of smoking behavior, found that secondary school students who were regular smokers were more likely to have parents who smoked than students who previously smoked but subsequently stopped. Thus, environmental influences seem to be paramount in the initiation of smoking, whereas both environmental factors and genetic dispositions may determine the persistence of the smoking habit.

The differential impact of the smoking habits of fathers and mothers on the smoking behavior of their sons and daughters has been investigated by Wohlford (1970; Wohlford and Giammona, 1969). In general, sons are more likely to smoke if their fathers smoke, and daughters are more likely to smoke if their mothers smoke (Banks et al., 1978; Horn et al., 1959; Salber and MacMahon, 1961; Wohlford, 1970). Since no relationships have been found between the smoking habits of fathers and daughters, nor between mothers and sons, same-sex parental modeling would appear to have a stronger impact on children's smoking behavior than genetic factors.

Spielberger et al. (1983) investigated the relationship between the smoking habits of parents and older siblings and the initiation and maintenance of smoking behavior in a sample of 955 college students. On the basis of previous research findings, positive relationships were expected between family smoking habits and the initiation of smoking, and between the smoking habits of fathers and sons, and mothers and daughters. With regard to the maintenance of smoking behavior, smokers were expected to be more likely to have parents and older siblings who smoked.

A self-report *Smoking Behavior Questionnaire* (SBQ) designed to elicit specific information about the smoking habits of students and their families was constructed for this study. Questionnaires used in previous investigations to evaluate family smoking habits (Clausen, 1968; Ikard et al., 1969; Leventhal and Avis, 1976) were carefully reviewed, and relevant items from these instruments were adapted for this study. The construction of the SBQ is described in detail by Spielberger et al. (1983). In responding to the SBQ, the students were instructed to indicate whether they were current smokers, occasional smokers, ex-smokers, or nonsmokers, and to report similar information for their mothers, fathers, and older siblings. These four categories were defined as follows:

1. Current smoker: Smokes one or more cigarettes every day.

2. Occasional smoker: Smokes cigarettes from time to time, but *not* every day.

3. Ex-smoker: Formerly either a regular or occasional smoker, but currently does not smoke.

4. Nonsmoker: Never smoked or only experimented briefly with cigarettes, but never became a regular or occasional smoker.

In evaluating relationships between family smoking habits and the initiation of smoking, students who reported that they were current, occasional, or ex-smokers were classified as "smokers," and the responses of these students were compared with those of students who reported that they had never smoked. In examining the relations between family smoking habits and the maintenance of smoking behavior, current, occasional, and ex-smokers were treated as separate groups and compared with each other.

The percentage of females and males classified as "smokers" was 49% and 37%, respectively. The finding that a higher percentage of the females were smokers was consistent with recent trends reported by Evans et al. (1979) of a decrease in smoking among male teenagers and adults, and a notable increase in smoking among females in their teens and twenties. Among the female smokers, 40% reported they were current smokers, 26% were classified as occasional smokers, and 34% were ex-smokers. The percentages of male smokers classified as current, occasional, or ex-smokers were 31%, 29%, and 40%, respectively.

Positive relationships were found between the smoking behavior of students and the smoking habits of their parents for both sexes. If one or both parents smoked, their sons and daughters were more likely to be smokers than if neither parent smoked. While these findings were generally consistent with results reported by other investigators, no association was found between the smoking habits of fathers and sons, nor between those of mothers and daughters, as have been reported in previous studies. Thus, there was no evidence of same-sex parental modeling in the present study.

Students with older brothers and/or sisters who smoked were more likely to be smokers than those with older siblings who did not smoke. Moreover, older sisters appeared to have a greater impact on their younger sisters than on the smoking behavior of their younger brothers, whereas older brothers seemed to have a similar influence on the smoking of younger siblings of both sexes. When the combined effects of the smoking habits of parents and older siblings were evaluated, older siblings appeared to have a much stronger influence than parents on the smoking behavior of their younger siblings. Indeed, the smoking habits of parents seemed to have little or no added influence on the smoking behavior of those students whose older siblings were smokers.

Students with no older siblings, or with nonsmoking older siblings, were themselves less likely to be smokers, but these students were more likely to take up smoking if one or both parents smoked than if neither parent smoked. Since no differences were found in the smoking habits of the parents or older siblings of current, occasional, or ex-smokers, the findings in this study suggested that family smoking habits, especially those of older siblings, influence students to take up smoking, but have little impact on the maintenance of smoking behavior.

The National Institute of Education (1979) of the U.S. Department of Health, Education and Welfare, investigated patterns of teenage smoking in a sample of 2,639 high school students who were interviewed by telephone to obtain information about their smoking behavior and the smoking habits of their families and friends. The findings for these high school students were quite similar to the results described above for college students: (a) The percentage of girls who smoked was larger than the percentage of boys (a decade earlier the percentage of boys who smoked was greater); (b) If one or both parents smoked, their children were more likely to smoke, although, there was little evidence of same-sex modeling; (c) If older siblings smoked, younger siblings were more likely to be smokers; and (d) The smoking habits of older siblings had a stronger influence on their younger siblings than did the smoking habits of parents.

The consistent finding for both high school and college students that smoking is more strongly associated with the smoking habits of older siblings than with parental smoking habits would seem to indicate that peer-group environmental influences are more important than constitutional-genetic factors in the *initiation* of smoking, as Eysenck's model would predict. Although college students in the present study were more likely to smoke if their parents and older siblings smoked, there was no direct evidence that family smoking habits influenced the *persistence* of smoking behavior once the students had begun to smoke, as would be predicted from Eysenck's theory. However, in the following section, findings that smokers and non-smokers differed in personality are consistent with Eysenck's Diathesis-Stress model, which assumes that constitutional-genetic factors contribute to the maintenance of smoking behavior.

Personality and Smoking Behavior

Some years ago, Matarazzo and Saslow (1960) published a comprehensive review of the research literature on the psychosocial and personality characteristics of smokers and nonsmokers. Noting that smokers have been found to differ significantly from nonsmokers in numerous studies, they observed that these differences were generally small, and that the overlap between smoker and nonsmoker groups was extensive, especially on measures of personality characteristics. In commenting on the cumulative research findings, Matarazzo and Saslow (1960, pp. 509–510) conclude:

> . . . a clear-cut smoker's personality has not emerged from the results so far published in the literature. This is not surprising when it is remembered that approximately 60 million Americans over the age of 18 smoke. It is hard to believe that they would share in common one personality "type." This is not to imply, however, that the various psychological dimensions along which smokers have been shown, as a group, to differ from non-smokers may not suggest an important single process, or processes, underlying these various demonstrated differences.

Following a decade of active research, the diverse and expanding literature on personality and smoking was subsequently reviewed by Smith (1970), who observed that smoking was associated with extraversion in 12 of 15 studies, with antisocial tendencies in 17 of 19 studies, and with impulsive behavior in 6 of 8 studies. Accordingly, he concluded that smokers were more extraverted and have stronger antisocial tendencies than nonsmokers, and that the evidence is "reasonably convincing" that smokers are also more impulsive. In addition, Smith noted that smoking was associated with neuroticism and anxiety in several studies, but considered these findings either inconsistent or based on too few studies to draw meaningful conclusions.

A similar interpretation of the research on smoking and personality was offered by Matarazzo and Matarazzo (1965), who were more impressed than Smith with the associations between tension, anxiety, and neuroticism, and smoking behavior. In their view, "The results, meager and poorly supported as they are, suggest the. . . . presence of a slightly higher number of 'extravert', and 'neurotic', and 'tense' individuals among the smokers as compared to the nonsmokers" (1965, p. 377).

Several studies published shortly after Smith's (1970) review provide additional evidence that smoking is associated with extraversion (Brackenridge and Bloch, 1972; Jacobs and Spilken, 1971; Jamison, 1979; Rae, 1975), but no relationship between smoking and extraversion was found in at least three studies (Floderus, 1974, cited in Costa and McCrae, 1981; McManus and Weeks, 1982). Eysenck (1980, 1983) has suggested two plausible explanations for the failure to find that smokers were more extraverted than nonsmokers in several recent studies. He points out that the Extraversion Scale of the Eysenck Personality Inventory (EPI) which was used in most of the early studies (Eysenck and Eysenck, 1964) contained items relating to both sociability and impulsiveness. When psychoticism was included in Eysenck's theory as a major dimension of personality (Eysenck and Eysenck, 1968, 1975), the EPI was revised to form the Eysenck Personality Questionnaire (EPQ), and some of the EPI impulsiveness items were incorporated into the EPQ Psychoticism Scale.

Eysenck concludes that these aspects of extraversion may have contributed to the positive relationship with smoking behavior that was found in the earlier studies. More recently, Eysenck (1983) has observed that there has been considerable change over the past twenty years in the social acceptability of smoking. Whereas socially oriented extraverts were previously reinforced for smoking by their peer groups, "Nowadays smoking behavior is socially disapproved and hence socially oriented extraverts might be put off smoking to some extent, thus lowering the expected degree of correlation" (Eysenck, 1983, p. 448).

Most studies published subsequent to Smith's review have reported that smokers score consistently higher than nonsmokers on Eysenck's Psychoticism Scale (Jamison, 1978; McManus and Weeks, 1982; Powell, 1977; Powell et al., 1979), which measures impulsive, antisocial behavior (Eysenck and Eysenck, 1968). A number of recent studies have also reported evidence that smokers are more neurotic, tense, and anxious than nonsmokers, as reflected in higher scores on variants of Eysenck's Neuroticism Scale (Brackenridge and Bloch, 1972; Gupta et al., 1976; McManus and Weeks, 1982; Powell et al., 1979), the Taylor (1953) Manifest Anxiety Scale (Houston and Schneider, 1973; Schneider and Houston, 1970), and measures of anxiety and anger reactions under stress (Thomas, 1978). However, Jamison (1979) found no relationship between neuroticism and smoking behavior in a large sample of 13- to 16-year-old school children.

The research evidence that smokers have higher scores than nonsmokers in extraversion, neuroticism, and psychoticism as measured by the EPI and the EPQ is generally consistent with Eysenck's Diathesis-Stress model. It should be noted, however, that most of the studies in which these relationships were reported were conducted in Great Britain, India, and Australia. Although Eysenck's personality scales are widely used in many different countries, these measures have been employed to investigate relations between personality and smoking in only one study with American subjects (McCrae et al., 1978). In this study, in which a brief eighteen-item form of the EPQ was used that did not assess psychoticism, smokers were found to have higher scores on neuroticism, but not on extraversion.

Personality and Smoking in American College Students

In the study described earlier, the *Eysenck Personality Questionnaire* (EPQ) and trait scales of the *State-Trait Personality Inventory* (STPI) were administered in group testing sessions to 955 American college students (Spielberger and Jacobs, 1982). The EPQ is the most recent form of a series of personality inventories developed by Eysenck and his colleagues over the past thirty years (Eysenck, 1952, 1958, 1959; Eysenck and Eysenck, 1964, 1975). It consists of ninety true-false items that assess extraversion, neuroticism, and psychoticism as personality dimensions. The STPI is a sixty-item self-report rating scale that assesses individual differences in anxiety, curiosity, and anger as emotional states and as personality traits (Spielberger, 1979).

Associations between individual differences in personality and the initiation of smoking in this study were evaluated by combining the data for current, occasional, and ex-smokers into a single group ("smokers"), and comparing the personality characteristics of the smokers with those of nonsmokers. The results indicated that the smokers had significantly higher scores than nonsmokers on the EPQ Extraversion, Neuroticism, and Psychoticism Scales. Although these differences were in the same direction for both sexes, the magnitude of the differences in extraversion and psychoticism were substantially larger for the females than for the males. The females also scored significantly higher on neuroticism and lower on psychoticism than the males, as would be expected on the basis of Eysenck's (1981) theory of personality.

Relationships between the personality dimensions and the persistence of smoking behavior were evaluated by comparing the EPQ and STPI scores of current, occasional, and ex-smokers. Current smokers of both sexes tended to score higher on extraversion and psychoticism than occasional and ex-smokers, but these differences were not statistically significant. A surprising finding was that women who smoked regularly had significantly *lower* EPQ Neuroticism and STPI Trait Anxiety scores than female occasional and ex-smokers. In the context of Eysenck's (1980) hypothesis that women who are high in neuroticism are more likely to take up smoking, this finding suggested that smoking may be effective in reducing the emotional tension and anxiety associated with neuroticism.

An interesting new finding in this study was that ex-smokers had significantly higher trait curiosity scores than current and occasional smokers (see Spielberger and Jacobs, 1982, Table 3, p. 400). This finding provides further evidence that individuals who stop smoking differ in many important respects from persons who continue to smoke on a regular basis. We may speculate that although curiosity may have been an important factor in motivating the ex-smokers to begin smoking, the greater curiosity of these students was not likely to stimulate them to continue to smoke after smoking was no longer a novel experience.

In summary, the results of our study of American college students were generally consistent with previous research in which smokers were found to be higher than nonsmokers in extraversion, neuroticism, and psychoticism, but the differences in extraversion and psychoticism were due primarily to the females. The surprising finding that female current smokers scored lower in neuroticism and trait anxiety than occasional and ex-smokers suggested that smoking may be an effective tension reducer for women who continue to smoke. Finally, the higher curiosity scores of the ex-smokers suggested that persons motivated by curiosity to take up smoking are less likely to continue to smoke.

Prospective Studies of Personality and Smoking

Most studies of personality and smoking are based on retrospective investigations in which personality measures and information about smoking habits are obtained concurrently. Consequently, it is not possible to make unequivocal inferences with regard to possible causal effects of the personality variables on smoking behavior. Cherry and Kiernan (1976, 1978) have reported findings from a longitudinal investigation of personality and smoking which appear to demonstrate that persons higher in extraversion and/or neuroticism are more likely to become smokers. The subjects in the Cherry-Kiernan study were 2,573 participants in a national survey of health and development in England who completed the short form of the Maudsley Personality Inventory (Eysenck, 1958) at age 16. At age 20, they completed a retrospective questionnaire that inquired about whether or not they smoked, when they had started to smoke, and the quantity of cigarettes they presently smoked. Similar information on the smoking habits was obtained at age 25. Cigar and pipe smokers were excluded from the study.

The male and female survey participants who were smoking regularly at age 16 were more extraverted and neurotic than nonsmokers and those who initiated the habit later. Moreover, participants of both sexes who did not smoke at age 16, but who had become regular smokers by age 25, were also higher in extraversion and neuroticism than nonsmokers. Extraversion and neuroticism appeared to have an additive effect on smoking; a larger proportion of the survey participants who were high on both personality dimensions were smokers, as compared to those high on only one dimension. In addition to providing further evidence that smokers are higher in extraversion and neuroticism than nonsmokers, these findings indicate that extraversion and neuroticism predated the smoking habit for those survey participants who began smoking after age 16.

Seltzer and Oechsli (1985) report prospective findings based on a comprehensive investigation of child development, from birth to late adolescence, of a large cohort of California boys and girls (Yarushalmy, 1969). In this unique longitudinal study, data on the psychosocial characteristics of the participants were obtained prior to the time that some of them began cigarette smoking as teenagers. The study participants were interviewed when they were 15 to 17 years old to determine if they smoked regularly at that time (as much as one cigarette a day) or were nonsmokers. Occasional smokers (less than one cigarette per day) represented a very small segment of the population and were excluded from the study.

The teenagers had been examined when they were 9 to 11 years old, and mothers' reports of their behavior at age 10 were also available. The mothers had responded to a true-false behavioral checklist consisting of 100 statements that described the psychosocial behavior and personality traits of their children (for example, "Hates to go to bed"; "Stubborn"; "Has lots of fears and worries"). The checklist items were subsequently grouped by experts into six distinctive subsets in order to derive measures of extraversion, neuroticism, psychoticism, anger, anxiety, and Type-A personality.

The scores of the teenage smokers on each of the six personality measures were compared by Seltzer and Oechsli (1985) to those of nonsmokers. The extraversion and Type-A personality scores of smokers of both sexes were significantly higher than those of nonsmokers; the anger and psychoticism scores of the female smokers were also significantly higher than those of female nonsmokers. In addition, teenage smokers of both sexes had significantly lower scores than nonsmokers on two tests of cognitive ability that were given to them when they were 9 to 11 years old. Thus, the findings in this study provide impressive evidence that the teenage smokers differed from nonsmokers on important personality and cognitive characteristics long before some of them developed the cigarette-smoking habit.

Motivational and Emotional Determinants of Smoking Behavior

The results of several recent studies that investigated motivational-emotional, cognitive, and situational determinants of smoking behavior are reported below. These studies focus on the internal states and processes that stimulate people to start smoking and that contribute to the persistence of the smoking habit. The reasons given by college students for beginning and continuing to smoke, reported in the next section, help to clarify the influence of specific cognitive and motivational-emotional factors on the initiation and maintenance of smoking behavior. Motivational-emotional, situational and personality factors that appear to influence the persistence and strength of the smoking habit are described in the final section.

Reasons for Smoking

In a pilot study conducted prior to the investigation of the smoking habits of American college students described above (Spielberger et al., 1983), a smoking behavior questionnaire that inquired about reasons for smoking was administered to 149 undergraduate students (52 males, 97 females) enrolled in introductory psychology courses. These students were also invited to participate in small group discussions of the reasons why college students start and continue to smoke; each student was offered $2.00 for participating in the discussion groups. The investigators met with a total of 81 students, in small groups of 7 to 10 students, for in-depth discussions of their reasons for smoking or not smoking. There were separate groups for current smokers ($N = 27$), ex-smokers ($N = 17$), and nonsmokers ($N = 37$), which permitted more focused discussions of the motivational factors that influenced the smoking behavior of these students. The group discussions were audio tape-recorded.

On the basis of an analysis of the students' responses to the smoking behavior questionnaire and a review of the audio tapes, the ten reasons that were most often reported spontaneously by the students as influencing them to begin smoking, and the ten reasons given most frequently as influencing them to continue to smoke were identified. One reason reported by some students as influencing them to start smoking—"Because television and newspaper advertisements made cigarette smoking seem appealing to me"— was rarely mentioned as influencing them to continue smoking. However, in order to clarify current controversy about the role of media advertising as a determinant of smoking behavior, an item designed to assess this topic ("Because of media advertisement") was included among the subset of reasons for continuing to smoke. The list of reasons for beginning and continuing to smoke appears below.

Smoking Behavior Questionnaire: Reasons for Smoking

I. Factors that influenced you to start smoking:

1. I wanted to see if I would enjoy it.
2. I thought there must be something satisfying about it because so many people smoke.
3. I wanted to try something new.
4. Because most of my friends smoke.
5. Because my parents smoked and seemed to enjoy it.
6. Because it made me feel more relaxed around my friends.
7. I did not want to refuse my friends when they offered me a cigarette.
8. My parents disapproved and I wanted to show my independence.
9. Most of my older brothers and sisters seemed to enjoy smoking.
10. Because television and newspaper advertisements made cigarette smoking seem appealing to me.

II. Factors that influenced you to continue to smoke:

1. Because I enjoy it.
2. I get bored when I do not smoke.

3. Because most of my friends smoke.
4. Makes me feel more comfortable around my friends.
5. Gives me something to do when I'm alone.
6. Helps me forget my worries.
7. It facilitates thinking and gives me inspiration.
8. Relaxes me when I'm upset or nervous.
9. Because of media advertisement.
10. Because it is stimulating.

Current, occasional and ex-smokers in the sample of 955 American college students were asked to report the extent to which each of the 10 reasons listed in part I had influenced them to begin to smoke, and to report how much each of the second set of 10 reasons listed in part II had influenced them to continue smoking. The amount of influence of each reason was rated on the following 4-point scale: "Not at all," "Some," "Moderate influence," "Strong influence"; these ratings were given weighted scores of "1," "2," "3," and "4," respectively.

The means, standard deviations, and the rank-order of the ratings given by females and males of the relative influence of the 10 reasons for *starting* to smoke are reported in table 3–1, in which it can be noted that "I wanted to see if I would enjoy it" was rated as most influential by both sexes. The same five reasons were ranked as most important by both male and female smokers, and by the male and female current, occasional, and ex-smokers, though the rank order and magnitude of influence were rated somewhat differently by the two sexes. In general, pleasure-seeking, curiosity, peer-group pressures, and, to a lesser extent, tension reduction, seemed to underlie the reasons rated as having had the most influence on the students to take up smoking.

The second group of five reasons for starting to smoke, which were rated substantially lower than the top-ranked reasons, reflect the influence of peer group pressures and family smoking habits. Rebellious nonconforming behavior ("My parents disapproved and I wanted to show my independence") was consistently ranked as the least important reason for starting to smoke by both sexes; however, it should be noted that women who were high on Eysenck's psychoticism dimension rated this reason as much more influential than women with low psychoticism scores. Media advertisements ("Television and newspaper advertisements made smoking seem appealing") and the smoking behavior of older siblings ("Most of my older brothers and sisters enjoy smoking") were also rated as having relatively little influence by both sexes.

The means, standard deviations, and the rank order of the ratings given by males and females as reasons for *continuing* to smoke are reported in table 3–2. "Because I enjoy it" and "Relaxes me when I'm upset or nervous" were

Table 3–1
Rank Order, Means, and Standard Deviations of Factors Reported by Male and Female College Students to Influence Them to Begin Smoking

Reason for Beginning to Smoke	Females (N = 294)		Males (N = 130)	
	Rank	$\overline{X}$ SD	Rank	$\overline{X}$ SD
See if I would enjoy it	1	2.61 0.95	1	2.52 0.92
Because most of my friends smoke	2	2.52 1.14	3	2.41 1.16
Try something new	3	2.44 0.97	4	2.32 0.92
Thought it was satisfying because other people smoke	4	2.37 0.98	2	2.48 0.98
Made me feel more relaxed around my friends	5	2.14 1.05	5	2.02 1.08
Parents seemed to enjoy smoking	6	1.58 0.89	7	1.53 0.85
Did not want to refuse friends	7	1.51 0.89	6	1.55 0.87
Older siblings enjoyed smoking	8	1.48 0.83	9	1.46 0.83
Media advertisements	9	1.46 0.73	8	1.48 0.74
Parents disapproved— show independence	10	1.32 0.73	10	1.31 0.69

consistently ranked by both sexes as the two most influential reasons for continuing to smoke. It can be noted in table 3–2 that women rated all ten reasons as having had a greater influence on them than did the men, which may account for the higher prevalence of smoking among women in recent years. The women also tended to give much higher ratings to tension-reducing motives ("Relaxes me when I'm upset"; "Helps me forget my worries") than the men.

Peer-group pressures ("Most of my friends smoke"), which ranked relatively high as a reason for starting to smoke, also seemed to have some influence on maintaining the smoking habit. However, stimulation-seeking motives ("Because it is stimulating"; "It facilitates thinking") were rated as relatively unimportant reasons for continuing to smoke by both men and women. "Media advertisement" was rated as having little or no influence on continuing to smoke and consistently ranked as least influential by both sexes.

The means, standard deviations, and the rank order of the reasons given by male and female current, occasional, and ex-smokers for continuing to

Table 3–2

Rank Order, Means, and Standard Deviations of Factors Reported by Male and Female College Students to Influence Them to Continue Smoking

Reason for Continuing to Smoke	Females (N = 294)		Males (N = 130)	
	Rank	$\overline{X}$ SD	Rank	$\overline{X}$ SD
Because I enjoy it	1	2.80 1.09	1	2.52 1.25
Relaxes me when I'm upset or nervous	2	2.62 1.12	2	2.05 1.12
Helps me forget my worries	3	2.12 1.15	7	1.59 1.01
Gives me something to do when I'm alone	4	2.11 1.10	4	1.72 0.98
Makes me feel more comfortable around my friends	5	2.10 1.11	3	1.83 1.08
Get bored when I do not smoke	6	1.86 1.08	4	1.72 1.00
Because most of my friends smoke	7	1.85 1.06	6	1.69 1.11
Because it is stimulating	8	1.72 0.90	8	1.54 0.83
Facilitates thinking	9	1.55 0.92	9	1.33 0.79
Media advertisements	10	1.17 0.54	10	1.14 0.58

smoke are reported in table 3–3. The six reasons listed in the top half of the table were each rated as significantly more influential by current smokers of both sexes than by occasional and ex-smokers. In contrast, "Because most of my friends smoke" was rated as significantly more important by ex-smokers of both sexes than by current and occasional smokers. The female ex-smokers also rated "Makes me feel more comfortable around my friends" as having had a greater influence on them than did the female current and occasional smokers. While "Media advertisement" was rated as the least important reason for continuing to smoke by all groups, female ex-smokers rated this reason as significantly more important than did female current and occasional smokers.

In general, current smokers gave higher ratings than occasional and ex-smokers to internal tension-reducing, pleasurable, and stimulation-seeking reasons for continuing to smoke, and ex-smokers of both sexes tended to give higher ratings than current smokers to external factors such as peer group

Table 3–3
Means, Standard Deviations, and Rank Order of the Ratings of Female and Male Current, Occasional, and Ex-Smokers of the Reasons That Influenced Them to Continue Smoking

Variable		Females				Males			
		Current Smokers (N=40)	Occasional Smokers (N=37)	Ex-Smokers (N=46)	F-Ratio	Current Smokers (N=117)	Occasional Smokers (N=75)	Ex-Smokers (N=94)	F-Ratio
Because I enjoy it	$\overline{X}$	3.37	2.35	2.45	33.79***	3.13	2.03	2.37	8.85***
	SD	0.89	0.86	1.16		0.97	1.23	1.29	
	Rank	(1)	(2)	(1)		(1)	(1)	(1)	
Relaxes me when I'm upset or nervous	$\overline{X}$	2.94	2.43	2.36	8.85***	2.53	1.81	1.83	5.84**
	SD	1.00	1.10	1.18		0.91	1.24	1.06	
	Rank	(2)	(1)	(3)		(2)	(2)	(4)	
Gives me something to do when I'm alone	$\overline{X}$	2.44	1.79	1.97	9.73***	2.00	1.35	1.78	4.62**
	SD	1.06	0.92	1.17		0.78	0.92	1.09	
	Rank	(3)	(5)	(6)		(4)	(6)	(5)	
Get bored when I do not smoke	$\overline{X}$	2.26	1.39	1.76	17.23***	2.18	1.43	1.57	6.78**
	SD	1.11	0.73	1.11		0.93	1.01	0.93	
	Rank	(4)	(8)	(7)		(3)	(5)	(6)	
Because it is stimulating	$\overline{X}$	1.85	1.52	1.71	3.06*	1.78	1.30	1.52	3.29*
	SD	0.92	0.84	0.90		0.77	0.78	0.89	
	Rank	(8)	(7)	(8)		(6)	(8)	(8)	
Facilitates thinking	$\overline{X}$	1.88	1.20	1.40	15.63***	1.63	1.11	1.24	4.78**
	SD	1.04	0.55	0.86		0.90	0.66	0.74	
	Rank	(7)	(9)	(9)		(8)	(9)	(9)	
Because most of my friends smoke	$\overline{X}$	1.55	1.75	2.30	14.99***	1.48	1.32	2.18	7.97***
	SD	0.87	0.96	1.19		0.64	0.97	1.35	
	Rank	(9)	(6)	(4)		(9)	(7)	(2)	
Makes me feel more comfortable around my friends	$\overline{X}$	1.99	1.88	2.41	6.00**	1.98	1.59	1.89	1.31
	SD	1.13	0.96	1.12		1.00	1.09	1.14	
	Rank	(6)	(4)	(2)		(5)	(3)	(3)	
Helps me forget my worries	$\overline{X}$	2.26	2.03	2.01	1.50	1.70	1.54	1.54	0.33
	SD	1.20	1.04	1.14		0.91	1.14	0.98	
	Rank	(4)	(3)	(5)		(7)	(4)	(7)	
Because of media advertising	$\overline{X}$	1.11	1.12	1.30	3.70*	1.20	1.05	1.15	0.63
	SD	0.45	0.40	0.70		0.52	0.66	0.56	
	Rank	(10)	(10)	(10)		(10)	(10)	(10)	

influence ("Because most of my friends smoke") and media advertisements. Occasional smokers of both sexes rated most of the reasons for continuing to smoke as less influential than did either current or ex-smokers. Occasional smokers also reported that they enjoyed smoking less than current smokers, and even less on the average than ex-smokers. It is interesting to note that the ratings of the occasional smokers were generally more similar to those of ex-smokers than current smokers.

Motivational-Emotional and Situational Determinants of Smoking Behavior

The six smoking motivational factors identified by Ikard et al. (1969) were extracted and replicated in several factor analyses of the responses of American smokers to the 23-item Horn-Waingrow Smoker Survey, which was developed to measure the four general types of smoking behavior postulated by Tomkins's Affect Control model. In responding to the Horn-Waingrow questionnaire, smokers rated the degree to which statements describing the stimulating, pleasurable, tension-reducing, and habitual-automatic effects of smoking were characteristic of them.

In a somewhat different approach, McKennell (1970) classified British smokers according to the occasions on which they were likely or unlikely to smoke. A checklist of 42 smoking occasions was presented to representative national samples of 564 adolescent and 775 adult smokers and ex-smokers. Factor analyses of responses to this checklist consistently identified seven types of smoking occasions which were labeled: Nervous Irritation Smoking; Relaxation Smoking; Smoking Alone; Activity Accompaniment; Food Substitution; Social Smoking; and Social Confidence Smoking. The first two factors correspond reasonably well with Tomkins's negative and positive affect control types: the Activity Accompaniment factor is similar to the Ikard et al. Stimulation factor. McKennell's two psychosocial factors (social, self-confidence smoking) and Food Substitution did not emerge among the factors identified by Ikard et al. (1969) because they are not included in Tomkins's model. Finally, McKennell's Smoking Alone factor appears to overlap several of the Ikard et al. factors.

Russell et al. (1974) attempted to link the McKennell (1970) occasions-for-smoking typology with the smoking motivation factors derived by Ikard et al. (1969) from Tomkins's model. They constructed a 34-item questionnaire which incorporated a number of affect-control and smoking-occasions items that were adapted from the Horn-Waingrow questionnaire and the McKennell checklist. New items intended to assess several additional smoking motives as conceptualized by the authors were also included. In responding to the Russell questionnaire, smokers rated each of the 34 statements on a 4-point scale in terms of whether it was characteristic of them "Not at all,"

"A little," "Quite a bit," or "Very much so." The Russell et al. smoking motivation questionnaire was given to 175 cigarette smokers at a London teaching hospital. The sample included doctors, nurses, students, patients, visitors, technicians, orderlies, and clerical and other hospital staff. This questionnaire was also administered to 101 persons attending two hospital clinics for smokers.

The same six factors emerged in both samples and were labeled: Stimulation Smoking; Indulgent Smoking; Psychosocial Smoking; Sensorimotor Smoking; Addictive Smoking; and Automatic Smoking. The Stimulation Smoking factor was defined by items adapted from the Ikard et al. Stimulation and the McKennell Activity Accompaniment factors. The Indulgent Smoking factor, which contained items related to smoking for pleasure in relaxed situations, was similar to the Ikard et al. Pleasurable Relaxation and McKennell Relaxation Smoking factors. The Sensorimotor Smoking factor consisted of items from the Ikard et al. Sensorimotor Manipulation and Stimulation factors, but appeared to be more closely associated with the former. A sensorimotor factor was not included in the McKennell typology of smoking occasions.

The Russell et al. Addictive and Automatic smoking factors were largely defined by items adapted from the Ikard et al. Addictive and Habitual smoking motivation factors, and appear to be quite similar to these factors. The Psychosocial Smoking factor appears to reflect a combination of McKennell's Social Smoking and Social Confidence Smoking factors. As previously noted, psychosocial smoking is not conceptually represented in Tomkins's model. Consequently, items describing this type of smoking were not included in the Horn-Waingrow Smoker Survey.

The smoking motivation factors extracted by Russell et al. (1974) differed in a number of important respects from the smoking occasions and affect control factors previously identified by McKennell (1970) and Ikard et al. (1969). There is, nevertheless, a remarkable correspondence of the findings in these studies, which is especially impressive when one considers the major differences in theoretical orientation and research methodology, and in the populations from which the samples were drawn. Moreover, the findings of Russell et al. suggest that the internal motivational states evoked by particular situations have more direct influence on smoking behavior than the parameters of the situations in which they are generated.

Although Russell et al. hypothesized a "sedative smoking" factor, and included specific items to measure it, this factor did not emerge in any of the analyses based on their 34-item questionnaire. Since Negative Affect Reduction and Nervous Irritation smoking were among the strongest factors identified, respectively, by Ikard et al. and McKennell, the failure to find a sedative (negative affect) factor was surprising. This may have resulted from an unfortunate choice of items for assessing sedative smoking. For example, none of the three items used by Russell et al. to assess sedative smoking directly inquired about reducing tension and anxiety. However, when Russell et al. restricted their analysis to the 18 items intended to assess the Ikard et al. factors, all six of the Ikard et al. factors emerged, including the sedative smoking (reduction of negative affect) factor.

Frith (1971) has also constructed a questionnaire designed to assess the extent to which 22 specific situations influenced smoking behavior. On the basis of the known effects of nicotine on cortical arousal and the relationships between personality and smoking postulated by Eysenck's Diathesis-Stress model, Frith reasoned that some people (extraverts) would be more likely to smoke to increase cortical arousal in boring situations in which low levels of cortical arousal are generally experienced. In contrast, persons characterized by high levels of arousal (neurotics) are more likely to smoke in stressful situations in order to reduce the unpleasant feelings of tension and anxiety associated with high levels of arousal typically experienced in such situations.

In order to evaluate these predictions, Frith administered his questionnaire, which described 12 high-arousal and 10 low-arousal situations, to 98 cigarette smokers (hospital employees and their friends). The high-arousal situations involved stress produced by external stimulation or mental activity; the low-arousal situations involved relaxation, boredom, and repetitive work. The smokers were instructed to imagine themselves in each situation, and then indicate by rating themselves on a 7-point scale, how much they would crave a cigarette in that situation.

In a factor analysis of the subjects' questionnaire responses, Frith reported only the results of a two-factor solution. Number of cigarettes smoked per day had the highest loading on the first factor; all of the smoking situations also had positive loadings on this factor. On the second factor, the high-arousal situations loaded in one direction and low-arousal situations loaded in the opposite direction. These findings suggest that negative affect (sedative) smoking and reduction in cortical arousal are associated with high-arousal situations, and that positive affect smoking and increased cortical arousal are associated with low-arousal situations. The two poles of Frith's bipolar second factor roughly correspond with the Nervous Irritation Smoking and Relaxation Smoking factors previously reported by McKennell. Frith also found that women reported a stronger desire to smoke in high-arousal situations, whereas men indicated a stronger urge to smoke in low-arousal situations. These findings are generally consistent with Eysenck's models.

Stanaway and Watson (1980) administered the Russell et al. (1974) and Frith (1971) questionnaires and the Eysenck Personality Inventory (Eysenck and Eysenck, 1964) to a heterogeneous sample of 115 cigarette smokers, ranging in age from 18 to 55. The subjects in this study were full-time and part-time students and members of the academic, clerical, and library staff at a British polytechnic institute. Separate factor analyses of the Russell and Frith questionnaires essentially replicated the findings in the original studies. The results of a series of factor analyses based on the combined data from the Russell and Frith questionnaires yielded complicated results which were summarized by Stanaway and Watson (1980, p. 379) as follows:

> . . . the questionnaires of Russell and Frith are relatively independent in terms of what they measure. A number of factors identified in the analyses of the separate questionnaires have also been found in the combined analyses. By making a judicious choice of items from the two questionnaires, and preferably rewording some of the items so that they are all in the same format, it should no doubt be possible to obtain reliable, valid measures of some or all of these factors.

Relationships between smoking behavior and scores on the EPI Neuroticism and Extraversion scales were also examined by Stanaway and Watson (1981). The smokers in this study had significantly higher neuroticism scores than nonsmokers. Although the smokers also had higher extraversion scores, this difference was not statistically significant. However, because of small sample size, the data for males and females were combined, making the results for extraversion difficult to interpret. Since the EPI does not contain a psychoticism dimension, Stanaway and Watson derived a measure of psychoticism, using items from the EPI and the Zuckerman Sensation Seeking Scale (Zuckerman et al., 1964). Consistent with Eysenck's theory, smokers were found to have significantly higher scores than nonsmokers on this derived psychoticism measure.

Best and Hakstian (1978) obtained ratings from a sample of 331 Canadian smokers of their urge to smoke in 50 different situations in which cigarettes are commonly smoked. For each situation, the subjects were instructed to rate, on a 7-point scale, "the typical strength of their urge to smoke relative to their average urge" (1978, p. 80). In separate factor analyses for males and females, eleven situational smoking factors were extracted for each sex. These factors substantially overlapped the situational factors previously reported by McKennell (1970) and Frith (1971), and also included smoking motivation factors similar to those identified by Ikard et al. (1969) and Russell et al. (1974). In addition, several relatively unique factors were found, which were different for males and females.

In summary, Russell et al. (1974) have demonstrated that most of the smoking motivation and smoking occasion factors identified by Ikard et al. (1969) and McKennell (1970) could be assessed with a single relatively brief questionnaire that included selected items from the questionnaires used in the earlier studies. Similarly, Stanaway and Watson (1980) administered the Russell and Frith questionnaires, and extracted factors based on the combined data for both scales that were similar to those identified in previous studies. It should be noted, however, that the relatively small samples of smokers in the Russell et al. and Stanaway and Watson studies did not permit them to conduct separate analyses for men and women. The findings reported in the following section were obtained in a series of studies based on large heterogeneous samples of smokers in which the smoking motivation of males and females was evaluated in separate analyses.

Motivational-Emotional Determinants of Smoking Behavior

The two major goals of our research were: (1) to construct a single questionnaire that would encompass the most important smoking motivation and smoking situation factors identified in previous studies; and (2) to evaluate the relationships between these factors and personality measures that have been found to be related to smoking behavior. Frith's and Best and Hakstian's questionnaires were selected for further study to insure an adequate representation of smoking situations. The Russell questionnaire was selected because it incorporates and integrates most of the factors identified and replicated in previous research with the Horn-Waingrow (1966) Smoker Survey and the McKennell smoking occasions questionnaire, with the exception of the strong Negative Affect Reduction and Nervous Irritation Smoking factors reported by Ikard et al. and McKennell.

Because of the theoretical importance of negative affect in the Tomkins and Eysenck models, the state scales of the State-Trait Personality Inventory (STPI) were adapted to assess anxiety and anger as smoking motivation factors. The STPI, as noted above, is comprised of six 10-item subscales for assessing anxiety, anger and curiosity as emotional states and personality traits (Spielberger, 1979). The STPI state scales, which normally assess the intensity of each of these emotional states at a particular time, were modified to assess the intensity of the "urge to smoke" associated with each emotion.

The first step in this research program was to administer the original items of the Russell et al. (1974), Frith (1971), and Best and Hakstian (1978) questionnaires to 160 smokers, consisting of 70 university students and 90 clerical, technical and factory workers. The Russell et al. (1974) questionnaire (34 items) was administered with the identical instructions ("Indicate the extent the item is true for you") and 4-point rating scale format ("Not at all," "A little," "Quite a bit," "Very much so") used in the original study. The instructions for Best and Hakstian's (1978) smoking situations questionnaire (50 items) were also the same as those used in the original study ("Imagine yourself in each situation and rate the typical strength of your urge to smoke, relative to your average urge to smoke"). However, their 7-point rating scale format was replaced with a simpler 4-point rating scale, in which the extreme points were defined as "Very little urge," and "Very great urge." These same urge-to-smoke instructions and 4-point rating scales were also used in administering the Frith questionnaire (22 items) and the modified STPI state anxiety, anger and curiosity scales (30 items).

Responses to the 136 individual items from the four questionnaires were factored together; separate analyses were carried out for males and females. The resulting eigenvalues and screen tests indicated that 9 to 11 factors could be extracted for both sexes; 5 to 7 of these factors were defined primarily by a combination of items from the Russell, Frith, and STPI questionnaires. The remaining factors were defined almost exclusively by items from the Best and Hakstian questionnaire. Inspection of the factors defined exclusively by the Best and Hakstian items revealed that the content of most of these factors was similar to that of the factors defined by the other three measures. These findings suggested that the Best and Hakstian factors were due primarily to method variance rather than systematic variance associated with the smoking situations. Therefore, the Best and Hakstian questionnaire was not included in further efforts to assess smoking motivation.

The Russell, Frith, and modified STPI questionnaires were administered to a second more heterogeneous sample of 237 smokers, ranging in age from 17 to 69, comprised of community college and university undergraduate students and managerial, technical, clerical, and sales workers. The data from this sample for the three questionnaires were combined with the data obtained on these measures from the 160 smokers in the previous study, and separate factor analyses were carried out for the 176 males and 202 females in the combined sample. The results of the unrotated analyses identified six factors for both sexes with eigenvalues greater than 1.0; however, screen tests strongly suggested the extraction to five factors. Therefore, five and six factor solutions were computed with varimax rotation. The 5-factor solutions were clearly superior, producing: (a) close approximation to simple structure, (b) highly similar (invariant) factors for males and females, and (c) meaningful psychological interpretations of each factor.

The items with salient loadings (.40 or greater) in the 5-factor solutions, and the questionnaire from which each item was taken, are reported in table 3–4, in which the remarkable similarity of the factor structure for men and women may be noted. Factors I and III were defined entirely by items from the STPI; the 12 items with salient loadings on Factor I all came from the STPI Anger and Anxiety scales, whereas Factor IV consisted entirely of STPI Curiosity items. These factors were labeled, respectively, Negative Affect Control and Intellectual Stimulation/Curiosity. The items with salient loadings on Factor II came from all three questionnaires; the content of these items led us to name this factor Restful and Relaxing Situations. Factors III and V were defined exclusively by items from the Russell questionnaire. Since the content of the three items with very high loadings on Factor III were all related to automatic smoking, this factor was labeled Automatic/Habitual Smoking. Social attractiveness and sensorimotor items had high loadings on Factor V; hence, this factor was named Social Attractiveness and Sensory Stimulation.

The next step in our effort to identify stable smoking motivation factors was to prepare and evaluate a preliminary Smoking Motivation Questionnaire (SMQ). The preliminary SMQ was comprised of the 44 items listed in table 3–4; all of these items had salient loadings on the five smoking motivation factors identified in the previous analyses. The preliminary SMQ consisted of two parts, each with different instructions. Part I was comprised of the 18 smoking-motivation items from the Russell questionnaire, which require smokers to rate the extent to which each item describes their smoking behavior. The second part consisted of the 4 Frith and 22 STPI items listed in table 3–4, but the instructions were modified from those used in the previous study. Rather than instructing the subjects to rate "your urge to smoke, relative to your average urge to smoke," which some respondents found confusing, they were asked to "rate the typical strength of your urge to smoke" in each situation.

The preliminary SMQ was administered to 651 smokers (324 males, 327 females) to determine if the smoking motivation factors identified in the previous studies could be replicated on a new, heterogeneous sample consisting of working adults employed in a variety of settings. The subjects ranged in age from 17 to 77 (mean age = 36.0), and included hospital staff, fire-fighters, and managerial, professional, technical, clerical, sales, and blue collar workers employed in a variety of government agencies, service industries, and manufacturing plants. The results of the factor analyses of the 44-item preliminary SMQ in the replication sample were strikingly similar to the findings reported in table 3–4. The same five factors were identified, the loadings of the individual items on each factor were quite similar to those previously obtained, and the factor structure was invariant for males and females. There was, of course, some shrinkage, but this was limited primarily to a few items with dual and/or smaller loadings in the original sample.

The 36 items with consistently high loadings on the same factor for both males and females in the original and replication samples were selected for the final form of the SMQ, which can be found in Appendix 3A. The 12 items with uniformly high loadings on Factor I, and the 6 items with the highest loadings, respectively, on Factors II, III, IV, and V were retained. In order to determine the factor structure of the final form of the SMQ, the data for the two samples were combined and the responses to the 36 items of the 1,029 subjects (500 males, 529 females) for whom complete data were available were refactored. The results of separate factor analyses for men and women are reported in table 3–5. Each of the five factors was clearly defined by the same items for which uniformly high loadings on these factors were found in the original and replication samples; only two of the 36 items had salient loadings on more than one factor. The numbers in tables 3–4 and 3–5 preceding each item (1 to 36) indicate the position of the item in the final form of the SMQ (see appendix 3A).

The factor structure of the SMQ was further evaluated to determine if the urge to smoke associated with negative emotions could be differentiated into

Table 3–4
Factor Analysis of the Preliminary Smoking Motivation Questionnaire

		Factor Loadings									
		I. Negative Affect Control		II. Restful and Relaxing		III. Intellectual Stimulation/Curious		IV. Automatic/Habitual		V. Social Attractiveness/Sensory Stimulation	
Item No.	Scale Item	M	F	M	F	M	F	M	F	M	F
Russell, Peto & Pate											
9.	Having a quiet rest			.63	.59						
2.	Comfortable and relaxed			.60	.69						
5.	Smoke automatically					.74	.67				
12.	Don't remember lighting up					.72	.72				
8.	Still have one burning					.68	.69				
13.	Rushed & have lots to do					.67	.50				
4.	Run out—unbearable					.54	.59				
11.	Gnawing hunger to smoke					.52	.53				
—	Helps me think and concentrate					.46	.53				
—	Busy & working hard					.42	.55				
6.	Look mature & sophisticated									.73	.70
1.	Enjoy handling a cigarette									.67	.67
7.	Enjoy lighting up									.62	.70
3.	Enjoy watching smoke									.57	.55
—	Pleasure to offer/accept cigs									.56	.59
10.	Confident with other people									.55	.54
—	Pleasure—something in mouth									.51	.61
14.	Attractive to opposite sex									.48	.67
Frith Questionnaire											
21.	Restful evening alone			.80	.78						
15.	Quiet evening with friends			.72	.67						
—	Solitary walk			.71	.59						
25.	Chatting at break			.62	.60						

State-Trait Personality Inventory

Item										
28. Feel like breaking things	.85	.82								
20. Feel angry	.84	.85								
24. Feel like yelling	.82	.78								
32. Feel irritated	.82	.83								
16. Feel furious	.79	.84								
34. Feel like hitting someone	.78	.80								
17. Feel tense	.77	.84								
36. Feel like swearing	.76	.74								
22. Worrying over misfortunes	.74	.81								
33. Worried	.73	.82								
26. Feel nervous	.73	.82								
29. Jittery	.68	.76								
30. Relaxed			.78	.76						
— Feel at ease			.77	.56				.45		
31. Feel mentally active			.51	(.23)			(.36)	.50		
23. Inquisitive							.71	.82		
18. Feel curious							.70	.65		
35. Feel eager							.59	.63		
19. Feel interested							.58	.80		
— Feel steady			.50				.50	.61		
— Feel stimulated							.43	.56		
27. In a questioning mood	.44						.43	.68		
Eigenvalues	8.5	8.7	5.8	4.1	4 0	3.7	3.5	4.5	3.4	3.6

Table 3–5
Factor Analysis of the Smoking Motivation Questionnaire

Item No.	Scale Item	I. Negative Affect Control		II. Restful and Relaxing		III. Intellectual Stimulation/ Curious		IV. Automatic/ Habitual		V. Social Attractiveness/ Sensory Stimulation	
		M	F	M	F	M	F	M	F	M	F
	Negative Affect Control										
32.	Feel irritated	.85	.86								
20.	Feel angry	.85	.85								
28.	Feel like breaking things	.80	.78								
16.	Feel furious	.79	.84								
24.	Feel like yelling	.79	.80								
34.	Feel like hitting someone	.78	.81								
36.	Feel like swearing	.78	.76								
33.	Feel worried	.78	.79								
26.	Feel nervous	.77	.79								
29.	Feel jittery	.77	.76								
17.	Feel tense	.76	.81								
22.	Worrying over misfortunes	.76	.75								
	Restful & Relaxing Situations										
30.	Relaxed			.80	.83						
21.	Restful evening alone			.77	.76						
2.	Comfortable & relaxed			.72	.73						
9.	When having a quiet rest			.69	.67						
15.	Quiet evening with friends			.67	.68						
25.	Chatting at break			.65	.61						
	Intellectual Stimulation/Curious										
23.	Inquisitive					.76	.83				
18.	Feel curious					.73	.76				
19.	Feel interested					.69	.71				
27.	In a questioning mood					.63	.74				

Item	8.6	8.5	4.0	3.8	3.5	3.5	3.0	3.1	2.9	2.7
35. Feel eager	.40				.57	.56				
31. Feel mentally active					.53	.48				
Automatic/Habitual Smoking										
12. Don't remember lighting up							.78	.75		
8. Still have one burning							.74	.69		
5. I smoke automatically							.72	.74		
4. Run out—unbearable							.55	.64		
13. Rushed & have lots to do		.40					.49	.49		
11. Gnawing hunger to smoke							.48	.57		
Social Attractive & Sensory Stimulation										
6. Look mature & sophisticated									.77	.76
7. Enjoy lighting up									.71	.68
3. Enjoy watching smoke									.67	.53
14. Attractive to opposite sex									.66	.72
10. Confident with other people									.61	.59
1. Enjoy handling a cigarette									.54	.57
Eigenvalues	8.6	8.5	4.0	3.8	3.5	3.5	3.0	3.1	2.9	2.7

separate smoking motivation factors for anxiety and anger. Toward this end the 12 items with high loadings on Factor I (Negative Affect Control) were evaluated in separate factor analyses for males and females. The results of these analyses, reported in table 3–6, indicated that separate anxiety and anger smoking motivation factors could be extracted. Although most of the items had strong loadings on only one of these factors, substantial dual loadings on both anxiety and anger were found for 4 of the 12 items for both sexes. These findings suggest that the arousal of anger and/or anxiety is a particularly potent stimulus for smoking, which presumably reduces the unpleasant feelings associated with these negative affects.

Independent scales for measuring anxiety and anger as smoking motivation factors were formed, consisting of the six items with the largest loadings on these factors (feeling irritated was assigned to the Anxiety factor), and the psychometric properties of these scales were evaluated. The Anxiety and Anger scales were found to have very strong internal consistency. The alpha coefficients and item remainder correlations reported in table 3–6 were remarkably high for such brief scales. These findings provide further evidence that the urge to smoke is stimulated by internal states of anxiety and anger

Table 3–6
Item Loadings for the SMQ Anxiety and Anger Smoking Motivation Factors, and Item Remainder Correlations and Alpha Coefficients of the Subscales for Assessing These Factors

Item No.	Scale Items	Factor Loadings				Item-Remainder Correlations			
		Anxiety		Anger		Anger Scale		Anxiety Scale	
		M	F	M	F	M	F	M	F
31.	Nervous	.87	.83			.86	.83		
21.	Tense	.82	.80			.81	.81		
27.	Worrying over possible misfortunes	.82	.82			.82	.78		
39.	Worried	.81	.83			.85	.83		
34.	Jittery	.76	.70	(.39)	.43	.81	.77		
38.	Irritated	.59	.68	.65	.60	.77	.83		
25.	Angry	.47	.66	.73	.58			.81	.80
20.	Furious	.43	.64	.70	.57			.76	.78
41.	Feel like hitting someone			.87	.86			.85	.85
33.	Feel like breaking things			.86	.86			.84	.81
29.	Feel like yelling at somebody		.40	.83	.80			.84	.83
44.	Feel like swearing			.81	.78			.83	.80
	Eigenvalues	4.4	5.1	4.7	4.2				
	Alpha Coefficients					.94	.93	.94	.94

that are clearly discriminated by smokers, even though these states may occur simultaneously, as reflected in the item overlap and the fact that they jointly defined the Negative Affect Control factor.

Correlations among the scales corresponding to the seven SMQ factors are reported in table 3–7. The Negative Affect Control scale was comprised of 12 items, and was further divided into two 6-item subsets for assessing anger and anxiety as smoking motivation factors. The scales for assessing the other four smoking motivation factors were each comprised of six items. The Negative Affect Control scale correlated highly with the Anger and Anxiety scales, as would be expected on the basis of item overlap, and these two scales correlated highly with one another. The three negative affect scales were also moderately correlated with the Automatic-Habitual scale. Thus, persons who smoke automatically report that the urge to smoke is strongest in emotionally arousing situations. It would appear that automatic smoking may help the smoker reduce anxiety and emotional tension, as has been previously reported (Ikard et al., 1969; Russell et al., 1974), and to control anger.

The Automatic-Habitual scale also correlated moderately with the Intellectual Stimulation/Curiosity scale, suggesting that positive feelings associated with states of curiosity and inquisitiveness may also stimulate automatic smoking. The finding that the scales based on the Restful-Relaxing Situations and Social Attractiveness/Sensory Stimulation factors correlated very little with one another, nor with the other smoking motivation factors, suggested that these factors were relatively independent. However, smokers who report a stronger urge to smoke in restful-relaxing situations were also somewhat more likely to smoke when feeling intellectually stimulated or curious.

Differences between males and females on each smoking motivation factor were evaluated by t-tests, which are included in table 3–7. Women reported a stronger urge to smoke when emotionally aroused by either anxiety or anger. These results are consistent with previous research in which female smokers were found to be higher in trait anxiety and neuroticism, and with Eysenck's hypothesis that women are more likely than men to smoke in order to reduce tension and anxiety. Women also reported a slightly stronger urge to smoke in restful and relaxing situations, presumably to enhance the positive affect of enjoyment as conceptualized by Tomkins.

Correlations of the SMQ scales with the EPQ Extraversion, Neuroticism, Psychoticism, and Lie scales are reported in table 3–8. The EPQ Neuroticism scale correlated positively with 5 of the 7 SMQ factor scales for both sexes. A small negative correlation was also found between Neuroticism and the Social attractiveness/sensory stimulation factor for males. Significant correlations were also found between the EPQ Extraversion and Psychoticism scales and the SMQ smoking motivation factors, but these correlations were quite small and none were significant for both sexes. The correlations

Table 3–7
Means, Standard Deviations, and Intercorrelations among the SMQ Factor Scores

SMQ Factors	Negative Affect Control		Anger		Anxiety		Restful-Relaxing		Social/Sensory		Automatic-Habitual		Intellectual Stimulation/Curious	
	M (500)	F (529)	M (500)	F (529)	M (500)	F (529)	M (500)	F (529)	M (500)	F (529)	M (500)	F (529)	M (500)	F (529)
Anger	.95	.96												
Anxiety	.93	.95	.77	.82										
Restful-Relaxing	.25	.29	.14	.22	.33	.35								
Social/Sensory	.20	.20	.20	.21	.17	.16	.17	.19						
Automatic-Habitual	.56	.48	.51	.44	.56	.47	.30	.25	.16	.15				
Intellectual Stimulation/Curious	.58	.52	.54	.50	.56	.50	.46	.45	.31	.26	.54	.45		
Mean	30.79	35.63	14.13	16.80	16.65	18.82	14.32	15.41	8.70	8.85	12.60	12.39	11.76	11.87
SD	11.22	11.14	6.28	6.31	5.64	5.35	4.42	4.51	2.84	2.83	4.26	4.09	4.25	4.43
t-test	6.92*		6.79*		6.33*		3.90*		0.89		−.81		.40	

Note: Correlations of .15 or greater are significant at $p < .001$.

*$p < .001$.

Table 3–8
Correlations of the SMQ and the EPQ Extraversion, Neuroticism, and Psychoticism Scales

SMQ Factors	Extraversion		Neuroticism		Psychoticism		Lie	
	M (463)	F (480)	M (470)	F (472)	M (449)	F (468)	M (453)	F (470)
Negative Affect	.00	−.07	.32***	.27***	.05	.01	.01	−.06
Anger	.04	−.05	.29***	.25***	.03	.00	−.01	−.06
Anxiety	.04	−.09*	.33***	.28***	.07	.03	.03	−.05
Restful-Relaxing	.02	−.10*	−.02	.01	.12**	.06	.14**	.03
Social/Sensory	.12**	−.04	−.13**	.07	.02	.01	−.08	−.01
Automatic-Habitual	−.06	−.12**	.27***	.21***	.06	.04	−.01	.01
Intellectual Stimulation/ Curious	.07	−.04	.20***	.23***	.06	.13**	.00	.07

Note: The N's reported in the table indicate the number of subjects for whom data on the EPQ were available. Due to missing data on several SMQ and EPQ Scales, the number of subjects on which each correlation was based ranged from 425 to 470 for males, and from 468 to 480 for females.

* $p < .05$
** $p < .01$
*** $p < .001$

between the EPQ Lie scale and the SMQ smoking motivation factors were essentially zero, indicating that the response set of putting up a good appearance has relatively little influence on smokers responses to the SMQ.

Correlations of the SMQ with the STPI Trait Anxiety, Trait Anger, and Trait Curiosity scales are reported in table 3–9. Small but highly significant positive correlations were found between the T-Anxiety and T-Anger scales for both sexes with the same five SMQ factors that correlated significantly with the EPQ Neuroticism scale. Thus, smokers who more frequently experience anxiety and anger are likely to feel a stronger urge to smoke when they experience these emotions. Since neurotics experience anger and anxiety more frequently than stable persons, the relations between the STPI and EPQ personality scales and the SMQ smoking motivation factors consistently indicate that the urge to smoke is stronger for neurotic persons when they experience anxiety and anger. These findings further suggest that smoking helps persons high in neuroticism to reduce the unpleasant negative affect associated with feelings of anxiety and anger. None of the correlations between the smoking motivation factors and trait curiosity were statistically significant.

Correlations of the SMQ smoking motivation factors and the EPQ and STPI personality scales with daily cigarette consumption are reported in table 3–10 for the replication sample of 651 subjects described above. Separate correlations were computed for current and ex-smokers, who were asked to report the number of cigarettes they presently or previously smoked each day by checking one of the following five categories: 1-5 (less than 1/4 pack); 6-10 (1/2 pack); 11-20 (1/2 to 1 pack); 21-40 (1 to 2 packs); more than 2 packs. Scores from 1 to 5, respectively, were assigned for these categories,

Table 3–9
Correlations of the SMQ with the STPI Trait Anger, Anxiety, and Curiosity Scale

	T-Anxiety		T-Anger		T-Curiosity	
SMQ Factors	M (324)	F (326)	M (324)	F (326)	M (324)	F (325)
Negative Affect	.27***	.25***	.30***	.31***	.03	− .07
Anger	.25***	.25***	.31***	.32***	.03	− .06
Anxiety	.26***	.21***	.25***	.27***	.02	− .06
Restful-Relaxing	.00	.03	.09	.01	.00	.04
Social/Sensory	.13*	.25***	.04	.15**	.05	.01
Automatic-Habitual	.27***	.19***	.25***	.19***	.03	.10
Intellectual Stimulation/ Curious	.22***	.17**	.20***	.14**	.08	.03

* $p < .05$
** $p < .01$
*** $p < .001$

Table 3–10

Correlations of Daily Cigarette Smoking with the Smoking Motivation Factors and the EPQ and STPI Scores of Current and Ex-smokers

Motivation & Personality Measures	Current Smokers		Ex-smokers	
	Male (215)	Female (246)	Male (77)	Female (62)
SMQ Factors				
Negative Affect	.34***	.39***	.22	.25*
Anger	.26***	.36***	.13	.20
Anxiety	.40***	.42***	.28*	.30*
Restful-Relaxing	.27**	.25***	.41***	.37**
Social/Sensory	.00	.11	−.01	.27*
Automatic-Habitual	.55***	.58***	.58***	.50***
Intellectual Stimulation/ Curiosity	.44***	.35***	.31**	.21
EPQ Scales				
Extraversion	−.15	−.06	.15	−.20
Neuroticism	.11	.02	.13	−.07
Psychoticism	03	−.06	−.08	−.15
Lie	.09	.07	.12	.03
STPI Scales				
Trait Anxiety	.04	.02	.09	−.04
Trait Anger	.09	.10	.04	−.14
Reaction	.14	.11	.13	−.08
Temperament	.02	.06	−.04	−.16
Trait Curiosity	.09	−.02	.00	.01
Daily Cigarettes Smoked				
Mean	3.40	3.21	3.56	2.71
SD	1.02	1.01	1.04	1.23

* $p < .05$
** $p < .01$
*** $p < .001$

with higher scores indicating more cigarette smoking. The mean number of cigarettes smoked daily, reported at the bottom of table 3–10, was approximately the same for male and female current smokers and male ex-smokers (between 1 and 1-1/2 packs per day); the daily cigarette smoking for female ex-smokers was somewhat less (1/2 to 1 pack).

The correlations of the EPQ and STPI personality scales with daily cigarette smoking were essentially zero for both male and female current smokers, as well as for ex-smokers of both sexes, as can be noted in table 3–10. Although smokers were found to score higher in extraversion, neuroticism, psychoticism, and trait anxiety in previous research, none of these personality measures predicted daily cigarette consumption. In contrast, six of the seven smoking motivation factors correlated positively and significantly with daily cigarette consumption for current smokers of both sexes. Significant positive correlations between the smoking motivation factors and daily cigarette consumption were also found for the ex-smokers, but the pattern of these correlations was different than for the smokers. Thus, while personality traits are positively related to smoking motivation (see tables 3–8 and 3–9), they do not predict daily cigarette consumption.

The SMQ Automatic-Habitual scale correlated more highly with daily cigarette consumption than the other smoking motivation factors for current and ex-smokers of both sexes. Significant positive correlations were also found between the Negative Affect Control (anger and anxiety) factors and number of cigarettes smoked for the current smokers, whereas only anxiety was consistently related to daily cigarette consumption for the ex-smokers. The Intellectual Stimulation/Curiosity smoking motivation factor correlated positively with daily cigarette smoking for current smokers and for male ex-smokers, but not for female ex-smokers. The female ex-smokers were the only group for whom the Social Attractiveness/Sensory Stimulation factor correlated significantly with number of cigarettes smoked. It would seem that male and female ex-smokers differ substantially from current smokers in their motivation for smoking.

In order to evaluate the extent to which various combinations of the smoking motivation factors predict daily cigarette consumption, separate step-wise multiple regression analyses were carried out for the male and female current and ex-smokers. Given the substantial item overlap between the Anxiety and Anger smoking motivation scales and the Negative Affect Control scale, the latter was not included in these analyses. The Automatic-Habitual smoking factor was, of course, the best predictor of daily cigarette consumption, as would be expected from the zero-order correlations reported in table 3–10. The finding that this factor was strongly associated with cigarette consumption was, of course, not surprising because the items that define Automatic-Habitual smoking seem to reflect a strong smoking habit, rather than the internal states and situational factors that stimulate smokers to smoke. Therefore, in order to evaluate the relative strength of the other smoking motivation factors, the Automatic-Habitual smoking scale was eliminated and step-wise multiple regression analyses were carried out for the remaining smoking motivation factors. The EPQ and STPI scales were also included in these analyses, in which number of cigarettes smoked was the dependent variable.

For the male current smokers, the Intellectual Stimulation/Curiosity factor was the single best predictor of daily cigarette consumption; Anxiety and Restful and Relaxing Situations also contributed significantly to the multiple correlation of .57. For female current smokers, the Anxiety Smoking motivation factor was the best single predictor of cigarette consumption, and

Curiosity and the EPQ Neuroticism scale added significantly to the multiple correlation of .46. The Restful and Relaxing Situations scale was the only smoking motivation factor that contributed to the prediction of daily cigarette smoking for ex-smokers, providing further evidence that the smoking motivation of ex-smokers is quite different from that of persons who continue to smoke.

Summary and Conclusions

Models of smoking behavior proposed by Tomkins and Eysenck to account for the prevalance and persistence of the smoking habit were reviewed and evidence relating to these theories was evaluated. Both theories have been successful in generating and guiding research and are supported by a substantial body of empirical findings. The two theories are similar in their focus on the stimulating and tension-reducing effects of smoking, but each emphasizes a different set of variables and neither directly addresses questions relating to the cognitive processes that may be associated with developing and maintaining the smoking habit. Since these theories do not generate conflicting hypotheses, they may be regarded as complementary rather than antagonistic. Therefore, integration of the two theories should provide a more comprehensive understanding of smoking behavior. Eysenck and Tomkins clearly recognize the importance of motivational and emotional factors as determinants of smoking behavior. Eysenck links smoking to cortical arousal associated with individual differences in personality, but does not attempt to specify the *psychological* nature of the internal states that stimulate a smoker to light up. The internal emotional states that stimulate smokers to smoke, and that are in turn modified by smoking, are at the core of Tomkins' theory. But Tomkins does not relate smoking behavior to specific affects, nor to individual differences in personality. Rather, the four categories of smokers postulated in Tomkins's model are defined on the basis of the use of smoking to control undifferentiated positive and negative affective states.

In this chapter, research findings relating to the effects of family smoking habits on the initiation and maintenance of smoking behavior were reviewed, and studies of relationships between personality traits, reasons for smoking, and smoking behavior were examined. The construction of a questionnaire to assess smoking motivation was also described, and the findings in a series of investigations in which this questionnaire was used to assess the emotional and motivational processes that maintain the smoking habit were reported in detail.

For both high school and college students, smoking behavior is more strongly associated with the smoking habits of peers and older siblings than parental smoking, although students with no older siblings are more likely to smoke if one or both parents smoke. These findings seem to indicate that environmental influences are more important than constitutional-genetic factors in the initiation of smoking. In contrast, constitutional-genetic factors, mediated by internal emotional states and personality dispositions, seem to have a greater influence on the persistence of the smoking habit.

Comprehensive reviews of the research literature indicate that smokers score consistently higher than nonsmokers in extraversion and neuroticism, and that smokers are more impulsive and have stronger antisocial tendencies than nonsmokers. In several recent studies, however, no relationships were found between extraversion and smoking, which may result from a decline in the social acceptability of smoking over the past 20 years. If socially-oriented extraverts are reinforced for smoking by their peers less often than in the past, this would reduce the degree of association between extraversion and smoking.

In the research reported in this chapter, pleasure-seeking, curiosity, and peer group pressures seem to underlie the reasons rated by students as most important in influencing them to take up smoking, whereas rebellious nonconforming behavior and media advertisements were rated as having relatively little influence. "Because I enjoy it" was consistently ranked by both sexes as the most influential reason for continuing to smoke. Regular smokers rated tension reduction and pleasurable stimulation as more important than occasional and ex-smokers. In contrast, ex-smokers of both sexes rated peer group influences and media advertisements as having greater influence on their continuing to smoke than current smokers. Thus, ex-smokers are more like occasional smokers than regular smokers, and regular smokers and ex-smokers differ markedly in their reasons for smoking, which appears to reflect important differences in their personality characteristics.

Five smoking factors were identified in the questionnaire studies of smoker motivation: Negative Affect Control, Restful and Relaxing Situations, Intellectual Stimulation/Curiosity, Automatic/Habitual Smoking, and Social Attractiveness/Sensory Stimulation. These factors were almost identical for men and women and similar to the smoking motivation factors identified in previous research. Among the five factors, internal states and motivational processes appear to have a stronger and more direct influence on smoking behavior than situations or personality traits. The urge to smoke seems to be stimulated most strongly by internal emotional states of anxiety and anger, which jointly define the Negative Affect Control factor, and smoking appears to have an ameliorative effect on these unpleasant negative affects.

References

Armitage, A.K., Hall, G.N. & Sellers, C.M. 1969. Effects of nicotine on electrocortical activity and acetylcholine release from the cat cerebral cortex. *British Journal of Pharmacology* 35, 152–160.

Banks, M.H., Bewley, B.R., Bland, J.M., Dean, J.R. & Pollard, V. 1978. Long term study of smoking by secondary school children. *Archives of Disease in Childhood* 53, 12–19.

Best, J.A. & Hakstian, A.R. 1978. A situation-specific model for smoking behavior. *Addictive Behaviors* 3, 79–92.

Borland, B.L. & Rudolph, J.P. 1975. Relative effects of low socio-economic status, parental smoking and poor scholastic performance on smoking among high school students. *Social Science and Medicine* 9, 27–30.

Brackenridge, C.J. & Bloch, S. 1972. Smoking in medical students. *Journal of Psychosomatic Research* 16, 35–40.

Cherry, N. & Kiernan, K.E. 1976. Personality scores and smoking behavior: A longitudinal study. *British Journal of Preventive and Social Medicine* 30, 123–131.

Cherry, N. & Kiernan, K.E. 1978. A longitudinal study of smoking and personality. In R.E. Thornton (ed.), *Smoking behavior: Physiological and psychological influences*. New York: Churchill Livingston.

Clausen, J.A. 1968. Adolescent antecedents of cigarette smoking: Data from the Oakland Growth Study. *Social Science and Medicine* 1, 357–382.

Coan, R.W. 1973. Personality variables associated with cigarette smoking. *Journal of Personality and Social Psychology* 26, 86–104.

Costa, P.T. & McCrae, R.R. 1981. Stress, smoking motives, and psychological well-being: The illusory benefits of smoking. *Advances in Behavior Research and Therapy* 3, 125–150.

Costa, P.T., McCrae, R.R. & Bosse, R. 1980. Smoking motive factors: A review and replication. *The International Journal of the Addictions* 15, 537–549.

Evans, R.I. 1976. Smoking in children: Developing a social-psychological strategy of deterrence. *Journal of Preventive Medicine* 5, 122–127.

Evans, R.I., Henderson, A.H., Hill, P.C. & Raines, B.E. 1979. Current psychological, social, and educational programs in control and prevention of smoking: A critical methodological review. *Atherosclerosis Reviews* 6, 203–245.

Eysenck, H.J. 1952. *The scientific study of personality*. London: Routledge and Kegan Paul.

Eysenck, H.J. 1958. A short questionnaire for the measurement of two dimensions of personality. *Journal of Applied Psychology* 42, 1–12.

Eysenck, H.J. 1959. *The manual of the Maudsley Personality Inventory*. London: University of London Press.

Eysenck, H.J. 1965. *Smoking, health and personality*. New York: Basic Books.

Eysenck, H.J. 1967. *The biological basis of personality*. Springfield, IL: Charles C. Thomas.

Eysenck, H.J. 1973. Personality and the maintenance of the smoking habit. In W.L. Dunn (ed.), *Smoking behavior: Motives and incentives*. Washington, D.C.: Winston/Wiley.

Eysenck, H.J. 1980. *The causes and effects of smoking*. London: Temple Smith.

Eysenck, H.J. (ed.). 1981. *A model for personality*. New York: Springer.

Eysenck, H.J. 1983. A note on "Smoking, personality and reasons for smoking." *Psychological Medicine* 13, 447–448.

Eysenck, H.J. & Eysenck, S.B.G. 1964. *The manual of the Eysenck Personality Inventory*. University of London Press: London.

Eysenck, H.J. & Eysenck, S.B.G. 1968. A factorial study of psychoticism as a dimension of personality. *Multivariate Behavioral Research Special Issue,* 15–32.

Eysenck, H.J. & Eysenck, S.B.G. 1975. *Manual of the Eysenck Personality Questionnaire.* London: Hodder and Stoughton.

Frith, C.D. 1971. Smoking behavior and its relation to smokers' immediate experience. *British Journal of Social and Clinical Psychology* 10, 73–78.

Gupta, A.K., Sethi, B.B. & Gupta, S.C. 1976. EPI and 16PF observations in smokers. *Indian Journal of Psychiatry* 18, 252–259.

Horn, D., Courts, F.A., Taylor, R.M. & Solomon, E.S. 1959. Cigarette smoking among high school students. *American Journal of Public Health* 49, 1497–1511.

Horn, D.H. & Waingrow, S. 1966. Some dimensions of a model from smoking behavior change. *American Journal of Public Health* 56, 21–26.

Houston, J.P. & Schneider, N.G. 1973. Further evidence on smoking and anxiety. *Psychological Reports* 32, 322.

Ikard, F.F., Green, D. & Horn, D. 1969. A scale to differentiate between types of smoking as related to the management of affect. *International Journal of Addictions* 4, 649–659.

Ikard, F.F. & Tomkins, S. 1973. The experience of affect as a determinant of smoking behavior: A series of validity studies. *Journal of Abnormal Psychology* 81, 172–181.

Jacobs, M.A. & Spilken, A.Z. 1971. Personality patterns associated with smoking in adolescents. *Journal of Consulting and Clinical Psychology* 37, 428–432.

Jamison, R.N. 1978. *Personality, antisocial behavior and risk perception in adolescents.* Master's thesis, University of London.

Jamison, R.N. 1979. Cigarette smoking and personality in male and female adolescents. *Psychological Reports* 44, 842.

Laoye, J.A., Creswell, W.H. & Stone, D.B. 1972. A cohort study of 1205 secondary school smokers. *Journal of School Health* 42, 47–52.

Leventhal, H. & Avis, N. 1976. Pleasure, addiction, and habit: Factors in verbal report or factors in smoking behavior? *Journal of Abnormal Psychology* 85, 478–488.

Leventhal, H. & Cleary, P.D. 1980. The smoking problem: A review of the research, theory, and research policies in behavioral risk modification. *Psychological Bulletin* 88, 370–405.

Matarazzo, J.D. & Matarazzo, R.G. 1965. Smoking. In D.L. Sills et al. (eds.), *International Encyclopedia of the Social Sciences.* New York: MacMillan.

Matarazzo, J.D. & Saslow, G. 1960. Psychological and related characteristics of smokers and nonsmokers. *Psychological Bulletin* 57, 493–513.

McKennell, A.C. 1970. Smoking motivation factors. *British Journal of Social and Clinical Psychology* 9, 8–22.

McManus, I.C. & Weeks, S.J. 1982. Smoking, personality and reasons for smoking. *Psychological Medicine* 12, 349–356.

Merki, E.J., Creswell, W.H., Stone, D.B., Huffman, W. & Newman, M.S. 1970. The effects of two educational and message themes on rural youth smoking behavior. *Journal of School Health* 38, 448–454.

National Institute of Education. 1979. *Teenage smoking: Immediate and long term patterns.* Washington, D.C.: U.S. Government Printing Office.

National Clearing House for Smoking and Health Publications. 1966. *Adult use of tobacco.* Washington, D.C.: Public Health Service, U.S. Department of Health, Education and Welfare.

Palmer, A.B. 1970. Some variables contributing to the onset of cigarette smoking among junior high school students. *Social Science and Medicine* 4, 359–366.

Powell, G.E. 1977. Psychoticism and social deviancy in children. *Advances in Behavior Research and Therapy* 1, 27–56.

Powell, G.E., Stewart, R.A. & Grylls, D.G. 1979. The personality of young smokers. *British Journal of Addiction* 74, 311–315.

Rae, G. 1975. Extraversion, neuroticism and cigarette smoking. *British Journal of Social and Clinical Psychology* 14, 429–430.

Russell, M.A.H. 1971a. Cigarette dependence: I. Nature and classification. *British Medical Journal* 2, 330–331.

Russell, M.A.H. 1971b. Cigarette smoking: Natural history of a dependence disorder. *British Journal of Medical Psychology* 44, 1–16.

Russell, M.A.H., Peto, J. & Patel, U.A. 1974. The classification of smoking by factorial structure of motives. *Journal of the Royal Statistical Society* 137, 313–346.

Salber, E.J. & MacMahon, B. 1961. Cigarette smoking among high school students related to social class and parental smoking habits *American Journal of Public Health* 51, 1780–1789.

Schneider, N.G. & Houston, J.P. 1970. Smoking and anxiety. *Psychological Reports* 26, 941–942.

Seltzer, C. & Oechsli, F. 1985. Psychosocial characteristics of adolescent smokers before they started smoking: Evidence of self-selection. A prospective study. *Journal of Chronic Diseases* 38, 17–26.

Smith, G.M. 1970. Personality and smoking: A review of the empirical literature. In W.A. Hunt (ed.), *Learning mechanisms and smoking.* Chicago: Aldine.

Spielberger, C.D. 1979. *Preliminary manual for the State-Trait Personality Inventory.* Tampa, FL: Human Resources Institute, University of South Florida.

Spielberger, C.D. & Jacobs, G.A. 1982. Personality and smoking behavior. *Journal of Personality Assessment* 46, 396–403.

Spielberger, C.D., Jacobs, G.A., Crane, R.S. & Russell, S.F. 1983. On the relation between family smoking habits and the smoking behavior of college students. *International Review of Applied Psychology* 32, 53–69.

Stanaway, R.G. & Watson, D.W. 1980. Smoking motivation: A factor-analytical study. *Personality and Individual Differences* 1, 371–380.

Stanaway, R.G. & Watson, D.W. 1981. Smoking and personality: A factorial study. *British Journal of Clinical Psychology* 20, 213–214.

Taylor, J.A. 1953. A personality scale of manifest anxiety. *Journal of Abnormal and Social Psychology* 9, 369–376.

Thomas, C.B. 1978. Personality differences between smokers and nonsmokers. *Maryland State Medical Journal* 27, 63–66.

Tomkins, S.S. 1966. Psychological model of smoking behavior. *American Journal of Public Health* 56 (supplement), 17–20.

Tomkins, S.S. 1968. A modified model of smoking behavior. In E.F. Borgatta & R. Evans (eds.), *Smoking, health and behavior.* Chicago: Aldine.

Wohlford, P. 1970. Initiation of cigarette smoking: Is it related to parental smoking behavior? *Journal of Consulting and Clinical Psychology* 34, 148–151.

Wohlford, P. & Giammona, S.T. 1969. Personality and social variables related to the initiation of smoking cigarettes. *Journal of School Health* 34, 544–552.

Yarushalmy, J. 1969. The California Child Health and Development Studies. Study design and some illustrative findings on congenital heart disease. Congenital malformations. *Excerpta Medica International Congress: Series No. 204.*

Zuckerman, M., Kolin, E.K., Price, L. & Zoob, I. 1964. Development of a sensative-seeking scale. *Journal of Consulting and Clinical Psychology* 28, 477–482.

Appendix 3A
Smoking Motivation
Questionnaire (SMQ)

I. *Instructions*: Please read each statement and indicate to what extent it is *true for you* by circling the number for the category that *describes you best*.

	Not At All	A Little	Quite A Bit	Very Much So
1. Handling a cigarette is part of the enjoyment of smoking it	1	2	3	4
2. I want to smoke most when I am comfortable and relaxed	1	2	3	4
3. Part of the enjoyment of smoking is watching the smoke as I blow it out	1	2	3	4
4. When I have run out of cigarettes I find it almost unbearable until I can get them	1	2	3	4
5. I smoke automatically without even being aware of it	1	2	3	4
6. I feel I look more mature and sophisticated when smoking	1	2	3	4
7. Part of the enjoyment of smoking comes from the steps I take to light up	1	2	3	4
8. I light up a cigarette without realizing I still have one burning in the ashtray	1	2	3	4
9. I like a cigarette best when I am having a quiet rest	1	2	3	4
10. While smoking I feel more confident with other people	1	2	3	4
11. I get a real gnawing hunger to smoke when I haven't smoked for awhile	1	2	3	4

	Not At All	A Little	Quite A Bit	Very Much So
12. I find myself smoking without remembering lighting up	1	2	3	4
13. I smoke more when I am rushed and have lots to do	1	2	3	4
14. I feel more attractive to the opposite sex when smoking	1	2	3	4

II. *Instructions*: Please read each statement and rate the typical strength of your urge to smoke in each situation by circling the number for the category that *describes you best*.

	Very Little Urge	Mild Urge	Mod-erate Urge	Very Great Urge
15. When you are having a quiet evening with friends	1	2	3	4
16. When you are worrying over possible misfortunes	1	2	3	4
17. When you are tense	1	2	3	4
18. When you feel curious	1	2	3	4
19. When you feel interested	1	2	3	4
20. When you feel angry	1	2	3	4
21. When you are having a restful evening alone reading a magazine	1	2	3	4
22. When you are furious	1	2	3	4
23. When you are inquisitive	1	2	3	4
24. When you feel like yelling at somebody	1	2	3	4
25. When you are relaxed	1	2	3	4
26. When you feel nervous	1	2	3	4
27. When you are in a questioning mood	1	2	3	4
28. When you feel like breaking things	1	2	3	4
29. When you are jittery	1	2	3	4
30. When you are chatting with friends during a coffee or tea break	1	2	3	4
31. When you feel mentally active ...	1	2	3	4
32. When you feel irritated	1	2	3	4
33. When you are worried	1	2	3	4
34. When you feel like hitting someone	1	2	3	4
35. When you feel eager	1	2	3	4
36. When you feel like swearing	1	2	3	4

Part III
Smoking: The Context of Society

4
Health Issues Relating to "Passive" Smoking

Domingo M. Aviado, M.D.

The exposure of nonsmokers to tobacco smoke in a confined space is known as "passive" smoking. In recent years, a considerable number of articles have appeared on the claimed health effects of passive smoking or, more precisely, exposure to environmental tobacco smoke. The medical complaints of certain persons exposed to environmental tobacco smoke are varied. These include nasal stuffiness, watering of the eyes, headache, difficulty in breathing, and chest pain. More recently, complaints of exposed nonsmokers include the fear of developing coronary heart disease, pulmonary disease, or lung cancer. Some reports suggest that expectant mothers' exposure to environmental tobacco smoke during pregnancy will potentially reduce the birth weight of their newborns and may even influence growth and development of their infants. Still other reports suggest that there is a relationship between smoking at home and both lung cancer in nonsmoking spouses and respiratory disease in children.

As the literature review contained in this paper indicates, however, there is no substantial evidence to support the view that exposure to environmental tobacco smoke presents a significant health hazard to nonsmokers. It is conceivable that a large portion of nonsmokers' reaction is due to the publicity surrounding the reported hazards of environmental tobacco smoke. Nonsmokers are bombarded with information about the "evils of tobacco smoke" from newspaper columnists such as Ann Landers and voluntary health associations such as the American Lung Association.

Recent developments have seriously brought into question the validity of certain claims about environmental tobacco smoke. One investigator warned in the 1970s that anginal patients can suffer harm during exposure to tobacco smoke, but the Environmental Protection Agency (EPA) has decided recently that these data were not sufficient to form the basis of its standards. A group of investigators who had contributed observations in 1981 which supported the possibility that environmental tobacco smoke can cause lung cancer subsequently questioned the significance of their own results (see subsection on Lung Cancer). Other investigators interested in the possible health consequences of environmental tobacco smoke met during a 1983 Workshop and concluded that "available evidence demonstrates that the possible effects of environmental tobacco smoke are not significant in comparison to the multitude of health problems facing society on a global scale."[1]

This chapter is intended primarily to review these recent developments, although attention will also be paid to the earlier studies that are responsible for the current fears and misconceptions about passive smoking. After reviewing the historical background on the subject, the chapter proceeds to a discussion of the possible influences of passive smoking on the circulatory and respiratory systems. Psychosocial aspects are discussed in the conclusion, since this subject may help explain the difficulties that sometimes arise between smokers and nonsmokers in society.

Environmental Tobacco Smoke Symptom-Complex

The reaction of many nonsmokers to environmental tobacco smoke has been described in anecdotal reports for the past 400 years (see section on Psychosocial Aspects). During the first half of this century, medical journals published isolated case reports of patients who claimed to be "allergic" to tobacco smoke. The medical profession regarded these reports as examples of hypersensitivity to extrinsic factors, including household dust, pollen, food constituents and occupational dust. The subjective symptoms of patients could not be measured other than by expressing their occurrence when the patient was exposed to tobacco smoke. Furthermore, the presence of tobacco smoke as the initiating factor of the reaction could not be proven. The sciences of inhalational toxicology and occupational medicine were in their infancy and the medical profession soon became aware that, although many substances are dangerous when inhaled, there is a threshold level that separated a safe or tolerable level from an unsafe or intolerable level.

The first measurements of environmental tobacco smoke in public places were reported by German investigators in 1957. Harmsen and Effenberger[2] measured the carbon monoxide levels inside trains in Germany. The levels were as high as 40 parts per million (ppm), and these were attributed to tobacco smoke. Since the tolerable level of 50 ppm carbon monoxide was being questioned at that time in Germany, some of their colleagues directed their efforts to measuring carbon monoxide in extreme situations, such as registering carbon monoxide levels of 90 ppm inside nonventilated automobiles with engines running, while stationary in a garage. Srch[3] attributed the intra-vehicular level to cigarette smoking of occupants, without considering the contribution of carbon monoxide from vehicular emissions. This observation, although isolated in occurrence and not subsequently confirmed inside vehicles or in public meeting rooms, triggered the concept that environmental tobacco smoke can produce unsafe levels of carbon monoxide. Although subsequent measurements indicated that carbon monoxide levels associated with cigarette smoke meet the applicable air quality standards, the extremely high levels reported under unrealistic circumstances in the 1950s and 1960s continue to be cited as evidence that environmental tobacco smoke is a health hazard. It should be recognized that these early measurements of carbon monoxide were based on the assumption that this product of combustion originates almost entirely from tobacco smoke. The publication of the initial results prompted other investigations that appeared to confirm, rather than to test, this hypothesis.

Although the claimed health effects of environmental tobacco smoke were first reported twenty-five years ago, there is no recognition in medical journals and text books of a specific disease associated with the exposure. The medical literature includes attributions to specific inhalants, such as polymer fume fever, asbestosis, byssinosis, and carbon disulfide angina. Several publications mention meat wrappers' asthma, pigeon breeders' disease, and marihuana fetal abnormalities as medical consequences attributed to substance inhalation. These diseases were recognized during the same period that symptoms associated with passive smoking were being reported. Yet to date, there is no valid documentation that patients suffer a specific adverse health effect due exclusively to exposure to environmental tobacco smoke. Medical publications of case reports have been anecdotal in nature. It has not yet been possible to definitely attribute a particular disease condition to passive smoking. Most claims of symptomatic effects of environmental tobacco smoke are based on epidemiologic studies that have been characterized in the 1984 Surgeon General's Report as "crude indices in general [that] ignore time spent with the smoker and the environmental factors known to influence smoke concentration."[4]

Although early attempts were made to estimate levels of environmental tobacco smoke exposure, subjective complaints reported by nonsmokers could not be expressed in quantitative terms for statistical analysis. Some investigators resorted to testing airway function and cardiac performance. However, the predictive nature of these tests in terms of indicating organic disease has been questioned. Since nonsmokers continue to complain of symptoms relating to the circulatory and respiratory systems which they attribute to environmental tobacco smoke, and since such subjective complaints are reported in the medical literature, the term "symptom-complex" is used in this chapter to describe such complaints. A causal relationship between these subjective complaints and environmental tobacco smoke has not been proven. The etiology of circulatory and respiratory diseases is complex and includes so many risk factors that it is difficult, if not impossible, to prove that a patient's symptoms originate from passive smoking.

The environmental tobacco smoke symptom-complex refers to the subjective complaints and medical fears of nonsmokers. Publications in medical journals relating to the symptom-complex have been used to support arguments for restriction of smoking in public places. The relevant publications are discussed below, with special emphasis on recent developments that may relegate the symptom-complex to perpetual uncertainty of etiology.

Circulatory System

As stated above, the suspicion that environmental tobacco smoke is hazardous to human health was initiated in 1957 by German investigators who reported unusually high levels of carbon monoxide in poorly ventilated vehicles in which cigarette smoking was either permitted[2] or experimentally conducted.[3] The two initial reports were followed by conferences and workshops which raised questions on several issues:

How much carbon monoxide can be generated by an ignited cigarette?

What is the concentration of carbon monoxide in a public place where smoking is permitted?

Are the prevailing levels of carbon monoxide from environmental tobacco smoke hazardous to human health?

In the midst of the health discussion regarding carbon monoxide and environmental tobacco smoke, occupational and ambient air quality standards were also being discussed. This led to a considerable amount of confusion. Animal experiments and epidemiologic studies were performed in an apparent effort to tighten air quality standards in the workplace and outdoor or ambient atmosphere. Results from these studies were being applied to the question of environmental tobacco smoke in public places, without recognizing the differences in duration of exposure: a few hours exposure in restaurants, theaters, and aircraft contrast sharply with eight hours in workplaces or with twenty-four hours daily for the ambient atmosphere. Clinical studies by a cardiologist showing that carboxyhemoglobin levels seen in the general population could influence anginal patients encouraged anti-smoking groups to recommend prohibition of tobacco use in public places. The same investigator also conducted studies on anginal patients exposed to vehicular pollutants, low levels of carbon monoxide, and environmental tobacco smoke. His unconfirmed results are discussed below (Coronary Heart Disease).

The use of carbon monoxide as an index of environmental tobacco smoke exposure has been reviewed recently by the author. He concluded that carbon monoxide is an acceptable index of environmental tobacco smoke exposure with four limitations. *First,* although carbon monoxide levels in an occupied space have been reported to be directly proportionate to the amount of tobacco product or cigarettes lighted, a mathematical relationship cannot be established because the amount of sidestream smoke is variable and unpredictable. Therefore, it follows that estimations of sidestream/mainstream ratio and cigarette equivalents to characterize environmental tobacco smoke exposure have limited use. *Second,* indoor carbon monoxide levels represent not only environmental tobacco smoke exposure, but also a variable fraction derived from indoor sources such as gas stoves and fuel combustion burners and outdoor sources such as vehicular and industrial emissions. *Third,* indoor levels of carbon monoxide measured when tobacco smoking takes place are within the applicable indoor air quality standards. The few reported instances that exceeded the standards reflect unrealistic situations in poorly ventilated enclosures with extremely high levels of cigarette smoke and indoor pollutants. *Fourth,* carbon monoxide absorption by the blood in the form of carboxyhemoglobin cannot entirely be predicted from fluctuating carbon monoxide levels in an occupied space. Further improvements in instrumentation are needed to permit continuous monitoring of carbon monoxide and carboxyhemoglobin levels. Since carbon monoxide measurements initiated the medical reports on the circulatory aspects of the symptom-complex, the early controversies and their recent resolution are recounted below.

Controlled Environmental Tobacco Smoke Exposure Experiments

Following the initial reports of carbon monoxide levels in trains and other vehicles, it became obvious to several investigators that any contribution from tobacco smoke could properly be evaluated by controlling air ventilation. Experiments were conducted in chambers and nonventilated rooms to determine the levels of carbon monoxide generated from cigarettes in the most extreme situation of insufficient air movement. The reported experiments have a number of common features: a known number of cigarettes were lighted, sidestream smoke was generated either by human or machine smoking, and human exposure levels were measured by using a carbon monoxide analysis inside the chamber or occupied room, a carboxyhemoglobin analysis of blood of exposed subjects, or by using both methods. The results summarized in table 4–1 are arranged according to increasing carbon monoxide levels in the exposure chamber: a room with windows and doors sealed or a poorly ventilated room.

Carbon Monoxide Levels. Of the 14 major published studies on carbon monoxide and environmental tobacco smoke,[5-18] 2 did not include measurements of carbon monoxide levels and 12 studies showed mean carbon monoxide

Table 4–1
Carbon Monoxide and Blood Carboxyhemoglobin Levels of Subjects in Controlled Chambers or Nonventilated Rooms

Study, Year	Number of Cigarettes/ hour/10 M^3	Carbon Monoxide (ppm)	Blood Carboxy- hemoglobin Control	Percent Change
Anderson & Dalhamn, 1973[5]	3.1	4.5	0.3	0
Seppänen, 1977[6]	3.8	16	1.6	+ 0.4
Grimmer et al., 1977[7]	1.4	17	—	—
Lawther & Commins, 1970[8]	4.7	20	—	—
Hugod et al., 1978[9]	2.5	20	0.7	+ 0.9
Hurschman et al., 1978[10]	—	20	—	+ 1.4
Polak, 1977[11]	6.7	23	2.0	+ 0.3
Pimm et al., 1978[12]	2.4	24	0.5	+ 0.3
Weber, 1976[13]	6.7	24	—	—
Klosterkötter & Gono, 1976[14]	13.3	28	—	+ 1.4
Harke, 1970[15]	3.1	30	—	—
Russell et al., 1973[16]	18.6	38	1.6	+ 1.0
Harmsen & Effenberger, 1957[2]	3.2	80	—	—
Dahms et al., 1981[17]	—	—	0.72	+ 0.4
Aronow, 1978[18]	2.4	—	5.92	+ 3.9

Source: Adapted from Rylander et al., 1984.[1]

Note: For complete bibliographic information on these studies, see endnote indicated.

levels that ranged from 4.5 to 38 ppm. A higher level of carbon monoxide was reported in one study that has not been replicated. Harmsen and Effenberger reported an extremely high level of 80 ppm in a room with exposure of 3.2 cigarettes/hour/10 M^3. This is not an excessive exposure since, as table 4–1 indicates, other investigators have more than doubled this amount of cigarette combustion—for example, Polak to 6.7 and Russell et al. to 18.6—with resulting carbon monoxide values of 23 and 38 ppm, respectively. Since the concentration of 80 ppm was reported in 1957 prior to the introduction of modern techniques, it is reasonable to exclude this study and generalize that in all controlled experiments with combustion of up to 18.6 cigarettes/hour/10 M^3, the maximal carbon monoxide level is about 40 ppm.

Carboxyhemoglobin Levels. The bodily uptake of environmental carbon monoxide was estimated by measuring carboxyhemoglobin levels in blood samples collected from nonsmoking subjects in 10 of the 15 experiments (see table 4–1). In spite of the wide range of carbon monoxide levels in the enclosed space (4.5 to 38 ppm), the exposure-related change in carboxyhemoglobin levels ranged from + 0.3 to + 1.4 percent. There is no direct relationship between both measurements because the duration of exposure (one to three hours) may not be sufficient to achieve pulmonary (alveolar air to capillary blood) equilibrium. Furthermore, the subjects did not have comparable preexposure levels; these ranged from 0.3 to 2.0 percent carboxyhemoglobin.

The two studies that report carboxyhemoglobin levels in compromised individuals involved patients suffering from either bronchial asthma[17] or angina pectoric[18]. The shortcomings of these studies are not limited to the investigators' failure to report exposure levels of carbon monoxide, a routine measurement for almost all investigations in this field. There are other criticisms relating to the significance of the tests in evaluating possible health hazards of environmental tobacco smoke exposure. Although there was a reported reduction in ventilatory measurements for chronic asthmatics, the effect was reversible and none of the patients actually developed an acute asthmatic attack. For the anginal patients, the earlier appearance of subjective chest pain during bicycle ergometry after exposure to cigarette smoke, compared to that prior to exposure, does not necessarily indicate a worsening of the disease process. That the carboxyhemoglobin levels of anginal patients reportedly rose by 3.9 percent was due either to the fact that (a) levels were not accurately measured, or (b) after two hours of exposure, the carbon monoxide level in the exposure room exceeded 38 ppm, which is the highest level reported in a study with combined measurements of exposure and uptake levels.[19] (See also the section on coronary heart disease for further discussion.)

Environmental Tobacco Smoke Exposure Indoors

Several publications on the use of carbon monoxide as an index of environmental tobacco smoke exposure relate to realistic situations indoors, such as offices, conference rooms, restaurants, bars, taverns, nightclubs, public enclosures, and workplaces (see table 4–2).

Offices and Conference Rooms. There are nine publications on carbon monoxide levels in offices and conference rooms.[19-27] One of the early studies on carbon monoxide levels associated with environmental tobacco smoke was conducted by Harke,[20] who examined two air conditioned buildings. Although smoking was permitted, values exceeding 5 ppm carbon monoxide were rarely observed. There were brief periods when carbon monoxide levels reached from 7 to 15.6 ppm and, in one case, the high levels were attributed to a lighted cigarette held close to the inlet of the measuring device. Since outdoor carbon monoxide levels were not measured, it is not possible to determine if indoor levels of less than 5 ppm were due entirely to cigarette smoke. A significant portion of indoor carbon monoxide is most likely derived from outdoor sources, according to other investigators who reported that indoor carbon monoxide levels are either equal to or slightly greater, but rarely lower, than outdoor levels. The peak indoor to outdoor differential reported can be as much as 10 ppm whereas the minimal differential can be as low as 0.2 ppm. The peak carbon monoxide levels reported inside offices and conference rooms are 20 ppm and 32.5 ppm (see table 4–2). These levels are not

Table 4–2
Indoor and Outdoor Carbon Monoxide Levels: Mean or Range

Investigators, Year	Carbon Monoxide (ppm)	
	Indoors	*Outdoors*
Offices and Conference Rooms		
Portheine, 1971[19]	5 to 24	—
Harke, 1974[20]	< 5 to 9	—
Chappell & Parker, 1975[21]	2.5 ± 1.0	2.5 ± 1.0
Beaucent et al., 1982[22]	10 to 20	8 to 10
Stehlik et al., 1982[23]	8 to 16	—
Coburn et al., 1965[24]	4 to 9	—
Dublin, 1972[25]	32.5	—
Slavin & Hertz, 1975[26]	8 to 10	1 to 2
Allen & Wadden, 1982[27]	4.5 to 13.0	4.2 to 13.3
Restaurants, Bars, Taverns, and Nightclubs		
Chappell & Parker, 1977[28]	4.0 ± 2.5	2.5 ± 1.5
	13.0 ± 7.0	2.5 ± 1.5
Sebben et al., 1977[29]	13.4	9.3
Seppänen & Uusitalo, 1977[30]	2.5 to 15	—
Badre et al., 1978[31]	2 to 23	0 to 15
Fischer et al., 1978[32]	0.5 to 5.1	0.4 to 4.8
Cuddebach et al., 1976[33]	3 to 30	—
Equitable Environmental Health Inc., 1976[34]	6.2	6.45
Nylander, 1978[35]	2 to 20	1 to 15
Workplaces		
Szadkowski et al., 1976[37]	2.78 ± 1.42	1.07 to 6.33
Weber & Fischer, 1980[38]	2.8	1.7
Fischer & Weber, 1980[39]		
Weber, 1981[40]		
White & Froeb, 1980[41]		
(smoking permitted)	3.1 to 29.4	—
(smoking not permitted)	3.2 to 13.8	—

Source: Adapted from Rylander et al., 1984.[1]
Note: For complete bibliographic information on these studies, see the endnote indicated.

exclusively generated by cigarette smoking since outdoor sources were not excluded.

Restaurants, Bars, Taverns, and Nightclubs. The carbon monoxide levels in eating, drinking and entertainment establishments[29-35] are generally less than 10 ppm with two reported exceptions: levels of 15 ppm[30] and 30 ppm.[33] There is no evidence that tobacco smoke is the sole contributor to carbon monoxide levels inside restaurants since other sources (cooking stoves, table-side food preparations) were not excluded. The indoor levels of carbon monoxide can originate in part from outdoors and the highest indoor-to-outdoor differential reported was 3.0 ppm.[32] The publications listed in table 4–2 refer not only to restaurants but also to supermarkets and hospital lobbies[29] and hotel lobbies and bus terminals.[35] One study relating to restaurants and theater lobbies[36] has been excluded from table 4–2 because carbon monoxide levels were stated as less than 10 ppm, rather than in specific numbers.

Occupational Exposure. The most recent studies on indoor exposure to tobacco smoke relate to workers without any description of the nature of the occupation. The studies characterize them as "office workers" with a subgroup of "passive smokers" working in the same room as smokers.[37] In spite of the 8-hour exposure in the offices with smokers, the nonsmokers had a reduction in mean carboxyhemoglobin levels from 0.82 percent to 0.63 percent. In another study of workers, there was a reported indoor-to-outdoor differential of 1.1 ppm carbon monoxide.[38] Although carboxyhemoglobin levels were not measured, it is safe to assume that there would not have been any significant change. In one study, some of the workers carried a portable carbon monoxide analyzer, and hourly mean differences from 0.1 to 4.7 ppm were reported between areas where smokers were allowed and areas where smoking was not permitted.[41] In all of these reports, since the work environment is not specified, the contribution of carbon monoxide sources other than cigarette smoke has to be considered. Machinery and production of industrial chemicals can contribute to measured carbon monoxide levels.

Coronary Heart Disease

Evidence that carbon monoxide could be detected in tobacco smoke, although in concentrations lower than vehicular emissions, resulted in claims that non-smokers are likely to suffer from carbon monoxide poisoning, with such symptoms as headache, disturbed mental activity, and loss of consciousness. However, it should be noted that the toxic effects do not appear until carboxyhemoglobin levels exceed 20 percent, and the controlled exposure studies showed that carboxyhemoglobin levels rarely exceeded 5 percent. Even so, Aronow and his colleagues questioned the safety of low levels of carbon monoxide in patients with coronary heart disease. They reasoned that since carbon monoxide reduces the oxygen-carrying capacity of the blood, even physiologically acceptable levels would be harmful to the heart. In a series of publications, Aronow et al. reported that anginal patients showed a reduction in tolerance to bicycling after exposure to freeway driving,[42] inhalation of carbon monoxide and air mixtures,[43,44] or exposure to environmental tobacco smoke.[18] The carboxyhemoglobin levels (as low as 1.8 to 3.0 percent) that provoked the shortening of exercise tolerance were below the accepted norm of 5 percent, based on the subjective description by the patient that chest pain had started.

The observations of Aronow et al., although unconfirmed by other investigators, were used by several groups to support the contention that passive smoking is dangerous to patients with coronary heart disease. The results were considered by federal agencies in the determination of occupational and ambient air quality standards. After a decade of debate on the validity of the publications by Aronow et al. on anginal patients, it was reported that the senior investigator had submitted falsified data to the Food and Drug Administration.[45] Furthermore, the results of a low level carbon monoxide project funded by the EPA were regarded as unacceptable for purposes of setting air quality standards.[46] The Aronow results relating to passive smoking can presently be set aside and viewed as unreliable. The 1983 Surgeon General's Report in fact does not mention the questionable studies, although they were discussed in the earlier Surgeon General Reports of 1972, 1979, 1980, and 1981.

Possible Health Effects of Carbon Monoxide Levels during Environmental Tobacco Smoke Exposure

The preceding review of reported levels of carbon monoxide associated with environmental tobacco smoke exposure necessitates a brief discussion on potential health hazards. The reported indoor carbon monoxide levels can be regarded as an index of environmental tobacco smoke exposure provided that other sources of carbon monoxide are recognized, measured and deducted to arrive at a net value for environmental tobacco smoke. It should be noted that although most reported indoor levels are less than 10 ppm, there are isolated instances exceeding 10 ppm and reaching as high as 38 ppm. These include situations of excessive smoking in poorly ventilated rooms and those in which the outdoor sources of carbon monoxide contributed to the measured carbon monoxide indoors.

Almost all published levels of carbon monoxide derived from environmental tobacco smoke are below the outdoor primary standards of 35 ppm for 1 hour and 9 ppm for 8 hours under realistic conditions. There is, therefore, little reason to suspect any adverse effect on human health from reported indoor carbon monoxide levels normally associated with environmental tobacco smoke. The general population should be protected from exposure to carbon monoxide that would result in carboxyhemoglobin levels of 5 percent or more. This recommendation is based on the review of the results from animal experiments and human observations on carbon monoxide exposure.[47-50] Moreover, a conclusion by a group of scientists at a recent international workshop, was that carbon monoxide exposure from environmental tobacco smoke "is not important from a health point of view."[1]

Respiratory System

The concept that the environmental tobacco smoke symptom-complex may involve the respiratory system did *not* originate from measurements of tobacco smoke constituents, as was the case for claims of carbon monoxide influence on the circulatory system. A review of the early reports indicates that the genesis of the respiratory aspects of the symptom-complex were based on the following assumption: since cigarette smokers are reported to have a higher incidence of respiratory diseases than nonsmokers, then nonsmokers exposed frequently to environmental tobacco smoke would also suffer from similar diseases. Studies were conducted to compare two subject groups: those exposed to environmental tobacco smoke and those from a "smoke-free" environment. The initial reports on vasomotor rhinitis and childhood respiratory diseases appeared in the 1960s, adult respiratory diseases in the 1970s, and lung cancer in the 1980s. The initial reports suggested that the group exposed to a "smoke-free" environment had lower incidences of vasomotor rhinitis, childhood respiratory diseases, adult respiratory diseases, and lung cancer. The shortcomings of the initial reports were subsequently defined and are discussed below.

Vasomotor Rhinitis

Individuals suffering from vasomotor rhinitis have varied histories of hypersensitivity to household dust, pollen and other environmental substances. In 1968, Speer reported on a group of 441 nonsmokers who complained of sneezing, running nose and other respiratory symptoms when exposed to environmental tobacco smoke.[51] He concluded that the reactions were irritative in nature, rather than a form of allergy involving the formation of immune antibodies. This initial publication was followed by a report that exposure to tobacco smoke caused a specific form of allergic rhinitis. Zussman selected at random a group of atopic patients, including some who complained that they could not tolerate exposure to tobacco smoke.[52] Most of these patients showed a positive skin reaction to tobacco extract. The author's interpretation of his results was that nonsmokers exposed to tobacco smoke develop allergy of the nose and allergic conjunctivitis and even serious cardiopulmonary diseases.

However, studies with tobacco leaf extract do not resolve the issue of whether cigarette smoke or any of its constituents is allergenic to humans.[53] One study conducted by Becker et al. reported the isolation of a large molecular weight molecule from tobacco smoke, which the authors claimed to be an allergen.[54] These authors later speculated that this molecule might be responsible for some health problems in both smokers and nonsmokers, ranging from cardiovascular disease and emphysema to sudden death.[55,56] However,

Stedman in reporting upon his own research and review of the scientific literature, stated that these authors used a separation technique which introduced a "substantial artifact" into the materials later used in biological tests.[57]

Accordingly, it is not surprising that McDougall and Gleich failed to find any evidence of tobacco smoke allergens in their tests of 30 subjects who reportedly experienced allergic type symptoms on exposure to tobacco or tobacco smoke.[58] Salvaggio and his colleagues have found no allergic response even in people who claim to be "smoke sensitive" and they suggest that the reported sensitivity may be due to psychological factors.[59] In his analysis of the tobacco allergy question, Taylor cautioned that "there is no proof that specific sensitization to tobacco smoke exists."[53] The above statement remains valid to the present day despite the fact that tobacco smoke continues to be described as an allergen of the mucosal membrane. The confusion has been compounded by the use of the term "allergen" to include direct irritation that is not strictly mediated by haptene-antibody reaction. (See also subsection on adult respiratory diseases.)

Childhood Respiratory Diseases

The 1984 Surgeon General's Report contains a review of the conflicting results on the possible influence of environmental tobacco smoke on children.[4] Although a small change in pulmonary function has been reported, the Report states that "the significance of this finding to the future development of lung disease is unknown." The circumstances surrounding the health issues relating to children exposed to environmental tobacco smoke are discussed below.

Questionnaire Surveys Suggesting Association. Parental smoking was first reported to be associated with childhood respiratory problems in a 1967 publication by Cameron, who conducted a telephone survey of 1,000 residences in Denver.[60] Since that time a number of studies have been conducted and their results relied upon for the frequent claims made today by some that parental smoking causes respiratory illness in children. Those making this claim point primarily to various questionnaire-type studies[61-63] and an occasional clinical study[64] which report that children of smoking parents have an increased incidence of respiratory symptoms or illness compared to children of nonsmoking parents. These studies are cited as proof of the causal theory, even though some of these studies also report a correlation between respiratory illness in the parents and similar such illnesses in the children, irrespective of smoking. For example, Weiss et al. reported an association between respiratory symptoms in children and parental smoking, but also reported a strong association between the occurrence rate of these symptoms in children and the prevalence of such symptoms in the parents.[65] Thus, the question recognized as early as 1976 by Colley et al.[66,67]—whether the children's respiratory illness is caused by cross-infection from the parents or by a genetic predisposition to such illnesses in both parents and children—is ignored by those who argue that environmental tobacco smoke is the established cause of the reported respiratory illness in these children.

Reliance on questionnaires for information about respiratory symptoms also casts doubt on the reported findings, and the investigators themselves have recognized this weakness. Ekwo et al., in reporting a significant association between parental smoking and respiratory symptoms in children, noted that "slight changes in the phrasing of questions can result in substantial differences in the type of responses one obtains."[62] Similarly, Schenker et al. observed that there was a significant difference in reported respiratory symptoms depending upon which parent completed the questionnaire.[63]

Epidemiologic Studies Questioning Causal Association. Studies claiming that parental smoking causes respiratory symptoms of illness in children tend to ignore studies from the United States,[68] Britain,[69] Europe,[70–72] and Africa,[73] which do not find such associations. A study by Schilling et al. reported that parental smoking does *not* cause respiratory illness in children or other family members.[74] These researchers studied respiratory symptoms, diseases and lung function in 376 families with 816 children in three New England communities and found no significant relation between parental smoking and respiratory symptoms or lung function in their children. They concluded that exposure to low levels of smoke produced by cigarette smokers does not result in chronic respiratory symptoms or loss of lung function among children or adults. Another clinical study by Kerrebijn et al. on chronic nonspecific respiratory diseases in children found that "smoking and nonsmoking parents have about the same proportion of children with respiratory symptoms. The number of cigarettes smoked by the parents has no influence on respiratory symptoms in their children . . ."[75] A study of 1331 children living in two different residential areas, one industrial and the other rural, reported a significant association between respiratory disease and residence in the industrial area and a strong association between the mothers' respiratory symptoms and the children's respiratory symptoms, but no association between maternal smoking habits and children's respiratory symptoms.[72]

In an editorial comment upon Colley's study[61] reporting an association between parental smoking and respiratory illness during the first year of life, Schilling and Bouhuys pointed to the lack of "firm evidence" that such illnesses "have a serious and lasting effect as no excess of respiratory illness or diminished lung function has been found in the older children of smoking parents." Their view is supported by Dodge and his colleagues, who in recent studies have reported an association between parental smoking and respiratory symptoms in children, but no association between parental smoking and children's lung function or lung growth.[76,77]

Confounding Risk Factors. The 1979 Surgeon General's Report suggested that other factors such as parental neglect may also play a role.[78] The Report recommended that "prospective studies are needed to define the relationship between parental smoking and the prevalence of respiratory illness and symptoms and pulmonary function status in children. Care should be taken to consider such confounding factors as socio-economic status and the smoking habits of the children." The Surgeon General's recommendation is supported by a later clinical study by Speizer et al. which found that children from households with gas stoves had a greater history of respiratory illness and decreased lung function compared to children from households with electric stoves;[79] these findings, further, were independent of both social class and parental smoking. In addition, the proceedings of the 1981 International Symposium on Indoor Air Pollution, Health and Energy Conservation[80] included presentations that help account for the alleged association between parental smoking and respiratory diseases in children. The reports cite cooking stove emissions, urea insulation, and other residential and outdoor pollutants as individually causative of respiratory disease in children. In addition, nitrogen dioxide levels emitted from stoves exceed those contributed by environmental tobacco smoke, and so need to be considered as well.[81]

The importance of controlling for confounding factors when studying the possible respiratory effects of environmental tobacco smoke was stressed in the report of the recent workshop on environmental tobacco smoke sponsored by the Division of Lung Diseases of the National Heart, Lung, and Blood Institute, which emphasized that any study which ignores them will be seriously flawed:

> The difficulty of controlling for potentially confounding variables was recognized. Such variables include: (1) unvented combustion products from different kinds of stoves used for both heating and cooking, e.g., gas, wood and kerosene, (2) other indoor pollutants such as formaldehyde and respirable particulate matter, (3) indoor pollutants of organic origin such as pollens, molds, mites, other allergens and infectious organisms, (4) characteristics of indoor environments such as temperature, humidity, and frequency of air exchanges, (5) socio-economic status, culture (ethnic), and such factors as crowding, number of siblings, household conditions, child care, reporting biases, etc., (6) demographic and medical characteristics of the study population such as age, sex, marital status, the presence of underlying respiratory conditions, atopy, infections, disability and/or co-morbidity, (7) parental symptoms such as productive cough which will affect reporting, (8) maternal smoking during pregnancy, (9) annoyance responses and other psychological or social responses to tobacco smoking in a nonsmoker. Extensive as this list of

potentially compounding variables may be, the importance of taking them into consideration in the study design and analysis cannot be overemphasized.[82]

Changes in Lung Function in Children. One recent study was reported by Tager et al., who observed a cohort of children for seven years in East Boston.[83] They reported that children of mothers who do not smoke have a larger annual increase in lung function compared to children of smoking mothers. It is noteworthy, however, that the reported differences in pulmonary function decreased over time. The investigators conceded that the reported decrements, if they really exist, have not been demonstrated to be clinically significant.

The results of Lebowitz et al. presented during the International Symposium showed that household aggregation or crowding affect the relationship of children's pulmonary function to parental smoking.[84] In fact, in Lebowitz' study, when household aggregation was taken into account, there was no relationship of children's pulmonary function values to parental smoking. It should be noted that the East Boston study omitted the variable considered by Lebowitz et al. Moreover, there were no measurements of primary air pollutants in the East Boston study, as reported by Lebowitz et al., nor does it appear that Tager et al. controlled for recognized confounding factors that may have resulted in lowered lung function measurements, such as colds, flu, allergies, bronchitis and other respiratory diseases. That maternal or parental smoking does not influence the incidence of respiratory symptoms or decrease lung function in children has also been demonstrated by investigators in Connecticut,[85] Sweden,[75] France,[86] Italy,[87] Canada,[88] and elsewhere.[67-73] Further study of the etiology of childhood respiratory symptoms and disease are indicated in light of the inconsistent and contradictory findings reported thus far.

Adult Respiratory Diseases

The first publications on adult pulmonary disease and environmental tobacco smoke appeared in the *Proceedings* of the Third World Conference on Smoking and Health, held in New York City in 1975. For the first time in this quadrennial meeting, the subject of passive smoking was discussed. In his presentation entitled "The Effects of Tobacco Smoke on Nonsmoking Cardiopulmonary Public," Tate cited one patient who "became so tight with wheezing and asthma that she could not get her breath" while working in an area where smoking was permitted.[89] The author pointed out that:

> For approximately 34 million people (AMA estimate) with sensitivity of the respiratory tract, i.e., nose and lung, the problem is real and extremely serious. Nine million people in this nation have asthma. Some 7 million days are lost from work and 6.5 million days from school; $125 million are spent on hospital and medical care for asthma and hay fever, and 2500 die each year.

These people must use public buildings, public conveyances and the recreational areas of this nation. They have a right to breath clean air and enjoy as much health as is possible. Tobacco smoke is one of the most serious problems they face in daily life.[89]

Except for this one patient, Tate did not cite any medical data to support his conclusion. He made the assumption that all asthmatics are allergic to exposure to tobacco smoke, which is contrary to the fact that tobacco smoke has not been proven to be an allergen. Tate cited the effects of statements regarding carbon monoxide made at the conference by an investigator whose results on passive smoking have been questioned by two U.S. governmental agencies.[90] It should also be noted that carbon monoxide is not known to be an allergen and is not a risk factor for chronic obstructive lung disease.

At the time the above-mentioned 1975 Conference was held, the available information showed that the concentrations of tobacco smoke in public places were unlikely to influence the respiratory system (see Carbon Monoxide section). The levels of benzo(a)pyrene in restaurants were below the accepted work environmental standards,[91] and this product of combustion may have originated from the kitchen. In addition, studies in experimental chambers with cigarette smoke reported levels of acrolein and acetaldehyde which were lower than the threshold limit values in the workplace.[92] Hinds and First calculated that the levels of nicotine in public places are so low that a nonsmoker is typically exposed to levels of tobacco smoke that are equivalent to a small fraction of a filtered cigarette per hour.[93]

More recently, Muramatsu et al. reported on a compact and lightweight device for personal monitoring of nicotine from environmental tobacco smoke.[94] Multiple samples were taken from each of the following places: offices, laboratories, conference rooms, hotel lobbies, tea rooms, restaurants, cafeterias, bus and railway waiting rooms, automobiles, trains, domestic airplanes, hospital lobbies, and dwellings. Atmospheric nicotine levels, calculated from 91 air samples collected over periods of up to 8 hours, ranged from 0.9 to 40 ug/hour. Thus, a nonsmoker exposed to environmental tobacco smoke under these conditions might inhale nicotine equivalent to smoking 0.001 to 0.044 ordinary cigarettes per hour. These estimates are about the same as those reported by Hinds and First.[93]

At the Fourth World Conference on Tobacco and Health held in Stockholm in 1979, Stahle and Tibbling revived the earlier controversy that tobacco smoke is an allergen and is likely to provoke acute bronchial asthma.[95] Although their Swedish asthmatic patients were reported to have a positive response to skin testing with tobacco leaf extract, it had been recognized that the extract is not the same as tobacco smoke, and this has been reiterated by a Swedish colleague.[96] In the United States, Dahms et al. reported in 1981 on the respiratory discomfort in asthmatics who were exposed to high levels of tobacco smoke in an experimental chamber.[17] The concentration of tobacco smoke was not realistic and there were no control nonasthmatics, a short-coming recognized by the investigators. The difficulties in breathing reported by the subjects might have been a psychological response, since several other studies failed to show that one- or two-hour exposures to tobacco smoke provoked an acute asthmatic attack.[97-99]

Another relationship between environmental tobacco smoke exposure and the respiratory system was suggested in 1980 by White and Froeb.[41] They reported that nonsmokers exposed to tobacco smoke in the workplace for 20 years or longer had lower values of small-airways function. The relevance of that finding was discussed by Lenfant and Liu in an editorial: "There is no proof as yet that the reported reduction in airways function has any physiological or clinical consequences."[100] This author expressed his disbelief that White and Froeb were able to identify a truly representative group of subjects who have work histories of 20 or more years without exposure to tobacco smoke.[101] Freedman contended that the study was "flawed" because White and Froeb used a lung function analyzer which fails to meet the technical recommendations of the American Thoracic Society.[102] Furthermore, Lebowitz criticized the study as improperly designed since thousands of subjects were excluded by White and Froeb without adequate explanation.[103]

This author has been witnessing the increasing severity and frequency of respiratory complaints comprising the environmental tobacco smoke symptom-complex. Nevertheless, it is his conclusion that a causal relationship has not been established,[104] an opinion that is shared by other investigators.[105-107]

Lung Cancer

The most publicized claim that has arisen in recent years is that environmental tobacco smoke causes lung cancer in nonsmokers. That allegation gained widespread public attention in early 1981 as a result of two studies: the Hirayama study from Japan,[108] and the Trichopoulos study from Greece.[109] Both studies reported a statistically significant increased risk of lung cancer in nonsmoking wives of smokers compared to nonsmoking wives of nonsmokers. The two studies, however, were criticized by the scientific community. Criticisms of the Japanese study were summarized at the 1983 Workshop on Atmospheric Tobacco Smoke: "[The Hirayama] study has been criticized in detail by other researchers from the point of view of questionnaire reliability, absence of histological diagnosis, statistical treatment, grouping of smoking habits among husbands and confounding factors such as air pollution from heating and/or cooking."[1]

There are additional serious methodological weaknesses in this study as well. For example, Hirayama controlled for the age of the husbands rather than the wives, who were the subject of the study. This presents a significant problem in Japan, where there is often a substantial disparity in the ages of husbands and wives. The author also failed to control for socioeconomic status.

Hirayama recently published an update of his study covering the period from 1971 through 1981.[110] Since the reported findings are substantially similar to those he published in 1981,[108] the criticisms of his initial publication on methodological and other grounds are equally applicable to this update. An update of the Trichopoulos study has also been published recently, in which the authors state that their reported findings are substantially the same as those contained in their 1981 paper. In their most recent publication, Trichopoulos et al. acknowledge that their study "was criticized (by ourselves and others) because of the small number of subjects, because several tumors lacked histological confirmation, and because controls and cases were from different hospitals." Having concluded their study, the authors concede that "doubt must remain about the histological evidence and hospital differences . . ."[111] One commentator, having reviewed the 1983 Trichopoulos paper, has found it even less convincing than the 1981 report.[112]

Given the methodological and analytical problems of the Hirayama and Trichopoulos studies, nothing can be determined from them without a well-designed replication study. Yet a seven-year prospective study such as Hirayama's would be impractical and expensive to replicate in Asian countries possessing different cultural and ethnic backgrounds, as well as differing disease patterns. Chinese women have a high incidence of lung cancer that is unrelated to smoking habits.[113,114] It would take another seven years to determine if Japanese women, like Chinese women, have a high susceptibility to lung cancer. For Americans, the results of the American Cancer Society study are more relevant. Garfinkel reported in 1981 that nonsmoking wives of smoking husbands have no statistically significant increased risk of lung cancer compared to wives of nonsmoking husbands.[115] This prospective study of several thousand subjects from several states is more significant than the case-control study by Correa et al. involving 30 lung cancer patients (8 males and 22 females) from Louisiana, which reported that nonsmokers married to heavy smokers doubled their risk of lung cancer.[116]

The most recent study dealing with environmental tobacco smoke and lung cancer was published in March, 1984 by Kabat and Wynder.[117] They reported negative results from a case-control study of nonsmoking patients with histologically confirmed diagnoses of primary lung cancer. Their analysis of tobacco smoke exposure involved a subset of the study population, 25 men and 53 women. The reported findings were negative: there were no differences between women patients and controls with regard to exposure to environmental tobacco smoke in the home or at work; and there were no differences between patients and controls in the proportion of smoking husbands among the women who were asked about their husband's smoking habits.

Similarly, there was no difference between the male patients and controls on the basis of exposure to environmental tobacco smoke in the home, and the number of male patients and controls who reported that their wives smoked was identical. Kabat and Wynder did report that more male patients than controls were exposed to tobacco smoke at work and claimed that "the difference is just statistically significant," but conceded that it "could be due to information bias."

In discussing their data, Kabat and Wynder acknowledge that "the plausibility of a role of [environmental tobacco smoke] in lung cancer can be questioned on several grounds."[117] The investigators also suggest that there are other possible explanations for the occurrence of lung cancer in nonsmokers, including exposure to ionizing radiation in the course of radiation treatment, healed tuberculosis scars, estrogen (since nonsmoker lung cancer is more common in women than it is in men), and carcinogens of nutritional origin.

In view of the above, it is not surprising that the 1983 Workshop arrived at the following conclusion: "An overall evaluation based upon available scientific data leads to the conclusion that an increased risk [of lung cancer] for nonsmokers from [environmental tobacco smoke] exposure has not been established."[1]

Despite this reasoned conclusion, an analysis has recently been published in which the results of Hirayama et al. have been combined with those relating to Seventh Day Adventists in an attempt to construct a numerical estimate of lung cancer among nonsmokers attributable to environmental tobacco smoke.[118] It is the opinion of this reviewer that results on Oriental women cannot be applied to Americans. This opinion has been strengthened by a recent study by Koo et al., who report that, contrary to Hirayama's report regarding Japanese women, exposure to environmental tobacco smoke does not influence the lung cancer incidence in Chinese women.[119] If the results of Hirayama et al. cannot apply to other Oriental women, it is even more unlikely that they can have any relevance to American or European women.

Psychosocial Basis for Environmental Tobacco Smoke Symptom-Complex

The preceding sections discuss the evidence that argues against a conclusion that tobacco smoke exposure causes diseases of the circulatory and respiratory systems. Briefly, the evidence consists of the following:

1. that carbon monoxide levels related to tobacco smoke in experimental conditions and in public places are acceptable since the levels are below the acceptable air quality standards for workplaces;

2. that exposure to substandard levels of carbon monoxide as an alleged health hazard to anginal patients was originally based on studies of an investigator whose experimental work has now been seriously questioned by at least two U.S. governmental health agencies;

3. that tobacco smoke has not been shown to be allergenic in humans;

4. that studies on children's respiratory diseases are inconclusive on the effect of maternal or paternal smoking;

5. that there are no adequate data on which to conclude that environmental tobacco smoke causes adult respiratory diseases, including bronchial asthma; and

6. that lung cancer in nonsmoking women has not been shown to be causally related to the smoking habits of their husbands.

Since there is no significant evidence that tobacco smoke exposure causes disease, the subjective complaints of nonsmokers who claim they are "sensitive" must be examined. The remaining possibility is that the environmental tobacco smoke symptom-complex is caused by a host of psychosocial factors discussed in the following paragraphs.

Social Acceptability of Tobacco Smokers

From the historical standpoint, the most widely quoted and most powerful opponent of smoking was King James I of England. In his Counter-Blaste to Tobacco published in 1604, he described the averseness of tobacco smoke to many nonsmokers. In the United States, the opposition to smoking started in the late 1800s by Lucy Page Gaston. A national campaign against cigarettes, but not cigars, pipe and chewing tobacco, began essentially the same way as the antialcohol movement of the same era. In recent years, the antismokers' movement to ban the use of tobacco joined forces with "nonsmokers' rights" groups to prohibit tobacco use in public places. With varying degrees of success, the two groups have used the reports of alleged health effects in their attempt to have public smoking regulated. In some quarters, cigarette smoking has become an unacceptable social practice (see note 120 for historical background on antismoking and nonsmokers' rights movement).

Psychological Effects of Environmental Tobacco Smoke Exposure

It has been suggested that many of the symptoms reported by nonsmokers may be due to psychological factors. This theory is supported by the study of Rummel et al. in which college students were first asked about their attitudes concerning tobacco smoke.[121] Subsequent exposure to tobacco smoke revealed that the students who "disliked" smoke had higher pulse rates after exposure than those who were "indifferent." It has also been suggested that the cardiac response "may come from anger rather than from the smoke itself."[122] Feinhandler suggested that upheavals in society and overcrowding have made people supersensitive to other people's behavior.[123] Since cigarette smoke is highly visible, some individuals have reacted against the smoker as "a ready target for general frustrations, anxiety and discontent."

Stone and his collaborators reported the results of psychological testing on nonsmoking volunteers who rated their annoyance to tobacco smoke while assigned to perform mental exercises.[124] They concluded that when nonsmokers were highly motivated by the assigned mental exercise, those exposed to environmental tobacco smoke reported significantly less annoyance than those not exposed. Shor and his collaborators questioned college students about their attitudes toward tobacco smoke and their reported symptoms from exposure.[125-127] There was a high correlation between the students' aversion attitudes and the incidence of symptoms.

Although the cardiovascular and bronchopulmonary systems are regulated by the involuntary or autonomic nervous system, there are several examples supporting the general proposition that emotionalism can influence both systems: anger causing tachycardia and high blood pressure, exercise and emotional upheaval triggering an acute asthmatic attack, and voluntary slowing of the heart rate by yogi practitioners. The nervous mechanisms that form a connecting link between the autonomic and voluntary nervous systems were reviewed by this author in 1955.[128]

There have been no psychological measurements conducted on patients manifesting symptoms which they claim result from environmental tobacco smoke. Such a study should focus on the behavioral differences of individuals who are susceptible to cardiopulmonary diseases and other conditions in contrast to those who are not. In other words, the study would help to determine if the behavioral profile is the cause of the symptom-complex and, in addition, whether the behavior has been affected by widely publicized health claims about nonsmokers exposed to environmental tobacco smoke.

The focus on psychological factors and their possible role in causing the environmental tobacco smoke symptom-complex does not ignore the fact that tobacco smoke under certain extreme conditions can be offensive to the normal nonsmoker. Many individuals have probably been in situations where it would have been better that no one smoked, such as poorly ventilated areas, warm rooms, elevators, and crowded buses. Nonsmoker annoyance under these conditions does not mean that anyone is being harmed; rather, it means that tobacco smoke can be a nuisance. Even given that such conditions sometimes exist, it still is difficult to explain scientifically why certain nonsmokers react so violently to the presence of tobacco smoke. Such individuals are not necessarily more sensitive than other nonsmokers; they simply are more prone than are others to the environmental tobacco smoke symptom-complex. The reason or reasons behind this difference will be elucidated by additional research, experimentation and investigation.

Concluding Remarks

The above review of the literature indicates that there is no substantial evidence to support the view that exposure to environmental tobacco smoke presents a significant health hazard to the nonsmoker. After a detailed consideration of the circulatory and respiratory disease studies, it is concluded that there are inadequate data on which to base a conclusion that exposure to environmental tobacco smoke causes such diseases. Consequently, in this author's view, nonsmokers should not use claims of adverse health effects as justification for not interacting with smokers in society.

Notes

1. R. Rylander, Y. Peterson, and M.C. Snella, "ETS—Environmental Tobacco Smoke." Report from a workshop on effects and exposure levels, *Eur. J. Resp. Dis.* (1984) 65 Suppl. 133:1–152. The report includes: D.M. Aviado, Carbon monoxide as an index of environmental tobacco smoke exposure, pp. 47–60.

2. H. Harmsen and E. Effenberger, "Tabakrauch in Verkehrsmitteln, Wohn- und Arbeitsräumen," *Arch. Hyg. Bakteriol.* (1957) 141:383–400.

3. M. Srch, "Ueber die Bedetung des Kohlenoxyds beim Zigarettenrauchen in Personenkraftwageninnern," *Dtsch. Gesamte Gerichtl.* (1967) 60:80–89.

4. U.S. Public Health Service, *Smoking and Health: Chronic Obstructive Lung Disease. A Report of the Surgeon General,* 1984.

5. G. Anderson and T. Dalhamn, "Health Risks Due to Passive Smoking," (Swedish) *Läkartidningen* (1973) 70:2833–2836.

6. A. Seppänen, "Smoking in Closed Space and Its Effect on Carboxyhemoglobin Saturation of Smoking and Nonsmoking Subjects," *Ann. Clin. Res.* (1977) 9: 281–283.

7. G. Grimmer, H. Böhnke, and H.P. Harke, "Zum Problem des Passivrauchens: Aufnahme von polycyclischen aromatischen Kohlenwasserstoffen durch Einatnen von zigarettenrauchhaltiger Luft," *Int. Arch. Occup. Environ. Health* (1977) 40:39–99.

8. J. Lawther and B.T. Commins, "Cigarette Smoking and Exposure to Carbon Monoxide," *Ann. N.Y. Acad. Sci.* (1970) 174:135–147.

9. C. Hugod, L. Hawkins, and P. Astrup, "Exposure of Passive Smokers to Tobacco Smoke Constituents," *Int. Arch. Occup. Environ. Health* (1978) 32:21–29.

10. L.G. Hurshman, B.S. Grown, and R.S. Guyton, "The Implications of Side-stream Cigarette Smoke for Cardiovascular Health," *J. Environ. Health* (1978) 41: 145–149.

11. E. Polak, "Le papier á Cigarette. Son Rôle dans la Pollution des lieux Habités. Tabagisme Passif: Notion Nouvelle Précisée," *Bruxelles Med.* (1977) 57:335–340.

12. P. Pimm, R.J. Shephard, and F. Silverman, "Physiological effects of acute passive exposure to cigarette smoke," *Arch. Environ. Health* (1978) 33:201–213.

13. A. Weber, "Luftverunreinigung und Belästigung durch Zigarettenrauch: Zum Problem des Passivrauchens," *Z. Krankenpfl.* (1976) 69:115–118.

14. W. Klosterkötter and E. Gono, "Zum Problem des Passivrauchens." *Zbl. Bakt. Hyg.* (1976) 162:51–69.

15. H.P. Harke, "The problem of 'passive smoking,' " *Münch. Med. Wochenschr.* (1970) 51:2328–2334.

16. M.A.H. Russell, P.V. Cole, and E. Brown, "Passive smoking: absorption by nonsmokers of carbon monoxide from room-air polluted by tobacco smoke," *Postgrad. Med. J.* (1973) 49:688–692.

17. T.E. Dahms, J.F. Bolin, and R.G. Slavin, "Passive smoking: effects on bronchial asthma," *Chest* (1981) 80:530–534.

18. W.S. Aronow, "Effect of passive smoking on angina pectoris," *N. Engl. J. Med.* (1978) 299:21–24.

19. F. Portheine, "Zum Problem des Passivrauchens," *Münch. Med. Wochenschr.* (1971) 18:707.

20. H.P. Harke, "The Problem of Passive Smoking. I. The Influence of Smoking on the CO Concentrations in Office Rooms," *Int. Arch. Arbeitsmed.* (1974) 33:199–204.

21. S. Chappell and R. Parker, *A Study of Carbon Monoxide Levels in Enclosed Public Spaces.* (Fredericton, New Brunswick, Canada: New Brunswick Council on Smoking and Health, 1975), 16 pages.

22. C. Beaucent, A. Grünewald, F. Brygoo-Butor, A. Cornet, and M. Philbert, "Pollution Atmosphérique dans un Bureau de Centre de Paris Ventilé par Gaines d'Aeration. Risques pour la Santé du Personnel," *Arch. Mal. Prof. Med. Trav. Secur. Soc.* (1982) 43:126–128.

23. G. Stehlik, O. Richter, and H. Altmann, "Concentration of Dimethylnitrosamine in the Air of Smoke-Filled Rooms," *Ecotoxicol. Environ. Safety* (1982) 6:495–500.

24. R.F. Coburn, R.E. Forster and P.B. Kane, "Considerations of the Physiological Variables that Determine the Blood Carboxyhemoglobin Concentration in Man," *J. Clin. Invest.* (1965) 44:1899.

25. W.B. Dublin, "Secondary Smoking. A Problem that Deserves Attention," *Pathologist* (1972) 26:244–245.

26. R.G. Slavin and M. Hertz, "Indoor Air Pollution," paper presented at the American Academy of Allergy Annual Meeting, San Diego, CA, 1975, 4 pages.

27. R.J. Allen and R.A. Wadden, "Analysis of Indoor Concentrations of Carbon Monoxide and Ozone in an Urban Hospital," *Environ. Res.* (1982) 27:137–149

28. S.B. Chappell and R.J. Parker, "Smoking and Carbon Monoxide Levels in Enclosed Public Places in New Brunswick," *Can. J. Publ. Health* (1977) 68:159–161.

29. J. Sebben, P. Pimm, and R.J. Shephard, "Cigarette Smoke in Enclosed Public Facilities." *Arch. Environ. Health* (1977) 32:53–58.

160 • *Smoking and Society*

30. A. Seppänen and A.J. Uusitalo, "Carboxyhemoglobin Saturation in Relation to Smoking and Various Occupational Conditions," *Ann. Clin. Res.* (1977): 9:261–268.

31. R. Badre, R. Guillerm, N. Abran, M. Bourdin, and C. Dumas, "Atmospheric Pollution by Smoking," (French) *Ann. Pharm. Fr.* (1978) 36:443–452.

32. T. Fischer, A. Weber, and E. Grandjean, "Luftverunreinigung durch Tabakrauch in Gaststätten," *Int. Arch. Occup. Environ. Health* (1978) 41:267–280.

33. J.E. Cuddebach, J.R. Donovan, and W.R. Burg, "Occupational Aspects of Passive Smoking," *Am. Ind. Hyg. Assoc. J.* (1976) 263–267.

34. Equitable Environmental Health Inc., *The Results of a Preliminary Survey of Indoor/Outdoor Carbon Monoxide Levels in Washington, DC*, 1976, 10 pages.

35. L.R. Nylander, Statement to the Chicago City Council, 1978, 5 pages.

36. J. Perry, "A Study on the Hazard of Tobacco Smoke Air Pollution to Health," *BR Columbia Med. J.* (1973) 15:304–305.

37. D. Szadkowski, H.P. Harke, and J. Angerer, "Body Burden of Carbon Monoxide from Passive Smoking in Offices," (German) *Inn. Med.* (1976) 3:310–313.

38. A. Weber and T. Fischer, "Passive Smoking at Work," *Int. Arch. Occup. Environ. Health* (1980) 47:209–221.

39. T. Fischer and A. Weber, "Passivrauchen am Arbeitsplatz," *Soz. Präventivmed.* (1980) 25:401–406.

40. A. Weber, "Passivrauchen Luftqualität, Massnahmen," *Soz. Präventivmed.* (1981) 26:182–183.

41. J.R. White and H.F. Froeb, "Small-Airways Dysfunction in Nonsmokers Chronically Exposed to Tobacco Smoke," *N. Engl. J. Med.* (1980) 302:720–723.

42. W.S. Aronow, C.H. Harris, M.W. Isbell, S.N. Rokaw, and B. Imparato, "Effect of Low-Level Carbon Monoxide Exposure on Onset and Duration of Angina Pectoris. A Study in Ten Patients with Ischemic Heart Disease." *Ann. Intern. Med.* (1973) 79:46.

43. W.S. Aronow and M.W. Isbell, "Carbon Monoxide Effect on Exercise-Induced Angina Pectoris," *Ann. Intern. Med.* (1973) 79:392–395.

44. W.S. Aronow, "Aggravation of Angina Pectoris by Two Percent Carboxyhemoglobin," *Am. Heart. J.* (1981) 101:154–157.

45. M. Mintz, "FDA, Citing Phony Evidence, Bans Drug Test by Researcher," *The Washington Post*, March 23, 1983.

46. C. Peterson, "EPA Probe Criticizes a Study Used in Air Quality Standard," *The Washington Post*, June 7, 1983.

47. U.S. Environmental Protection Agency, *Air Quality Criteria for Carbon Monoxide*. EPA, 1979, 600/8-79-022.

48. R. Rylander and J. Vesterlund, "Carbon Monoxide Criteria," *Scand J. Work Environ Health* (1981) 7 Suppl. 1, 39 pages.

49. World Health Organization and the UN Environmental Programme, *Environmental Health Criteria 13. Carbon Monoxide* 1979, 125 pages.

50. National Academy of Sciences—National Research Council, *Medical and Biologic Effects of Environmental Pollutants. Carbon Monoxide*. Washington, 1979, 239 pages.

51. F. Speer, "Tobacco and the Nonsmoker," *Arch. Environ. Health* (1968) 16:443–446.

52. B.M. Zussman, "Tobacco Sensitivity in the Allergic Patient," *Ann. Allergy* (1970) 28:371–377.

53. G. Taylor, "Tobacco Smoke Allergy—Does it Exist?" *Scand. J. Resp. Dis.* (1974) Suppl. 91:50–55.

54. C.G. Becker, T. Dubin, and H.P. Wiedemann, "Hypersensitivity to Tobacco Antigen." *Proc. Nat. Acad. Sci. USA* (1976) 73:1712–1716.

55. C.G. Becker and T. Dubin, "Activation of Factor XII by Tobacco Glyco-protein," *J. Exp. Med.* (1977) 146:457–467.

56. C.G. Becker and T. Dubin, "Tobacco Allergy and Cardiovascular Disease," *Cardiovasc. Med.* (1978) 3:851–854.

57. R.L. Stedman, Statement Submitted to a Hearing before the Subcommittee on Tobacco of the Committee on Agriculture, House of Representatives, 95th Congress, Second Session, September 7, 1978. Serial No. 95-000. Effect of Smoking on Nonsmokers, pp. 82–85.

58. J.C. McDougall and G.J. Gleich, "Tobacco Allergy—Fact or Fancy?" *J. Allergy Clin. Immunol.* (1976) 57:237.

59. S.B. Lehrer, J. Taylor, and J.E. Salvaggio, "Immunological Evaluation of Tobacco Smoke 'Sensitive' Individuals by Skin, Radioallergosorbent and Precipitin Tests," *J. Allergy Clin. Immunol* (1981) 67·49

60. P. Cameron, "The Presence of Pets and Smoking as Correlates of Perceived Disease," *J. Allergy* (1967) 40:12–15.

61. J.R.T. Colley, "Respiratory Symptoms in Children and Parental Smoking and Phlegm Production," *Brit. Med. J.* (1974) 2:201–204.

62. E.E. Ekwo, M.M. Weinberger, P.A. Lachenbruch, and W.H. Huntley, "Relationship of Parental Smoking and Gas Cooking to Respiratory Disease in Children," *Chest* (1983) 84:662–668.

63. M.B. Schenker, J.M. Samet, and F.E. Speizer, "Risk Factors for Childhood Respiratory Disease," *Am. Rev. Resp. Dis.* (1983) 128:1038–1043.

64. D.G. Sims, M.A.P.S. Downham, P.S. Gardner, J.K.G. Webb, and D. Weightman, "Study of 8-year-old Children with a History of Respiratory Syncytial Virus Bronchiolitis in Infancy," *Brit. Med. J.* (1978) 1:11–14.

65. S.T. Weiss, I.B. Tager, F.E. Speizer, and B. Rosner, "Persistent Wheeze: Its Relation to Respiratory Illness, Cigarette Smoking, and Level of Pulmonary Function in a Population Sample of Children," *Am. Rev. Resp. Dis.* (1982) 122:697–707.

66. S.R. Leeder, R. Corkhill, L.M. Irwig, W.W. Holland, and J.R.T. Colley, "Influence of Family Factors in the Incidence of Lower Respiratory Illness during the First Year of Life," *Brit. J. Prev. Soc. Med.* (1976) 30:203–212.

67. S.R. Leeder, J.R.T. Colley, R. Corkhill, and W.W. Holland, "Respiratory Symptom Prevalence in Adults: The Comparative Importance of Smoking and Family Factors," *Am. J. Epidemiol.* (1977) 105:530–533.

68. I.B. Tager, S.T. Weiss, B. Rosner, and F.E. Speizer, "Effect of Parental Cigarette Smoking on the Pulmonary Function of Children," *Am. J. Epidemiol.* (1979) 110:15–26.

69. Y.C. Wang, C.S. Beardsmore, and M. Silverman, "Pulmonary Sequelae of Neonatal Respiratory Distress in Very Low Birth Weight Infants: A Clinical and Physiological Study," *Arch. Dis. Child* (1982) 57:418–424.

70. B. Holma and O. Winding, "Housing, Hygiene, and Health: A Study in Old Residential Areas in Copenhagen," *Arch. Environ. Health* (1977) 32:86–93.

71. A. Mandi, E. Galabmos, G. Galgoczy, M. Szabo, and K. Kollar, "Relationship between Lung Function Values and Air Pollution Data in Budapest School Children," *Pneumonologie* (1974) 150:217–255.

72. E.J. Camacho, P.R. Colomer, and J.L.D. Betoret, "Pulmonary Symptoms and Pulmonary Functional Tests among Children in Relation to the Area of Residence," *Eur. J. Resp. Dis.* (1982) 63:165–166.

73. D. Kossova, M. Xaba, F. Shabalala, F. Shoba, L. Haynes, T. Cocorozis, and J. Morfopoulous, "Smoke-Filled Rooms and Lower Respiratory Disease in Infants," *S. Afr. Med. J.* (1982) 61:621–624.

74. R.S.F. Schilling, A.D. Letai, S.L. Hui, G.J. Beck, J.B. Schoenberg, and A. Bouhuys, "Lung Function, Respiratory Disease and Smoking in Families," *Am. J. Epidemiol.* (1977) 106:274–283.

75. K.F. Kerrebijn, H.C.A. Hoogeveen-Scroot, and M.C. Van De Wal, "Chronic Non-Specific Respiratory Disease in Children: A Five Year Follow-Up Study," *Acta. Paediat. Scand.* (1977) 261:1–49.

76. R. Dodge, "The Effects of Indoor Pollution on Arizona Children," *Arch. Environ. Health* (1982) 37:151–155.

77. R. Dodge, B. Boyer, C. Ellis, and B. Burrows, "The Respiratory Health and Lung Function of Anglo-American Children in a Smelter Town," *Am. Rev. Resp. Dis.* (1983) 127:158–161.

78. U.S. Public Health Service, *Smoking and Health: A Report of the Surgeon General*. Chapter 11: Involuntary Smoking. (Washington, D.C.: U.S. Government Printing Office, 1979), pp. 11–32.

79. F.E. Speizer, G. Ferris, M.M. Bishop, and J. Spengler, "Respiratory Disease Rates and Pulmonary Function in Children Associated with NO_2 Exposure," *Am. Rev. Resp. Dis.* (1980) 121:3–10.

80. J. Spengler, C. Hallowell, D. Moschandreas, and O. Fanger, eds., "Indoor Air Pollution. Proceedings of the International Symposium on Indoor Air Pollution, Health and Energy Conservation, Amherst, MA, October 13–16, 1981." *Environ. Int.* (1982) Special Issue.

81. J.D. Spengler, C.P. Duffy, R. Letz, T.W. Tibbitts, and B.G. Ferris, Jr., "Nitrogen Dioxide Inside and Outside 137 Homes and Implications for Ambient Air Quality Standards and Health Effects Research," *Environ. Sci. Technol.* (1983) 17:164–168.

82. U.S. Public Health Service, *Report of a Workshop on Respiratory Effects of Involuntary Smoke Exposure: Epidemiologic Studies*. U.S. Department of Health and Human Services, 1983.

83. I.B. Tager, S.T. Weiss, A. Munoz, B. Rosnar, and F.E. Speizer, "Longitudinal Study of the Effects of Maternal Smoking on Pulmonary Function in Children," *N. Engl. J. Med.* (1983) 309:699–703.

84. M.D. Lebowitz, D.B. Arnet, and R. Knudson, "The Effect of Passive Smoking on Pulmonary Function in Children," *Environ. Int.* (1982) 8:371–373.

85. R.S.F. Schilling, A.D. Letai, S.L. Hui, G. Beck, J.B. Schoenberg, and A. Bouhuys, "Lung Function, Respiratory Disease and Smoking in Families," *Am. J. Epidemiol.* (1977) 106:274–283.

86. S.L. Fortmarker, D. Klein Walker, F.H. Jacobs, and H. Ruch-Ross, "Parental Smoking and the Risk of Childhood Asthma," *Am. J. Publ. Health* (1982) 72:274–278.
87. R. Ronchetti, F. Martinez, S. Cirscione, F. Macri, G.M. Tramutoli, G. Antognoni, G. Ciofetta, and C. Imperato, "Influenza di Fattori Familiari e Ambientali sulla Prevalenza della Sindrome Asmatica e della Sindrome Bronchitica del Bambino," (Studio Epidemiologico su 2500 Scolari Romani), *Riv. Ital. Ped.* (1982) 8:755–765.
88. "Conference Told Smoke Didn't Hurt Children's Lungs," Regina Leader Post, Sept. 27, 1984. (Roland Hosein of the University of Toronto interview).
89. C.F. Tate, *The Effects of Tobacco Smoke on the Nonsmoking Cardio-Pulmonary Public*. Proceedings of the 3rd World Conference on Smoking and Health. DHEW Publication, 1977, NIH 77-1413C:329–335.
90. W.S. Aronow, *Effect of Passive Smoking on the Cardiovascular and Respiratory Systems*. Proceedings of the 3rd World Conference on Smoking and Health. DHEW Publication, 1977, NIH 77-1413C:883–890.
91. V. Galuskinova, "3,4-Benzpyrene Determination in the Smokey Atmosphere of Social Meeting Rooms and Restaurants: A Contribution to the Problem of the Noxiousness of So-Called Passive Smoking," *Neoplasma* (1964) 11:465–468.
92. H.P. Harke, A. Baars, B. Frahm, H. Peters, and G. Schultz, "Zum Problem des Passivrauchens. Abhängigkeit der Konzentration von Rauchinhaltsstoffen in der Luft Verschieden Grober Raume von der Zahl der Verrauchten Zigaretten und der Zeit," *Int. Arch. Occup. Health* (1972) 29:323–339.
93. W.C. Hinds and M.W. First, "Concentrations of Nicotine and Tobacco Smoke in Public Places," *N. Engl. J. Med.* (1975) 292:844–845.
94. M. Muramatsu, S. Umemura, T. Okada, and H. Tomita, "Estimation of Personal Exposure to Tobacco Smoke with a Newly Developed Nicotine Personal Monitor," *Envir. Res.* (1984) 35:218–227.
95. I. Tahle, and L. Tibbling, "Tobaksallergi hos Patienter med Asthma Bronchiale," *Läkatidningen* (1978) 75:1711–1713.
96. G. Bylin, "Tobacco Allergy—Does It Exist?" (Swedish), *Läkartidningen* (1980) 77:1530–1532.
97. R.J. Shephard, *The Risks of Passive Smoking* (London: Croom-Helm, 1982), p. 73.
98. R.J. Shephard, R. Collins, and F. Silverman, "Passive Exposure of Asthmatic Subject to Cigarette Smoke," *Environ. Res.* (1979) 20:392–402.
99. Wiedemann et al., "Lung Function and Airway Reactivity in Stable Asthmatics after Passive Exposure to Cigarette Smoke," *Am. Rev. Respir Dis.* (1983) 127:92.
100. C. Lenfant and B.M. Liu, "(Passive) Smokers versus (Voluntary) Smokers," *N. Engl. J. Med.* (1980) 302:742–743.
101. D.M. Aviado, "Small-Airways Dysfunction in Passive Smokers," *N. Engl. J. Med.* (9180) 303:393.
102. A. Freedman, "Small-Airways Dysfunction in Passive Smokers," *N. Engl. J. Med.* (1980) 303:292.
103. M.D. Lebowitz, cited by L.H. Fountain, "White-Froeb Study Discredited by Scientists," *US Congressional Record*, 97th Congress, 2nd session, December 16, 1982.

104. D.M. Aviado, Statement on Carbon Monoxide Levels in Public Places. In *Effect of Smoking on Nonsmokers*. Hearing before the subcommittee on Tobacco of the Committee on Agriculture, House of Representatives, September 7, 1978. Serial No. 95-000:185–194.

105. H. Schievelbein, "Are There Really Important New Findings about Passive Smoking?" (German) *Oeff. Gesundheitswes.* (1982) 44:454–456.

106. H. Schievelbein, "Lungenkarzinov bei Passivrauchern," *Münch. Med. Wochenschr.* (1981) 123:668–669.

107. T.D. Sterling, H. Dimich, and D.M. Kobayashi, "Indoor Byproduct Levels of Tobacco Smoke: A Critical Review of the Literature," *J. Air. Pollut. Control Assn.* (1982) 32:250–259.

108. T. Hirayama, "Non-Smoking Wives of Heavy Smokers Have a Higher Risk of Lung Cancer: A Study from Japan," *Br. Med. J.* (1981) 282:183–185.

109. D. Trichopoulos, A. Kalandidi, L. Sparros, and B. MacMahon, "Lung Cancer and Passive Smoking," *Int. J. Cancer* (1981) 27:1–4.

110. T. Hirayama, "Passive Smoking and Lung Cancer: Consistency of Association," *Lancet* (1983) 2:1425–1426.

111. D. Trichopoulos, A. Kalandidi, and L. Sparros, "Lung Cancer and Passive Smoking: Conclusion of the Greek Study," *Lancet* (1983) 2:677–678.

112. W.D. Heller, "Lung Cancer and Passive Smoking," *Lancet* (1983) 2:1309.

113. W.C. Chan and S.C. Fung, "Lung Cancer in Non-Smokers in Hong Kong," In E. Grundmann, ed., *Cancer Campaign: Geographical Pathology in Cancer Epidemiology* (Stuttgart: G. Fischer Verlag, 1982), 6:199–202.

114. K. Shanmugaratnam, "Respiratory Tract Cancers in Asian Populations: A Review," *Cancer Bull.* (1975) 13:21–26.

115. L. Garfinkel, "Time Trends in Lung Cancer Mortality among Nonsmokers and a Note on Passive Smoking," *JNCI* (1981) 66:1061–1066.

116. P. Correa, L.W. Pickle, E. Fonthain, Y. Lin, and W. Haenszel, "Passive Smoking and Lung Cancer," *Lancet* (1983) 2:595–597.

117. G.C. Kabat and E.L. Wynder, "Lung Cancer in Nonsmokers," *Cancer* (1984) 53:1214–1221.

118. J.L. Repace and A.H. Lowrey, "An Estimate of Nonsmokers' Lung Cancer Risk from Passive Smoking," cited in *New York Times*, November 3, 1984, pending publication in *Environmental International*.

119. L.C. Koo, J.H.C. Ho, and D. Saw, "Is Passive Smoking an Added Risk Factor for Lung Cancer in Chinese Women?" *J. Exp. Clin. Cancer Res.* (1984) 3:277–233.

120. R.E. Shor, M.B. Hor, and C.B. Williams, "The Distinction Between the Antismoking and Nonsmokers Rights Movement," *J. Psychol.* (1980) 106:129–146.

121. R. Rummel et al., "The Physiological Effects of Inhaling Exhaled Cigarette Smoke in Relation to Attitude of the Nonsmoker," *J. School Health* (1975) 45:524–529.

122. M. Halberstam, "Smoking and the Nonsmoker," *New York Times*, May 12, 1978.

123. S. Feinhandler, Statement, US Congress, House Committee on Agriculture, Subcommittee on Tobacco, "Effects of Smoking on Nonsmokers," Hearing, 95th Congress, 2nd Session, September 7, 1978. Washington: Government Printing Office, 1978, pp. 56–63.

124. J.D. Stone, S.T. Breidenbach, and N.W. Hemistra, "Annoyance Response of Nonsmokers to Cigarette Smoke," *Percept. Mot. Skills* (1979) 49:907–916.

125. R.E. Shor and D.C. Williams, "A Brief Survey of Beliefs about the Effects of Tobacco Smoke Pollution on Intellectual Performance in College Classrooms," *Psychol. Rep.* (1978) 43:1047–1050.

126. R.E. Shor and D.C. Williams, "Reported Physiological and Psychological Symptoms of Tobacco Smoke Pollution in Nonsmoking Students," *Psychol. Rep.* (1979) 101:203–218.

127. R.E. Shor, D.C. Williams, and M.B. Shor, "An Investigation of Reported Symptoms and Attitudes on Tobacco Smoke Pollution as a Function of Expositional Context, Smoking Status, and Gender," *Addict. Behav.* (1981) 6:271–282.

128. D.M. Aviado and C.F. Schmidt, "Reflexes from Stretch Receptors in Blood Vessels, Heart and Lungs," *Physiol. Rev.* (1955) 35:247–300.

5
The Social Role of Smoking

Sherwin J. Feinhandler

Since the reports on smoking of the Royal College of Physicians in 1962 and the U.S. Surgeon General in 1964, a plethora of literature on smoking has been produced. Early studies, largely physiological in focus, were followed by psychological and, later, sociological studies. For the most part the psychological studies focused on individual needs and motivations and on the personality of the smoker; the sociological literature was primarily concerned with demographic characteristics of smokers contrasted with nonsmokers.

In the 1979 Surgeon General's report, tobacco use is analyzed in the context of a medical model (16:10–13), and the studies selected for review are assessed within this framework. The report supported this model by reviewing studies which gave little consideration to the social role of smoking. Although the importance of environmental influences is frequently mentioned (16:13,17; 17:5,21; 19:32), and casual references made to "social," "cultural," "ritual," and "cognitive" factors, the real implications of these influences and factors are seldom pursued in any thorough way (16:14; 17:8). Rather, the norm is a brief statement on the need for a better understanding of these aspects (16:13,17; 17:9,21; 19:35). The dominant view, sometimes expressed and other times implied, is that smoking is a behavior best interpreted with a medical model.

However, some authors have argued that:

> a simple medical model is inadequate to explain smoking attitudes and behavior: normative considerations are probably the crucial factor. [Nuehring and Markle, 1974]

> A medical model would suggest that people smoke cigarettes in order to ingest nicotine. . . . consumption measured in pounds of tobacco/year has declined steadily over the past two decades. [But today the] . . . average cigarette . . . contains less tobacco. . . . Thus, people seem to measure smoking satisfaction not only physiologically, but also in social psychological or normative ways not related to nicotine consumption. [Markle and Troyer, 1979, p. 619]

The medical model explanation of tobacco use is inadequate because it cannot begin to account for the rapid spread of smoking after its discovery in the New World at the end of the sixteenth century, or its persistence throughout the world. Smoking exists as a set of culturally regulated behaviors that can be interpreted at three levels: as personal behavior pattern, as interpersonal convention, and as cultural mechanism; it is these levels that are so often ignored.

Various authors have, however, recognized these levels. Mausner (1973) discussed smoking as part of a complex social ritual that can be an important expressive behavior which helps to define the individual's self-concept.

Other views have held:

[Smoking] not only yields a variety of pleasurable sensations but, more important, helps the smoker cope with the demands of life, eases and promotes his or her social interactions and is a valuable aid to the establishment of a sense of identity. [Mausner, 1973]

Smoking is a ritual that welcomes strangers, provides companionship in solitude, fills "empty time," marks the significance of certain kinds of occasions and expresses individual identity and personal style. [Feinhandler, 1978]

The state of social research on smoking was summarized by Mettlin (1973, p. 145):

. . . no investigation has provided a means whereby the effects of several different forms of [social] influence may be examined simultaneously. . . . The study of smoking behavior has been approached as though cigarette smoking had little continuity with other kinds of social acts.

While recognizing the problem, Mettlin did not consider smoking in its social context. Other studies have recognized the relevance of situational factors in relation to smoking: Best and Hakstian (1978) asked smokers to rate their desire to smoke in conventional smoking situations; Meade and Wald (1977) asked smokers to report the number of cigarettes they smoked during different parts of the working day; Glad and Adesso (1977) observed smoking behavior, but in artificially constructed situations.

Hoffman and Boyko (1969) examined the relationship of game role to smoking rate in bridge tournaments. Mausner and Platt (1974) analyzed the effect of smoking status on the choice of partners by a group of college women. Clark (1977, 1978) asked smokers, ex-smokers, and nonsmokers to summarize their awareness of others' smoking in social interaction. Tryon, Vaughter, and Ginorio (1978) studied responses of male and female smokers to social cues in streets and waiting areas. These studies, while conducted in natural settings, are restricted either by a limited choice of situation or by a narrow specification of smoking acts and they completely ignore the symbolic components of smoking.

Throughout its history, smoking has been seen both as socially desirable and as anathema. In the last two decades smoking has been subject to a variety of attacks. These attacks have a great deal to do with the symbolic meanings which surround smoking. In order to understand why cigarette smoking retains its importance even though it is under attack, one must first examine its symbolic meanings for contemporary society both historically in the West and cross-culturally.

A Brief History

From the beginning, tobacco has had a symbolic role during times of war—and peace. It still does. We're all familiar with the Indians' use of the peace pipe when settling a dispute. Passing the peace pipe was a gesture of friendship and good will. Today, in many parts of the world, cigarettes are offered along with tea and coffee before the start of peace or trade negotiations. In the Philippines and in Pakistan, this practice even takes place during marriage negotiations . . . [SSA, 1977]

The ritual use of tobacco by New World natives was a most curious sight to Columbus's crews and their followers. What were they to make of these smoke-breathing people? Clearly they were people, yet so vastly different in appearance and behavior that European minds boggled at the confrontation. Strange enough that they existed at all, with their peculiar dress and custom; stranger still that they inhaled and exhaled clouds of smoke, inviting the newcomers to do likewise.

If people were all descended from Adam and Eve, how could some—without even the knowledge to build great ships—have crossed vast seas? No, these could not be children of God. Who else, then, could have placed them here but Satan? And was their smoke not evidence of their association with hellfire and brimstone? So reasoned the Spanish conquistadors and their priests. Yet, however abominable their origins and practices, Christian duty required that they be saved, just as loyalty to the crown demanded that they be controlled so their land and goods could be acquired.

Now in order to save and control the natives, they had to be persuaded to abandon their beliefs and customs in favor of those brought by the Spaniards. But while the Spanish leadership devised ways to bring this about, their own men were finding reason to adopt the ways of the natives. Hardship and loneliness undermined many distinctions between good and evil, right and wrong. However loudly the priests proclaimed tobacco an evil weed, and its smoke symbolic of alliance with the devil, their followers found it difficult to resist the social and medicinal benefits of smoking. In clouds of shared smoke, they found welcome, a very pleasant light-headedness, and even relief from certain stomach complaints the New World diet had inflicted on them.

Historical texts leave no doubt that tobacco played an important role in the cultural struggle between Spaniard and native. The clerical position was well represented by Monardes, who wrote of tobacco in 1571: "And as the devil is a deceiver and knows the virtues of herbs he showed them the value of this plant so that they might see imaginary things and fantasies which it reveals to them, and thus he deceives them." (Dickson 1954, p. 87)

Even priests had apparent difficulty with the devil's seduction, as Father Nobrega revealed in a letter of 1550:

> All the food is difficult to digest, but God has remedied this with a plant, the smoke of which is in much aid of digestion and for other bodily ills and to drive out moisture from the stomach. No one of our brothers uses it, nor does any other of the Christians, in order not to imitate the unbelievers who like it very much. I need it because of the dampness and my catarrh, but I abstain—not what is useful for myself [do I want] but what is good for many that they might be saved. [Dickson, 1954, p. 62.]

The natives themselves revered tobacco and its smoke. For them, as for many other nontechnological societies that later adopted it, smoking symbolized welcome, unity, communication with the gods and spirits, and the healing power to drive out diseases. To differentiate themselves from the pagans, the Spaniards officially pronounced it abominable, disorganizing, a pact with the devil. Only its medicinal properties escaped their condemnation, sometimes leading them to call the devil's weed "God's remedy."

While the New World clergy waged its losing battle, tobacco was already infiltrating Europe. Although the first sailor to bring it back to Spain from Columbus's earliest voyage was jailed by the Inquisition, he found the imported weed spreading rapidly by the time he was released. Its medical value was soon widely touted and a lucrative trade developed as Spain, then France and England, acquired a taste for smoke. By the last decade of the sixteenth century, tobacco was spreading to Holland, Central and Eastern Europe, and Russia. Colonial and mercantile interests introduced it; its spread was accomplished primarily by travelers, students, colonists, soldiers, and seamen, whose inroads were quickly followed up by merchants.

In Elizabethan England, the pleasurable use of tobacco was readily acknowledged in addition to its medical value. Old and young, men and women, and even children smoked—schoolboys being urged to do so as purification of their lungs against disease. For a time, the negative connotations of smoke seemed quite forgotten. But, with restoration of the monarchy in 1660, English culture changed, and smoking practices reflected the changes with powerful symbolism.

The exiled Charles II returned from France to establish a court that had to differentiate itself from a rising merchant class made newly rich by commerce and a new country gentry who had acquired land under Cornwall. The courtiers distinguished themselves by wearing fancy French dress of brocade and lace, bringing with them also the dainty and ostentatious habit of snuffing: tobacco use in a new and smokeless form. By contrast, the new gentry's pipes were crude and polluting. Eventually the social classes separated and ordered themselves by their tobacco habits and an elaborate social/moral code. Courtiers snuffed in a rarefied atmosphere; ladies kept their parlors pure while their men retired to smoking rooms in special smoking jackets and lavishly embroidered caps. The lower classes and rebellious bohemian youth continued to smoke in the streets and coffee houses. Thus the Victorians established order in their lives.

Meanwhile, the New World organized its tobacco habits along geographic lines. In South America and Mexico, cigar smoking became ever more popular, even among women. In the Southern colonies, the profitable farming and trade of tobacco made its use readily acceptable. But the Puritan stronghold in the North, gaining little tangible benefit from the weed, revived all its negative symbolic meaning and passed many laws to restrict its use. Only when cigarette manufacture gave the North a stake in the tobacco economy and a rapidly developing technology brought social liberalization, did smoking become symbolic of maturity in young men and independence in women.

Today tobacco is used socially, ceremonially and instrumentally. It is used in a variety of contexts: in Pacific Island courtship rituals; in African councils, clan gatherings and marriage negotiations; in North and South American Indian divination and healing ceremonies; to seal bargains in Asia; and for hospitality in the Middle East. Social Systems Analysts, Inc., a social and behavioral research and consulting firm in Watertown, Massachusetts, has conducted cross-cultural studies on 183 societies directed at discovering the place of tobacco and its use in society (SSA, 1977). These studies focused on the social and symbolic functions of tobacco. We were able to identify types of behavior which are indices of social and personal functions of tobacco use in dominant American culture, and the relationships of these functions to situational factors.

As we move from traditional to more urban societies, ceremonial and sacred contexts for tobacco use are displaced by more secular contexts, and its use becomes less determined by social categories and more by social contexts. Social structure and systems of cultural meanings are shared within ethnic and subcultural groups and vary from one group to another. Therefore, one must expect that the behavior and meanings surrounding tobacco use will differ among these groups.

Given the recent increase of female smoking in the West, we were interested in regularities of tobacco use among women across cultures. Women smoke in 127 of the 183 societies in our sample. In Asia, South America and the Pacific there is relative approval for smoking by women, while in North America and the Mediterranean there is relative disapproval. There is a strong tendency for women to smoke in societies using tobacco in social contexts such as courtship, hospitality, and dispute mediation. In their study of smoking behavior and the sexes, Tryon et al. (1978, p. 341) found that "In the development of smoking habits and on-going smoking behavior, the influ-↓ ence of social and situational cues are significantly greater for women than for men." The highly probable explanation of these patterns is that smoking carries different meanings and achieves different ends for women than it does for men.

Our observations (SSA, 1979) indicate that groups of women, more often than men, share cigarettes as a group-defining device. Over the last decade the percentage of males who smoke has decreased, while the percentage of females who smoke has been on the increase. Compared to male non-smokers, a far smaller proportion of male smokers are college educated. The difference is greatest among young men. Among women, however, a higher proportion of smokers are college educated than are nonsmokers.

A comparison of age groups shows that nearly all differences occur among women between fifty and seventy years of age. For younger women education seems to make no significant difference in rates of smoking and nonsmoking. Among the young, the less educated women may have caught up with the better educated in their values concerning sex roles, and may therefore show an increased smoking rate. Abstinence and bodily purity constitute a basis for experiencing moral superiority among antismokers. However, for many women, equality, not superiority, is what smoking has come to symbolize (Feinhandler, 1983a). Women may be participating in what were formerly exclusively male roles, and thus exhibit the same smoking behavior as men, but with a time lag.

In a study of the social functions of smoking in the Boston metropolitan area, we found important ethnic differences in smoking behavior (SSA, 1979). Where ethnicity is strong, it influences what a person smokes, when, where, and with what kinds of personal and social consequences. For example, there was some evidence that smoking "styles" of Blacks, particularly when smoking with other Blacks, are very different from those of Irish. These styles take on additional meanings for both Blacks and Irish when they interact socially in ethnically homogeneous groups. In these situations styles of smoking appear to communicate more to participants, more cigarettes are smoked, but more slowly, and more frequent exchanges take place than in ethnically mixed situations.

Thus, in less than five hundred years, tobacco spread inexorably around the world—a dramatic example of diffusion—acquiring in each time and culture a set of social meanings. Nontechnological cultures tended to adopt its original meanings into their own ceremonial rites of marriage, tribal negotiations, healing, and communication with the spirit world. Developing industrial cultures gave tobacco many new meanings—sometimes in strong opposition to the original meanings, sometimes as translations of old meanings into appropriate new forms. But however the symbolism of smoking changed, symbolism it was, and very powerful symbolism at that.

The latest symbolism attached to smoking is that of pollution. In the mounting campaign of antismokers, each cigarette seems a tiny representation of an industrial smokestack, fouling the air and threatening all those who breathe it. No longer are smokers and nonsmokers divided along class or religious lines; the categories themselves of "smoker" and "nonsmoker" are coming to represent an important social division. Is this an entirely new view of smoking, yet another historical and cultural meaning given to it? Is tobacco simply a pervasive and convenient substance to which a vast variety of symbols can be attached? Or is there some underlying structure that links and makes sense of all the disparate attitudes toward smoking across cultures?

To answer these questions and find some coherent pattern, we must look more closely at the domains—social, religious, medical, and boundary—in which conflicting views of tobacco have arisen.

The Social Context

Whatever the framework in which we view smoking, we find both negative and positive values attributed to it. This is certainly clear at present, with efforts toward and resistance against the segregation of smokers commanding public attention. The negative side of this issue is the social offensiveness of smoke, an attitude reminiscent of England after the Restoration and earlier referrals to tobacco as a foreign and barbarous substance. James I contrasted the willingness of the English to adopt the savage practice of smoking with their refusal to adopt civilized French manners. Note that his crusade followed the widespread—almost universal—adoption of smoking into English culture. To support his argument that smoking was offensive to others and an uncivil habit, he recalled its origins in order to pronounce it foreign and intrusive.

Much of the Victorian crusade against smoking focused on other negative images of cultural intrusion. The smoking habit had been spread by foreign travellers, students, sailors and soldiers—powerful images of the outsider. When these images were identified with the lower classes, who smoked widely and publicly, the upper classes separated themselves effectively by their nonsmoking or by their rigid adoption of different smoking practices. Thus the Victorians maintained the social order they decreed by class distinctions, reinforced with the symbolism of alien and intrusive smoke.

The offensiveness of smoking in Victorian literature runs quite counter to earlier rationales for its pleasantness. Elizabethans, from courtier to peasant, were not addicted to bathing and found their social gatherings easier in the presence of a smoke cloud that eased olfactory burdens. Tobacco had thus served a valuable function in covering offensive odor, its own smell seeming fresh and welcome by contrast. *Read's Weekly* of 21 February 1761 gives us a poem written in 1669, entitled "Tobacco"

> At Celia's toilet dost thou claim a right—
> The nymph so famed for teeth, like ivory white.
> For breath more fragrant than the vernal air,
> Blest with thy aid, makes every swain despair.

Where tobacco was welcome, we also find the association with foreigners or strangers reversed so completely that smoke was empowered to turn strangers into friends (reminiscent of the original native meaning of peace-pipe circles). At coffee houses, which proliferated throughout England in the seventeenth century, strangers met to share a pipe and a taper with which to light it. As Rowlands wrote in the "Knave of Clubbes"

> . . . Come into any company,
> Though not a crosse you have,
> Yet offer them Tobacco,
> And their liquor you shall have.
> They say old hospitalitie
> Kept chimnies smoking still,
> Now what our chimnies want of that
> Our smoking noses will.

A contributor to the *Spectator* (1714) comments on lighting a pipe at the candle that stood before a company of strangers, "and after having thrown in two or three whiffs amongst them, sat down and made one of the company." He further observed how "lighting a man's pipe at the same candle is looked upon by brother-smoakers [*sic*] as an overture to conversation and friendship."

These opposing social meanings of tobacco—offensive smell and intrusion on one hand and pleasant odor and welcoming friendship on the other—recur at different times and places throughout the history of smoking. Clearly they are still in evidence today, when the exchange of cigarettes can make a person welcome in a new group while offending others within reach of the same smoke.

The Religious Context

We have already seen the first conflict between tobacco as the holy herb of New World natives and the devil's bane of Spanish priests. While the former offered smoke to their gods and received powers of communication and healing in return, the latter saw only pagan evil in the practice. That view was to be revived when James I (1604) attributed more than negative social meaning to the substance, stating, "In your abuse thereof sinning against God. . . . the blacke stinking fume therof, neerest resembling the horrible stygian smoke of the pit that is bottomless."

In 1614, only a few years after this tirade, William Barclay called upon the Bishop of Murry to defend "this sacred herb," and, indeed, the good bishop rose to the occasion, declaring tobacco to have "much heavenlie vertue in store." America, he added, was "the countrie which God hath honoured and blessed with this happie and holy herb." In Spenser's *Fairie Queen* we find reference to "divine tobacco," and other clerics pronounced it "holy." What some called "Stygian smoke" in fact was often used to deodorize churches where horses were stabled, and we can find old church-wardens' ledgers with entries for tobacco and frankincense as single expenditures.

In the religious context, there is considerable debate over the moral consequences of tobacco use. Nor were the lines always drawn between clergy and laity. Fra Convertino, a Franciscan, wrote in 1650: " . . . smoking expelled the humors from the brain and body, with the result that smokers were less liable than others to the temptations of the flesh . . . those ecclesiastics who smoked or took snuff usually found it easier to overcome such temptations than those who were ignorant of the habit" (Corti, 1931).

Perhaps the most ingenious rationale for tobacco use in all its history was that of Father Desa de Cupertino, who died in 1686 and was later canonized —after the prohibitions against clerical use of tobacco had been rescinded. He argued that snuff hid the odor of sanctity about his person and soul; that without it, he would have been guilty of the sin of pride (Dickson, 1954).

In England, the clergy preached that tobacco inspired contemptuous feelings by inducing indolence. Loitering, profligacy, and the weakening of moral fiber in various ways were also attributed to smoking. Many a young nobleman's estate, it was said, "is altogether spent and scattered to nothing in smoke. This befalls after a shameful and beastly fashion, in that a man's estate runs out through his nose, and he wastes whole days, even years, in drinking of tobacco; men smoke even in bed . . . You see that tobacco is a phantastick temper . . . " (Corti, 1931). Thackeray, on the other hand, pronounced its virtue, saying: "The pipe draws wisdom from the lips of the philosopher, and shuts up the mouth of the foolish; it generates a style of conversation, contemplative, thoughtful, benevolent and unaffected" (Laufer, 1924).

Thus we see, among clergy and laity, considerable dissent. The user of tobacco was sinful, indolent, and profligate according to some; virtuous, thoughtful, and modest according to others. Among colonial Puritans in America, laws, practices, and pronouncements can be seen to reflect the same opposing views.

The Medical Context

Medical views of tobacco through history reveal still another opposition which generally takes the form of "tobacco as cure-all" versus "tobacco as cause of illness." Its medical virtues, we may recall, were an effective counter to its perception as a pagan evil when tobacco was first introduced into Spain. An early error of classification—confusion with yellow henbane, a member of the nightshade family—was perpetuated in Latin taxonomies, as well as in their French, English and Dutch translations. Therefore, a panacea–poison dichotomy persisted for some time, generating much argument among doctors throughout Europe.

Even before this misclassification, Spaniards in the New World described relaxing effects of smoking together with medical benefits. Oviedo, among others, wrote that "the inhaling of a certain kind of smoke which they call tobacco . . . produce[d] a state of stupor . . . until they became unconscious and lay sprawling upon the earth like men in a drunken slumber." Many claimed that smoke filled the brain and dulled the senses, though the above passage from Thackeray and numerous non-Western sources, indicate quite the opposite: that smoking clarifies thought and keeps one awake. Even that ardent antismoker James I documented these contradictions: "being taken when a man is sleepie and drowsie, it will, as they say, awake his braine, and quicken his understanding."

Modern knowledge of *Nicotiana tabacum* makes many historically-described effects of tobacco, as panacea or poison, relaxant or stimulant, suspect, although it is possible that the effects of various species were observed at different times.

Particularly interesting is the recurring concept of contagion. The current view that ill effects of smoking are passed on to nonusers who are present has its counterparts in the past, when it was claimed, for example, that nonsmokers were forced to smoke in self defense, much as people could overcome the unpleasant effects of garlic on others' breath by partaking themselves.

Opposing the theme of contagion were arguments that tobacco could halt the spread of disease. Clearly, notions of contagion were still confused in the seventeenth century, when a letter was written, praising tobacco smoke as "one of the wholsemest sents that is against all contagious airs, for it overmasters all other smells." Yet such beliefs took firm enough hold that, at the height of the 1665 plague, schoolboys at Eton were required to smoke a pipe every morning as a measure against contagion. Samuel Pepys, after visiting the houses of plague victims in 1667, wrote: "It put me into an ill conception of myself and my smell, so that I was forced to put some roll-tobacco to smell to and chaw, which took away the apprehension."

To summarize, the dichotomies of meaning given to tobacco in the medical domain are relaxant–stimulant, poison–panacea, and agent for spreading or halting contagion. Contagion, particularly, is a notion laden with symbolic content, and illustrates the way in which cultural ideas are generated around anomalous substances when knowledge is inadequate for explaining the mechanisms behind visible phenomena. The medical concept of contagion around tobacco clearly extends to other domains, such as the social context. A strange, foreign substance, introduced by strangers or foreigners, threatens social order by threatening to bring about disorder—whether through actual illness or other means. Such ideas are most easily defined by viewing tobacco in a fourth domain.

The Boundary Context

The Victorians, as we saw, used smoking behavior to draw symbolic boundaries between classes, as the Spanish in the New World had used it to distinguish themselves symbolically from the pagan natives. Presently, smoking itself categorizes people who are not otherwise divided. "Smoking" or "non-smoking" sets boundaries between people, and increasingly does so between the physical areas they occupy.

In contrast to this notion of separation by boundaries, smoking also serves the function of inclusion. Symbolically, the "smoke-filled room," whether or not it actually contains smokers, connotes the sacred inner circle of persons with common status and cause. Certainly some of the mystique of unifying native ritual persists in this image. In less esoteric groups, the sharing of tobacco in English coffee houses and American coffee breaks permits entry into a group even when no other basis for comradery exists. And we can still observe group distinctions by type of tobacco use. Just as the Victorians segregated themselves by snuffing, cloistering in smoking rooms, and so forth, we find academic circles identified by their pipes, businessmen by good cigars, and liberated women by long slim cigarettes.

In segregating smokers and nonsmokers in airplanes and other public spaces, the boundaries often become unifying factors on either side. As nonsmokers become more vocal in their opposition, the "vice" across the boundary becomes a common topic of discussion, as does the vice itself within the circle of its practitioners. Everyone is thus increasingly aware of the boundaries, more concerned with extending their own territory, and more threatened by incursions.

Tobacco is thus something of an anomaly, with ambiguous or changing boundaries, and cultures tend to make special provisions for anomalies. Meaning is difficult to pinpoint when categories are not firmly established; magical, transcendant meanings can thus be assigned. Anomaly or ambiguity in categories invokes notions of attributed power and related concepts of danger. The ambiguities surrounding tobacco lend to it the status of an object to which symbolic meanings are readily attached in a cultural system. It is these symbolic meanings that give rise to the personal, social, and cultural uses to which tobacco is put.

Douglas (1966) lists five ways of coping with such ambiguity: choose one interpretation, control or eliminate the anomalous item, avoid it, attribute danger to it, or incorporate it into ritual. Complex societies, however, may have too many competing interests to resolve, avoid or incorporate the ambiguity. Rather, they keep it salient by generating sets of contradictions—opposing attitudes and meanings—around anomalous matters. This seems to be what happened as tobacco spread throughout Western civilization. If we look at some of these oppositions within their own contexts, a pattern begins to take shape.

Underlying Structures of Opposition

Once we see that every meaning given to tobacco use and every symbol attached to it has its opposite regardless of domain (social, religious, medical, boundary), we can seek a more fundamental structure to account for the surface attitudes. The usefulness of underlying dimensions will depend on the relative predictive power of the alternatives we can posit. Let us examine a few candidates for basic oppositional meaning.

Good versus Evil. Clearly smoke is good when it symbolizes the sacrificial or purifying fire, and when it is itself considered a purifying agent. Equally obvious is the connotation of evil when smoke represents hellfire, pagan sacrilege, and contagion. Thus, the good-evil dimension has explanatory value in both religious and medical domains. This link is strengthened when we note historical uses of tobacco to cleanse and purify in religious and medical rituals. All cultures regard the purified soul and the purified body as intrinsically good. Social and boundary domains, however, seem less appropriately characterized by good–evil distinctions.

We versus They. Social and boundary domains have much to do with notions of inside and outside. The relationship of group to group is always a matter of "we" and "they" from the participant point of view. Rituals of hospitality are essentially mechanisms for transforming a stranger into a friend, or temporarily making a member of a rival group into a member of one's own group: making one of "them" into one of "us." Tobacco, as we have seen, has been and still is used to gain such entry—or to preclude it through differences in smoking style.

On an individual level, every culture has concepts of personal space, a territorial aura every person carries around his or her body. Rules of hospitality also regulate the ways in which others are treated inside this space. Individuals regard personal space as personal property and feel assaulted when this space is invaded. For the smoker, this space is often defined by a personal cloud of smoke and may willingly be shared with a stranger's mingling cloud. Nonsmokers, on the other hand, will see the same cloud of smoke as alien territory or the intrusion of another's space across his or her own boundary. Ownership of space in which smoking does or does not occur has become an important issue in our own culture.

When smoke is used to cover a foreign odor, such as that of horses in church or people at a social gathering, it can be seen as a countermove to invasion of territory. When smoke itself intrudes, via the pipes of the gentry amidst snuffing courtiers, in the Victorian parlor, or in a nonsmoking section of an airplane, it constitutes invasion of space controlled by others. To make foreign space his own, the Spanish missionary tried to persuade natives to abandon their smoking habit.

Own space, own smell, own customs, define the "we" opposed to foreign space, foreign smell and foreign customs belonging to "them." We may share what is ours with those whom we welcome, preserve it against those we do not, and lose it to aggressive intruders. Symbolism for all these events has been attached to tobacco use in various ways throughout history. Smoking has been used to share space or defend it, to transform offensive odor or produce it, to preserve social order among groups—all ways of preserving distinctions between our "we" and "they." This dimension links social and boundary domains effectively.

Hints of it can also be found in religious and medical domains, particularly in the former. But in both contexts, the good–evil dimension is more fundamental. Thus, if we are to find a single predictive dimension, we must find one common to both the good–evil and we–they oppositions with respect to smoking.

Purity versus Pollution. We already noted that purity is not necessarily derived from or related to ideas of hygiene, but represents a strong element in religion. In both domains, purity expresses uncontaminated order—the opposite of disorder—whether sacred or secular. Decisions about what constitutes order are a cultural matter, and it follows that definitions of disorder—whatever violates order—must also be culturally determined. If disorder is thought to be produced by an outside agent or force, rather than by internal disintegration, the culture identifies a pollutant.

It is easy to demonstrate the cultural relativity of pollution. While perfectly hygienic, a brand-new pair of shoes on the breakfast table is polluting because shoes don't "belong" on a table. A dog licking its master's face, while unhygienic, is not polluting to us. Goats in the house, by contrast, are polluting in our culture, but not in many others. Without culture there would be no concept of pollution and in nature there would be no pollution in the absence of human society.

Notions of purity and pollution are readily extended into the social context. Social groups and social activities are so structured that it is often quite clear whether they are pure or polluted. We know who and what belongs, that is, is part of the order, and who or what does not. Smoke was required to purify the air in churches that doubled as stables, but clearly polluted the air in others. The nonsmoker at a cocktail party has been, until recently, almost as disordering as a smoker in the theatre. The Victorian order was rife with notions of purity and pollution with respect to smoking, as was the Puritan tradition in America.

The boundary context is also readily amenable to structuring along a purity–pollution dimension, for it is precisely when pollutants enter "pure" territory that they become pollutants. "Foreign" persons and "foreign" substances are only so designated when outside their own space, intruding into another.

If we understand purity and pollution as symbols of order and disorder, yet another aspect of smoking fits our framework. Anxiety, tension, and other forms of dysphoria are essentially violations of an ordered mood state. The smoker who experiences such states can frequently restore order by smoking, despite the fact that tension and anxiety may simultaneously be produced in nearby nonsmokers! These effects may inhere in the ritual and symbolism of smoking, rather than in its pharmacological effects. Thus, segregating smokers, transforming strangers into friends by offerings of tobacco, smoking to appease gods or demons, soothing anxiety with smoke and forbidding smoking are all purification rituals against disordering pollution.

Occasionally in history, Elizabethan England and twentieth-century America for example, smoking has become extremely widespread in a culture, but more usually we see an ordered pattern of smoking and nonsmoking. When tobacco is a sacred substance, used in religious and/or political ritual, its purity is preserved by restricting its use to certain people and occasions. To the Spanish, hellfire was a symbol of purification, in that it preserved order by tormenting sinners, but smoke from hellfire was seen as disordering here on earth.

Symbolically, healing and purification are almost synonymous in their meaning of restoring order, both to the individual and to the society in which he or she functions. Medicinal substances are generally reserved for healers unless society decrees that ordinary people may have access to them for minor ailments or preventive measures. Recall that Elizabethan schoolboys were actually required to smoke.

Social distinctions preserved by different practices and attitudes around smoking preserve pure order by minimizing pollution in similar ways: the culture decrees who shall smoke and not smoke and which smoking materials shall be consumed by various groups (even today's liberated women do not chew tobacco). Boundary maintenance is also a measure against pollution, ordering society by designating air and group space appropriate or inappropriate for smoking.

We conclude, then, that the purity–pollution dimension is more fundamental than either the good–evil or we–they dimensions, these latter being transformations of the underlying dichotomy as it is expressed in different contexts or domains. It is interesting to note that the good–evil distinction in our terms is not found in the nontechnological tribal societies which have adopted tobacco use. There, tobacco is seen as inherently good, becoming "bad" only if it is too weak to exert the power required of it: cleansing outsiders who must be brought into the culture according to exogamous marriage rules, driving possessing demons out of bodies, bringing gods into communication with people, making friends of enemies, and so on. Tobacco use "out of place" is less likely where its meaning and use is widely respected. Only in complex societies, containing multiple subcultures, will the meanings of a substance like tobacco become a source of conflict.

These symbolic components, although they appear structurally valid, are on too abstract a level to have a direct effect on behavior in daily life. The components do, however, underlie much of the social process. In order to investigate the power of symbols as they motivate decisions and behavior, it is necessary to make them more concrete. This can be done by investigating the ways in which tobacco use functions in daily contexts.

Functions of Tobacco Use

As stated earlier, all of the studies cited at the beginning of this paper suffer from the same shortcoming: none takes account of the actual situational factors present or the social process surrounding smoking, and most rely on self-report. It is only by observing and analyzing smoking as it occurs in the flow of daily activities that one can begin to understand its social and cultural roles, and its consequent importance to those who engage in it.

In previous studies (SSA, 1979, 1980; Feinhandler, 1981), we have been able to describe a number of the functions of smoking, including exchange, affect management, group definition, and boundary mediation. Our past research has lead us to conclude that most tobacco use is as much culturally patterned as it is individually determined. Tobacco use functions on a social as well as a personal level. The functions of smoking must be understood in the context of the situations in which people smoke. Furthermore, those situations are defined by social structure and shared systems of culturally-defined meanings.

In spite of the recognition of shared behavior, there still seems to be a need for some authors to reduce the explanation of smoking behavior to simpler physiological or psychological levels, for example:

> Smoking is possible under a wide variety of circumstances and settings. These numerous settings become discriminative for smoking and often come to serve as learned reinforcers for smoking. An urge is subjectively experienced when these situations are encountered. . . . the pleasure and relaxation associated with using alcohol, finishing a meal, or drinking coffee, and the perceived diminution of unpleasant affective states of anxiety, tension, boredom, or fatigue . . . [Lichtenstein, 1982]

> [self-reports from smokers] suggest they smoke to regulate a variety of externally induced states: to reduce anxiety, to provide stimulation, to alleviate boredom, to keep occupied, to have something to 'fiddle with,' as well as to reduce stress, anger and irritability, induced by abstention. [Leventhal and Cleary, 1977]

The situations in which people smoke are varied: some relaxed, some anxiety provoking, some alone, some in company—yet each individual tends to smoke in all of them, but differently in relation to the situation. If smoking is really a matter of personal psychological motivation and individual desire for nicotine, situational factors should produce different individual behavior, reflecting unique minds and bodies. We know that tobacco contains nicotine, but that does not explain why smoking in particular situations, and not in others, became customary.

There seems to be great agreement on the meanings underlying smoking for smokers and nonsmokers alike. Smoking in this society is informal, sociable, and a marker of time and space. Even the most virulent antismoker "understands" the meaning of smoking regardless of his or her attitude toward it. Spatial considerations are almost unimportant in a decision about the appropriateness of smoking. A children's playground is appropriate for smoking if it is coded as "outdoors," but not if it is coded as children's space. Space becomes important as a negotiating item when there is conflict in the meaning of a situation.

Through observational studies of smoking (Feinhandler et al., 1983b; SSA, 1980) we have been able to categorize smoking behavior as having personal, social, and ordering functions. The personal uses are related to the notion of habit in that an individual learns to accomplish certain ends and repeats behavior for that purpose. The social functions are primarily interpersonal in nature. The ordering functions relate to customary ideas of segmenting time and events and otherwise imposing order on situations.

Personal functions include the management or enhancement of negative and positive affect, the presentation of self and the preparation of self for possibly stressful situations. Social functions include the definition of social space by mediating and maintaining boundaries, the building of social cohesiveness by defining groups and sharing and exchanging within groups. Ordering functions deal with marking events, focusing attention, measuring time, marking time out, and filling time.

Personal Functions

Presentation of Self. Individuals may use tobacco with its related paraphernalia and smoking styles to express a specific self-image.

Positive Affect Enhancement. Smokers often smoke to enhance positive emotional states such as relaxation, gratification and stimulation.

Negative Affect Management. Smoking and its attendant behavior can function to reduce negative feelings such as fear, anxiety, stress, or anger.

Social Functions

Boundary Mediation. The circles of personal space or group space are formidable social barriers. No one steps up to a stranger or a group and begins a conversation without some sort of ice-breaker, an event or object external to the participants. A smoker has a ready-made ticket into a circle of other smokers. Smoking can aid in breaking down the social barrier around a group of people.

Group Definition. Smoking as a common activity tends to reinforce and affirm the relationship among members of a group and aids in defining the participants as a group.

Exchange. The offering or accepting of a cigarette or light serves to cement and bond social relationships. Social relationships are most often established by performing acts or giving objects of minor, but appreciated value. To accept an object or a service rendered is to incur an obligation or a debt, which, when repaid, establishes a pattern of exchange.

Boundary Maintenance. People tend to evaluate their personal association with others according to whether the others are on the inside or outside of various social boundaries. Rituals of hospitality are essentially mechanisms for transforming a stranger into a friend, or temporarily making a member of a rival group into a member of one's own group. Tobacco has served to exclude people from, or to distinguish, groups—to maintain boundaries.

Interactional Transition. When wishing to change the topic of conversation or proceed to another mode of communication, a Kikuyu speaker may say, "Let us now take a pinch of snuff." Smoking behavior is often used to facilitate or mark a shift in the primary interpersonal activity.

Ordering Functions

Pacing. Smokers often use the amount of time it takes to smoke a cigarette to measure the duration of such external events as, for example, co-occurring activities.

Focusing Attention. Smoking can add structure to tasks. It has been noted that smoking is an aid to concentration (Wesnes and Warburton, 1981).

Time Filling. To occupy oneself before the start of an event over which one has no control, one may smoke a cigarette.

Time Out. Time out is a break or relaxation period from other activities. Smokers may commence these other activities at leisure, with the act of smoking to mark time out. Because smokers can almost always carry their cigarettes with them, they have a portable symbol of this "break time." They can mark a situation as their own by lighting up.

Event Marking. Smoking often occurs before or after an event, acting to mark a beginning or ending. Smoking thus serves to frame the event and reflect the human propensity to categorize and organize events so that they are both bounded and sensible.

Summary

This paper argues that the medical models focusing on tobacco pharmacology or the tobacco habit are not adequate to explain the prevalence and persistence of its use. These approaches, further, are unable to explain historical or cross-cultural variations in the attitudes toward tobacco and the functions of smoking. To address the social and cultural import of tobacco and smoking, we have examined its symbolic meanings for society historically, cross-culturally and, in contemporary society, among women and certain ethnic groups.

While there have been many studies of smoking, most have been oriented by a medical model and many have assumed physiological dependency. Those that have focused on behavior have largely ignored the sociocultural context of the behavior; they completely ignore its symbolic and meaning components.

Historically, the social, religious, medical, and boundary domains in which conflicting views of tobacco have arisen reveal a coherent underlying structure that links attitudes toward smoking. This structure consists of symbolic dimensions of "good" vs. "evil" and "we" vs. "they." At a deeper level these dimensions have "purity" vs. "pollution" underlying them. It is partly the anomalous status of tobacco that predisposes it as a salient object to which symbolic meanings can be attached.

These meanings give rise to important social functions for many members of all classes in modern American society. These functions were investigated in a variety of natural settings and are presented. The social and cultural roles of smoking and tobacco use in society force us to recognize the inadequacy of physiologically or psychologically based habit models. By recognizing the social and cultural factors related to tobacco use we can understand its persistence in society.

Some Concluding Thoughts

The underlying dimension of "purity–pollution" in tobacco symbolism makes today's conflict between smokers and nonsmokers easier to understand. While antismoking campaigns are at present ostensibly based on medical opinion, it is difficult to believe that so many people would be suddenly concerned with their fellow citizens' health. We might account medically for the cessation of smoking in those who fear it will pollute and make ill their own bodies, but why the new concern about smoking at large?

If we take the term "pollution" literally, a new meaning appears, for pollution indeed is a major issue of our times. Industrial wastes, chemical food additives, automobile exhausts and other pollutants in our air, water, soil, and food threaten our health and well-being, our entire order. Much earlier we stated that the cigarette has become a tiny representation of the industrial smokestack; perhaps now that symbol is more prevalent. For if smoking—especially with sides drawn for and against the practice—has represented the deep dimension of purity vs. pollution, then its association with the real and major problem of technological pollution was virtually inevitable.

Understanding this makes it easier to understand the vehemence of the antismoking campaign. Technological pollution is a serious threat to us all, and if smoking symbolizes that threat, then we will take the smoking issue very seriously, at least as seriously as the Spanish conquistadors took it when it seemed to threaten their own culture, and probably more so.

Given that symbols are culturally determined and that we have seen how tobacco symbolism has been repeatedly shifted from one pole of each of its underlying dimensions to the other, it is worth asking whether smoking is a serious threat in itself. The smoker's smoke is immediate and visible; not so the technological pollutants we rightly fear. Therefore, smoking is an easier target for attack. With considerable social outrage and energy, we might even succeed in eliminating smoking from our culture, but if we did so, would the overall threat to existence have been reduced? Or might we have been effectively distracted from the task of purifying our air, not to mention our water, soil and food?

References

Best, J.A. & Hakstian, A.R. 1978. A situation-specific model for smoking behavior. *Addictive Behaviors* 3, 79–92.

Clark, R. 1977. *Smoking: A social interaction theory of cigarette smoking and quitting.* Oceanside, New York: Dabor Science Publications.

———. 1978. Cigarette smoking in social interaction. *The International Journal of the Addictions* 13(2), 257–269.

Corti, E.C. 1931. *A history of smoking.* London: Geo. G. Harrap.

Dickson, S.A. 1954. *The panacea or precious bane.* New York: New York Public Library.

Douglas, M. 1966. *Purity and danger.* London: Routledge & Kegan Paul.

Feinhandler, S.J. 1978. Testimony before the Subcommittee on Tobacco, Committee on Agriculture, House of Representatives. Serial No. 95-000. Washington: U.S. Government Printing Office.

———. 1981. Social function as a component of market value. In *Analysis of Consumer Policy.* Philadelphia: Wharton Applied Research Center.

———. 1983a. Anti-smoking and the body politic. Unpublished paper.

Feinhandler, S.J., Harford, T.C., O'Leary, C. & Dorman, N. 1983b. Drinking in bars: An observational study of companion status and drinking behavior. *International Journal of the Addictions* 18(7), 937–950.

Glad, W. & Adesso, V.J. 1977. The relative importance of socially induced tension and behavioral contagion for smoking behavior. *Journal of Abnormal Psychology* 85(1), 119–121.

Hoffman, D.T. & Boyko, E.P. 1969. Cigarette smoking by tournament bridge game participants. *The Psychological Record* 19, 585–589.

Laufer, B. 1924. Introduction of tobacco into Europe. *Anthropology Leaflet Series*, No. 19. Chicago: Field Museum of National History.

Leventhal, H. & Cleary, P.D. 1977. Why haven't more people quite smoking? *The Sciences* 17(7), 12. New York: Academy of Science.

Lichtenstein, E. 1982. The smoking problem: A behavioral perspective. *Journal of Consulting and Clinical Psychology* 50, 804–819.

Markle, G.E. & Troyer, R.J. 1979. Smoke gets in your eyes: Cigarette smoking as deviant behavior. *Social Problems* 26(5), 611–625.

Mausner, B. 1973. An ecological view of cigarette smoking. *Journal of Abnormal Psychology* 81(2), 115–126.

Mausner, B. & Platt, E.S. 1974. Smoking: A behavioral analysis. *American Journal of Sociology* 79(4), 1049–1051.

Meade, T.W. & Wald, N.J. 1977. Cigarette smoking patterns during the working day. *British Journal of Preventive and Social Medicine* 31, 25–29.

Mettlin, C. 1973. Smoking as behavior: Applying a social psychological theory. *Journal of Health and Social Behavior* 14, 144–152.

Nuehring, E. & Markle, G.E. 1974. Nicotine and norms: The re-emergence of a deviant behavior. *Social Problems* 21(April), 513–526.

Social Systems Analysts, Inc. 1977. A cross-cultural study of smoking. Unpublished report.

———. 1978. Situational factors in smoking appropriateness. Unpublished report.

———— . 1979. The social functions of smoking: An observational study. Unpublished report.

———— . 1980. The social role of smoking. Unpublished report.

Tryon, W.W., Vaughter, R.M. & Ginorio, A.B. 1978. Smoking behavior as a function of social cues and sex: A naturalistic study. *Sex Roles* 3(4), 337–344.

U.S. Surgeon General. 1979. *Smoking and Health*. U.S. Department of Health, Education and Welfare.

Wesnes, K. & Warburton, D.M. 1981. Smoking, nicotine, and human performance. *Pharmae Therapy* 21, 189–208.

6
Smoking, Human Rights, and Civil Liberties

Douglas J. Den Uyl

> Irrational creatures cannot distinguish between injury and damage, and
> therefore, as long as they be at ease, they are not offended with their fellows;
> whereas man is then most troublesome when he is most at ease, for then it is
> that he loves to show his wisdom and control the actions of them that govern
> the commonwealth. [Thomas Hobbes]

Nineteen eighty-three was a landmark year for antismoking forces. It
was in 1983 that Proposition P, otherwise known as the Smoking
Pollution Control Ordinance was passed in San Francisco. The ordinance, hotly contested and only narrowly passed, marked the first instance
in this country of a government regulation whose effects are likely to mean
the prohibition of all smoking in many places of work. Prior to Proposition P,
legislation such as Connecticut's Clean Indoor Air Act (1979) was either much
more limited in the range of places covered by the act or required separation
of smokers and nonsmokers rather than prohibition, as in Minnesota's Clean
Indoor Air Act of 1975. Even though the San Francisco ordinance is only a city
ordinance, its logical implications are more pervasive than those of preceding
pieces of legislation. Furthermore, the media exposure given to the San Francisco ordinance—through a segment of the popular television news program
"60 Minutes" aired on 29 January, 1984—has turned an otherwise local af-
fair into a national one. However one feels about smoking, the more aggressive regulatory posture of the San Francisco ordinance combined with the
national attention the ordinance has received should give one pause for reflection and concern.

In this paper we shall discuss the propriety of the San Francisco ordinance as well as some criteria that might be used for evaluating the rights of
smokers and nonsmokers in "public places." The discussion which follows is
formulated in a context that would be most familiar to readers in the United
States. However, a brief appendix is provided which discusses the political
philosophy exhibited by the World Health Organization's campaign against
smoking. For purposes of this paper we shall assume that smoking is at least

offensive and perhaps harmful. We are not *arguing* or *conceding* that smoking is offensive or harmful to smokers or nonsmokers. Rather, we start with this assumption in order to more clearly identify the rights in question and to avoid the accusation that the following analysis depends upon an overly benevolent interpretation of controversial smoking issues. Before discussing smoking directly, however, we must first lay the foundations that will be used in our analysis of the smoking issue. To that task we now turn.

Human Rights, Civil Liberties, and Government Intervention

Rights and Liberty

One of our most treasured national documents is the Declaration of Independence. This document is not simply a historical statement of our desire to break from English rule, but is (perhaps more importantly) an expression of a political and moral philosophy. That philosophy is contained in the following familiar passage:

> We hold these Truths to be self-evident, that all Men are created equal, that they are endowed by their Creator with certain unalienable Rights, that among these are Life, Liberty, and the Pursuit of Happiness—That to secure these Rights, Governments are instituted among Men, deriving their just Powers from the Consent of the Governed, that whenever any Form of Government becomes destructive of these Ends, it is the Right of the People to alter or to abolish it, . . .

This passage has been cited so often in so many speeches and articles that it is now trite and, because of overuse, almost meaningless. Nevertheless, the very triteness of the passage masks the quite substantial theses contained within it. These theses deserve renewed attention because they do say something significant about the role and purpose of government. Moreover, the principles enumerated in the Declaration constitute the framework within which the smoking controversy will be analyzed below. Here are a few of the significant principles mentioned in the passage cited from the Declaration:

1. People, by their very nature, have certain rights which are neither created by government nor alterable by government.
2. These basic rights are foundational—that is, they are not defined in terms of anything but themselves (not, for example, in terms of social utility, public welfare, state security, and so on).
3. All persons have the same rights—not collectively, but individually.

4. The function of government is to protect these rights. Indeed, governments are legitimately established for this end *and no other*.

5. Laws which violate these rights should be abolished or altered so that they no longer violate these rights. The same can be said about governments which systematically violate basic rights.

Jefferson included life, liberty, and the pursuit of happiness among the basic rights. This was a paraphrase of John Locke's triad of life, liberty, and property.[1] There is no disagreement here between Jefferson and Locke. Both saw property as a basic right and as an integral part of the pursuit of happiness.

Of the three terms in the triad of basic rights, "liberty" seems to be the most crucial. Equal pursuit of happiness, for example, is merely the expression of the freedom to pursue individual interests. And given the diversity of human interests, the state would be protecting the right of divergent pursuits of interest in protecting basic rights. Notice that Jefferson does not say that the state should guarantee our happiness nor even that it should outline the paths we should take toward that end. The Declaration also does not say that the government should keep us from falling into unhappiness. The role of the state consists simply in not interfering with our *pursuit* of happiness even if we are mistaken about what will in fact bring us that happiness. Since we possess equal basic rights, the same protection must be provided to all, which usually means protecting us from the interference of others and others from our interference.

The centrality of the concept of liberty with respect to our basic rights indicates that these rights are essentially negative. They impose obligations of noninterference on each of us vis-à-vis others' pursuit of happiness. Interference by the state is legitimate only when some person or group has first crossed the boundaries of noninterference (through a criminal act, for example). Individuals, however, are not the only violators of basic rights. States can violate them too, and this is why Jefferson was insistent that a Bill of Rights be added to the Constitution. Violations of rights by states are actually more serious than violations by individuals, since states possess a virtual monopoly on the use of force. Rectification of a rights violation perpetrated by the state, thus becomes difficult or impossible.

Clearly, applying these rights in concrete practice can be complicated and can raise numerous questions and difficulties. Nevertheless, the heat of the moment should not make us lose sight of the basic principles involved, especially when it is possible to have our basic rights eroded piecemeal by laws. The Declaration urges us to stand back every now and then from more specific disputes and to reflect upon general principles. We are permitted this detached perspective because our particular laws and social policies are meant to be evaluated in terms of principles more fundamental than themselves—our "unalienable rights."

Traditionally our "unalienable rights" were called "natural rights." That terminology has since gone out of fashion. Today the phraseology is likely to be "human rights." In either case, we are said to possess certain basic rights that cannot be legitimately violated by either our fellow citizens or government and which can be used to evaluate the actions of either. Herein lies the difference between a moral perspective on an issue and other types of approaches. If a lawyer or legal theorist were writing on our topic, for example, he would have to operate within the framework of existing law. The legality of the San Francisco ordinance would have to be challenged or defended in terms of existing law or legal procedures. By the same token, an economist must evaluate social utility in terms of current desires and interests. Jefferson's remarks in the Declaration, however, indicate that an issue can be examined from a point of view that need not pay particular attention to existing law or what will currently maximize social utility. We can instead evaluate an issue from a *moral* point of view.

In matters of public policy, the moral point of view translates into a discussion of basic rights.[2] Since the purpose of the state is to protect people's rights, public policies can be assessed by analyzing whether rights are in fact being protected. No prediction need be made about whether the correct course of action will in fact be taken, nor are we limited to using the term "rights" in a narrowly legalistic fashion. We may instead be concerned with what *ought* to be the case, even if practical realities are biased in an alternate direction. With Jefferson, therefore, we shall assume that there are basic human rights, that the concept of liberty best expresses the essence of these rights, that these rights are foundational in the sense that they morally override policies that do not respect them, and that the function of government is to protect these basic rights. These values, finally, are not necessarily peculiar to the United States. Many Western Liberal Democracies claim to be grounded in similar values. Thus it is upon this bit of theoretical scaffolding that we shall build the case that follows.

Legal Paternalism

If we agree that governments are acting legitimately when they keep us from violating each others' rights, do they have a further obligation to insure that we use our liberty in ways that keep us from harming ourselves? The belief that governments ought to protect people from harming themselves is known as legal paternalism, and governments often act in legally paternalistic ways. Because of its intervention under this principle, for example, people have limited access to pornography, marijuana, laetril, and prostitutes. There are also more subtle forms of paternalism, such as Federal Trade Commission regulation of advertising in the name of the most gullible members of society, or Securities and Exchange Commission regulation of the stock market on roughly the same principle. It is hard to know where the authority for such paternalistic acts comes from. I may wish to have my self-harming actions regulated, but it is not clear how I can legitimately impose such restrictions upon you, especially if you can be (or are) made easily aware of the risks you are taking. Furthermore, it is not clear where I would derive the right to use *your* resources in financing a government program to protect *me* from self-harm (or vice versa).

Nevertheless, some philosophers have argued for the legitimacy of legal paternalism. Many of these thinkers can be dismissed as having little sympathy for the principle of liberty mentioned above. Others, however, do deserve to be described as civil libertarians in the sense that they give the benefit of the doubt to the principle of liberty. These thinkers would generally hold that there is a prima facie case against government interference with self-harming actions, but allow for certain interferences in appropriate cases. The following principle has been offered by Joel Feinberg to help determine when such interference is justified: "A man can rightly be prevented from harming himself (when other interests are not directly involved) only if his intended action is substantially nonvoluntary or can be presumed to be so in the absence of evidence to the contrary."[3] The key terms here are obviously "other interests," "nonvoluntary," and "absence of evidence to the contrary." But let us resist the temptation to discuss each of these concepts in turn, and instead take the passage as a whole and apply it to the topic at hand—smoking.

At another point in the article from which the preceding passage was taken, Feinberg claims that we would run "serious risks of governmental tyranny" if those who voluntarily chose to smoke were prevented from doing so.[4] However, he also makes the following statement:

> The way for the state to assure itself that such practices [smoking] are truly voluntary is continually to confront smokers with the ugly medical facts so that there is no escaping the knowledge of what the medical risks to health exactly are. Constant reminders of the hazards should be at every hand and with no softening of the gory details. The state might even be justified in using its taxing, regulatory, and persuasive powers to make smoking . . . more difficult or less attractive.[5]

It is hard to imagine how the state could use its "taxing, regulatory, and persuasive powers" and not seriously threaten individual liberty. Furthermore, it would seem to follow from the desire to make an action "truly voluntary" that the state would have to supply any *contrary* evidence to smokers and nonsmokers alike. And this does not even begin to address the troublesome question of why the resources of voluntary smokers should be expropriated (through taxation and regulation) for a program that will inevitably diminish their freedom and pleasure in smoking.

The chief difficulty, however, with the passage on smoking is that it violates the principle for justified legal paternalism mentioned earlier. Notice that the principle of legal paternalism allows for state interference only when an individual's action is "substantially nonvoluntary." On the other hand, the passage just cited implies that the state may interfere to insure that our actions are "truly voluntary." Obviously "substantially nonvoluntary" and "truly voluntary" are rather different concepts, with the latter concept implying the most complete and rationally correct assessment of the evidence that is humanly possible. Indeed, "truly voluntary" is the kind of concept that *could* be used by the state to reject any form of deviant behavior, since any form of deviant behavior can be interpreted as "irrational" according to conventional norms.

Clearly Feinberg is not using "truly voluntary" in a way that would usher in the totalitarian state. It is evident, though, that "substantially nonvoluntary" is the preferred expression because it is a more manageable concept and because it is more likely to inhibit state intervention. In the smoking controversy, then, a substantially nonvoluntary action would be one that was performed in ignorance of any medical evidence of the alleged adverse effects of smoking. Moreover, "substantially nonvoluntary" must also mean that information about smoking was significantly inaccessible to the average smoker. In both cases there can be no presumption in favor of legal paternalism for smoking. Not only is there a widespread belief that smoking is harmful (continuously reinforced by television advertisements), but in addition a warning is printed on each package. I might add that when Feinberg made these statements about smoking in 1971, which was prior to the cigarette labeling law, there was still a widely held belief that smoking was harmful to health. Thus even before the current widespread public controversy on smoking, it would not be easy to claim a smoker's actions were substantially nonvoluntary.[6]

What is clear from the foregoing analysis is that there are no grounds for legal paternalism with respect to smoking. Furthermore, the expenditure of public funds on attempts to convince people not to smoke is also an illegitimate form of legal paternalism. To ask people to finance campaigns against their own choices, even if those choices are irrational, neither secures the protection of rights nor enhances the prospects of such protection.

Rights and Harms

If the coercive power of the state cannot be legitimately used to protect individuals from any harm to themselves that smoking may cause, perhaps it can be used to prevent harm to others. To answer this question an examination of the relationship between rights and harms is required. Is protecting someone from harm the same thing as protecting someone's rights? Can one be harmed and not have one's rights violated? And alternatively, can one not be harmed and yet still have one's rights violated? These questions must be addressed before an intelligent assessment of the smoking controversy can be made.

Consider the following case: a person is running at full speed. During the run another person steps in front of the runner and throws his body at the runner, breaking the runner's nose. It is clear that the runner has been harmed. Is it also clear that the runner has had his rights violated? The answer to this question must be no, because too little information is provided. Suppose, for example, that the event just described took place during a professional football game. The tackler may regret that the runner's nose was broken, but the runner knowingly and voluntarily agreed to face the risk of such injuries when he agreed to join the football team. Thus, although a harm was certainly the result of the interaction between tackler and runner, no one's rights were violated.

Consider another case: a burglar enters my house by picking the lock. At the time he enters no one is home. The burglar looks around, finds nothing of value, and leaves. I return home later and find nothing out of order. The lock on the front door has not been damaged and nothing inside the house has been disturbed. The only reason I know a burglar has entered my house is that he left a note saying: "Please find a better job so that you can afford to buy something worth stealing—your local cat burglar." My acute embarrassment causes me to finally have the courage to quit my job, and I subsequently find another one at twice the salary. From this case it is clear that I have not been harmed by the burglar's actions. Indeed, I may even have benefited by those actions. Nevertheless, the burglar's trespass violated my rights, because his entry into my house was not gained with my permission.

These two cases indicate that when a person is harmed, his or her rights have not necessarily been violated, and also that one's rights may be violated even if one is not harmed. A recent paper by J. Roger Lee has detailed more sufficiently than we can here the points made by our preceding examples.[7] Lee's basic argument is that it is not the harmfulness of an action per se that ought to concern legislators, but whether the harm was accompanied by a lack of consent by the one who suffers the harm. Lee further points out that consent does not mean what one would *like* to happen but what one *might reasonably expect* to be the risks and benefits of an action. Broken bones are clearly a risk voluntarily incurred by one who plays professional football even though no one who suffers such injuries would *like* to have them and even though football players would *prefer* to play without receiving any injuries. Thus, if the proper concern of legislators ought to be to protect us from violations of our rights (protection from nonconsensual interferences), the regulation of activities to protect us from harms may extend beyond the province of legitimate governmental authority.

Lee's own argument operates within what he calls a framework of rational expectations.[8] We need not explore the technical details of Lee's discussion to see its main point. If a person enters a situation containing possible risks, harms, or other unpleasant features which were known to the person or could reasonably be presumed to be known, then it is plausible to conclude that the person has consented to those risks, harms, or unpleasant features. If those risks, harms, or unpleasant features then do come about, no one's rights have been violated. If, on the other hand, someone introduces a component into the situation which the person could not plausibly have been said to have consented to in the sense just mentioned, then there is evidence that the person's rights have been violated. Although people tend to complain only when the factor to which they did not consent is harmful, it is important to realize that it is not the harm itself that matters here, but rather the fact of lack of consent.

Real-life cases can be complicated, and that to which a person can be reasonably expected to consent (given cultural circumstances and knowledge) can also be unclear or changeable at times. Nevertheless, borderline or complicated cases do not detract from the validity of the position that causing harm does not necessarily violate rights (or vice versa). Given that the proper function of government is to protect rights, it would therefore not necessarily follow that the government should "do something" if being around smokers is either harmful or offensive. But the question of the extent to which government should or should not interfere with smoking needs more exploration. The next two sections are designed to provide the needed additional discussion based upon the principles just discussed.

Smoking and Property Rights

The Nature of the San Francisco Ordinance

Section 1001 of the San Francisco Smoking Pollution Control Ordinance states:

> Because the smoking of tobacco or any other weed or plant is a danger to health and is a cause of material annoyance and discomfort to those who are present in confined places, the Board of Supervisors hereby declares that the purposes of this article are (1) to protect the public health and welfare by regulating smoking in the office workplace and (2) to minimize the toxic effects of smoking in the office workplace by requiring an employer to adopt a policy that will accommodate, insofar as possible, the preferences of non-smokers and smokers and, if a satisfactory accommodation cannot be reached, to prohibit smoking in the office workplace.

Additional sections of this ordinance spell out the meaning of the points contained in Section 1001. The ordinance is not a complete ban on smoking in the workplace, although in certain cases smoking may have to be banned to accommodate the terms of the ordinance. Rather, the ordinance was intended to institute a two-stage approach. The first phase involves businesses attempting to work out an arrangement that would satisfy both smoking and non-smoking employees. If that cannot be accomplished, that is, if there is even one nonsmoking employee who remains dissatisfied with the arrangement, then smoking must be banned from the workplace.

The ordinance is explicitly weighted in favor of the nonsmoking employee (section 1003), but there are exemptions to the ordinance. "Public places" such as stadiums, bars, and restaurants are exempted; however, medical waiting rooms, libraries, museums, and hospitals do fall under the ordinance. Offices inhabited exclusively by smokers (even if nonsmokers visit) are exempt, as are offices in private homes and offices rented by a single contractor. The ordinance also states that employers are not required to undertake any expenditures to accommodate smoking or nonsmoking employees. Of course, if an employer fails to undertake expenditures to satisfy a nonsmoking employee, the employer may end up having to ban smoking from the workplace entirely.

A number of anomalies are contained in the statement of purpose (section 1001) cited above. First of all, if smoking is such a "danger to health" it seems inconsistent to "accommodate" smokers at all. In hazardous industries such as the chemical industry, the government tends to regulate exposure by *anyone* who comes in contact with the chemical. The government certainly does not allow those who may wish to play with toxic chemicals to risk the health of fellow workers and then ask those workers to "accommodate" their more chemically playful colleagues. In a similar fashion, it is hard to understand how one "minimizes toxic effects" by accommodating producers of those effects. It would seem, therefore, that "public health" is more a ploy to gain legal respectability than a substantive feature of the ordinance. That, of course, leaves "annoyance and discomfort" as the chief justification for the ordinance. Secondly, the ordinance repeatedly refers to accommodating smokers; yet it is difficult to understand what accommodating smokers means here, since it is the nonsmoker who is being accommodated. Logically this must be the case, for there would be no purpose to the ordinance if it did not assume that smokers were already being accommodated. "Accommodation" could, of course, mean a *mutually* acceptable arrangement between smokers and nonsmokers, but if this is its meaning, then the bias in favor of the nonsmoker contradicts the intent of the term. The ordinance could have simply required mutual accommodation and left each office to its own devices about how to secure such accommodation; or it could have required relieving any employee (smoker or nonsmoker) of his position if he refused to bargain in good faith. These are not recommendations on my part, but rather indications of the sloppy or incomprehensible logic of the ordinance.

The preceding arguments are merely minor swipes at an ordinance that has much more serious defects. These defects include excessive governmental intrusion into the liberties of citizens and a violation by government of property rights. We have already discussed many of the background principles needed to make such charges stick. But some additional theorizing is needed to insure that the defects of the ordinance are fully clarified.

Liberty and Property

The connection between liberty and property is one that advocates of governmental power would like to sever. Men like Jefferson and Locke were quite convinced that the surest way for the government to erode the liberty of its citizens was to take control of the property of its citizens. Today the erosion of property rights has gone so far that people no longer associate the right to property with the concept of civil liberties. But as we noted in the first section of this paper, what a government does and what it ought to do are not always the same. Our contention is that "economic liberties" ought to be respected in the same way and for the same reasons as "civil liberties."

Consider, for example, what a civil liberty like freedom of speech would mean without property rights. It would mean that the microphone, newspaper, magazine, or book that you are using to express yourself would be controlled by the state. The potential thus exists (and is likely to be realized) for censorship of views the state finds unacceptable (usually expressed by such phrases as "against the public interest"). With property rights, however, an individual may "censor" the views of those with whom he/she disagrees by excluding the views from his/her magazine or publishing house, but an individual cannot *generally* exclude contrary opinions from society at large as the state can. The same type of reasoning applies to other standard examples of civil liberties, such as freedom of assembly.[9] Civil liberties divorced from property rights therefore represent simply what will be allowed by the currently dominant social power.

In the United States, the term "civil liberties" has come to mean the rights guaranteed by the amendments to its constitution (primarily amendments one through ten and fourteen). These were rights *against* government interference. There is, however, no amendment that refers explicitly to the right of property. This is because the Founding Fathers believed that the separation of powers and the system of checks and balances would be sufficient to protect private property rights. Recent scholarship further indicates that the Founders intended Article I, section 10 of the Constitution to prohibit state intervention with the obligations of contracts.[10] In addition, Bernard Siegan has argued that judicial review of economic liberties and the application of substantive due process to economic matters were part of constitutional law until relatively recently.[11] Thus despite present tendencies to conceptually distinguish economic liberties from other civil liberties, the political and social theory advanced here is not without legal precedent.

For our purposes a distinction must be drawn between government regulation of private property and government protection of private property rights. The latter is a legitimate function of government; the former is not. Ordinary discourse often conflates these two notions by calling legitimate protection of private property rights "regulation."[12] For example, if corporation X promises that its product will perform *p, q* and *r* tasks and the product only performs *q*, it is not "regulation" to require the corporation to make good on its promise or offer compensation. Rather, government action in this case is a protection of my property rights which are infringed if my property (my money) is taken under false pretenses. On the other hand, if corporation X informs a consumer that its product performs *p, q,* and *r* and the state disapproves of *r*, then it would be regulation to prevent corporation X from selling the product with feature *r*. The difference between the two cases is that in the latter some end other than the protection of rights is being sought. Voluntary exchange (my money for the product) between consenting parties is being limited to enhance some end, such as preventing self-harm, beyond the propriety of the exchange itself. The former case, however, recognizes that *both* parties have property rights and seeks to ensure that the exchange of property was a voluntary one.

Notice that the "protection of property rights" has less to do with things and objects than it does with voluntary exchange or use of those objects. We noted above that the concept of "voluntary" can become complicated in certain cases, but this does not detract from the central point: no (property) rights have been violated if A (either group or person) exchanges with B and B with A something to which each is entitled (that is, was not obtained by force or fraud) and of which A and B understand, or can be presumed to understand, the nature, consequences, or uses. Conversely, a person's property rights have been violated if something to which that person is entitled has been taken under false pretenses or (what amounts to the same thing) has been taken in exchange for something whose uses, nature, or consequences the person could not reasonably be expected to understand. To illustrate these general principles with a controversial example, if I (a cancer victim) agree to exchange some money for your bottle of laetril knowing full well the scientific scepticism about the usefulness of that product and in the absence of any claims on your part that the drug will in fact cure cancer, then no one's property rights have been violated by the exchange. If, on the other hand, I purchase your bottle of laetril because you told me it cures cancer and not only does it not perform as promised but also I could not be expected to know the risks I was taking, then my property rights have been violated.

Furthermore, if the government prevents or restricts my informed purchase of the drug or prevents or restricts your sale of the drug despite your willingness to inform the consumer about the possible risks, then both our property rights have been violated. Lee's concept of rational expectations would obviously have some role to play here, since complicated technology may imply a reasonable presumption of ignorance on the part of consumers with respect to certain products. Nevertheless, a regulatory attitude will tend to imply a different sort of approach to this problem than will a "rights protecting" attitude. A regulatory attitude will tend to decide *for* consumers what they ought or ought not to have or purchase; a rights protecting attitude will instead tend to concern itself with consumer information, leaving it up to the consumer to decide what he ought or ought not have or purchase.

The current government posture is regulatory rather than rights protecting; but that is beside the point for present purposes. The rights protecting posture is the one that is consistent with the traditions of individual liberty on which our argument is based. All that remains, therefore, is the application of these principles to the San Francisco ordinance.

Limiting Governmental Power

In discussing the limitations of governmental power over private property, it is first necessary to be clear about the meaning of private property. Property is private if it is owned by an individual or group of individuals and not by the state. Contrary to the San Francisco ordinance's classification scheme, bars and restaurants are not public property. Opening one's doors to the public does not thereby transform private property into public property. The resources are still being controlled and used for the benefit of the owners which, in such cases, is not the government. Museums and libraries, however, may be public property because they are owned by the state and run with tax dollars. To "open one's doors to the public" simply means that one is advertising the terms of an agreement for an exchange to any and all comers. It does not mean that one has a public responsibility to others beyond living up to the terms of the agreement, nor are the owners of such properties implying by their advertisement that they wish to relinquish control of their property to the state.

Despite commonly misleading terminology, companies whose stock is held by large numbers of persons are also not public companies but private companies. The number of owners does not transform a piece of property from private to public. All such companies are claiming when they sell stock is that a share in the equity of the company can be purchased for a certain price. They are not thereby necessarily inviting the state to become business partners. Clearly, then, workplaces qualify as private property, since such places are owned by and are part of private businesses. The obligation of government would therefore be to protect the property rights of those who own these businesses as well as those who trade with these businesses.

One way to trade with a business is to offer services in exchange for money or other forms of remuneration. Protecting property rights in such cases would mean insuring that both parties live up to the terms of their agreement. It obviously does not mean dictating the terms of that agreement. Employers and employees are thus free to come to whatever terms both find mutually agreeable. "Mutually agreeable" here does not mean what either or both parties *wish* to be the case, but rather what conditions are necessary for an exchange to take place. If no exchange takes place, the presumption must be that the terms were not mutually agreeable. If an exchange does take place, the presumption is that the terms were mutually agreeable. The only remaining question would then be whether it is reasonable to assume that both parties understood the terms in question.

It is important to realize that if both parties understood the terms of the agreement, it is quite irrelevant whether one or both parties are harmed by the agreement. A theory which respects rights and liberty must also respect the possibility, even likelihood, that people might willingly undertake risks that could result in harm to them. Since a reasonable presumption exists that people do not wish to harm themselves without an understanding of the risks they are taking, parties to an exchange can expect to be informed of the risks about which they could not reasonably be expected to know. The state may intercede in an exchange on behalf of one party if the other has hidden certain pertinent facts or misled the other party about such facts. If, on the other hand, the risks are understood and an exchange takes place, the person(s) subject to those risks can be understood as having consented to them, leaving no ground for state action.

According to the standards just enumerated, the San Francisco ordinance is a clear violation of property rights and an illegitimate extension of governmental power. It is the employer who has the right to decide the smoking policy of the firm and not the city of San Francisco. If the working conditions with respect to smoking are known to the employee when he or she considers a job offer, then that person has accepted those working conditions in accepting the job. The state's (here the city of San Francisco) imposition of additional restraints upon the employer turns a voluntary agreement into an involuntary one, since state action would be unnecessary if the employer would have voluntarily offered terms like those stated by the ordinance.

One might object that either a) the employees cannot be presumed to understand the claimed health or discomfort effects of working in an environment with smokers, or b) the employees cannot be presumed to understand that there would be smokers in their work environment. Assuming the employer gave no information to the employee about a or b, I find both quite implausible. Smoking has been common enough in workplaces that a person can expect to have coworkers who smoke. Moreover, smoking is common enough for a person to have experienced the "discomforts" of being around smokers. And finally, the possible "negative" health effects of smoking have been sufficiently publicized to warrant the presumption that being around smokers might be risky. Of course, if some of the essays in this volume and elsewhere about the lack of sufficient evidence on the alleged detrimental effects of ambient smoke are true, then the case for government intervention is removed entirely.[13]

Someone may doubt the accuracy of my statements about the cultural expectations of employees accepting jobs in environments with smokers. However, even if I am wrong about these expectations, it affects the argument in only a minor way. If people cannot be expected to know they will be working with smokers, that problem could be solved by an ordinance requiring that firms clearly state their policy on smoking to prospective employees (current employees already know what that policy is).[14] To require that firms inform prospective employees about its smoking policy is in no way similar to the current San Francisco ordinance. Under the proposed "information ordinance," a firm could tell a prospective employee that no smoking anywhere will be allowed, or that it requires smokers and nonsmokers to share desks and that smokers must blow smoke in the nonsmoker's face every five minutes (or anything in between). Although it seems to me that this "information ordinance" would be a superfluous bit of legal posturing, it is at least not inconsistent with individual freedom of choice. The present ordinance, on the contrary, *requires* a certain form of behavior or policy.

It might also be thought that the San Francisco ordinance is not as pernicious as I have implied since its main intention is to accommodate both smokers and nonsmokers. This objection fails to understand the principle involved, which is that employers *have* no social obligation to accommodate either smokers or nonsmokers. Obviously a firm which discriminates completely against smokers or nonsmokers pays an economic cost if more qualified job candidates are sacrificed for adherence to a smoking policy; but that is the firm's business and not the state's. This is all we need show as far as the political nature of smoking in the workplace is concerned.

Private Alternatives

Although companies have the right to adopt whatever smoking policies they choose, it is likely that the market will tend to reflect the desires of prospective employees. In an article in the *San Francisco Chronicle* explaining the smoking ordinance, it was noted that many firms have already adopted smoking policies.[15] In many cases, these were more "anti" or "restrictive" smoking policies than permissive ones, but the general point is worth noting. If most employers have employees who object to working around smokers, the market will begin to reflect this. Not only will employers find ways to satisfy the desires of their employees, but prospective employees will begin looking for firms whose policies best reflect their own smoking habits.

State intervention in market processes such as the San Francisco ordinance is almost always detrimental for reasons other than the ones given above. Because laws must be universal and essentially static, and because actors in the market never universally fall into one behavior pattern or necessarily have the same desires over time, restrictive legislation such as the San Francisco ordinance is invariably inconvenient to many people. Given the general effectiveness with which the market tends to respond to changing desires and attitudes, it seems quite unnecessary and excessive for coercive state action to intervene in that process. Moreover, it is almost comical to observe that those workplaces most plausibly subject to government control—"any property owned or leased by state or federal governmental entities"—are exempt from the San Francisco ordinance.[16]

Smoking and Public Property

Harm and Ambient Tobacco Smoke

Since a restricive case for state control of smoking on private property cannot be made, our attention must be turned to smoking on public property. Public property differs significantly from private property because it is owned by the public and controlled by the state. Unlike private ownership, the owners of public property cannot exclude each other or transfer their shares of the property. Moreover, the resources of the owners are forcibly expropriated to support the management of the public property. In a sense, then, the rules that would govern use of public property would be rules that apply to people who are "stuck" together whether they wish to be or not. And the significant difference between public and private property may make a difference in how we evaluate smoking in such places.

One thing, however, does not seem to change in our movement from private to public property. Paternalism seems no more justified in the public case than in the private. To ban smoking in public places simply because the state has decided its citizens should not smoke is to manage a piece of property against the interests of some of its owners. Unless one can show that people utilize public property for paternalistic purposes, there is no reason to believe that paternalism suddenly becomes a function of government on public property.

On the other hand, the concept of harm does seem to factor in more significantly with respect to public property than with private property. Since owners cannot exclude each other or transfer ownership rights there is virtually no choice about one's associates or possibility of avoiding (or accepting) the potential harms one may face. Thus, preventing harmful or risky behavior on public property would be a legitimate function of the state. If exposure to ambient tobacco smoke is in fact harmful, it could be legitimately banned from public places. We must therefore devote a moment to the question of whether ambient tobacco smoke is harmful.

Although public discussion may proceed as if the negative health effects of ambient tobacco smoke were solidly established, the evidence for such effects is either weak or nonexistent. Certain studies, such as those by White and Froeb, claim to show negative health effects of ambient tobacco smoke.[17] But such studies have been seriously criticized on both methodological and substantive grounds.[18] Furthermore, a number of other studies showing contrary results have been conducted.[19] Statements and supporting evidence to this effect can be found in other essays in this volume, and we are in no position in this essay to judge the validity of the scientific claims and counter-claims on this issue. Nevertheless, a fair reading of *all* evidence on ambient tobacco smoke should generate, even in the layperson, a high degree of scepticism that there is sufficient evidence to support claims that ambient tobacco smoke is harmful.

In this section of the paper, therefore, we shall operate under the assumption that ambient tobacco smoke is not a health hazard. Instead we shall assume that a significant number of people find it annoying to be around smokers. On the basis of this assumption we shall discuss the principles that might apply to offensive behavior on public property.

The Balance of Interests Approach

One of the remarkable aspects of the San Francisco ordinance is that it does not cover hallways, lobbies and office lounges.[20] On the face of it, it would seem more plausible for the state to regulate such "public places" than it would for it to control the activities of private offices. Of course, the argument could be made that, unlike an office, the limited exposure to tobacco smoke one would face in lounges and hallways does not justify state regulation of smoking in such places (beyond what the Fire Marshall may require). This argument may be true, but it concedes a great deal. Since public buildings are analogous to lounges and hallways with respect to public usage, this argument suggests that smoking should be permitted on similar terms in public buildings. Secondly, the argument admits that at least limited exposure to ambient smoke is not a health problem. And finally, the argument seems to imply that smoking is sufficiently inoffensive to most other people that the state need not concern itself with smoking in such "public places."

We cannot, however, assume that all regulators will use the same type of logic that seems to be exhibited by the San Francisco ordinance. Therefore let us keep our assumption that smoking offends a significant number of people even if it does not harm them. Remembering that all citizens are technically co-owners of public property with the government serving as their trustee, the question now is what principles might be advanced for determining when the government can legitimately ban "offensive" behavior from public places?

In a well known essay Feinberg outlines the principles that ought to apply to offense behavior in public places.[21] Feinberg's purpose was to derive a set of principles that would mediate between reasonable and unreasonable offense. Some people, for example, might be "unreasonably" offended by the sight of an interracial couple kissing in a public place. It does not seem to Feinberg that the state should prevent such "offenses." On the other hand, erecting pornographic billboards in Times Square does seem to be a form of behavior that the state might "reasonably" prevent. Thus Feinberg sought to develop a set of principles that would not call for state intervention in the first case but would in the second.

Feinberg selects three principles which are designed to solve the aforementioned problem.[22] The first of these is the "standard of universality," under which the behavior in question must be offensive to a vast majority of people, with "vast majority of people" meaning "any person chosen at random, taking the nation as a whole, and not because the individual selected belongs to some faction, clique, or party."[23] The second standard is the "standard of reasonable avoidability." If an action qualifies as offensive under the first principle, there may still not be sufficient grounds to prevent it if individuals can avoid experiencing the offensive act without undue inconvenience. As Feinberg points out, thrusting pornographic pictures into people's hands on a public street violates this second principle; but if those same pictures are contained in a book that one neither has to purchase nor open, the second principle does not permit state intervention. It is important to note that this second principle should be concerned with normal people: "No respect should be shown for *abnormal susceptibilities*," Feinberg states.[24] Finally, if a person is constrained by law for offensive behavior, such a person "must be granted an allowable alternative outlet or mode of expression."[25] We shall assume that this third principle applies only if a behavior can be shown to be offensive by the first two principles. This assumption is justified because the third principle begins with the notion that someone's behavior was restricted for offensive behavior.

If we apply these principles to public smoking, we see that the first principle does not justify state intervention with smoking. Since we can safely assume a) that smokers do not mind being around other smokers, b) that there is a significantly large population of smokers, and c) that many nonsmokers have no objection to being around smokers, there is no reason to suppose that any normal adult picked at random from the nation at large would object to smoking in public places.[26] Given this answer to the first principle, it would seem that there is little reason to call upon the second. Nevertheless, to avoid any biases and to account for the possibility that some random samples would not suggest anything definitive, let us consider the second principle.

The second principle would seem to support antismoking advocates. After all, it is not easy to avoid cigarette smoke once it is in the air. However, given our assumption that ambient tobacco smoke is not harmful, the burden of proof under this balancing of interests approach rests with the antismoker and not the smoker. The antismoker is the one calling upon intervention with an activity that is a common occurrence. Thus, the antismoker must show that there are no reasonable ways to avoid smokers. If this can be shown, then the state is obligated *not* to ban smoking in most places, but only to provide alternatives for antismokers. Further, providing alternatives for antismokers is not the same as providing alternatives for nonsmokers, since not all nonsmokers can be presumed to be antismokers. It is only under a condition where most of society is filled with antismokers that public property may have to make special provisions for the smoker. Thus under current conditions smoking should be permitted in public places.

One may still wish to argue that although most nonsmokers may not mind that much being around smokers, they would, given a choice, *prefer* not to be around smokers. It should be remembered, however, that smokers are legitimate owners of public property also. Mere preference therefore is not sufficient grounds for restricting their liberty. I, for example, would prefer not to be around people with body odor or loud and ill-mannered individuals in public places, or children on field trips to the museum as I seek to contemplate the artifacts in silence. My preferences do not, however, justify a claim to exclude such individuals or groups, especially if I can find alternate times to visit a public place when the likelihood of confronting such individuals is lessened. The bias must always be in favor of freedom of action, and this bias places the burden of proof squarely on the shoulders of those who would restrict another's actions—not the other way around.

Some may claim that the foregoing argument gives the benefit of the doubt to the smoker when really it should be the other way around. After all, the "natural" state of things is for there not to be smoke in the air. Since the smoker initiates an action against others of which they may disapprove, this places the burden of proof on the smoker. Of course, erecting a building is not "natural" either; but this argument may be saying that individuals have a right to clean air and that the smoker is someone who pollutes that air. Hence a moment must be spent discussing this type of argument.

The Rights Approach

Pollution need not be harmful to qualify as pollution. If I dump my trash on your yard, I have "polluted" your yard even though the type of trash involved may only be papers so that no issue of a health hazard arises. Public smoking might be viewed in a similar vein. Even though the smoke from my cigarette may not harm you, it does enter your airspace and thus could be seen as a form of "pollution." Of course, I have the right to "pollute" my own airspace provided I do not infringe upon yours (and vice versa).

As some recent work has suggested, the rights approach remains unmoved in the face of pleas to consider the costs or inconveniences to polluters.[27] Polluters must refrain or be made to refrain from polluting regardless of costs or inconvenience. But the rights approach is not as simplistic as first appearances might suggest. The preceding sentences do not imply that all pollution must be halted. Rather, the implication is that pollution can occur on one's own property provided it does not spread to the property of others without their consent. What is needed, therefore, are unambiguous rights claims—not necessarily the cessation of all pollution. Since private property establishes relatively unambiguous rights claims, a solution to the pollution problem consistent with individual rights is to privatize unowned or public resources. Oddly enough, a certain "meeting of the minds" is now occurring on this issue between philosophers (who argue from a theory of individual rights) and economists (who tend to view matters in cost/benefit terms). A number of thinkers in both groups are calling for the privatization of public resources as a means of solving the pollution problem.[28]

It can safely be assumed that privatization is already established in places that are now private. Consequently, our section on smoking and private property shows that there is no significant pollution problem with respect to smoking and private business establishments. As we noted above, firms have the right to make whatever arrangements they wish regarding smoking. Although privatization will go a long way towards removing the ambiguities involved in solving conflicts of interest over public resources, we must assume that there will always be some public property, since the government will, at the very least, need buildings from which to operate.[29] What, then, can be said about an alleged form of nonharmful pollution in areas that must remain public?

Ostensibly the rights approach would not answer the foregoing question by an appeal to cost–benefit (or "risk–benefit") analysis or by an appeal to "balancing interests." This is because a theory of individual rights such as the one outlined in this paper tends to see such approaches as subsuing the individual into some sort of social aggregate. The sphere of permissible behavior for the individual is thus defined in terms of some overall social good (for example, that the benefits to society exceed the costs), rather than the social good being a function of the protection of individual rights. Under the aggregating method an individual's interest will be respected only to the extent that a sufficient number of others have the same or similar interest. If only a few have the same interest, then that interest will tend to lose in the face of an overwhelming majority of contrary interests. But if there are sufficient numbers on both sides of an issue, some procedure for balancing the interests would have to be found.

The rights approach, on the other hand, places little or no emphasis on how many people line up on one side or the other of an issue. Hence, if an individual has a right to a certain resource, his freedom to use that resource cannot be restricted (assuming that his use does not violate any one else's rights) *even if society would be "worse off" by that individual's use of his property*. With respect to the public smoking issue, then, someone might argue that if ambient smoke violates the airspace of even one individual, the inconvenience to smokers is irrelevant to the legitimacy of requiring that they refrain from such activities. Certainly this argument places the burden of proof on the smoker's shoulders in a way that the argument of the preceding section may not have.

The rights argument works if the premise about violating another's airspace can be established. Keeping in mind, however, that the resource in question here is *necessarily* public and cannot be subject to privatization, both the smoker and nonsmoker can lay equally justified claims to exactly the same airspace. The nonsmoker has no more right to say that the air must be free of smoke than the smoker has the right to say it can be full of smoke, since both are owners of the same air.[30] Here we have a true and irreconcilable conflict of interest, for without clearly distinguishable rights claims (allowing exclusion and transferability), there is no basis to decide in favor of one interest to the exclusion of the other. The only way to handle such a case, therefore, is to employ the "second best" solution of trying to balance interests as discussed in the last section. In essence, public property is not amenable to analysis in terms of individual rights.[31] Given our assumption that the property in question is necessarily public and that no impending threat of serious harm exists, something like the balancing of interests approach discussed above is all that can be used in conflict of interest cases.

It is interesting to note that the foregoing argument has something significant to say about broader problems of pollution. Except perhaps in cases where an obvious, immediate and serious threat to health is present, those who wish to solve the pollution problem by turning over more and more resources to the state are in essence asking that more and more resources become subject to irreconcilable conflicts of interest. Recent trends in the politics of pollution seem to bear this point out.[32] In contrast, the establishment of private property rights in the marketplace provides a system whereby individuals can express their true values on how much pollution they wish to avoid or be exposed to. Of course, *if* public smoking were taken to be a form of pollution, it would be on a much more limited and minor scale than externalities such as acid rain or toxic wastes.

We can now conclude this section by noting that, since the balance of interests approach must be employed in situations of necessarily public property, no case can be made for banning smoking from public property at this time. Indeed, only under certain limited conditions—conditions where the antismoker must be given an outlet—can a case be made for segregating smokers and nonsmokers. Of course the particulars of this analysis may change if the vast majority of people become antismokers or if they become prosmokers. If the pendulum swings significantly in either of these directions, the minority of advocates left on the other side will be losers. That is the inherent difficulty with public property, as we noted above.

Conclusion: Markets, Manners and Public Policy

In this chapter we have tried to discuss the limits of governmental intervention in the smoking controversy. We have assumed that smoking is either harmful or offensive in order to clarify the role of government under a "worst case" scenario. Of course, if smoking is neither harmful nor offensive, especially to others, then the case for government involvement is weakened considerably. "Offense," however, is a rather subjective concept and it is doubtful that smoking (or any other adult pleasure) will ever be free from being offensive to somebody. Furthermore, however misguided the San Francisco ordinance may be, its even marginal political acceptability does indicate some significant disapproval of smoking by many people.[33] Significant disapproval does not, on the other hand, mandate a public policy on smoking, and herein lies one of the chief problems with current thinking about public policy.

Since the ultimate weapon of the state is the use of coercive physical force, one would expect a civilized society to call upon such a weapon only as a last resort and only when evidence of nonconsensual risk is beyond reasonable doubt. As we noted at the end of the second section, state action tends to be universal and inflexible and thus tends to ignore differences of desire and circumstance. A law such as the San Francisco ordinance may speak of accommodation, but everyone knows that the bottom line has more to do with obedience than accommodation. It is unfortunate, therefore, that instead of calling upon the state last, people today look to the state first to reform behavior which some find objectionable. The hysterical claims and missionary-like zeal exhibited by groups who wish to impose their vision of the good upon others is symptomatic of certain asocializing forces in our society.

The reasons for this disturbing trend could range from the theory that members of wealthy urbanized cultures have the proximity and leisure to concern themselves with the behavior of others to the idea that vocal publicity is an effective means of tapping public resources for one's own ends. Speculation about such causes is best left to sociologists and economists, but there is one consideration we can offer in this context—the widespread ignorance of the meaning of political liberty and its practical correlate, the free market. Despite the rhetoric about competition, we need to understand that the marketplace is an instrument of accommodation and socialization and not, as its critics charge, a vehicle for asocialization. On the other hand, state power that extends beyond what is necessary for individuals to enjoy peace and security is destructive of social life.

Because a free market is defined by freedom of exchange, the benefits of exchange can only be enjoyed if individuals find mutually agreeable terms according to which they make their exchanges. Thus the incentives of the marketplace are all towards accommodation. Joseph Schumpeter noted long ago that one of the reasons it would be unlikely for businessmen to lead the fight against the erosion of economic liberties is that such people develop habits of accommodation instead of conflict. Businessmen cannot afford to alienate potential customers, and although this may not generate the kinds of feelings one finds in a family, it will tend to diminish dogmatic and self-righteous attitudes.

If, on the other hand, the value of political liberty is unappreciated, the social benefits of market processes will be ignored or rejected. Problems will then become politicized, creating incentives opposite to the ones just mentioned. Apart from the inherent moral problems that arise from a disrespect of liberty, reliance upon state-imposed solutions will tend to generate rather than alleviate social alienation. If social winners and losers are defined by the extent to which their policies can be imposed upon others through state action, it is clear that some gain *at the expense of* others, rather than by agreement *with* others. The public smoking controversy is a good case in point. Both smokers and nonsmokers feel victimized by whatever public policy is adopted. If no policy against smoking in public is issued by the state, nonsmokers believe that they are not being protected. If restrictive smoking policies are adopted, smokers believe that they are being unfairly abused. It seldom occurs to either side that maybe the public smoking question is not an issue that should be conceived in public policy terms at all.

Under the assumption that the case for the negative health effects of ambient tobacco smoke is negligible or nonexistent, the market and good manners are more than adequate to solve any problems between smokers and nonsmokers. Businesses can try various smoking policies to meet the needs of their customers, clients, and employees. These policies will tend to reflect the desires of those customers, clients, and employees without generalizing to the circumstances of other businesses. For example, one restaurant may find that most of its customers are nonsmokers and therefore adopt more restrictive smoking rules than another restaurant whose customers are mostly smokers. Why, in all fairness and justice, should the policies of one of the businesses have to apply to another? Similarly, private individuals in their own personal relations will function in a market-like manner as well. The value a person places on being around smokers or nonsmokers will tend to influence the choices that person makes in social contexts.

Leaving the issue to the marketplace might seem like a submission to pro-smoking forces. A little reflection, however, will indicate that there is nothing in the preceding suggestion that formally supports either smoking or non-smoking forces. That would depend on social attitudes at any given moment.

It is interesting to note that despite the reputation the tobacco industry has for being all-powerful, it has not been that effective in reversing the trend towards negative attitudes about smoking, even among many smokers. And as one might expect, the market is beginning to reflect these attitudes without the help of the state.

Finally, a word must be said in defense of good manners. However well the market works, we often find ourselves in situations where the smoking preferences of those around us are unknown or different from our own. In general, good manners suggest that we consider the interests of others and defer our own desires to theirs if the demands for doing so are not too excessive. It seems quite rude for a smoker to light up in a room full of non-smokers who have made their distaste of smoking known. By the same token, it is excessively boorish for a nonsmoker to hysterically demand that a room full of smokers put out their cigarettes or to lecture them on the "evils" of smoking. Both parties can excuse themselves periodically or suffer some inconvenience for a time. Certainly the state cannot serve as a surrogate for good manners, since rules of etiquette are useful in precisely those cases which the general perspective of the state can never anticipate or comprehend.

Perhaps the general point of this paper, then, is that the habit of calling upon the state to relieve any inconvenience is more dangerous than current presumptions about the habit of smoking itself. To ask public authorities to take responsibility for what can and should be the responsibility of individuals is always a threat to liberty. Thus although the factual assertions about the smoking controversy may dominate public discussion, deeper issues of political and social philosophy may lie beneath those more visible disputes. And in the end, the deeper issues may be more significant for public policy than the factual assertions will ever be.

Notes

1. See Saul K. Padover, *Jefferson* (New York: Mentor Books, 1952), p. 35.
2. The moral point of view per se is broader than the rights issue, however. It should also be mentioned that even if one does not adopt a natural rights perspective, the argument of the following pages holds, because it depends on a commitment to the central value of liberty which some may arrive at by means other than a natural rights approach. However, it is my view that the natural rights approach best secures the central value of liberty. Moreover, this is still the language of much political debate on moral and political values.
3. Joel Feinberg, "Legal Paternalism," in *Rights, Justice, and the Bounds of Liberty* (Princeton: Princeton University Press, 1980), p. 129.
4. Ibid., p. 121.
5. Ibid.
6. Someone might wish to argue that the allegedly "addictive" character of smoking makes the action substantially nonvoluntary. The thesis that smoking is addictive,

however, is thoroughly discredited by the large and ever growing number of people who quit smoking. Smoking is at most a habit (perhaps a strong one). But habits are not "substantially nonvoluntary" actions. Indeed, one of the first great moralists—Aristotle—claimed that the whole purpose of morality was to "habituate oneself to virtue." Thus "habit" and "voluntariness" are not in conflict. All the term "habit" implies is a degree of difficulty in altering behavior.

7. J. Roger Lee, "Choice and Harms," in T. Machan and M.B. Johnson, eds., *Rights and Regulation* (Cambridge, Mass.: Ballinger, 1983), pp. 157–173.

8. Technically defined by Lee as: "If a person truly and knowingly enters into situation A, which has the rational-expectation framework (p,q,r,s, not-t), then if that person objects to the consequence of an event described by 'p', that person owes an explanation why p is objectionable and further, why, knowing that p would eventuate, he/she entered into situation A. The fact that he/she entered into situation A is strong evidence that the occurrence of p does not violate his/her rights. Similarly, if the rational-expectation framework for situation A clearly excludes t, then if t occurs when a person B enters into A and if t was a consequence of an act of a second person C toward B in situation A, then there is evidence that C has violated B's rights" (p. 169).

9. See Tibor R. Machan, *Human Rights and Human Liberties* (Chicago: Nelson Hall, 1975).

10. Bernard H. Siegan, *Economic Liberties and the Constitution* (Chicago: University of Chicago Press, 1980), p. 5 and Ch. 2.

11. Ibid., Ch. 1ff.

12. See Tibor Machan, "Should Business Be Regulated?" in T. Regan, ed., *Just Business: New Introductory Essays in Business Ethics* (New York: Random House, 1984), pp. 202–234.

13. Of course, some nonsmokers may still find being around smokers "offensive." But if the government has no business dictating acceptable risk, it surely has no business dictating acceptable offenses.

14. This parenthetical remark may seem too facile for some. It must be remembered, however, that the smoking case is not comparable to a situation where a substance previously thought to be harmless has suddenly been discovered to be toxic. In such emergency situations the state might intervene *temporarily* to insure that people understand the risks involved. Claims against smoking (even exposure to ambient smoke), on the other hand, have been around for a long time. Most nonsmokers have grown up around parents or peers who smoke. Continued association by nonsmokers with smokers suggests a degree of scepticism about the hyperbolic claims made against exposure to ambient smoke. Thus it is unlikely that employment patterns would change significantly even if some minor long term risks could in fact be established. In any case, *if* a thoroughly substantiated risk were discovered, employers could give current employees a reasonable period of time to decide whether they wish to accept the firm's smoking policy.

15. Marshall Kilduff, "How Smoking Law Will Affect Firms and S.F. Workers," *San Francisco Chronicle*, 10 November 1983.

16. Section 1004 of the Smoking Pollution Control Ordinance.

17. J. White and H. Froeb, "Small-Airways Dysfunction in Non-Smokers Chronically Exposed to Tobacco Smoke," *New England Journal of Medicine*, 1980 (302), pp. 720–723.

18. A summary of such criticisms is contained in the *Congressional Record*, 16 December 1982, submitted by The Honorable L.H. Fountain.

19. Statement by Michael D. Lebowitz to Public Health Commission, County of Los Angeles.

20. Kilduff, "Smoking Law."

21. Joel Feinberg, "Harmless Immoralities," in *Rights, Justice, and the Bounds of Liberty* (Princeton: Princeton University Press, 1980), pp. 69–95.

22. Ibid., pp. 88–92.

23. Ibid., p. 88.

24. Ibid., p. 90.

25. Ibid., p. 91.

26. Remember, that those who have a vested interest in seeing smoking increased or banned are excluded from Feinberg's random selection.

27. Tibor Machan, "Pollution and Political Theory," in Tom Regan, ed., *Earthbound: New Introductory Essays in Environmental Ethics* (New York: Random House, 1984), pp. 74–106.

28. For a good discussion of this point and the whole pollution question, see Peter H. Aranson, "Pollution Control: The Case for Competition," in *Instead of Regulation* (Lexington, Mass.: D.C. Heath and Company, 1982), pp. 339–393.

29. Nevertheless, in a rightly ordered society, the amount of public property would be negligible. Even streets and roads need not be public. For example, see Walter Block, "A Free Market in Roads," in *The Libertarian Reader* (Totowa, N.J.: Rowman and Littlefield, 1982), pp. 164–183.

30. It might be argued that the nonsmoker has a clear right to his lungs and what goes into them even if he does not have the same right with respect to the air. But of course the smoker has the same right. And since it is the same air that must be used to exercise either right, the conflict of interest remains.

31. Even in the case of harm, it is not individual rights that justifies state action, but rather that balancing interests and excluding harm cannot be reconciled, so excluding harm is given priority.

32. See B. Peter Pashigian, "The Political Economy of the Clean Air Act: Regional Self-Interest in Environmental Legislation," Center for the Study of American Business, Formal Publication Number 51, Oct. 1982.

33. The point is not limited to the San Francisco area. California has had statewide referendums on smoking similar to the San Francisco ordinance. Although these were defeated, opponents of smoking did not fail to generate some significant support.

Appendix 6A
The Political Philosophy of the World Health Organization

Since smoking is not a practice limited to the United States, the smoking controversy is also not similarly limited. In this appendix I will briefly indicate the type of political philosophy exhibited by the World Health Organization (WHO)—the major force behind the international antismoking campaign. The attitudes of WHO and the implications of those attitudes will be mentioned, so that the reader may draw his or her own conclusions about the value of WHO's approach. The arguments advanced in the body of the paper would apply to much of the antismoking legislation recommended by WHO. To avoid the tedium of discussing every minor difference in legislative style found around the world, it is enough simply to note the social and political assumptions behind the WHO campaign against smoking.

In 1982 a WHO-commissioned study entitled *Legislative Action to Combat the World Smoking Epidemic* was published.* This study can serve as a basis for evaluating the central social and political assumptions underlying WHO's campaign against smoking as well as the assumptions of various other antismoking groups and governments. From this study one discovers that the political and social principles of WHO and certain governments can be summed up under three categories: 1) paternalism, 2) social engineering, and 3) crude utilitarianism. We shall discuss each in turn.

As we noted in the body of the paper, paternalism is the view that governments ought to direct their citizens to what that government believes are appropriate forms of behavior. Liberty or freedom of action takes a distinct second place to government control of behavior for the desired end. The study refers to the argument based on liberty used by the tobacco industry as "specious" and claims that there is a "fundamental interest of governments

---

*Ruth Roemer, *Legislative Action to Combat the World Smoking Epidemic* (Geneva: World Health Organization, 1982). Page references will be cited in the body of this appendix. The beginning of this document contains a disclaimer saying that the views of the study do not necessarily represent those of WHO. But since this study was commissioned by WHO, and since the contents of the study indicate WHO's approach to the smoking issue, what follows should fairly accurately represent the WHO position.

in protecting public health" (p. 15). This may sound plausible, but in fact the study draws no distinction between possible self-harm and harm to others. "Protection" actually means control of *personal* as well as public behavior. Throughout the study, governments are invited "to discourage adults [not just children] from smoking" (p. 49). A case in point is the push to restrict or ban cigarette vending machines. The study claims that "such legislation is important because it reduces the general availability of cigarettes and eliminates the suggestion of public approval of cigarettes associated with their wide availability in vending machines" (pp. 49–50). Clearly, WHO and its affiliates have adopted an explicitly paternalistic policy toward those who smoke irrespective of effects upon others.

What is implicit is even more astounding than what is explicit in the WHO study. We are told, for example, that public transport workers should reduce or eliminate their smoking to avoid "the risk of sudden cardiac arrest" that could affect their passengers. On the basis of this kind of reasoning, governments would have the right to control the weight, cholesterol intake, sleeping habits, personal pressures, and exercise programs of anyone transporting another person. On a more principled level, WHO's paternalistic program is further exemplified by a redefinition of key concepts. WHO's Expert Committee on Smoking Control defines "freedom" as follows: "freedom should be seen not as the freedom of the manufacturer to promote a known health hazard but rather as the freedom and ability of society to implement public health measures" (p. 16). This definition implies that whatever "society" considers to be for the public good is freedom. Thus one can be forced to be free, if one's voluntary actions do not conform to state determinations of the public good. It takes little imagination to recognize the authoritarian implications of such a conception of freedom.

It is obvious from the foregoing that a great deal of social engineering will have to take place if governments are going to alter the behavior and desires of their citizens. In this connection it is enough to quote a 1979 statement by Dr. H. Mahler, described as the Director-General of WHO. The passage from the WHO study quoted below comes after Dr. Mahler has given the standard line on the health hazards of smoking. His remarks are further described as being "even more important" than controlling the health hazards of smoking:

> There are encouraging indications . . . that some political parties with a vision of a new kind of post-industrial society are beginning themselves to put the quality of life on their platforms and are taking the initiative of urging a reassessment of economic and social values, including the values that lie at the root of so much smoking. (p. 51)

If such a statement had not come from a "responsible" source, it would not be necessary to mention that the very definition of social engineering is a politician or other public authority who has a "vision" for a "new kind" of society and who is willing to "urge" (coerce) "a reassessment of economic and social values."

Finally, we come to the category of crude utilitarianism. Utilitarianism is generally known by the phrase "the greatest good for the greatest numbers." A crude version of this philosophy would be characterized by a readiness to sacrifice individual and minority rights if more people would even be slightly better off by doing so. This type of utilitarianism tends to aggregate individuals into classes and then attempt a simplistic form of cost–benefit analysis on the competing interests of the groups. The WHO study is not bashful on either count. For example, we are told explicitly that a government may have to "infringe some individual rights" in order to protect public health (p. 15). Moreover, the study conceives the smoking problem to be one of weighing the "rights" of smokers against nonsmokers (p. 59). There are, however, no "rights" of smokers or nonsmokers. There are only the rights of individuals which, as we have seen, WHO believes can be sacrificed if they stand in the way of some conception of the public good.

One further concept, favorably referred to in the WHO study (p. 58), combines elements of all three categories mentioned above. This is the concept of "rule-switching." The National Board of Health of Finland explains this concept as follows: "The philosophy in our approach has been one of 'rule-switching': instead of allowing smoking unless specifically forbidden the general rule now is that smoking in all public places is *prohibited unless specifically allowed*" (p. 16, emphasis in original).

The implications of this principle are staggering. For centuries political philosophers have agreed that one of the most important safeguards of liberty is that citizens have the right to pursue those actions they desire to pursue unless specifically prohibited by government. The burden of proof was always on the state to demonstrate the need for prohibition of actions often taken by its citizens. By reversing or "switching" this rule, the burden of proof now rests with the citizen to prove that actions other than those designated as acceptable by the state are justified. However harmful smoking is alleged to be, the totalitarian specter raised by "rule-switching" is the most serious threat to liberty advocated by WHO.

The social and political principles assumed or utilized by WHO render the facts about smoking irrelevant to anyone who values liberty. Paternalism, social engineering, and crude utilitarianism should be opposed even if unequivocal agreement develops on the claimed effects of tobacco smoke. And it is a sad commentary on our contemporary world when commercial enterprises such as the tobacco industry understand more about the nature of liberty than do the authoritative bodies instituted to "safeguard" it.

7
Smokers versus Nonsmokers

William F. Shughart II
Robert D. Tollison

I
n many locations today there is an important public policy struggle taking place between smokers and nonsmokers. The City of San Francisco, for example, recently enacted an ordinance banning smoking in a wide variety of public areas, and requiring employees to establish smoking rules for the workplace that satisfy their nonsmoking employees. San Francisco was not the first jurisdiction in the United States to mandate the segregation of smoking and nonsmoking employees. Five states and fourteen cities and counties had passed workplace smoking laws before San Francisco's voters approved Proposition P. Six other cities have since adopted similar restrictions. (Public smoking ordinances in another six cities include voluntary provisions for the private workplace; at least three dozen other jurisdictions have adopted smoking restrictions that affect only local government employees.)

Typical state laws restricting smoking are summarized in table 7–1. To illustrate, the Connecticut statute calls for nonsmoking areas in most restaurants, no smoking in a variety of public places, and the promulgation of workplace smoking rules by firms having fifty or more employees. As of late 1984, similar legislation was pending in five states (Massachusetts, Michigan, New Jersey, New York, and Pennsylvania), and various local ordinances restricting smoking in the workplace were under consideration in twenty-one cities and counties.[1] Moreover, the Civil Aeronautics Board voted to ban smoking on all airline flights lasting two hours or less, but subsequently reversed its decision when the Chairman changed his mind.

These legislative initiatives are by no means confined to the United States. Laws that restrict or ban "public" smoking to varying degrees are on the books in at least seventeen industrialized nations, notably France, Sweden, and Canada. Antismoking regulations have also begun to appear in a number of developing countries.

[Economists tend to see this widespread conflict between smokers and nonsmokers as a matter of certain environmental property rights. Smokers have historically held these rights either by custom or by default, and still do in most settings. Nonsmokers are now seeking, whether for perceived medical

Table 7–1
State Laws Restricting Smoking

State (Date of Adoption)	Employer's Responsibilities	Enforcement/ Penalties	Other Public Smoking Restriction Areas
Connecticut (June 1983)	Establish written rules governing smoking and nonsmoking, post and provide copies to employees. "The rule may include the designation of nonsmoking areas."	Not specified for private workplace. Other smoking laws carry $5 fine for violation.	Restaurants (75+ persons), health care facilities, elevators, retail food stores, public meetings, classrooms of public schools or colleges.
Montana (March 1979)	Designate nonsmoking areas, designate smoking areas, or designate entire areas as smoking. Post signs accordingly.	Enforcement by local boards of health. Penalty to employer (added in 1981) maximum $25.	Restaurants, stores, trains, buses, education and health facilities, auditoriums, arenas, public meeting rooms, elevators, museums, libraries, state/local government offices.
Nebraska (May 1980)	"To prohibit smoking in those places of work where the close proximity of workers or the inadequacy of ventilation causes smoke pollution detrimental to the health and comfort of nonsmoking employees" or "to make reasonable efforts to prevent smoking in the workplace" by "arranging seating to provide a smoke-free area," posting signs, asking smokers to refrain upon request of a client or employee suffering discomfort from the smoke.	Department of Health enforces. Fines up to $100 per violation by smoker or employer. Department of Health, local health board or any affected party may ask for injunction.	Restaurants, retail stores, public conveyances, education and health facilities, auditoriums, arenas, meeting rooms.

Utah
(August 1976)

Make "reasonable efforts" by posting signs and "arranging seating to provide a smoke-free area." May use existing physical barriers and ventilation.

Enforcement by local boards of health. Fine up to $299 per violation by employer or smoker. Also, up to 90 days in jail for employer violation.

Restaurants, retail stores, public conveyances, health facilities, auditoriums, meeting rooms, buildings supported by tax revenues, any place that proprietor posts as no smoking. Regulations also include hotels, motels, and resorts.

Minnesota
(June 1975)

By regulation, "Shall make arrangements for an acceptable smoke-free area" separated by 56" high barrier or by 4' space; or meeting specific ventilation standards; or meeting specific carbon monoxide limits. Must determine preferences of employees and other users, may designate smoking areas proportional in size to preference, using existing physical barriers and ventilation systems.

State and local boards of health enforce. Violation by smoker gets fine up to $100. Injunctive action against employer.

Restaurants, retail stores, public conveyances, education and health facilities, auditoriums, arenas, meeting rooms, state/local government offices. Hotels, motels, and resorts are included by regulation.

Source: The Tobacco Institute.

or nuisance reasons, to have these property rights reassigned. They view tobacco smoke as a negative externality and argue through their representatives for restrictions on smoking behavior. Seen in this light, we have a contest for property rights and externality control. More importantly, it is argued that since the market has "failed" to provide a solution, government has a legitimate role to play in resolving the issue.

The purpose of this chapter is to call this interpretation of the atmospheric tobacco smoke or public smoking issue into question. In so doing, we offer an alternative hypothesis based on income redistribution from smokers to nonsmokers to explain the salient facts of the present situation.

The Social Costs of Public Smoking Are Proximately Zero

Two key targets of the antismoking movement have been smoking in the workplace and "public" facilities such as bars, restaurants, and airplanes. Legislation is being designed by city, county, and state governments to place strict limits on the rights of smokers on the job and in other settings where they may come in contact with nonsmokers. Economic theory will not support such legislation. In a basic sense, where a regime of private property rights prevails, the social costs of environmental tobacco smoke are zero.

The bar, the restaurant, the airline, and the firm are privately-owned entities with a residual claimant(s). In each case, the owner has an economic incentive to provide the type of environment that workers and customers want. For example, firms hiring employees in a competitive labor market will provide certain workplace environments as part of the optimizing compensation package. This may involve smoker–nonsmoker segregation on the job, investment in smoke-removal devices, paying smokers or nonsmokers a wage premium to work in a given environment, and so on. The point is that the owner will internalize the costs of smoking in the workplace.

Consider some examples. Suppose that all workers prefer to smoke on the job, but that the owner of a firm objects strongly to tobacco smoke in the workplace. Clearly, the owner must bear the costs of indulging his preferences. If he requires that his employees not smoke on the job and offers only the going market wage, no one will be willing to work for him. To induce his employees not to smoke, the owner must pay, over and above the competitive wage, a premium that is just sufficient to make employment in his firm as attractive as alternative jobs where there are no restrictions on smoking. On the other hand, the owner can offer the market wage, allow smoking on the job, and invest in smoke-removal devices that bring the air quality to his liking. In either case, the costs of imposing a given smoking policy are internal to the firm.

Now suppose that the owner is indifferent between smoke-filled and smoke-free environments, but that some of the workers wish to smoke on the job and others prefer no tobacco smoke in the workplace. How does the owner reconcile these conflicting preferences? There are several alternatives. As before, the owner can ban smoking and pay a wage premium to smokers. Similarly, he can allow smoking on the job and compensate nonsmokers. Other options are to segregate smoking and nonsmoking employees or to install smoke-removal equipment. Which of these is chosen will depend on such factors as the mix of smokers and nonsmokers in the firm's work force, the cost and effectiveness of air cleaners, and the nature of the firm's production process, that is, can workers be separated without adverse effects on overall productivity? Market forces will lead the owner to select the smoking policy that achieves the desired result at minimum cost. In a competitive market, we would therefore expect to observe a variety of smoking policies adopted across firms, each of which is optimal for the given circumstances.

Exactly the same argument applies to the owner of a restaurant, bar, or any other private firm that serves a public composed of smokers and nonsmokers. The market for dining out, for example, will discipline firms in the restaurant industry to provide preferred eating and drinking environments. This involves the mechanisms mentioned previously: smoker–nonsmoker segregation, smoke-removal devices, price–environmental tradeoffs, and so forth. If the owner bans smoking, smokers will patronize the establishment only if the price–quality combination offered is as attractive as alternative eating places where smoking is allowed. The opposite applies for nonsmokers if smoking is permitted. The owner can indulge his own preferences at a cost. Thus, a variety of smoking policies will arise in the marketplace, and in the process the social costs of smoking in restaurants and bars are minimized.

In sum, with private property and residual claimants in place, the social costs of public smoking are proximately zero. Another way of making the same point is to say that even if nonsmokers were given the relevant underlying property rights, private entrepreneurs would not set out to change existing workplace and restaurant environments, since by our argument these environments are already optimally determined. This is just the Coase Theorem at work in this case. The implication, of course, is that government intervention cannot improve the situation; there are no relevant externalities left to internalize. Efficiency considerations therefore do not provide a rationale for laws restricting smoking in a private market setting.[2]

An Alternative Explanation

The need for an alternative interpretation of the origin of laws against public smoking is apparent. Private entrepreneurs have adopted social-cost-minimizing smoking policies, yet we observe various antismoking activists using the machinery of government to impose additional restrictions on smoking behavior in the workplace and other private establishments. We argue that, as in the case of many other laws, the avowed "public-interest" motivation of the nonsmokers may be based on a more ordinary form of self interest.

Consider the example of smoking in the workplace. By banning smoking on the job, nonsmoking employees impose costs on actual and potential smoking employees. To the extent that such bans make the smoking workers less productive on the job, less likely to be hired, and so on, the wages of nonsmokers will rise relative to smokers. There is thus a simple redistributive basis for laws prohibiting smoking in the workplace—they transfer wealth from smokers to nonsmokers.

We can see how this effect operates in a few of the possible settings. Take the case where a firm has an established policy of allowing smoking on the job and is paying nonsmokers a wage premium that is just enough to induce them to work in the firm. Current employees who do not smoke clearly gain from a law which bans smoking in the workplace: the legislation allows them to get both the higher compensation and the working environment they prefer. The wage premium is transformed into a rent; nonsmokers are now being paid more than the amount necessary for them to have been willing to accept employment in a firm where no smoking is permitted. Moreover, potential employees who do not smoke also benefit. It will now be cheaper at the margin for the owner to hire nonsmokers than to pay a wage premium to induce smokers to work in the mandated workplace environment. In short, nonsmokers have made it more difficult for smokers to compete for their jobs.

These gains are of course only transitory. In the long run, competition among nonsmokers for jobs will drive wages down to the amount just necessary for them to accept employment in their preferred workplace environment.[3] In the interim, however, nonsmokers earn rents, and these short-run returns provide a sufficient incentive for them to support no-smoking legislation.

Alternatively, suppose the firm has banned smoking and is currently offering a wage premium to smokers. We have argued that this additional compensation was necessary to attract smokers away from their next best alternative, namely, employment in firms that permit smoking on the job. Legislation which mandates the prohibition of smoking across the board reduces the need to compensate smokers. If no employer is able to offer jobs where smoking is permitted, smokers have fewer employment alternatives, and they therefore command smaller wage premiums. Accordingly, smokers suffer a real reduction in their economic welfare.

What about bars and restaurants? Here the argument is only a bit more complicated. In the absence of government intervention, some establishments offer smoke-free environments while others allow smoking under various conditions. An across-the-board ban on smoking forces restaurants and bars in the latter category to convert to no-smoking operations. The supply curve of smoke-free eating and drinking environments accordingly shifts to the right and, other things equal, this tends to lower the money price of dining out in a no-smoking atmosphere. Nonsmokers who eat out clearly gain from such an outcome: they obtain their preferred environment at a lower price. On the other hand, smokers and restaurant owners lose. As the price of meals eaten out declines, some restaurant owners will not be able to cover their opportunity costs; they will be forced to exit from the industry. (Exiting firms will most likely be those establishments where the cost of converting to no-smoking operations is high.) Smokers who buy meals out lose to the extent that the market price does not fall by enough to compensate them for having to dine in the mandated restaurant environment. This is just an extension of our earlier argument. A portion of the wealth transferred to nonsmoking employees by general prohibitions on smoking in the workplace comes at the expense of firm owners.

The interest-group explanation thus suggests that firms and smokers will generally oppose laws restricting smoking behavior, while nonsmokers advocate them. In particular instances one group wins over the other, depending on such factors as the costs of organizing the respective coalitions and of influencing the political process. In any event, it would appear to be interest groups and wealth transfers and not concern over an externality that drives public policy in this area.

Concluding Remarks

Our basic point is that considerations of redistribution, not economic efficiency, guide legislation about public smoking behavior. The Coase Theorem implies that in most private contexts, the relevant social costs of smoking are zero. Bans on smoking behavior appear to emanate from nonsmokers who seek wealth transfers from smokers and from the owners of firms in the economy. In this respect, public policy toward smoking operates like many other regulatory programs, with wealth transfers as its central focus. Any positive explanation of policy in this area must confront this fact.

Notes

1. For example, the Board of Supervisors of Sacramento County, California, is currently considering an amendment to the county code entitled "The Crime of Smoking."

2. Obviously, not all environments where smoking takes place are privately owned. Government facilities—local federal buildings, post offices, and city halls, to name a few—are not operated on a value-maximizing basis. Policies toward smoking in

such settings will therefore be in the nature of administrative decrees driven by maximands other than economic efficiency. The argument that follows in the text offers grounds for understanding what type of smoking policies might be established on public property.

3. See Gordon Tullock, "The Transitional Gains Trap," *Bell Journal of Economics* 6 (Autumn 1975):671–678.

8
A Sociological View of the Antismoking Phenomenon

Peter L. Berger

A famous professor at a German medical school in the nineteenth century is said to have opened a lecture with the following statement: "Gentlemen: I will now expound to you the omnipotence of God on the basis of the anatomy of the louse." The theological assumptions of this proposition, alas, cannot be pursued here. The professor, however, was also expressing an important insight about the character of scientific inquiry, namely, that reality is all of one piece and that looking at any slice of it can give us a sense of the whole. This is as true of social reality as it is of the physical universe. It also describes both the motive and the quality of my own interest in the antismoking phenomenon. That phenomenon, frankly, is only of limited interest to people who are not either members of an antismoking movement or employees of the tobacco industry. In an age of apocalyptic anxieties, most of us have many other things to worry about than the allegedly nefarious consequences of smoking. So do I.

The antismoking phenomenon is something I stumbled on by accident a few years ago and it has remained very marginal to my interests as a sociologist (which are centered on problems of modernization and Third World development). I have found, though, that this particular phenomenon is interesting, not so much in itself, but in terms of the light it sheds on wider social and cultural trends in our society. I might, then, open this chapter with a slight paraphrase: "Ladies and gentlemen: I will now expound to you certain features of Western advanced industrial societies on the basis of the anatomy of the antismoking phenomenon."

Put differently, this chapter is an attempt to use sociological categories to place the antismoking phenomenon in a wider context. Some principal features of such a sociological approach will be spelled out in the next section. From the outset, however, the reader is entitled to some answers to the following questions: What is the evidence on which the author is basing his observations? What is the author's bias? Does he have any vested interests of his own in the matter under discussion?

I first noticed the antismoking phenomenon through the increased aggressiveness of some of its activists in the United States. Irritated by this, I wrote a brief article about this.[1] This article was brought to the attention of some individuals in the tobacco industry and subsequently I did a moderate amount of consulting with that industry. My most intensive contact with the antismoking phenomenon was attendance, as a consultant for the tobacco industry, at two international conferences on smoking and health held under the auspices of the World Health Organization (Stockholm 1979 and Winnipeg 1983). Although I have not undertaken primary research of my own on the subject, since about 1978 I have read a good deal of antismoking literature and have conversed with a considerable number of individuals engaged on both sides of this issue. I have used an unpublished study, Michael Thompson et al., "The Political Culture of Anti-Smoking Groups" which compares such groups in the United States and Britain.[2]

Sociology has always purported to be a "value-free" science (the phrase was coined by the classical sociologist Max Weber). This means that, insofar as sociological propositions are scientifically valid, individuals with different, even contradictory values can agree on them. In this precise sense, the present chapter will also seek to be "value-free." Concretely this means that the analysis presented here could, in principle, be accepted or rejected by people on either side of the current controversy over smoking.

At the same time, sociologists in particular are sensitive to the fact that one's own biases and vested interests inevitably color one's perceptions of evidence. For this reason it is good practice to be very up-front about these, allowing readers to decide for themselves whether one's analysis is or is not as "value-free" as it purports to be. My bias, then, is against the antismoking phenomenon (I might say, paraphrasing again, that I'm an "anti-antismoking" person). This bias is political: I perceive the antismoking movement as tending toward further intrusion by government into private life, and I don't like such intrusion. Do I have vested interests in the matter? I'm not employed by the tobacco industry and would not have served as a consultant to it if it had not been for the aforementioned bias; my consulting fees have been an exceedingly small fraction of my income and would hardly be a reasonable motive (indeed, I wonder if I might not have a pecuniary motive to switch sides on this issue). I *do* have one vested interest in the matter that should be avowed: I am myself a smoker and as such have been personally annoyed by antismoking activism. Obviously, no one likes a habit one derives pleasure from to be castigated as a cosmic pestilence. On the other hand, this particular vested interest is lessened by the fact that I smoke pipes and cigars rather than cigarettes—the principal villains in the antismoking campaign.

There is one further and important point to be made about the status of this chapter: no competence is claimed here on the scientific controversy regarding smoking and health, and the sociological analysis presented is not dependent on any conclusions regarding this controversy. This point is important enough to be spelled out a little more. Very few people are professionally qualified to evaluate the scientific evidence on smoking and health. Let it be stipulated that medical researchers, physiologists, biochemists, and perhaps statisticians can arrive at an independent judgment on the weight of this evidence. The rest of us, having no independent access to "the truth of the matter," must take our opinions second-hand and on the basis of some sort of faith. This faith (which, of course, must also be very largely faith in this or that authority) is precisely what can be analyzed sociologically—regardless of what an independent scientific judgment might finally be. Nothing in what follows, then, is to be construed as implying that the scientific evidence cited by antismoking advocates either is or is not as valid as they suppose it to be.

A Sociological Approach

Sociology, of course, always seeks to place specific human phenomena in a broader context of societal structures and change. The approach employed here, however, is somewhat more specific. It is the approach commonly called that of the "sociology of knowledge." While the assumptions and implications of this approach can be and have been elaborated to a vast extent,[3] the basic thrust of the sociology of knowledge can be stated rather simply: ideas are plausible to people in specific social contexts. Put a little differently, ideas do not float around in some Platonic heaven detached from social forces, but rather, they link up with specific and empirically researchable groups in society, and ipso facto with the interests of these groups.

This root proposition of the sociology of knowledge is expressed by the concept of "plausibility structure." This refers to whatever social context is required for an idea to be credible to people. For example, there is the idea that witches cast spells that cause disease. If I were to propose this idea in Boston in the mid-1980s, it is very unlikely that I would find a responsive audience, except perhaps in this or that occultist subculture. On the other hand, people who put forth this proposition in New England in the seventeenth century found a very responsive audience indeed (much to the inconvenience of the alleged witches). This historical difference can be described by saying that contemporary Boston lacks the plausibility structure for a belief in witchcraft, while colonial Salem, Massachusetts, did provide this plausibility structure. It further follows that an individual in the latter location in time and space had no difficulty whatever taking a proposition about disease-causing witches very seriously—perhaps even taking the underlying worldview for granted—while I and my contemporaries would have to invest considerable effort before we could even entertain such an idea as a hypothesis.

Indeed, we very probably would have to immerse ourselves in the aforementioned occultist underworld before we could bring ourselves to the point of taking the matter seriously. Conversely, I and my contemporaries readily explain this or that pathological condition by the categories of psychoanalysis, which to a citizen of colonial Salem would appear as crazy as witchcraft appears to us. It should be noted that these statements do not hinge on any final judgments as to whether witchcraft or psychoanalysis are or are not scientifically valid; they refer to *socially defined* reality, not to reality as it may be deemed to be by this or that science. Thus let it be imagined that, sometime in the future, scientists might decide that witchcraft is an empirical phenomenon after all; this interesting discovery would not force us to revise the statement that witchcraft had a plausibility structure in New England in 1692 and lacked it in 1984. History, sad to say, is not governed by scientific truth, and the period when people did not believe in witches will just have to be put down as another of those ages of superstition to which the human race seems prone.

Some ideas take the form of norms: They enjoin us to do this or to refrain from doing that. All norms, however, rest upon cognitive presuppositions. Thus someone may proclaim a crusade against witches: "Witches are evil. They must be driven out." This *normative* program, however, rests on the *cognitive* presuppositions that 1) there *are* witches and 2) that they are bad news. It may be assumed that an antiwitchcraft crusader, especially one who has been crusading for a long time and derives power, prestige, or income from antiwitchcraft activities, will not take kindly to the proposition that witches are a figment of his or her imagination or that witches perform a commendable community service.

This last observation leads to a central concern of the sociology of knowledge, namely, the relation between ideas and vested interests. It is possible to distinguish two different kinds of vested interests, already alluded to in what has just been said about the cognitive defensiveness of the antiwitchcraft crusader. There are material and ideal interests. When people speak of vested interests, they usually mean the material ones: I am an antiwitchcraft specialist, and by virtue of this fact I have a fulltime appointment as an officer of the Inquisition (we are now, let us assume, in Seville rather than Salem), a powerful and prestigious job that also supplies me with a considerable, reasonably secure livelihood. It is obvious in this case that I will have a vested interest in the crusade against witches—and, by the same token, in the ideas about witchcraft on which the crusade is predicated. But there can also be vested interests of a nonmaterial sort: I'm *not* an employee of the Inquisition and I derive my livelihood from a professorship at the University of Seville; but I have written two books on witches (perhaps books that established my reputation as a scholar), my notions about witches are connected with a lot of other ideas that I have espoused (religious ideas, political ideas, and perhaps others), and in any case I have reached the age at which one is reluctant to revise ideas that one has held for many years. Such ideal interests will also affect the way in which I look at the issue of witchcraft.

A moment's reflection about a phenomenon as remote from one's own context as witchcraft will lead to the insight that vested interests of either sort are never limited to one party only; they always build on both sides of any disputed issue. The alleged witches themselves, needless to say, have vested interests in the matter—of a particularly pressing, material variety. But so do the employees of (let us imagine) the Witches Antidefamation Society and so does that other professor, who has written several books arguing that witches do not exist. This particular sociology-of-knowledge insight can be formulated in precise scientific prose by saying that, when it comes to vested interests, what is good for the goose is always good for the gander as well. Another point that should be very clearly made in this connection is this: to say that people's thinking is affected by their vested interests in no way implies that people are insincere. On the contrary, the great majority of people believe with the utmost sincerity that their vested interests coincide with the truth. Most Inquisitors sincerely believe that witches are wicked and most witches, equally sincere, believe that they are innocent. The reason for this is probably quite simple too: insincerity always requires a considerable effort, which most people are unwilling or unable to make (the great Machiavellians are a very small minority of the human race); it is much easier to hold one's beliefs sincerely.

Probably the concept that has passed most widely from the vocabulary of the sociology of knowledge into general usage is that of "ideology." An ideology, in its simplest definition, is an idea that expresses a vested interest. It follows that not all ideas are ideological; it follows further that just about any idea can, under certain circumstances, take on ideological functions, and some ideas start off that way. The most commonplace of ideologies is in politics—that is, in activities that have to do with the acquisition and the wielding of power. In politics, ideologies are part and parcel of the power game: "ideas as weapons." Once again, at the risk of being repetitious, one must stress that to describe an idea as ideological says nothing about whether this idea may be judged to be true or false, or a mixture of truth and error, by an objective observer standing outside this particular political fray.

The preceding, and necessarily sketchy, description of this particular sociological approach has deliberately avoided any reference to the antismoking phenomenon. It is applicable to just about any situation in which ideas enter into conflicts between social groups. The reader will have had no difficulty, however, in applying it mentally to the phenomenon at issue. The antismoking phenomenon too has a particular plausibility structure, and one of the tasks of sociological analysis must be to delineate its boundaries. The normative messages of the antismoking campaign intended to restrain or remove smoking must be understood as based on cognitive presuppositions, about the allegedly nefarious consequences of smoking, that most people are poorly equipped to evaluate. Most importantly, there are vested interests on *both* sides of the issue, and *both* sides take ideological stances—that is, use ideas as weapons in the conflict.

The antismoking movement uses the phrase "smoking interests," which refers, of course, to the tobacco industry. Fair enough: the tobacco industry obviously has enormous vested interests in the outcome of the current conflict, and these interests have an ideological aspect. Thus the tobacco industry has an obvious interest in questioning propositions about the negative effects of smoking. One might speculate that, if some scientist appeared who produced alleged evidence to the effect that smoking is a sure cure for leprosy, the tobacco industry would be sympathetically inclined, while the antismoking group would take a dim view of the hypothesis. And these predispositions would be at least relatively independent of the eventual scientific outcome of this particular argument, though in the end the weight of evidence would probably compel either side to draw back from its predispositional attitude. When leprosy disappears, say, from the Republic of Bongobongo in precise correlation, year by year, with the increase in smoking among its citizens, the antismoking movement might concede that perhaps smoking is good for lepers, though it may still point out that the causal connection can only be established once the cause of leprosy is known. In short, there are smoking as well as antismoking interests. The smoking interests are not difficult to identify. They consist of the tobacco industry, its political allies, especially in tobacco-producing areas, and, although only in a passive and politically unreliable manner, those portions of the public who smoke and are annoyed by those who want to stop or penalize the habit. The ideological predisposition of this group, obviously, is negative or at least skeptical toward allegations that smoking is inimical to health. But what is good for the smoking goose is also good for the antismoking gander. Thus the politics and the ideology of the antismoking interests must also be the subject of sociological analysis.

The Politics of Antismoking

Broadly speaking, the antismoking interests are constituted by all those who derive power, prestige, or income from the antismoking campaign. While correct, this statement is too broad, and a further differentiation is useful.

Looking at the antismoking phenomenon, one is impressed by its bifurcation into two distinct, though increasingly related, segments—the antismoking *movement* and various organizations constituting an antismoking *bureaucracy*. Thompson et al., looking at the phenomenon both in the United States and in Britain, have referred to the same bifurcation, using the slightly awkward terms "sects" and "castes," the former being voluntary activist groups campaigning against smoking, the latter various "establishment" groups who have taken up the antismoking cause. In the American case, groups such as ASH (Action on Smoking and Health) and GASP (Group Against Smokers' Pollution) represent the movement, while the Office on Smoking and Health represents the antismoking cause within the Federal government; the bureaucratic aspect of the phenomenon is also represented by nongovernmental agencies such as the American Cancer Society and the American Lung Association in the United States and the Royal College of Physicians in Britain. This distinction, of course, is at first purely formal, but it has significant implications.

The movement groups are, by their very nature, democratic and to some extent charismatic; they live by the enthusiasm of their voluntarily committed membership, and their leaders retain credibility only as long as they can enlist members' enthusiasm. In consequence, this sort of group tends to be highly activist and "single issue" in orientation. By contrast, bureaucracies are hierarchically organized, and authority rests not on charismatic appeal (there are no "members") but on formal credentials. The politics of bureaucracy tend to be cautious, multiple-issue in orientation, and ipso facto more inclined toward the politics of compromise. These characteristics are reflected in the literature emanating from these two camps within the antismoking campaign.[4] There are differences in all this between the United States and Britain, but they are of only marginal interest to the matter at hand.

It is, of course, the movement groups that think of antismoking in terms of a crusade. Antismoking is not only their sole ideological interest, it is the very reason for their existence. Absolutist, aggressive attitudes toward smoking follow logically. By contrast, the bureaucratic agencies concerned with the issue are *also* concerned with many other issues; they do not depend on smoking or nonsmoking for their existence; and they can afford to be more relaxed about the matter. Indeed, one might make the case that such bureaucratic agencies are not so much interested in the abolition of smoking as in its regulation. It follows that these bureaucratic agencies are more amenable to rational negotiations and compromises with the tobacco industry, while the movement portrays the industry as an evil force with which no morally acceptable dealings are possible. This difference appears to be borne out in the experience of tobacco industry people.

One sociological generalization that is widely supported empirically is that movements, qua movements, do not last.[5] There are several reasons for this; an underlying one is that enthusiasm is a fugitive emotion and a group that wants to survive over time has to find a more durable foundation. Thus, movements either disappear after a while as their adherents take up another, new and more exciting cause, or change into more structured groups which, under modern conditions, means that they become bureaucratized. Thompson et al. have put this in their own terms by saying that sects become castes.

One would, therefore, hypothesize as Thompson et al. did that the movement and the bureaucratic components of the antismoking phenomenon would, over time, tend to amalgamate.

This hypothesis is strongly supported by what could be observed at the Winnipeg conference. The symbiosis, again as one would expect, is both organizational and ideological. Organizationally, the movement has become itself much more bureaucratized and has entered into complex relationships with the existing bureaucracies, especially in government. Parallel to this development, there has been, if not an amalgamation, at least an approximation of the two ideological constellations: the ideology of the movement has become somewhat less aggressive (less "sectarian") as the bureaucratic agencies have officially espoused the antismoking point of view. This will be discussed again in the final section of this chapter; it is a development of considerable significance.

The antismoking phenomenon is originally and to a large extent still a phenomenon of Western advanced industrial societies, strongest in North America and in Northern Europe (one is almost, at least in a metaphorical sense, tempted to call it a phenomenon of "cultural Protestantism"). In these countries, the antismoking movement is one of many voluntary groupings banded together to push a cause, while the bureaucratic agencies that have taken up the antismoking cause are embedded in the vast structures of the Western welfare state. In recent years, however, the phenomenon has been internationalized and has become worldwide in its intended strategy. The major vehicle for this internationalization has been the World Health Organization (WHO), not the most prestigious of United Nations' (UN) bodies, but still one with great resources and prestige. The injection of the antismoking cause into the UN universe of discourse has had ideological as well as organizational ramifications. The UN is, above all, an organization of Third World governments. Logically enough, the antismoking cause has here become entangled with other strands of Third World ideology, notably hostility to multinational corporations. The tobacco industry has thus become targeted as yet another nefarious manifestation of multinational capitalism. There has been an important brake on this development though—the simple but far-reaching fact that tobacco is an important component in the economies of many Third World societies.

One other way of looking at the internationalization of the antismoking campaign is in terms of the vested interests of the Western as well as international bureaucracies involved. Just as international capitalism has created networks of power that transcend national boundaries, so there now exist international networks of bureaucrats. It is tempting to speak here of "welfare state imperialism": just as capitalists have pushed into new areas of the world in search of markets, so do the international bureaucrats—not only those of the UN but also of the agencies of Western governments with concerns for

Third World development. Thus, Third World participants at both the Stockholm and the Winnipeg conferences were brought there at the expense of the Scandinavian development agencies. Third World ideologists, in talking about the relation between multinationals and local economic interests, like to use the term "dependency" to describe this relationship. "Welfare state imperialism," it seems, establishes very similar relationships, by which power and privilege are distributed in the Third World by institutions centered elsewhere.

There is another important point to be made about the politics of antismoking: its class-specified character. In Western countries, especially in the United States, there are sharp class differences in terms of smoking behavior: lower-income people smoke more than upper-income people. This is important, not just because the antismoking movement is largely upper-middle-class in its constituency—that, after all, is characteristic of most organized movements rallied around causes (the upper-middle-class, for reasons that cannot be pursued here, is most prone to enlist in cause-related campaigns). But this particular movement targets a component of lifestyle—one which is particularly concentrated in the working class now. Thus the antismoking campaign stands in a long tradition of movements that have sought to impose upper-middle-class values and lifestyles on the lower strata of the class system and to use government power to enforce this imposition. The temperance movement in the United States is a perfect earlier example. That particular experiment was a failure, but it would be rash to predict similar failure in this instance.

The conventional phrase "upper middle class" may no longer suffice in describing the class dynamics in play here. A category used recently is that of the "new class" or "knowledge class." Put simply, this class is composed of all those people who derive their livelihood, not from the production and distribution of material goods and services, but from the production and distribution of symbolic knowledge. These are all the people employed in education, the media, the therapeutic and counseling agencies, and the institutions engaged in planning and administering the "quality of life."

Though obviously a minority of the population, this class exercises considerable power due to its access to the major communication channels of the society. Its interests are often in conflict with those of the old middle class, or "bourgeoisie," which is centered in business and industry. A very important fact about this class is that a major part of it depends directly or indirectly upon government subsidization. Accordingly, it has a strong vested interest in the expansion of government services, especially in the expansion of the welfare state. In this perspective, the antismoking campaign is a small part of a much larger process—namely, the process whereby this new class seeks to enlarge its power in society. The wider ramifications of this, however, go beyond the limits of this paper; the matter of class interests will, however, be taken up once more in the discussion of ideology.

The Ideology of Antismoking

The antismoking campaign, especially in its movement form, is charged with strong moral sentiment: here is a great evil that must be combatted. Indeed, very strong language is customary in the antismoking rhetoric—smoking is supposed to be "the single most important preventable cause of death," an "epidemic," a "pestilence," and the tobacco industry is given such attractive epithets as "merchants of death." In other words, the campaign is strongly normative in tone. As previously indicated, however, normative injunctions make no sense without the appropriate cognitive premises. The most important of these premises—indeed, in some ways the only one—is that smoking is unhealthful. The antismoking campaign, therefore, is a battle for health against disease and death.

Within antismoking circles, it is assumed that scientific evidence on this matter is conclusive, and that anyone denying this is motivated either by vested interests (the spokesmen for the tobacco industry) or by wishful thinking (recalcitrant smokers). As previously stated, the present analysis must bracket the question of the weight of this scientific evidence. Two observations, however, can be made. First, the evidence is clearly complex, and much of it is statistical in nature; therefore, it is important, from the viewpoint of the antismoking cause, that the cognitive presuppositions be frequently and emphatically—even ritually—repeated. Second, there is a considerable degree of defensiveness (one may say, "cognitive defensiveness") about the evidence on *both* sides of the issue; that is, there is nervousness about any data that might throw doubt on one's own position. This is easily understandable in the case of the tobacco industry. The defensiveness of the antismoking camp, however, is somewhat more difficult to understand, and, to an outside observer, suggests that the evidence may not be as conclusive as that camp would have one believe.

Antismoking is a theme that is not isolated; inevitably, it is located within a wider ideological and cultural configuration. This configuration in turn can be located within the class system of Western societies. Further research would be required to make this latter location definitive, but it may be hypothesized that it is primarily in the upper middle class, more narrowly in that portion of it that has been called the new knowledge class. If so, one would expect that antismoking will show strong linkages to other ideological themes popular in this class; one would also look for class interests in the matter. As far as the available evidence goes, the linkages are fairly prominent; the matter of class interests must remain more speculative—all one can really do is to point to the *general* interest of this class in the expansion of the welfare state (this general interest being distinct from the specific vested interests of antismoking staffs in the promotion of their cause).

The strongest linkage, of course, is with what may be called an overall "health cult." Here health becomes an ultimate, virtually sacral, goal. One should be careful here: if smoking is indeed the peril that these people purport it to be, then it is rational to be against it. What is suggestive, though, is the extravagant claims made in the antismoking literature not only against smoking, but, by implication, in favor of a healthful lifestyle liberated from smoking. The point here is that the antismoking cause is not alone in this view. Western cultures, with America probably in the lead, are replete with various health movements which all suggest that, if only one does this and avoids that, one will attain a joyful, wholesome, and (above all) long life. The enormously powerful place attained by the medical establishment is a logical consequence of this cultural theme: doctors are the priesthood of this cult, hospitals are the sanctuaries, and government is urgently expected to support and universalize this new "established religion." It is likely that this emphasis on health and longevity is related to secularization—that is, to a decline in plausibility among many people, especially in the knowledge class, of older religious beliefs. Be this as it may, the emotional violence of the antismoking movement becomes more understandable in the light of this particular linkage: if health is a quasi-religious goal, then any threat to health must take on a devilish quality. Once more, the analogy with the temperance movement is striking (the liquor industry, of course, played the villain role then).

There are also clear linkages with the environmentalist and the consumer movements. Ecological imagery abounds in the antismoking literature. Smoking is a form of pollution; indeed, smokers are polluters. Conversely, the ideal of a "smoke-free world" (now the official slogan of the antismoking movement) is portrayed in the imagery of ecological soundness. The linkage with the consumer movement is explicit, and in a number of countries consumer groups have taken up the antismoking cause: here is a hazardous product being marketed by allegedly unscrupulous businesses, and consumers band together to combat this danger. In the UN context, as already remarked upon, there is also a linkage with the wider anticapitalist ideology: the tobacco industry is supposed to be a particularly clear case of the evils of multinational corporations, especially as they allegedly dump harmful products on the innocent peoples of the Third World. This theme is muted in the antismoking literature within Western countries, and one can only speculate on the place it has in the thinking of people who belong to a class with generally left-leaning political opinions.

Crusades not only mobilize people against an evil, but they also conjure up utopian visions of a world freed from this particular evil. Some of this, no doubt, is a functional requirement of political mobilization: people will not make much of an effort on behalf of a cause deemed trivial or minor. But one may surmise that in this case more is involved than political tactics. The linkage with the cult of health suggests that there is a real utopia—one that is actually plausible to the people who evoke it rhetorically. As already indicated, it is a utopia of a joyful, long life, a sort of eternal youth. Allied to this is the vision of a life in which risks have been reduced to a minimum—especially by way of government action. The utopia, then, implies not only energetic health and youth, but a careful protection against all threats to the same by a benevolent and powerful government. One senses a certain contradiction here, a strange symbiosis of liberationism and hypochondria. But then utopias have never been exercises in logic.

There is one more very interesting ideological point to be made. At least in terms of Anglo-Saxon political culture, there is the general assumption and value that individuals have the right to do whatever they want unless they harm others; while government is obligated to protect one individual against the harm that others might do to him, it is not the function of government to protect an individual against himself. This political value creates an obvious problem for the antismoking campaign: after all, people smoke voluntarily and, if they become ill in consequence, they only harm themselves. It is precisely this logic that lies behind the campaigns to "decriminalize" drug abuse, sexual deviance among consenting adults and other "victimless crimes." The antismoking movement, however, is precisely intent on (so to speak) "criminalizing" smoking—at least to the extent of increasingly "stigmatizing" it (the term is actually used in antismoking literature). The strategy, quite overtly, is to progressively stigmatize smoking, segregating the smoker in all public places, and eventually to eliminate smoking as a socially acceptable custom.

How is this to be made politically palatable? The answer is clear: by suggesting that smoking harms, not only the smoker, but various categories of "innocent bystanders." For this reason, there are three pivotal issues in the antismoking campaign: the issue of "passive smoking," the issue of "children," and the issue of "social costs." "Passive smoking" is the term (a very imaginative one) used to describe the claimed effect of an individual's smoking on others in his or her immediate environment. The antismoking literature uses two arguments in this connection: that passive smoking is an annoyance and that it actually causes disease. The former is a point not dependent on scientific evidence; undoubtedly there are people irritated by smoke and they can be mobilized to insist on their right to be freed of this irritation in public places. The second argument is based on rather sparse and apparently disputed evidence to the effect that, for example, spouses of smokers are more susceptible to a number of diseases.

Whatever the state of the scientific evidence, the issue of passive smoking is important for the antismoking demand that smoking be at least segregated if not banned in public places, which increasingly is so defined as to include the workplace. Children, of course, are "innocent bystanders" par excellence. Therefore, the alleged harm of smoking to children is much emphasized in the literature (again, this involves passive smoking as well as children smoking themselves). It is interesting that in some of the literature the term "children" includes all teenagers. Contrast this with the terminology employed by advocates of abortion: a sixteen-year-old will be a "young woman" if she seeks an abortion; here she appears as a "child" if she smokes. There is also much emphasis on the alleged harm to fetuses ("unborn children," as prolife advocates might put it) from the smoking of their mothers.

The most ample, and elegant, extension of the notion of the "innocent bystander" is undertaken by means of the concept of "social costs." Here we *all* become "innocent bystanders." The concept refers to any costs accruing to society as a whole from the actions of individuals. For example, it is argued that an individual driver who fails to buckle up his safety belt and is seriously injured in an accident because of this failure harms not only himself but society as a whole, because others have to pay more to take care of his medical costs or, if he dies, to support his family. Thus, everyone's insurance or tax rates will go up, and society may also be partially or totally deprived of his own productive contribution. The same argument is made here in the case of the smoker. To buttress this argument, allegedly scientific econometric calculations are brought forth to show the aggregate costs of smoking to society. Not surprisingly, the tobacco industry has been parading its own calculations to demonstrate what its elimination would cost society. Whatever the merits of these competing econometrics, the concept of "social costs" is very useful to the antismoking movement in calling for government interventions in what most people still think of as an area of private behavior.

From Stockholm to Winnipeg

The antismoking movement has been around for many years now. It has its veterans, its hero figures (such as Sir George Godber of England), even its martyrs (such as Joseph Califano, former head of the U.S. Department of Health, Education and Welfare, supposedly driven from his post because of his opposition to smoking). When antismoking veterans meet, they have common battles to reminisce about and common biographical reference points to recognize each other by. The WHO conferences, meeting in four-year intervals, are important as reference points of this sort, signposts for the progress of the movement. It is, therefore, appropriate to conclude this paper by a comparison of the Stockholm and Winnipeg conferences (1979 and 1983).

There were, of course, considerable continuities. One significant change was in the relative emphasis on scientific information and advocacy techniques. The Stockholm program contained a larger number of scientific papers; the Winnipeg program was dominated by "how to" sessions—how to organize campaigns, how to lobby, and so on. The implication is clear: the scientific evidence is all in; the agenda now is a practical one. There continues to be a bifurcation between movement and bureaucratic elements within the antismoking camp, but the impression obtained is one of much greater amalgamation. In striking support of the thesis presented earlier by Thompson et al., what has emerged now is a sort of international antismoking conglomerate. Bureaucrats from governmental and international agencies happily spout the rhetoric of the movement. More important, the various movement groups appear to have become much more professionalized. Their staffs appear to be much more technically competent, matter-of-fact in their approach to strategy, and exhibit remarkable political know-how. One might sum all this up by saying that the antismoking movement presented itself as having come of age at Winnipeg. It is no longer a small voluntary crusade fighting against the odds for its cause, but a large and self-confident array of organizations enjoying wide support from government and other prestigious institutions.

Another interesting validation of the Thompson thesis comes from a shift in tactics. Thompson et al. had concluded from their content analysis that the antismoking "sects" stressed a punitive approach to smokers, while the "castes" stressed health and adopted a more benign attitude toward smokers, seeing them as victims rather than villains. Therefore, as "sects become castes" (in our terminology, as the movement becomes bureaucratized), one would expect that the rhetoric within the movement groups would also become more positive and benign. This is exactly what came out at Winnipeg. Vilification was pretty much limited to the tobacco industry. The approach to smokers, recommended in paper after paper, was benevolent, "user-friendly." In Stockholm the favored "educational" tool still appeared to be fear—images of people coughing their lungs out, and the like. Winnipeg was aglow with imagery of healthy, young people cavorting in blissful surroundings, and the like. In the words of one speaker, the goal should be not frightening people but "selling a lifestyle." Nonsmoking, in other words, is to be presented as part and parcel of a desirable lifestyle. Some of this new imagery was literally visual, through films, TV programs, and posters; it also permeated the verbal presentations.

There is a curious aspect to this tactical shift. The shift is, in effect, from an ascetic to a hedonistic stance. Nonsmoking used to be, almost by definition, abstemious, while smoking, by contrast, was always suggestive of enjoyment, relaxation, living well. Needless to say, the latter imagery has been very prominent in tobacco advertising. The new lifestyle approach of the antismoking movement expropriates, as it were, the hedonistic theme for its own ends. It remains to be seen how successful this shift will be.

Two new themes surfaced in the Winnipeg program—feminism and religion. There was one very well-attended session led by a British feminist and antismoking activist which tried to define smoking as a women's issue. This was not altogether easy, not only because the feminist movement has until now shown little interest in the subject, but because data indicate that women smoke more as they enter the labor force—placing the antismoking feminist in an ideological double bind. The religion session was poorly attended and probably of little significance, except for one point: the discussion of data indicating that antismoking has become an important emphasis of fundamentalist movements in various Muslim countries. An Egyptian physician who served as chairman of the session expressed the opinion that antismoking might become an important cause for the "Muslim masses." If he is right, and given the strength of Islamic fundamentalism in large portions of the globe, this could become significant in the near future.

As it presented itself in Winnipeg, the antismoking movement is confident in itself, its future prospects, and its ultimate victory. One may be skeptical as to whether ultimate victory is ever possible for this kind of cause. It remains true that the movement can look back on impressive successes, both in the decline in smoking in Western countries (outside the West, to its chagrin, the story is very different) and in the increasing willingness of government to take measures against smoking as well as against the tobacco industry. Official pronouncements of the movement confidently refer to further steps in the direction of the situation already existing in several Scandinavian countries (the promised land of the movement) where, as was repeatedly and proudly stated, smoking is well on the way to being a disreputable activity engaged in by consenting adults in private.

There is much reason for giving credence to this confidence. One growing problem in Western countries, however, may well be the aforementioned class distribution of both smoking and antismoking. The working classes of Western societies have shown strong resistance to the imposition of upper-middle-class values in other areas of life, and they may show comparable resistance to the antismoking campaign. As long as Western societies are democracies, this may mean political problems for the movement. A further problem may be the growing sentiment in the same countries that government regulation over the lives of individuals has gone too far. In both these problem areas the prospects of the antismoking phenomenon would seem to be linked to the prospects of the new knowledge class, which is its principal protagonist. To the extent that this class succeeds in consolidating and expanding its position in society, especially via the mechanisms of the welfare state, the future of the antismoking cause will indeed be bright.

Notes

1. "Gilgamesh on the Washington Shuttle," *Worldview*, November, 1977.

2. Michael Thompson et al., "The Political Culture of Anti-Smoking Groups," unpublished study, Institute for Policy and Management Research, 1979.

3. See Peter L. Berger and Thomas Luckman, *The Social Construction of Reality* (Garden City, NJ: Doubleday, 1966) and Peter L. Berger, Brigitte Berger, and

Mansfreid Kellner, *The Homeless Mind: Modernization and Consciousness* (New York: Random House, 1973).

4. Thompson et al. engaged in a content analysis of these materials. See their "Political Culture."

5. Max Weber developed this idea in his well-known theory of the "routinization of charisma."

Part IV
Smoking: The Context of the Economy

9
The Economic Contribution of the Tobacco Industry

H. Peter Gray
Ingo Walter

T he aim of this chapter is to outline the economic contribution of the tobacco industry in the context of national economies. We begin by defining the nature of the economic contribution of an industry and describing problems involved in its measurement. We then present available data on the tobacco industry's economic contribution in various countries around the world. A separate section of the paper is devoted to the industry's fiscal contribution, a particularly important issue in the case of tobacco products. We conclude with an overall assessment of the industry's economic role.

The Meaning of "Economic Contribution"

The concept of "economic contribution" of an industry or sector must be interpreted according to a set of economic targets established by national governments.[1] As such, economic contribution is a multidimensional concept; obvious dimensions such as employment and value added are supplemented by many additional dimensions that will tend to have varying degrees of importance in different countries. Such a list of objectives is provided in figure 9–1.

The "general objectives" are those likely to be systematically included in all national lists of economic objectives, and the tobacco industry's contribution to these goals may vary substantially according to the type of activity involved (leaf growing, processing, manufacture, distribution, and so on). In addition, there are "specific objectives" featured in the policy goals of industrial nations mainly in turbulent economic times as well as in developing countries.

Any practical analysis of an industry's economic contribution should consider all of these dimensions. In practice, however, very few of them permit quantification.[2] Several dimensions have to be reported in a "qualitative" sense that does not, despite the potential importance of such activities, allow much more precision than the indication of a positive or negative contribution by the industry.[3]

	Weight	Growing	Processing	Manufacturing	Exporting	Importing	Distribution	Retailing	Overall
GENERAL OBJECTIVES									
1. Income generation									
a. direct									
b. indirect									
total									
2. Employment generation									
a. direct									
b. indirect									
total									
3. Capital formation									
a. direct									
b. indirect									
total									
4. Labor-force augmentation									
5. Technology augmentation									
6. Residual growth effects									
7. Price-level effects									
8. Fiscal contribution									
9. Income redistribution									
SPECIFIC OBJECTIVES									
1. Balance of payments effects									
2. Regional balance									
3. Sectoral balance									
4. Social balance									
5. Infrastructure									
6. Externalities									

Figure 9–1. Pro-Forma Activity-Impact Analysis

The general objectives specified in figure 9–1 are easily identified. "Output" includes the value added by the industry itself as well as its indirect contribution through supplier industries (upstream contributions) and through downstream industries. Similarly, the employment contribution of the industry exceeds the level of employment in the industry itself by virtue of its indirect contributions. The measurement of this indirect contribution is much more difficult than for the industry proper because upstream and downstream activities usually include the focus industry as one activity among many. Labor-force augmentation is concerned with enhancement of the skill levels of labor, and technology augmentation with the technological base available in the economy. Labor-force augmentation can include the generation of skills which are both industry-specific and general while technology augmentation is likely to involve process technologies that permit production activities to be performed more efficiently. For the tobacco industry, the fiscal contribution is important to the point that it is treated separately in this paper.

Figure 9–1 thus provides a matrix which allows, at a highly abstract level, the concept of contribution to be spelled out. Some of the cells will contain numbers, but these are often surrogates for judgmental values. The matrix can be custom-designed for an individual country and at a particular point in time.[4] It cannot be applied through time or across countries without adaptation; there is danger in any attempt to develop a simple standard technique to assess an industry's contribution. Information on a nation's target weights must be obtained from local sources, such as national planning documents and reports of economic advisory groups and blue-ribbon committees to the executive and legislative branches of government. On occasion, country analyses undertaken by bodies such as the World Bank or the United Nations will be useful.[5]

One final distinction must be observed. The first three "general" targets in figure 9–1 are likely to dominate the goals of developed or industrialized nations for most industries (although revenue generation will be equally important for some countries). These are essentially short-run goals concerned with the level of output or employment and the rate of economic growth—the day-to-day functions of economic policy. In contrast, it is the other general targets as well as many of the specific targets which assume much greater importance for developing countries. These tend to be long-term goals that focus primarily on growth and social values.

Analysis and Measurement

Despite the obviously qualitative character of some of its dimensions, "economic contribution" implies measurement. This section briefly considers the problem of transforming abstract concepts into tangible realities and, particularly, the problem of measurement of the target variables in terms of the tobacco industry.[6] In keeping with the distinction drawn in the previous section between industrialized, developing and less-developed countries, these problems will be examined separately for the three groups.

Industrialized Countries

The policy emphasis for industrialized countries focuses directly on the short-run problems of capacity-utilization and price stability. The allocative mechanisms in the economy, involving both governmental policy and the decentralized system of markets, can be relied upon in relatively tranquil economic times to ensure the steady evolution of the economy in terms of growth. The political system in liberal democracies will tend to incorporate prevailing social criteria into the process of economic evolution. The focus of economic contribution is heavily dependent on what the industry generates in terms of output, employment, and spending power.

Short-run considerations of economic contribution by the tobacco industry can be measured by approaching the problem through the level of output or expenditures. On the presumption that an economy is not pushing against the limits of its aggregate output capacity, an industry's contribution to demand varies according to the value of goods supplied by that industry as the value added is divided among payments to suppliers—wages, salaries, and profits.[7]

An industry does not produce all of the value of its own sales in the same way that its payroll and other expenditures do not constitute its complete contribution to spending power. The use of goods produced by other industries and other sectors in the production of tobacco products (backward linkages) generates output and spending power indirectly by the tobacco industry. In turn, these supplier industries have their own suppliers. The industry's own value added may be considered its *direct* contribution, and the value added which it generates in feeder industries is the industry's *indirect* contribution. Similarly, other industries are used in the process of bringing the tobacco products to the ultimate consumer—wholesale and retail distribution—and these generate downstream indirect contributions. If the target measure of contribution is employment (instead of the monetary value of output or spending), the same relationship holds. The industry's contribution to employment consists of jobs generated in the industry itself and the employment generated in upstream (backward) and downstream (forward) economic activities.

To identify the economic contribution of an industry to national economic performance, at least in its quantitative dimensions, it is useful to consider the effect on national output and/or employment of a hypothetical contraction of the industry.[8] The advantage of specifying a contraction is that it precludes the possibility that all industries together are pushing against the limits of total production and, in this way, generating an inflationary situation. The postulated contraction consists of a reduction in the industry's sales and output.

The direct effect of an industry's contraction is the reduction of its contribution to total national output. Here the role of foreign suppliers is important.

A reduction in a domestic industry's level of output will reduce the demand for goods and services from all suppliers. A reduction in demand from foreign sources of supply does *not* reduce the level of output of the national economy. Thus, the more important imports are as a percentage of domestic sales, the less important the industry's contribution to the national economy and the damage done by a fall-off in the industry's level of output will be. Imports in this context can comprise final goods sold in the distribution chain or imported goods destined for use in some stage of the direct contribution of the industry. In contrast, a reduction in domestic sales will not affect sales made to foreigners. The more important exports are, the less important the fall-off in national output will be as the value of sales of the industry in the home market declines. Imports are a part of the indirect effects of an industry, while exports are a part of its direct effects.

The effect on employment also reflects the "chain of repercussions" through the economy, and depends on the degree to which the industry itself and its suppliers use labor. A reduction in the output of a supplier industry that uses a great deal of labor will have a much greater effect on the industry's contribution to employment than a reduction in a highly automated activity.

The industry's own contribution will, if capital formation is taking place, exceed the value of its output. If an industry expands its capacity by building additional facilities, this will generate additional output on the part of industries which supply the capital goods.

The measure of contribution in terms of the sum of the direct and the indirect contribution is now fairly well defined. An industry's contribution comprises its total effect on output and/or employment irrespective of whether the employment or output is generated in the industry itself or in related industries. The problems of measurement lie in the determination of the indirect effects. For example, in an industrialized country in which detailed input–output (I–O) tables specify the backward and forward linkages with a fair amount of accuracy, the tasks will be technically complex but conceptually straightforward.[9] Any capital formation activities will have indirect effects on quite different distributions of activity in supplier industries.

One further problem must be confronted. If the contribution of an industry is measured by its demand effects (the level of spending), then the problem of potential induced expenditures exists.[10] If an economy has spare capacity, a reduction in the direct and indirect contribution of an industry will lead to a reduction in spending by individuals associated with that industry. This reduction will have repercussive effects on other industries, as less of their goods are purchased. In turn, these industries will reduce their value added, employment, and so on. This is the famous multiplier effect of Keynesian macroeconomic analysis.

Thus, a given reduction in sales of the tobacco industry could be seen as having larger effects on the national economy if the induced spending effects are included in the measure of contribution. While the logic of the mechanism is valid, the industry-specific magnitude of the effect is not clearly identifiable.[11] Even in an economy for which a detailed I–O table is available, the effect of induced expenditures could not be distinguished according to the focus industry—the relationship is too tenuous. The crucial point at issue is the time frame of "contribution." If the focus of concern is short-run, it is arguable that the induced effect should be included. If the focus is longer-term, involving a period of, say, more than two years, then the induced effect should not be included in the measure because money not spent in one industry would find another outlet with equal (undistinguishable) induced effects. Another reason for exclusion of the induced effect from the measure of industry contribution is that it has the same value for any industry and is, therefore, in no way industry-specific.

This question is not negligible. The inclusion of the induced effect can have a very large bearing on the estimate of an industry's contribution to output and employment. Moreover, in the context of the tobacco industry—which makes large contributions to government revenues—there is a built-in counteraction. If sales of tobacco products were to be reduced, for example, by the imposition of increased excise taxes, the proceeds of those taxes would, under assumptions of a balanced budget, reduce taxation elsewhere in the economy or result in increased expenditures, which would have equivalent induced effects. Alternately, if the central government were seeking ways in which to reduce a fiscal deficit (so that taxes could be raised without any compensating increase in expenditures or offsetting tax reductions on other products or tax bases), then the direct and indirect effects of different means of reducing the deficit might vary, but the induced effects would still be indistinguishable. Later in this chapter when we report on studies of the economic impact of the tobacco industry that include induced effects in their estimating techniques this point will be mentioned explicitly.

In any measurement of induced or indirect effects, the availability of an I–O table is important because it represents the only precise means of measuring linkages between different industries and sectors in complex economies.[12] The accuracy or refinement of an I–O table depends upon the number of sectors identified separately within the table.

Unfortunately, the cost of creating an I–O table increases rapidly with any increase in the number of sectors identified separately. There is a tendency, then, for I–O tables to be more aggregative than is desirable for measures of contribution. It is this aspect that helps explain the inability to distinguish usefully between induced effects of different industries. It is a matter of some concern that the row and the column of an I–O table which represent the tobacco industry have characteristics that closely reflect the values for the industry itself.[13] It is this potential problem which points to the single most desirable feature of any analysis of the contribution of the tobacco industry to a national economy. Analysts must show that the industry's profile is well represented by "its" column, or they must add another row or column to the existing I–O table and, in this way, isolate the tobacco industry.[14] Such a step clearly demands a significant resource commitment. All five domestic stages of production could be contained in different columns in the existing I–O table. Here, common sense and budget constraints must intervene. What matters is the size of any discrepancy and the relative quantitative importance of the individual activities.

Developing Countries

Developing countries are those which have attained a significant rate of economic growth, with consequent and concomitant social evolution, but which have not yet achieved self-sustaining growth. This state of affairs typifies the newly-industrializing countries, such as Brazil, Korea, Mexico, Taiwan, and Yugoslavia. In these countries, national economic policy is preoccupied with maintaining the dynamism of the economy and ensuring the continuation of the sources of growth. The focus of policy is, then, long-run.[15] Equity considerations become secondary to the dynamics of economic development in the full understanding that, at some stages of development, too much concern with gross disparities of income distribution and equity could rob the growth process of its momentum.[16] Similarly, sustained high rates of economic growth normally improve the welfare of a great number of people, so that equity considerations are automatically and partially met by the continued dynamism of the economy. The inequality of living standards between those involved in the modern sector and those remaining in the traditional sector is aggravated, but this is an inevitable concomitant of growth and economic development.

The quantitative measures of an industry's contribution remain important. It is highly probable that high levels of capacity utilization will accompany successful economic development. But in developing countries, the measures of industry's output (direct and indirect), employment, and capital formation may be expressed as percentage increases and measured relative to the same measure of the economy as a whole.[17] The weights will also differ from those used in the industrialized countries—because of the positive weights being given to other, specific objectives, the sum of the three weights must be less. Among the three weights, that of capital formation is likely to be rather large relative to that of the value of industry's output and employment.

Balance-of-payments considerations become another, potentially important and quantitative short-run target. Most developing countries require large amounts of foreign exchange (obtained by means of exports of goods and services or by borrowing) to meet the required service on existing debt and to acquire capital goods and necessities that cannot be produced at home.[18] A shortage of foreign exchange may prove to be a serious constraint on the development process. The role of an industry as a supplier of foreign exchange or as a source of goods that were previously imported can prove to be a major factor in a developing nation. In contradistinction to the attitude toward foreign-exchange contributions in a developed nation where this particular role is likely to be spasmodic, the balance-of-payments problems faced by a developing country may be chronic, and the capacity of the industry to generate foreign exchange then becomes a permanent constituent of the objective function and does not acquire a positive weight only in times of foreign-exchange crises.

Labor-force augmentation in the sense of upgrading the skills of the labor force is fundamental to the growth process, and, therefore, important in a development context. It is, however, difficult both to isolate on an industry basis and to measure. Industries should become more aware of their own contributions to a national economy in such subtle dimensions as this, and should be able to supply data on this policy target to national bodies when called upon to do so.

Technology augmentation is also difficult to measure, and frequently it is hard to separate the contribution made by the domestic industry (whose contribution is being considered) and that obtained from foreign sources for which foreign exchange is being disbursed. In this respect, the separate stages of production become particularly important. It is in the leaf-growing, processing, and manufacturing activities that the tobacco industry is most likely to enhance the nation's technological base, although process technology may be introduced in the distributive stages and may spread quickly. In the leaf-cultivation activity, it is probable that labor force augmentation and technological augmentation go hand-in-hand.

Certainly the development of leaf cultivation in Brazil is symptomatic of this synergy. One county, Santa Cruz do Sul, is completely dependent upon the tobacco crop, uses very modern methods of cultivation and processing (both of which are labor-intensive) and ranks among the richest counties in the country. By its contribution to rural employment, the industry plays another role by absorbing some of the excess labor in the countryside and eliminating the pressure of labor inflows on the large cities. The ratio of farm owners to employees in cultivation is about five to one, and provides substantial stability to the region.[19]

In contrast to the role of technology in cultivation, the technology used in manufacturing may not be as beneficial, particularly when surplus labor is available in the local economy.

Just as the contribution of labor-force and technology augmentation can be very important but, at the same time, impossible to quantify, so too is the industry's contribution to infrastructure. For many economists, the provision of infrastructure is one of the main tasks allocated to government, and should be financed from tax revenues. While this may be true under ideal circumstances, industries must frequently provide their own infrastructure, particularly with respect to communications, in regions to which the government has not yet turned its attention. This provision of infrastructure is likely to have spillover benefits to the local economy in excess of the benefits gained by the investing industry.

Superficially at least, the fiscal contribution of the tobacco industry is no different from that in industrialized countries—it serves as an alternative to higher rates of direct taxation. But in a developing country, the efficiency of the alternative means of tax collecting may be markedly inferior. In Brazil, the fiscal contribution of the tobacco industry is huge by any standard. Robert Fendt, Jr., reports:

> The tax revenue raised from the tobacco industry (in Brazil) reaches levels which are difficult to evaluate without a comparative scale. It is worthwhile to note that the tax contribution from tobacco in 1982 (Cr$ 554,400 million) is a sum which would be enough to carry out all the federal government's regional development plans or to cover the government investments in energy and mineral resources, and still end up with 53 percent of the revenue left over.[20]

Measurement of the economic contribution of an industry is, clearly, a much more complex process in a developing than in an industrialized country. The relatively straightforward quantitative measures that were acceptable as a first measure for the industrialized or developed nations lose their dominance in a developing nation, and the number of noteworthy dimensions in the objective function increase substantially.

The concept of economic contribution is best identified, again, by the question, What would happen to the rate of economic development in the absence of the tobacco industry, or if the industry's growth were to be severely curtailed? An answer to this question is extremely difficult to generate and, because of the need to rely on the judgments of the analyst, will be difficult to substantiate in the face of hostile and unsympathetic criticism. Not every activity of the industry which contributes to the performance of the economy can be substantiated by numerical measures. However, the empirical studies surveyed below unambiguously point to the strong overall contribution of the tobacco industry to national economies in both developed and developing countries.

Less Developed Countries

Many countries are trapped in a state of stagnation or such slow growth that progress is hard to identify. Here, without any inherent momentum, growth-enhancing forces are few and must wage an uphill battle against all of the stagnant and stagnating institutions that surround them. In countries such as these, the agricultural sector is usually dominant, and manufacturing tends to be a small urban enclave. The labor force is generally not highly skilled, although it may respond quite well to training, at least in rudimentary tasks.

In such countries, the introduction of tobacco cultivation can have major beneficial effects and provide the impetus for local processing and manufacturing operations. Not only does tobacco generate improved incomes in the rural sector, but, in addition, processing—usually carried out in rural areas—provides additional employment, and the tobacco crop itself improves the yield of other crops that grow in rotation. The growth can be spectacular. From the introduction of flue-cured Virginia tobacco to Malaysia in 1959, the (direct and indirect) value of the industry was about $200 million in 1982, as described below.[21]

For the concept of "economic contribution" to have meaning, it may be necessary to limit its applicability to an economy which enjoys much of the structure of a modern economy. Stagnant countries do not allow economic contribution to be measured in any way other than a litany of the activities which can be traced to the industry on the assumption that, without the industry's presence, there would be no replacement activity worthy of note.

Measurement of Economic Impact

Actual studies of the economic impact of the tobacco industry have been undertaken in recent years for a number of countries and regions, both in the developed and in the developing world. With respect to the former, studies have focused on the United States, the European Economic Community (EEC) member countries as well as Spain and Portugal in Western Europe, Australia, and Canada. In the developing countries, economic impact studies have been undertaken for Argentina, Malaysia, and Zimbabwe, although some of these do not provide a comprehensive profile of the industry's bearing on the national economy as a whole. As is obvious from what has been stated here, the way in which the industry's economic contribution is estimated will vary widely between countries in the absence of a common, detailed format and, even if the format and methodology were to be carefully defined beforehand, institutional variations among countries and dissimilarities in the availability of data would induce substantial variation in the quality and reliability of the results. Thus, any given study can be seen as providing country-specific information of some value, but intercountry comparisons must be treated with caution.

United States

According to a 1985 study of the economic impact of the tobacco industry on the American economy,[22] a total of 414,217 persons were employed directly in the tobacco industry in 1983, or about 0.46% of the U.S. labor force (see table 9–1). Their earnings were about $6.7 billion, or 0.34% of labor income in the United States economy. The industry generated total expenditures of $31.5 billion directly and through upstream and downstream economic linkages. An additional $52.2 billion in expenditures is attributed to the "income multiplier effect" of employees' spending on consumer goods and services, for a total of $82.1 billion in contribution to GNP (see table 9–2). The multiplier effect can be questioned on methodological grounds, however, so it is advisable to focus primarily on the $31.5 billion in direct and indirect contribution of the industry itself. This represents roughly 1.0% of U.S. GNP. As table 9–3 indicates, the industry was a large contributor to federal and state/local tax revenues, with 1983 payments of $8.02 billion at the federal level and $5.44 billion at the state/local level. Of the $13.46 billion total, $9.79 billion represented excise and sales taxes. In the case of the United States, therefore, the tobacco industry turns out to be a relatively small sector in terms of its share of national output and employment, but a very large factor in tax collection at both the federal and state/local levels.

Unlike a number of other developed countries, the United States is an important supplier of tobacco leaf to international markets, exporting roughly one-third of its crop in unmanufactured form. In 1981, the value of tobacco leaf produced in the United States was $3.3 billion. No price supports were received from the government, although acreage limitations were in force

Table 9–1
Direct Impact of Tobacco Core Sector on National Employment and Compensation, 1983

Sector	Value of Sales ($ Millions)	Average Annual Employment	Average Annual Compensation[e] ($ Millions)
Tobacco Farming	2,497[a]	100,000	610.7
Auctions	2,409[b]	9,240	90.8
Manufacturing	15,800[c]	76,900	2,837.0
Wholesale Trade	24,000[d]	35,357	883.9
Retail Trade	28,348[d]	192,720	2,303.1
Total	—	414,217	6,725.5
Percent of United States Total	—	0.46	0.34

Source: Chase Econometrics, Inc., "The Economic Impact of the Tobacco Industry on the United States' Economy in 1983," Executive Summary, May 1985.
[a]Production value of tobacco harvest based on U.S.D.A. data.
[b]Gross producer sales from U.S.D.A.
[c]Includes Federal excise taxes.
[d]Includes Federal, state and local excise taxes, and retail sales tax in retail trade.
[e]Includes supplements to wages and salaries (i.e., fringe benefits) and employer contribution to social insurance.

Table 9–2
The Impact of the U.S. Tobacco Industry: Selected Economic Indicators, 1983
(billions of dollars)

Indicator	1983 U.S. Totals	Core and Supplier Impact	Expenditure Induced Impact
Gross National Product	3,304.8	31.5	50.6
Consumer Expenditures	2,155.9	28.3	33.3
Gross Private Domestic Investment	471.8	1.3	20.5
Net Exports of Goods and Services	−8.2	1.9	−3.7
Government Purchases of Goods and Services	685.5	0.0	0.5
National Income[a]	2,646.7	18.9	48.3
Compensation of Employees[b]	1,984.9	14.1	30.9
Proprietors' Income	121.7	1.0	3.3
Rental Income	58.3	0.0	0.0
Net Interest	256.6	0.3	6.4
Corporate Profits	225.2	3.5	7.7
Federal Government Receipts	641.1	10.0	8.8
State and Local Government Receipts	478.2	5.7	5.4
Employment (millions)	93.28	.71	1.59

Source: Chase Econometrics, Inc., "The Economic Impact of the Tobacco Industry on the United States' Economy in 1983," Executive Summary, May 1985.

[a]Includes all income taxes.
[b]Includes other labor income and employees' contributions to social insurance.

and a loan program is available to growers. This sum amounted to 4.5% of farm receipts from all crops. Two features of the leaf-growing sector suggest that its contribution is qualitatively above average. Because of soil conditions, output is concentrated in five states. Thus, any diminution of tobacco output would lead to severe local hardship and presumably take a long time to overcome. In addition, leaf growing employs, for relatively short periods, a large number of workers who have very limited skills and few alternative employment opportunities. Any measure of economic contribution must assume that the return earned on a factor of production measures that factor's opportunity cost in terms of its potential output contribution in an alternative industry. This assumption is unlikely to hold true for low-skilled agricultural workers in the United States, whose alternative job opportunities are rather scarce.

Western Europe

A 1985 study of the impact of the tobacco industry on the national economies of Western Europe is equally revealing. With respect to the labor force, it is

Table 9–3
Direct Impact of Tobacco Core Sector

Tax Category		Receipts ($ Millions)
Federal Tax Receipts		
FICA Taxes on Employee Wages		882.4
Employee Personal Income Taxes		974.4
Corporate Income Taxes		1,392.8
Tobacco Excise Taxes		4,770.0
Total		$8,019.6
State and Local Tax Receipts		
Social Insurance		54.4
Employee Personal Income Taxes		198.4
Corporate Income Taxes		165.4
Net Tobacco Excise and Sales Taxes		5,023.4
Cigarette Excise Taxes (State)	4,206.3	
Sales and Other Tobacco Taxes (State, City, and County)	817.1	
Subtotal		$5,441.6
Grand Total		$13,461.2

Source: Chase Econometrics, Inc., "The Economic Impact of the Tobacco Industry on the United States' Economy in 1983," Executive Summary, May 1985.

estimated that 1.6 million people were employed, either directly or indirectly, in the tobacco industry in the European Community in 1982.[23] Of these, 102,200 were employed in tobacco manufacturing, 98,600 in supplier industries to the tobacco sector, and 529,650 in specialized tobacco outlets (see table 9–4). If Spain and Portugal are added, the total figure for Western Europe (except Norway, Sweden, Finland, and Turkey) comes to almost 1.8 million.

The raw labor force figures may well overestimate the total employment effects of the tobacco industry, however, because of the seasonal nature of part of the agricultural employment in the industry. Table 9–5 indicates the corresponding full-time-equivalent (FTE) employment figures. These indicate that in 1982, a 694,200 FTE level was reached in the industry, or somewhat under one-half of the raw employment figures. The FTE estimate is a valuable aspect of the Western European study which is not present in the U.S. study. The actual employment impact probably lies somewhere between the total (head count) employment and the FTE figures, since seasonal employment tends to have a disproportionately large effect on family incomes and regional economic activity in tobacco-growing areas.

Overall, the contribution of the tobacco industry and linked sectors to the level of personal income in the Western European economies amounted to 5.8 billion European Currency Units (ECUs) in 1982, or about $6 billion (see table 9–6).

Table 9–4
Persons Engaged in the Tobacco Industry in the European Economic Community, Portugal, and Spain, 1982

	Tobacco Manufacturing	Backward Linkages	Number of Persons Engaged	Number of Persons Engaged in Specialized Tobacco Outlets	Total[b]
Belgium	6,350	2,400	3,300	15,250	27,800
Luxembourg	350	150	—		
Denmark	2,300	1,500	—	2,450	6,250
France	8,400	6,450	87,750[c]	86,000	188,600
Germany	22,500	26,650	17,650[d]	47,700	114,500
Greece	4,050	1,450	414,800	90,000	510,300
Ireland	2,200	1,350	—	6,100	9,650
Italy	14,800	5,750	316,400	123,750	460,700
Netherlands	8,850	6,300	—	10,400	25,550
United Kingdom	32,400	46,600	—	148,000	227,000
Total EEC	102,200	98,600	839,900	529,650	1,570,350
Portugal	1,900	2,350	6,700[e]	111,350	122,300
Spain	13,150	6,500	50,100	32,400	102,150
Total Twelve	117,250	107,450	896,700	673,400	1,794,800

Source: Data from Planning and Economic Consultants, *The Tobacco Industry in the European Community, Portugal and Spain* (Edinburgh: PEIDA, 1985), tables 4.1, 5.4, 6.5, 6.6, 6.7, 7.2, and 7.6.
[a]See table 7.2 for details.
[b]Includes figures of absolute number of persons engaged in tobacco growing and first processing and in specialized tobacco distribution outlets.
[c]Includes employment in tobacco reconstitution, but not in first processing.
[d]Excludes employment in tobacco first processing: data not available.
[e]Excludes employment in tobacco first processing: data not available.

Table 9–7 indicates that the data on tax revenues contributed by the tobacco industry is not complete. About $8.4 billion was contributed in the United Kingdom, $1.2 billion in the Netherlands, $888 million in Denmark and $789 million in Belgium. Given tax rates in these countries, however, it seems likely that the overall fiscal contribution of the tobacco industry in Western Europe is comparable to that in the United States.

Australia

In Australia, value added by the tobacco industry amounted to about $A 1.4 billion in 1978/79, or about 1.36% of GNP. Of this amount, $A 56.3 million was accounted for by locally-grown leaf, a value which is exaggerated by the high level of tobacco tariffs imposed by Australia.[24] The industry accounted for 1.6% of total employment. Indirect (sales and excise) taxes attributed to the industry were estimated at $A 777 million at the federal level and $A 85 million with respect to political subdivisions.

Table 9–5
Full-time Equivalents (FTEs) in the Tobacco Industry in the European Economic Community, Portugal, and Spain, 1982

	Tobacco Manufacturing	Backward Linkages	Tobacco Growing/ First Processing	Retailing	Total[a]
Belgium	6,350	2,400	600	6,000	15,850
Luxembourg	350	150	—		
Denmark	2,300	1,500	—	2,400	6,200
France	8,400	6,450	17,450[b]	17,700	50,000
Germany	22,500	26,650	3,400[c]	38,500	91,050
Greece	4,050	1,450	141,100	9,900	156,500
Ireland	2,200	1,350	—	3,600	7,150
Italy	14,800	5,750	70,550	24,700	115,800
Netherlands	8,850	6,300	—	7,500	22,650
United Kingdom	32,400	46,600	—	79,300	158,300
Total EEC	102,200	98,600	233,100	189,600	623,500
Portugal	1,900	2,350	2,800[d]	5,400	12,450
Spain	13,150	6,500	17,300	21,300	58,250
Total Twelve	117,250	107,450	253,200	216,300	694,200

Source: Data from Planning and Economic Consultants, *The Tobacco Industry in the European Community, Portugal and Spain* (Edinburgh: PEIDA, 1985), Tables 4.1, 5.4, 6.5, 6.6, 6.7, 7.2, and 7.6.
[a]Includes full time equivalent figures for tobacco growing and first processing and for forward linkages.
[b]Includes employment in tobacco reconstitution, but not in first processing.
[c]Excludes employment in tobacco first processing: data not available.
[d]Excludes employment in tobacco first processing: data not available.

Table 9–6
Summary of Pretax Personal Incomes Attributable to the Tobacco Industry in the European Economic Community, Portugal and Spain, 1982
(million ECU)

	Tobacco Manufacturing	Backward Linkages	Tobacco Growing/ First Processing	Forward Linkages	Total
Belgium	73	24	3	68	174
Luxembourg	4	2	—		
Denmark	33	18	—	35	86
France	127	81	96	185	489
Germany	391	367	16	503	1,277
Greece	33	11	438	47	529
Ireland	34	15	—	31	80
Italy	169	57	208	210	644
Netherlands	130	97	—	118	345
United Kingdom	555	536	—	608	1,699
Total EEC	1,549	1,208	761	1,805	5,323
Portugal	11	10	11	20	52
Spain	150	65	54	118	387
Total Twelve	1,710	1,283	826	1,943	5,762

Source: Data from Planning and Economic Consultants, *The Tobacco Industry in the European Community, Portugal and Spain* (Edinburgh: PEIDA, 1985), Tables 4.3, 5.5, 6.9, and 7.8.

Table 9–7
Summary Tax Revenues Raised in Association with the Tobacco Industry, 1982
(million ECU)

	Excise and VAT	Corporation Taxes	Income Taxes	Social Security Contributions	Total
Belgium	624	4	34	38	789
Luxembourg	89				
Denmark	845	13	28	2	888
France	2,180	n.a.	31	144	—
Germany	6,211	n.a.	220	375	—
Greece	384	n.a.	n.a.	n.a.	—
Ireland	403	2	13	11	429
Italy	3,087	n.a.	48	69	—
Netherlands	985	11	70	126	1,192
United Kingdom	7,694	187	311	202	8,384
Total EEC	23,122	—	—	—	—
Portugal	272	n.a.	5	10	—
Spain	778	4	32	30	844
Total Twelve	24,172	—	—	—	—

Source: Data from Planning and Economic Consultants, *The Tobacco Industry in the European Community, Portugal and Spain* (Edinburgh, PEIDA, 1985), Tables 8.1, 8.4, and 8.5.

Canada

The Canadian tobacco industry likewise served as a major source of revenue for the federal government in 1983, as well as for the provinces and their political subdivisions.[25] Excise taxes, excise duties and sales taxes (plus customs receipts) amounted to Can $1.2 billion—approximately 8% of the federal receipts from indirect taxation. Revenue raised for the provinces in this manner were about Can $1.2 billion.

Malaysia

The role of leaf growing is quite important in Malaysia, where agricultural technology seems to have been very much improved by the activities of industry-promoted extension services.[26] In consequence, the agricultural economies in those relatively limited areas in which conditions are right for leaf growing have enjoyed a remarkable growth in prosperity and have contributed to the political and economic stability of the country. In the context of some of the specific targets identified earlier, the success of leaf growing has provided other farming activities with a standard by which their performance can be measured. One important beneficial effect is to reduce the natural resistance of agricultural communities to the introduction of new crops. At the time of the so-called green revolution, the process of persuading small-scale agricultural producers to use new types of seed was one of the principal obstacles to increased tobacco output.

As Table 9–8 shows, the Malaysian tobacco industry in 1982 employed over 182,000 full- and part-time workers, or about 75,000 FTEs, in addition

Table 9–8
Economic Impact of the Tobacco Industry on Malaysia

Item	Farmers	Curers	Manufacturers	Distributors	Retailers	Total
Employment (thousands)						
Direct						
Full- and part-time	88.20	21.50	3.83	2.97	65.93	182.43
Full-time equivalent	32.08	10.03	3.83	2.97	26.37	75.28
Indirect: Full-time equivalent	1.73	0.79	10.06	0.51	—	13.09
Induced: Full-time equivalent	3.69	0.58	3.42	0.03	—	7.72
Total						
Full- and part-time	93.62	22.87	17.31	3.51	65.93	203.24
Full-time equivalent	37.50	11.40	17.31	3.51	26.37	96.09
Income/salary (In million $)						
Direct	38.10	26.95	53.41	15.64	99.02	233.12
Indirect	5.40	4.09	61.82	2.56	—	73.87
Induced	0.82	4.31	43.92	2.18	—	51.23
Total	44.32	35.35	159.92	20.38	99.02	358.22
Company net income (In million $)						
Direct	—	14.75	138.05	7.26	—	160.06
Indirect	3.23	2.43	36.93	1.54	—	44.13
Total	3.23	17.18	174.98	8.80	—	204.19
Investments (Any sector) (In million $)						
Direct	n.a.	10.74	54.68	n.a.	n.a.	n.a.
Indirect	n.a.	0.97	14.77	0.62	n.a.	n.a.
Total	n.a.	11.71	69.45	0.62	n.a.	n.a.
Government Revenue (In million $)						
Import/Excise/Sales	—	—	381.70	—	—	381.70
Direct company	—	6.08	64.42	2.96	11.00	84.46
Indirect company	1.29	0.97	14.77	0.62	—	17.65
Total	1.29	7.05	460.89	3.58	11.00	483.81

Source: Data from Frank Small and Associates, *Economic Assessment of the Impact of the Malaysian Tobacco Industry* (Kuala Lumpur: Council of Malaysian Tobacco Manufacturers, 1983). For notes on derivation of data, see Small and Associates.

to indirect employment of over 13,000 for a total of 203,000. Total income generated was in excess of $358 million, in addition to $204 million in net company income and $483 million in government revenues.

Zimbabwe

Data on the role of the tobacco industry is less available in the case of Zimbabwe, although some interesting findings have been made.[27] The industry is estimated to employ 101,270 workers directly, in addition to indirect employment of 22,150. This is a respectable number of workers in an industry that is quite competitive on world markets, as indicated by the importance of the industry's exports. Table 9–9 summarizes available data on Zimbabwe.

Table 9–9
The Tobacco Industry in Zimbabwe: Selected Employment Effects
(Estimate of Persons Employed)

Direct Employment	
Growing Sector	
Tobacco Farmers	
Flue-cured	1,160
Burley	3,000
Labour-Total	88,000
Training	110
Research	250
Service Companies	1,390
Growers' Associations	50
Marketing Sector	
Auction Floor	800[b]
Tobacco Marketing Board	50
Processing Sector	5,300[a]
Manufacturing Sector	1,160
Total	101,270
Related Employment	
Fertilizer and Chemical Industries	650
Distributive Sector	1,500
Transport Sector	1,000
Government Services	
(including energy sources and maintenance)	18,000
Miscellaneous	1,000
Total	22,150

Source: Data from Zimbabwe Tobacco Industry Council, *Tobacco and Its Economic Contribution to Zimbabwe* (Harare: Tobacco Industry Council, 1984).
[a]Full-time
[b]Seasonal

Table 9–10
**Cigarette Industry Significance in the Argentine
Economy, 1983**

Contribution to Gross National Product	1.24%
Contribution to Gross Industrial Product	5.18%
Contribution to D.G.I. Real Revenues	11.95%
Labor Force Employed by Cigarette Industry	5.573%
Position of Remunerations Paid in Relation to Other Industrial Sectors	1

Source: Data from Camera de la Industria del Tobaco, "Value Added in the Argentine Tobacco Industrye" (Buenos Aires: Camera de la Industria del Tobaco, 1984).

Argentina

In the case of Argentina, the tobacco industry was estimated to contribute value added of $811 million or 1.24% of gross national product in 1983.[28] Tax revenues were $747 million, or 11.9% of total collections. A total of 368,573 workers were employed in the industry, as well as in upstream and downstream firms, representing approximately 5.5% of the economically active population, as noted in table 9–10.

The Special Role of Fiscal Contributions

Some products or groups of products have proved their ability to serve as a reliable and productive source of tax revenues by virtue of their ability to carry disproportionately high and discriminatory rates of indirect taxation without rapid erosion of sales volumes. Products that are subjected to very high rates of indirect taxation may be luxury goods, where the intent of the high tax rates is presumably to "soak the rich" by exploiting that group's relative insensitivity to increased product costs. A second class of goods subjected to high rates of indirect taxation is used by a wide range of income classes which prove to have a relatively price-inelastic demand.

In some countries the capability of these goods to carry high rates of indirect taxation was discovered "by accident": The goods in question were referred to as "demerit goods," and it was deemed righteous and benevolent economic policy to discourage their consumption.[29] But if demand is price-inelastic, then taxation reduces the consumption of so-called demerit goods but little and instead provides a steady source of revenue to the government. Coffee has traditionally been used as a vehicle for raising revenue in Austria and Germany—possibly because it is a noncompetitive import and there is no domestic industry to complain about the inequitable treatment of its product. Tobacco products bear high and discriminatory indirect tax rates almost everywhere.

Governments, like all public institutions, are creatures of habit and are likely to take the line of least resistance in accomplishing any difficult task. When the task is to raise additional revenue, politicians are likely to look to existing forms of taxation and to tried-and-true products such as tobacco with heavy existing indirect tax rates. Governments can, therefore, act as a monopolist and by levying indirect taxes, increase the prices of the products of all the firms in the industry more or less equiproportionately. They can place a relatively heavy burden on both the user of the product and the industry producing it.

Indeed, the practice of relying upon some goods as a means of raising revenues has become so well established in the minds of both taxpayers and the politicians imposing the taxes that the process is seldom, if ever, questioned. Once a group of products has been identified as being a superior base for indirect taxation, shortfalls in anticipated revenues serve as perennial temptations to raise further the existing tax burden. Beyond some point, demand must become price-elastic. When this happens, the producing industry, the distributing network and the consumer are all burdened to no purpose. The intent of the tax is to raise revenues, and it loses its effectiveness once revenues begin to decrease.

There are, then, two issues: (1) The ability of a tax-burdened industry to generate an unduly high proportion of government revenues; and (2) The possibility that the rate of taxation will, by the government's own standards, be excessive. The ability to generate revenues is a feature of the industry's economic contribution (see figure 9–1). The likelihood that the critical or "excessive" tax rate will be exceeded is positively related to the perceived needs of governments for additional revenues, the level of popular resistance to other forms of taxation, and the degree of automaticity with which politicians rely on discriminatory excise taxation of certain familiar products. Whether the level of provision of public goods is inadequate or excessive makes very little difference to the role of the industry providing the tax-burdened product. The taxes raised by indirect taxation can be seen as substitutes for other ways of raising revenues, independently of the issue of the most desirable rate of provision of public goods. The contribution of the industry may be seen as greater when the other sources of revenues run into rapidly diminishing returns. Then the ability to provide additional public goods or transfers depends directly upon the capacity of the group of goods to generate more taxes.

Figures 9–2 and 9–3 identify the characteristics of products that can serve as standard bases for discriminatory and high rates of indirect taxation, and identify the (conceptual) limit of the maximum efficient tax rate. Consider the relationship between the rate of indirect taxation (measured horizontally) and the revenues raised by the tax. Figure 9–2 shows the relationship for a good with negligible tax-generating capacity. Demand for the

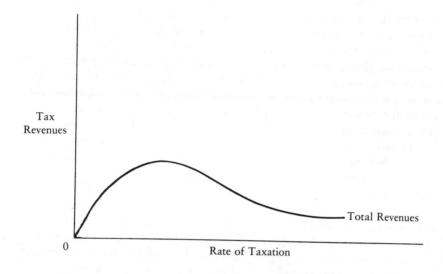

Figure 9–2. Tax Revenues and Tax Rates: I

good is very elastic to discriminatory rates of indirect taxation. An increase in the rate of excise tax will raise the cost of the good to the user, and decrease the number of units sold.[30] This is a standard weakness, for example, of the argument for relying on tariffs on imports as a source of revenues. The

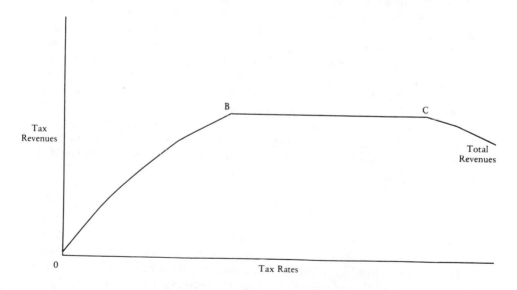

Figure 9–3. Tax Revenues and Tax Rates: II

increase in the revenue to be derived from taxing such a product depends on the preexisting rate of taxation and the price-elasticity of demand.

If the rate of tax is quite low, an increase in the tax rate of some magnitude will have only a small effect on total price, and the percentage increase in tax revenues would be quite high even for goods with moderately elastic demand schedules. As the tax rate continues to be increased, total revenues will quickly peak and further tax increases will reduce revenues absolutely. Such a revenue/tax-rate relationship is depicted in figure 9–2. Maximum revenues are small and extremely sensitive to the rate of tax.

Figure 9–3 shows the same relationship for a product which renders an "economic contribution" by virtue of its ability to raise tax revenues. Total revenues rise with the rate of indirect taxation until tax rate B is reached. Revenues are more or less constant between rates B and C and decline absolutely for rates in excess of C. The demand for the product is mildly price-inelastic over the range BC because the increase in tax rates generates a constant flow of tax revenues, and quantity of goods sold will be decreasing. Total revenues, including both industry's receipts and tax revenues, will be decreasing. In practice, the curve is unlikely to be completely flat (perfectly constant tax revenues) over the range BC, but it can be thought of as being "effectively flat" in the sense that econometric analysis will not be able to reject either a negative or a positive slope.

A tax rate can be considered "excessive" when it imposes marginal costs on society in excess of the benefits derived from marginal revenues raised. As noted, the marginal benefits can be reckoned in terms of the benefits derived from a failure to increase other forms of taxation or in terms of the public goods provided with the revenues. As long as a tax has some social cost, an increase in the tax rate that does not also increase revenues will be excessive. The existence of social costs from high rates of taxation makes any optimum tax lie to the left of B.

The social costs of increasing tax rates do increase for virtually every form of taxation. Direct taxes (personal income and corporate profits taxes) reduce incentives and the willingness of industry to invest. There may be some tax illusion here, in the sense that reduced incentives may follow from an increase over some concept of normalcy or from an announcement-effect rather than from an insidious increase in tax rates as a result of, say, a combination of inflation and a progressive tax structure.

Higher rates also lead to greater effort being made in tax saving, if not tax evasion. They can encourage smuggling and thus require that preventive measures be taken. These measures cost money, so that increases in indirect tax rates must have their effects measured in terms of net receipts. Higher indirect tax rates burden consumers whose tastes place heavy reliance on the goods being taxed[31] and reduce the profitability of the supplies, so that the industry's direct taxes are reduced.

There is a particularly serious likelihood that tax rates levied on tobacco (and similar) products will be excessive in countries in which different levels of government set their tax structures independently of each other. The classic example exists in a federal system where a central government has responsibility for certain tasks and another set of tasks devolves upon the provincial or state governments. In this country, states have traditionally tended to rely upon indirect taxation and the federal government has generated most of its revenues through direct taxation.[32] When federal governments encounter substantial resistance to increases in direct taxation, they tend to "poach" on the tax preserves of states and provinces. With two sets of governments levying indirect taxes on the same good more or less independently of each other's actions, the possibility for excessive total tax rates becomes great.

A particularly unhappy interaction between central and provincial governments was enacted in Canada and has since been reversed in response to recommendations of a Task Force on Alcohol and Tobacco Tax Indexation. The probability was that total taxation of tobacco products would become excessive. In fact, there was no limit to the rate of taxation. The central government had attempted to index the rates of excise duty and excise taxes on tobacco products to the rate of increase in the retail price of those products. Every September 1, the excise duty and taxes levied on cigarettes (used here as a representative tobacco product) was to have been adjusted to reflect any increase in the retail price of cigarettes as officially computed in the previous year. Starting with an increase in the retail price of tobacco products, the excise duty and tax would rise. When the federal excise taxes rose, the provincial sales taxes would also increase since the base for the provincial sales tax included the federal excise duty and tax. This would raise the retail cost of cigarettes (unless the provinces were to reduce their sales tax rates in a given year) and increase the federal excise duty and taxes on the following September 1. This process could have continued forever, even given constant prices set by the industry and unchanging tax rates on the part of the provinces.

It is important to note that the definition of an excessive rate of indirect taxation is determined in terms of the interests of society or the government and not the interests of the industry producing the good or the user of the good. It is the benefits which society garners from the taxes raised on tobacco and similar products when the tax rates are efficient that constitutes this dimension of "economic contribution."

In a significant number of developing countries, the revenue from tobacco accounts for 10% or more of the total government tax receipts. In one developing country, Jamaica, despite a high incidence of taxes on cigarettes, revenues from taxes on tobacco products are relatively low: 0.4% of government revenue from taxation. This may be explained by low taxes on non-cigarette tobacco products such as cigars.

In the majority of industrialized countries with high taxes on cigarettes, tobacco taxes as a share of government tax revenues range from 1.7% to 3.0%. Income from tobacco taxes, however, is much higher in several European Economic Community countries, notably the Federal Republic of Germany (7.3%), the United Kingdom (5.6%), and Ireland (5.6%).

The significant differences in the share of tobacco tax among some industrialized countries with extremely high taxes on cigarettes can probably be explained by the very different tax mixes used in both direct and indirect tax systems in these countries—the Federal Republic of Germany and France, for example, have a tax incidence of 75% and 77% respectively, but tobacco accounts for 7.3% of tax revenue in the Federal Republic of Germany compared to 2.0% in France.

Summary and Conclusions

In order to estimate the economic impact or contribution of something in the real world, it is vital that the contribution be considered in the light of a set of benchmarks that form the frame of reference for the study. This chapter has developed, very briefly, the dimensions of a government's set of economic goals (its objective function). The objective function comprises many dimensions, and not all of these lend themselves to relatively precise quantitative measurement. Some can be considered only in qualitative terms. The importance of a variable in the objective function will be determined by an individual government at a particular point in time. The objective function is subject to change through time and across countries and cultures according to the prevailing political context. It is particularly important to recognize that the benchmarks used in a developing country will tend to place greater stress on longer-run considerations, and that industrialized countries may tend, except in times of turbulence, to place greater emphasis on narrow measures of the contribution of an industry to high rates of capacity utilization. One dimension—the ability to serve as a base for government revenues—seems to rank high among the separate criteria in both industrialized and developing countries.

This distinction in the impact of the tobacco industry across countries is quite apparent. The benefits of leaf growing in a number of developing countries are very significant: as a conduit for improved agricultural technology, for value added, and, because of the labor-intensity of the operation, as a source of rural employment. To the extent that the intent of the government is to spread sources of development widely across the country and to reduce a seemingly natural tendency for manufacturing to develop in densely populated urban areas, the tobacco industry provides regional balance. For some of these countries, the contribution of the leaf-growing process is, in addition, a means of generating or economizing on scarce foreign exchange.

The manufacture of tobacco products and their distribution is an important source of employment in many countries, and the industry has backward linkages that are widely spread across the primary-products and the industrial sectors. This derives from the relative price-inelasticity of demand for tobacco products, which enables the government to capture, through the imposition of value-added and excise taxes, the economic surplus that a pure monopolist could achieve. There is a clear danger that governments could excessively rely on tobacco products as a source of revenue to the extent that the policy generates less than maximum yield and, at the same time, penalizes both producers and users. Of course, there exist other means of capturing the monopoly rent than through the imposition of indirect taxes. France, among other nations, lodges responsibility for the manufacture of tobacco products in a state-owned monopoly. If the monopoly is efficient, this system will generate profits for the state at the same rate that an optimum tax structure would achieve. The degree of efficiency achieved by government-owned monopolies is, of course, debatable.

Because of the country specificity of the objective function, the contribution of the tobacco industry may be expected to vary substantially across countries. While there does seem to be a general pattern of behavior observable in the developed world, the focus and techniques of measurement and the interpretation of any findings must be considered in the light of the features of the country under study. They cannot be transferred among nations.

Notes

1. Any discussion of the role of government and economic policy must draw heavily on J. Tinbergen, *On the Theory of Economic Policy* (Amsterdam: North-Holland Publishing Co., 1952). Many of the terms used here are drawn directly from Tinbergen's classic work.

2. On the question of the relationship between measurable entities and abstract concepts, see Henry Margenau, "What is a Theory?" in Sherman Roy Krupp, ed., *The Structure of Economic Science* (New York: Prentice-Hall, 1966), pp. 25–38.

3. The implications of this caveat for industry-impact analyses are self-evident. Some of the practical effects are given further consideration below.

4. Obviously, it is logically possible to have a consistent series of target variables for all countries provided that some carry zero weight; in the text all weights are assumed to be positive.

5. Multinational corporations are particularly likely to bask in the political spotlight because they are considered "foreign," and attitudes towards such firms can change relatively quickly.

6. There are some problems of definition and measurement with both output and employment; these are considered in Section II.

7. Enhancement of quantity is likely to be of interest only in developed nations; quality enhancement will be important in all nations.

8. This aspect of contribution is very important in any consideration of the role of the tobacco industry.

9. A short technical summary of input–output analysis is available in Paul R. Gregory and Robert C. Stuart, *Comparative Economic Systems* (Boston: Houghton Mifflin, 1980), pp. 152–154.

10. Axel Leijonhufvud, "Effective Demand Failures," *Swedish Journal of Economics* 75(1) (1973):27–48.

11. The authors wish to acknowledge invaluable correspondence with Ron Edwards on this point.

12. See Wassily Leontief, "The Distribution of Work and Income," *Scientific American* 247, (3), (1982):188–204.

13. An I–O table is created for an economy over a specified time period and can never be up to date. In the absence of severe shocks, relationships tend to evolve only gradually so that the error caused by the lapse of time can usually be considered negligible.

14. Whether it is necessary to adjust the row and column from which the tobacco industry will have been taken out depends upon the quantitative importance of the tobacco industry within that aggregate.

15. The separate listing of the price-stabilizing and residual-growth effects is probably ascribable to the times in which we live and the recognition of the current importance of inflationary forces as impeding the smooth functioning of the economy.

16. See James E. Meade, "A New Keynesian Approach to Full Employment," *Lloyds Bank Review* (October, 1983):1–18 and Leontief, "Distribution of Work and Income."

17. In fact, employment may become a variable of lesser significance since it will not measure the rate of capacity utilization directly and, if the workers used are highly-skilled and scarce, their employment in an industry may have high opportunity costs. Employment of low-skilled labor might prove to be a more useful measure.

18. See Hollis B. Chenery, "Transitional Growth and World Industrialization," in Bertil Ohlin et al., eds., *The International Allocation of Economic Activity* (London: Macmillan, 1977), pp. 457–490.

19. Robert Fendt, Jr., "Brazil, The Occupation of 2,000,000 People," in *Tobacco: Generator of Wealth* (London: World Tobacco, 1983), p. 109.

20. Ibid., pp. 111–112.

21. Fendt, *Tobacco,* pp. 11, 18, and 79.

22. Chase Econometrics, Inc., "The Economic Impact of the Tobacco Industry on the United States Economy in 1983," Executive Summary, May 1985. See also, Wharton Econometric Associates, *A Study of the U.S. Tobacco Industry's Economic Contribution to the Nation, Its Fifty States, and the District of Columbia* (Philadelphia: Wharton Econometric Associates, 1982).

23. Planning and Economic Consultants, *The Tobacco Industry in the European Community, Portugal and Spain* (Edinburgh: PEIDA, 1985).

24. University of New South Wales and University of Queensland, *The Impact of the Tobacco Industry on Regional, State and Australian Economies* (Sydney: Tobacco Institute of Australia, 1981).

25. Peat, Marwick, and Mitchell, *Economic Impact of the Tobacco Industry in Canada* (Toronto, PMM, 1979).

26. Frank Small and Associates, *Economic Assessment of the Impact of the Malaysian Tobacco Industry* (Kuala Lumpur: Council of Malaysian Tobacco Manufacturers, 1983).

27. Zimbabwe Tobacco Industry Council, *Tobacco and Its Economic Contribution to Zimbabwe* (Harare: Tobacco Industry Council, 1984).

28. Camera de la Industria del Tabaco, "Value Added in the Argentine Tobacco Industry," (Buenos Aires: Camera de la Indusria del Tabaco, 1984).

29. See Richard A. Musgrave and Peggy B. Musgrave, *Public Finance in Theory and Practice* (New York: McGraw-Hill, 1973), pp. 304–305.

30. Note that the elasticity will be quite different if an equiproportionate sales or excise tax is imposed on all products: price elasticity is a partial equilibrium concept and is, therefore, concerned with discriminatory rates of taxation.

31. The reduction in consumer welfare is analogous to the traditional partial-equilibrium analysis of the effect of a tariff on imports on consumer welfare in the levying country. Of course, if an increase in one rate of indirect taxation is countered by a decrease in the rate on another product, no certain answer exists.

32. See Musgrave and Musgrave, *Public Finance,* p. 190.

10
Smoking and Market Failure

Stephen C. Littlechild

Governments in all countries attempt to regulate smoking. The measures adopted include taxation of tobacco products, restrictions on sale and advertising of tobacco, restrictions on smoking in certain places, mandatory health warnings, provision of information, publicity campaigns, and so on. In many countries there is currently pressure to increase the severity of these restrictions. Some people would like public smoking completely banned, and there are occasional suggestions to outlaw tobacco itself.

By what criteria should government policy be decided? What should determine whether smoking should be regulated, and if so, how? Some framework of analysis is required within which the advantages and disadvantages of any proposed policy can be evaluated. In this chapter, we shall examine the case for regulation of smoking as a means of correcting "market failure."* This is a conceptual framework much used (and sometimes misused) by economists. It has often been invoked (either directly or implicitly) in the smoking debate.

The analysis of market failure poses two fundamental questions: 1) Is there reason to believe that the market process pertaining to a particular activity is significantly flawed, so that the net benefits of this activity are less than they might be, or even negative? and 2) If so, is there reason to believe that some form of intervention by government can help to remedy this defect without generating further problems elsewhere? In the case of smoking, two kinds of market failure are frequently alleged. First, smoking is claimed to involve risks to their own health of which most smokers are unaware. Second, smoking is claimed to adversely affect *non*smokers in various ways, chiefly a) by burdening nonsmokers with the medical expenses of smokers, and b) by annoying or impairing the health of nonsmokers. The first alleged market failure represents a case of "imperfect information," the second a case of "externalities." The aim of this chapter is to assess the validity of these arguments,

---

*The economic analysis of market failure deals with choice by adults.

and to consider what implications should be drawn for government policy toward smoking. For further discussion of this and related topics, see Little-child (1981) and Littlechild and Wiseman (1984a,b).

The concept of market failure is not the only way to approach the evaluation of public policy towards smoking, nor is it necessarily the best way. There are many other important considerations to be taken into account, such as the preservation of liberty in a free society and the protection of those unwilling or unable to make "sensible" decisions. This chapter does not attempt to specify how values such as liberty and paternalism should be balanced against each other or against the correction of market failure. Some of these questions are treated elsewhere in this volume, particularly in chapters by Douglas Den Uyl, Peter L. Berger, William F. Shughart II and Robert D. Tollison, and J.J. Boddewyn.

The Correction of Market Failure

The analysis of market failure is based on the concept of rational choice as expressed through properly functioning markets. When one chooses to spend money on a particular bundle of goods and services, one presumably prefers that bundle to any other bundle which one could have bought, but chose not to. If markets function properly, the prices of the various goods and services will accurately reflect the relative costs of producing them. The "fundamental theorem of welfare economics" asserts that, under these circumstances, the allocation of resources in the economy will be *efficient*. That is, it will not be possible to use the resources available in society to produce a different pattern of goods and services in such a way that everyone is better off. It will only be possible to make someone better off by making someone else worse off. Note that this analysis is not concerned with equity in distribution. It is not claimed that the outcome will be socially desirable, nor that the initial distribution of income is socially just. The assertion is simply that, if markets function properly, the outcome will be efficient in the sense that there is no "slack" in the economy with which some people could be made better off without making others worse off.

If markets function properly, government intervention is not warranted as a means of increasing economic efficiency. Intervention has to be justified in terms of other goals, such as to redistribute income or to secure specified national goals. As noted earlier, yet other arguments for government action might be advanced to protect children, for example, but these lie outside the model of rational choice.

In practice, of course, markets do not necessarily function properly: there may be "market failure." Three kinds of market failure are commonly identified: monopoly power, imperfect information, and external effects. For various reasons, prices may not properly reflect costs of production and consumption. As a result, the allocation of resources may not be efficient. A different pattern of production of goods and services could exist which could make some people better off without making anyone worse off.

Simple numerical examples will help to illustrate the concept of market failure.

Monopoly. Suppose a company charges $10 for a product which costs $6 to produce. Some potential customers would be willing to pay $9 for the product, which would cover incremental costs of production of $6, but are unable to buy because it is not in the company's self-interest to lower price—if the company reduced prices its total profit would fall. At the margin, social benefit is $9 (what people are willing to pay for more of the product) whereas social cost is $6 (what it costs to produce more of the product). There is a market failure here because output is lower than what an openly competitive market would produce.

Imperfect Information. Suppose a company charges $6 for a product which costs $6 to produce, and (at the margin) the consumer values this product at $6, but unknown to the consumer the product will need repairing at a cost of $2. At the margin, social benefit is $6 but social cost is $8 ($6 + 2). There is a market failure here because output is higher than economic efficiency requires. That is, given better information, the consumer would realize that the true cost of the product is $8 and would reduce purchases accordingly.

Externalities. Suppose a company charges $6 for a product which costs $6 to produce, and (at the margin) the consumer values this product at $6, but every time a consumer purchases this product his neighbor incurs a cost of $1. At the margin, social benefit is $6 but social cost is $7 ($6 + 1). There is a market failure here because output is higher than economic efficiency requires. If the neighbor's costs are counted, less of the product would be produced.

If a market is not functioning properly—that is, if there is market failure—it may be possible for the government to intervene to correct the failure, or at least to improve the situation. Depending upon the type of failure, this intervention may take the form of regulating prices or production, providing information or preventing misinformation, taxing or subsidizing, and so on.

To justify government intervention, however, it is not sufficient merely to identify a "market failure." Just as there may be "market failure," so there may be "government failure." One has to consider how a particular government body or regulation will *actually* work, rather than compare what an "infallible" government might do with how a "real" market works. In sum, to justify government intervention, it is necessary to show how a particular kind of intervention could generate a significant improvement in the working of the market so that, on balance, the benefits of this intervention outweigh the disadvantages.

To illustrate this point, consider the case of alcohol (Leu 1983). The continued production and sale of alcohol is a prima facie indication that the benefits to the purchasers outweigh the costs of production. However, it is argued by some that excessive consumption of alcohol can lead to physical, psychological, or emotional harm *to others* (for example, through accidents or distress to family members). In such cases of "externality," the economist's traditional remedy is a tax equal to the value of harm caused to others. In theory, a tax on alcohol would force the drinker to take into account the full consequences of drinking. In practice, however, it is impossible for a tax to distinguish between situations where externalities may be high (such as a heavy drinker driving home after a party) and situations where externalities may be slight (such as a light drinker having a nightcap before bed). A tax on alcohol would reduce consumption indiscriminately. It would therefore reduce the satisfaction otherwise experienced by millions of sensible drinkers without necessarily reducing the harm caused by a few excessive drinkers. In sum, although the market for alcohol may be characterized by an element of "market failure" due to externality, nevertheless, government intervention in the form of a further tax on alcohol cannot be justified on the grounds of correcting this particular market failure. Make no mistake about it, drinking and driving is an "externality" problem. The point of this example is simply that a tax on all drinking is not necessarily the most effective means to control this behavior. Other remedies, such as stiffer fines and prison sentences for convicted drunk-drivers, would constitute a more sensible policy approach to this problem.

Imperfect Information about Smoking

It is sometimes claimed that smoking involves a risk to the health of smokers, and that inadequate or misleading information about this risk would be provided by the market. Government intervention is therefore required to correct this market failure. How far is this argument valid?

It is often argued that the market does not provide information about the risks associated with certain goods or services. But when does consumer ignorance call for government intervention? The absence of "perfect" information is certainly not sufficient, since markets do not require perfect knowledge to function adequately. (Could the stock market even exist with "perfect knowledge"?)

The market process is one of continual learning—from observation, advertising, conversation, and, especially, past experience. Where repeated purchases are common, one would not normally expect significant ignorance on the part of consumers. If intervention is proposed for a particular product, an explanation is necessary for why users of this product are significantly more ignorant than users of other products for which intervention is not proposed.

Advertising

One possible source of consumer ignorance or misinformation is misleading advertising by producers. (Even in the absence of government regulation, of course, this may be disciplined by the increasing willingness of companies to expose unacknowledged defects by named rivals.) Where the consequences of misleading advertising may be deleterious to health, there may be a strong case for controlling advertising.

However, such a "market failure" has a *general* cause rather than being concerned with the advertising of a particular product or market. Any controls should apply to the advertising industry generally, not merely to a single product. Such controls will mainly concern the truth or accuracy of claims made in the course of advertising and will not limit the frequency or location of advertising. In most developed countries, such controls already exist, often operated by the advertising industry itself. There may be scope for debate as to their adequacy, but the debate should concern advertising as an activity rather than the advertising of specific products. As regards smoking, the tobacco companies are not alleged to be advertising in a misleading way. There seems no case for imposing greater restrictions on the advertising of tobacco products than on other products on this particular ground.

Provision of Information

There are certain circumstances in which the government has a public duty to disseminate information—for example, if the government has access to data not available to others, such as statistical records collected for demographic or fiscal purposes. Insofar as such data could be brought to bear on public policy issues, it can usefully be published. (Formally, the efficient allocation of resources requires that publication should be undertaken if the incremental outlays required to do so are less valued than the expected benefits.)

Broadly speaking, one can expect a market participant to make available information about his products which is of interest to consumers, wherever the participant's own product is likely to be perceived as superior to those of his rivals. In some cases, also, market arrangements do develop which expose flaws in products common to all producers; an example is the promotion by retailers of TV rental and insurance schemes in the days before the quality of picture tubes was adequate.

However, one cannot always rely on producers to supply information which will restrict the market as a whole. Market participants will have an incentive to conceal relevant information if its revelation would be against their financial interest. Consumers, for their part, will not demand information where they are exposed to risks of which they are unaware. Those other people or organizations (such as research laboratories), which could supply information about risks, may not have the financial incentive to acquire or publicize this information because there is no effective demand. Where there is clear "market failure" of this kind, a case can be made for government intervention to supply the information or to subsidize its publication. There is, however, one crucial ground rule that must be respected, namely, that the information provided should not go beyond the limits of what has been scientifically established. Similarly, the techniques used in conveying this information should not exceed what is appropriate to the content of the information.

In the case of tobacco, it would seem that the tobacco companies did provide information on those attributes (for example, strength and taste) which smokers deemed most relevant in the days before health became an issue. Tobacco advertising continues to make reference to those attributes which are perceived as important by smokers, such as tar yield. The significant recent shift in purchasing patterns makes it clear that many customers desire low tar cigarettes and therefore find this new information relevant. The health risks alleged to be associated with smoking have been well-publicized by medical organizations, independent scientific researchers, pressure groups such as ASH (Action on Smoking and Health), and indeed by various governmental bodies. In many countries, cigarette packets and advertisements are required to carry a government health warning. Given the volume of this information, it cannot seriously be argued that the general population is ignorant of the risks allegedly associated with tobacco. From the standpoint of correcting market failure, it appears that little more can appropriately be done with respect to the provision of information about smoking.

Externalities and Their Possible Remedies

Before considering the specific case of smoking, it will be helpful to review the economic analysis of externalities in general. It has been argued that the use of certain products ought to be curtailed or prohibited because of their claimed adverse effects on *other people*, or on social life generally. Following Pigou (1920), economists have argued that such external effects lead to a divergence between private cost (the price that a consumer pays) and social cost (defined as private cost plus the sum of the value of the adverse consequences to everyone else). The consumer will purchase any good or service to the point where, at the margin, its value to him in consumption is equal to the price he pays for it. But this private cost will be less than the cost to society: at the margin, the benefit to the consumer is less than the social cost. The level of consumption of this good is thus greater than economic efficiency dictates. If consumption were cut back slightly, those who would otherwise be harmed would gain more than the consumer would lose. To remedy this situation, it is argued that a tax on this good or service equal to the value of the external harm would bring private cost (price plus tax) into line with social cost. The externality would thereby be "internalized." Consumption would be reduced to the point where the benefit to the consumer equalled the price of the product *plus* the tax. In other words, the consumer would be taking into account the harm caused to others.

We have already noted, however, the impracticality of such a tax in the case of alcohol. Other measures, therefore, should be considered. In some cases a complete ban may be indicated; in other cases it may be more efficient to take no action at all. Properly interpreted, the market failure criterion states that government intervention is only appropriate where the benefits exceed the costs. Nowadays, economists are not so convinced that corrective taxation or outright bans are the solution to externalities. Since the pioneering work of Coase (1960), it has increasingly been recognized that externalities reflect an imperfection in the system of property rights. If an action by person A inflicts harm on person B, then B is evidently not protected by a property right, or at least it is too expensive for B to enforce this right. If B did have a property right which he could cheaply enforce economically, A would have to take into account the cost of violating B's property right, and there would be no externality. (Indeed, even if A rather than B owned the property right, B could offer to pay A not to exercise this right, provided the costs of negotiating were relatively low; here too, A would have to take into account the cost of harming B since doing so would sacrifice the offered payment.) Externality problems thus arise where property rights are not well-defined, or where so many people are involved that the costs of negotiating and enforcing the property rights are prohibitively high.

This work has suggested a somewhat different role for public policy towards externalities. Rather than looking for corrective taxes or outright bans, economists are increasingly looking to strengthen property rights or to reduce the costs of enforcing them. In cases where property rights already exist and would not be expensive to enforce, the fact that they are seldom enforced suggests that the externality cannot be very severe. An apparent "problem" may not be much of a problem after all.

The Alleged Externalities of Smoking

A typical expression of the "externalities" view was given in a newspaper column by guest writer Peter Fetherstone (1979) under the heading "Selfish, Arrogant Smokers." He begins by describing the litter generated by smokers, continuing:

If you could quantify the cost to the nation in any one year of the cost of treatment to the National Health Service of complaints caused or worsened by smoking, the damage done to property by fires started by cigarettes; the cost of cleaning up the mess smokers leave behind in our streets, trains and buses; the man-hours lost by people leaving their work to have a quick smoke, and the value of clothes and carpets ruined by cigarette burns, it would probably amount to far more than the revenue from tax on tobacco. Even if it did not, the unhappiness, misery and suffering it causes to non-smokers and smokers alike, and to animals used in experiments with cigarettes, would surely justify radical steps to restrict cigarette smoking.

The writer concludes by advocating a series of policy measures, including a ban on smoking in public places and on public transport, education in schools concerning the dangers of smoking, a substantial increase in cigarette taxes, a limit on cigarette advertising expenditures, and a ban on advertisements which glamorize smoking.

Some of these claims seem more important than others. Whatever mess smokers leave behind, it is probably small compared to that left by people eating sweets and fish and chips. Any argument against smoking on this ground would apply with much greater force to many food products. Similarly, clothes and carpets may be damaged by food and drink just as much as by smoking. Intuitively, one suspects that the costs of enforcing restrictions on smoking and other products would greatly outweigh the costs of any damage prevented.

This passage also confuses costs which are externalities with costs which are not. "The man-hours lost by people leaving their work to have a quick smoke" is not an externality if the people in question are paid according to their output. Any loss in output is reflected in a lower wage. This is a cost borne directly by the smoker, and incurred only if the benefit of smoking outweighs this cost. Preventing such smoking would reduce the smoker's welfare without increasing that of others.

Where wages are not related directly to output, it might be argued that smokers exhibit reduced work competence which imposes cost on others—for example, where the output and wages of coworkers are reduced by the smoker's absence. The evidence that this actually occurs is not convincing. The fact that payment schemes are not designed to take it into account suggests that the adverse effects, if they exist, cannot be very significant. No specific public policy measure seems to be indicated.

Fetherstone argues that a smoker affects others insofar as he causes friends and relatives to be concerned for him. This might be true for a wide variety of activities, such as eating, drinking, or engaging in dangerous sports and occupations. There is no obvious reason to single out smoking. Furthermore, it is not clear that the concern of others should take precedence over the concern (or lack of it) of those engaging in these activities.

It is increasingly claimed (though not by Mr. Fetherstone) that tobacco smoke is the cause of disease in nonsmokers. Elsewhere in this volume Domingo Aviado shows that there is no persuasive scientific evidence that tobacco smoke in the atmosphere is a health hazard to nonsmokers. Even if some causal relationship were to be established, this would not necessarily call for government bans or restrictions on smoking. Any increased aversion to sitting or working next to smokers would induce owners to modify their rules and facilities accordingly. Once again, there is no reason to expect market failure sufficient to justify wholesale remedial action by government.

Smoking and the Burden of Medical Expenses

A popular claim (the first made by Fetherstone) is that smokers are more liable to certain illnesses, but that with a National Health Service or similar system the expense of treating these illnesses is borne by nonsmokers as well as smokers. As it is sometimes put, the cost of smoking to society as a whole is greater than the private cost to the individual smoker. In effect, the smoker is being subsidized to smoke. This may lead him to smoke more than he otherwise would. It also effectively redistributes income from nonsmokers to smokers.

The case for government intervention in smoking rests largely upon the claim that smoking is the cause of illnesses with which smoking is statistically associated. However, it is by no means scientifically established that smoking *causes* these illnesses. An alternative possibility, sometimes called the "constitutional hypothesis," is that certain physical or psychological characteristics are associated with both a propensity to smoke and a propensity to develop certain diseases. In his survey of the empirical evidence, Eysenck (chapter 2, this volume) concludes that the constitutional hypothesis is equally as plausible as the more popular causal hypothesis.

If the constitutional hypothesis is true, and smoking is *not* the cause of these diseases, then smokers impose no burden of expenses on nonsmokers. Restrictions on smoking would reduce the satisfaction gained by smokers without creating any compensating benefits. There is thus a dilemma for public policy which may be related to the statistician's dilemma of Type I and Type II errors. To allow smoking if it in fact *is* harmful may be costly (in terms of illness); but to ban smoking if it is *not* in fact harmful is also costly (in terms of satisfaction foregone). The market failure framework would seem to require an assessment of the costs in either case and of the likelihood of each alternative hypothesis being true. Eysenck's chapter in this volume deals with the latter issue. We may comment briefly here on the costs involved.

It is not clear that it is more expensive to treat smokers than nonsmokers, if the cost of health care over the whole lifetime is taken into account. If smokers tend to die earlier than nonsmokers (which, as just noted, does not mean that smoking is the *cause* of such earlier deaths), less expense is incurred in treating those diseases which would otherwise tend to be incurred in old age. In fact, some calculations suggest that the medical costs of smokers are *lower* than those of an average person. This point is discussed at some length by Woodfield (1981), who reviews a large number of empirical or "quasi-empirical" studies from several countries. The claim about the burden of medical expenses is not generally made by economists. The more serious economic studies (even those arguing for restrictions on smoking) point out that the long-run consequences of stopping smoking may be to increase medical costs rather than decrease them (DHSS, 1972; Atkinson and Meade 1974; Atkinson and Townsend 1977; Leu 1982).

It is worth emphasizing that, if there were a perfectly functioning market in health care so that each person paid precisely the costs of his own medical treatment, the claim that smokers were subsidized by nonsmokers would not arise, regardless of the relative costs of treatment. Medical expenses would be a private cost, which the smoker would take fully into account and balance against the satisfaction of smoking. Accordingly, if there is a claim that smokers are subsidized by (or impose costs on) nonsmokers, it is because of the whole system of health care delivery that actually exists.

Medical expenses are in fact not usually charged wholly or directly to the patient. In the United Kingdom, the bulk of health services are provided by the publicly-funded National Health Service rather than by private markets. The alternative system of private medical insurance does not usually provide complete coverage, even in the United States, and public funds are becoming widely used in that country too. This means that the basic source of the "subsidy problem" is the nature of the health care system, which does not require those receiving treatment to pay its full cost. If the main purpose of public policy were to ensure that people bear their own health costs in full, this would imply a redesign of the health care system. If, instead, the aim is to ensure that medical treatment is available to all regardless of income, this presumably includes all illnesses however incurred. There seems to be no particular reason to discriminate against those persons affected by illnesses statistically associated with smoking.

Smoking as a Nuisance

Smoking is often alleged to be an unpleasant nuisance to nonsmokers, and there are calls to ban smoking altogether in public places. Smokers naturally resist this suggestion. At first sight, the problem is a difficult one. There seems no reason to believe that the "right amount" of smoking will take place—that any nuisance of smoking will be offset against the satisfaction of smoking.

Market failure seems obvious. But what is the solution? An "all-or-nothing" regulation seems to be necessary, yet a "no-smoking" rule seems unfair to smokers, while unrestricted smoking seems unfair to nonsmokers. It is not at all clear which of the two solutions is more efficient: banning smoking deprives smokers of satisfaction, but allowing smoking deprives nonsmokers of satisfaction. To some economists, the situation would seem to call for a cost–benefit approach, to measure and compare the monetary values attached to the two types of satisfaction, with government legislation following accordingly.

But is the dilemma really as severe as it at first appears? Is it necessary to choose between no action and an all-out ban? Is there, in fact, a market failure at all? If we reexamine the problem in terms of the property rights paradigm, it will become apparent that the extent of public smoking does indeed reflect the preferences of nonsmokers as well as smokers, and to a much greater extent than is commonly realized. In the absence of a ban, therefore, nonsmokers are not necessarily disadvantaged; indeed, the imposition of a general ban would almost certainly reduce rather than increase the general level of satisfaction.

Smoking is just one example of an activity which may, at certain times or places, annoy other people. Playing radios, eating, drinking, chewing gum, fooling around, kissing, even talking and laughing—all these activities, while generally unobjectionable in private, may be objectionable to some in public. How then are all these potentially offensive activities controlled? There are two broad restraining forces. The first is natural courtesy: the feeling of consideration for others. It is reflected in the question, "Do you mind if I smoke?" Social mores are continually changing to reflect changes in individual preferences; conversely, individual preferences reflect changing social mores. This is not of course to claim that everyone is completely altruistic, but rather that consideration *is* usually given to the effects on others. This is especially true in small groups and confined spaces, where smoking and other activities may present greatest annoyance. In private places such as people's homes, the host may endeavor not to seat a heavy smoker next to someone known to dislike smoking. He may suggest smoking be deferred until after dinner. He may even take into account views about smoking when selecting his guests. But there is nothing special about smoking here. It is just one of the considerations to bear in mind when attempting to organize a harmonious social gathering.

The second important force is that of property rights transacted in the market. In most situations, there is one person or organization which has the legal right to define what activities can or cannot be pursued. This is the "residual claimant" to the profits or losses which follow from this decision. For example, the owner of a restaurant can prescribe whether, or under what conditions, smoking is to be allowed there. In exercising this property right, the owner typically does not refer only to his *own* preferences: he takes into account the preferences of *all* his potential customers. Further, he typically does not impose a complete ban on smoking: he looks for ways of reconciling the preferences of smokers and nonsmokers.

If the restaurant owner imposes no restrictions on smoking, he will tend to lose the custom of nonsmokers who are offended by smoke. If, on the other hand, he bans smoking altogether, he will tend to lose the custom of smokers. He will therefore look for acceptable compromises: perhaps smoking in the lounge but not in the dining room, or smoking on certain nights only, or cigarettes but not pipes or cigars, and so on. He may also consider installing improved ventilation so that smoking does not annoy anyone. It will be in the owner's commercial interest to select that pattern of facilities and regulations which most closely reflect the preferences of all his potential customers: insofar as he fails to do this he loses money. Different restauranteurs will take different views of the situation, bearing in mind the different preferences of their clientele. (See chapter 7 by Shughart and Tollison in this volume for more on this issue.)

Exactly the same pattern of behavior is observed in other commercial contexts, such as cinemas and transport. The general conclusion must be that, in competitive markets, the pattern of facilities and regulations is likely to reflect consumer preferences in an efficient way. This is not to say that everyone is satisfied. But given the state of technology and the fact that people of different tastes have to interact with each other, there is no market failure. It is not possible to make everyone better off by government regulation. Government intervention in the form of an outright ban on smoking cannot be justified on the basis of market failure: on balance it will aggravate the situation rather than remedy it.

How far does this argument carry over into public places—those where the government, in one form or another, is the owner? Nationalized industries and municipal enterprises are quasi-commercial organizations. A similar pattern of behavior is observed there. For example, British Rail and the London Underground have separate no-smoking carriages, and on London Transport buses there is no smoking downstairs. What about government office buildings? Typically these are monopolies—there are no competitors for receiving income tax or paying out social security. The preferences of the customers will have less weight with the "owner" than in a commercial context, and the preferences of the management and employees will carry greater weight. Nevertheless, this does not mean that no consideration is given to nonsmokers. The management and employees want a congenial environment in which to work, and if the government as owner fails to ascertain and reflect their preferences in its rules and facilities with respect to smoking, then it will have greater difficulty in securing adequate staff. Here again individual preferences are not ignored. There is no obviously significant market failure by which a general ban on smoking in public places could be justified.

Conclusions

Those who advocate increased restriction on smoking often invoke economic considerations to support their arguments. Economic theory does indeed provide a framework in the concept of market failure within which public policy can be evaluated. Where markets function properly, the presumption is that freedom of choice will lead to greatest efficiency in satisfying consumer preferences. The onus is on those who wish to curtail freedom of choice to demonstrate (a) that there is in fact a "market failure" and (b) that government intervention is the best means of remedying it.

Our examination suggests that there are not, in fact, any significant market failures with respect to smoking. More precisely, our major findings are as follows:

1. If users of tobacco were being misinformed by false or misleading advertising, there would be a case for supervision to ensure "truth in advertising." There is no evidence of this, however, and in fact mechanisms to deal with such problems are already in effect in most developed countries.

2. There is a case for governments to disseminate information concerning the smoking and health controversy. Such information should not go beyond the bounds of what is scientifically established. However, there is now a general awareness of health claims about smoking, and no further measures seem called for.

3. There is no convincing evidence to suggest that smokers impose additional health care costs on nonsmokers. In any case, such a problem must be considered in the context of the total system of health care delivery. Where patients pay their own medical expenses, there is no market failure. Elsewhere, smokers should not be singled out to pay for their own medical costs where the health care delivery system does not require others to do so.

4. Common sense, courtesy, and market forces are likely to resolve most of the problems associated with smoking annoying nonsmokers. The design of present rules and facilities does in fact reflect the preferences of non-smokers as well as smokers.

In the light of these findings, the market failure argument provides no case for increased restrictions on smoking—whether in the form of increased taxes, stronger warnings, further prohibitions on advertising, or bans on smoking in public places. This is not to say that such policies could not be advocated on other noneconomic grounds. Any change in public policy has to be assessed in the light of a variety of often-conflicting criteria, such as the paternalistic desire to protect versus the libertarian desire for freedom. Economic efficiency and market failure are only one consideration amongst several. Nonetheless, economic analysis does have a role to play. It suggests that there is no outstanding market failure with respect to smoking which further government intervention could be expected to remedy.

References

Atkinson, A.B. & Meade, T.W. 1974. Methods and preliminary findings in assessing the economic and health services consequences of smoking, with particular reference to lung cancer. *Journal of the Royal Statistical Society* A, Part 3, 297–312.

Atkinson, A.B. & Townsend, J.I. 1977. Economic aspects of reduced smoking. *Lancet*, September 3, 492–494.

Coase, R.H. 1960. The problem of social cost. *J. Law Econ.* 3 (October), 1–44.

Department of Health and Social Security (DHSS), United Kingdom 1972. *Smoking and health.*

Fetherstone, P. 1979. "Selfish, arrogant smokers." *Times*, 2 December.

Leu, R.E. 1983. What can economists contribute? In M. Grant, M. Plant & A. Williams (eds.), *Economics and alcohol.* London: Croom Helm.

Leu, R.E. 1982. "Smoking and health care costs: Plus or minus?" Paper presented at HESG Meeting, Glasgow.

Littlechild, S.C. 1981. Advertising, brand loyalty and habit. In *Analysis of consumer policy*, Papers presented at Wharton Applied Research Centre Conference, 18–19 May 1981, Philadelphia, Pennsylvania.

Littlechild, S.C. & Wiseman, J. 1984a. Principles of public policy relevant to smoking. *Policy Studies*, January.

Littlechild, S.C. & Wiseman, J. 1984b. Principles of public policy relevant to goods with possible adverse health effects. Unpublished manuscript, February.

Pigou, A.C. 1920. *The economics of welfare.* London: MacMillan; Fourth ed., 1962.

Woodfield, A.E. 1981. Cost-benefit analysis of consumer policy: framework and critique. In *Analysis of Consumer Policy*.

11

The Incidence of Taxes on Tobacco

William F. Shughart II
James M. Savarese

Tobacco products are heavily taxed commodities. Currently, cigarette excise taxes in the United States vary from 2¢ per pack (North Carolina) to 26¢ per pack (Connecticut and Massachusetts), and generate over $4 billion in annual tax revenues for state governments, a sum representing about 2.5% of the total taxes collected by the states. (The revenues generated from cigarette excise taxes are by and large added to the states' general funds, but are earmarked for usages such as education, conservation, or construction in some instances.) In addition, the federal government imposes an excise tax of 16¢ per pack, and cigarettes are considered a taxable item under the sales tax in a majority of states. When these three items are combined, taxes account for anywhere from 25% to over 55% of the average retail price of cigarettes. Some cities and other localities also impose taxes on tobacco products. To illustrate, in 1976 New York City adopted an excise tax of 8¢ per pack as a replacement for a system begun in 1971 which had tied the local tax rate to the tar and nicotine content of cigarettes sold.[1]

The revenue-generating aspects of the cigarette tax usually become important only when government faces a "fiscal crisis," which brings about a need to raise additional tax dollars. Given that tobacco product consumers are in the minority, the majority of voters often find them to be a convenient target for higher tax rates. At other times, the normal rationale for imposing a tax on cigarettes is that the majority, not liking tobacco product consumption, uses the excise tax as a way of imposing its will.[2]

In spite of the other issues surrounding the tobacco tax, the question of who pays remains important. In general, the burden of the tax is shared by consumers in the form of higher prices, producers of tobacco products in the form of reduced profits, and tobacco farmers in the form of lower returns from growing tobacco (Buchanan and Flowers, 1980, p. 439). But an evaluation of tax equity must also consider how the burden is distributed within these three groups. For consumers, one normally compares the way in which taxes are assessed across individuals against some standard of fairness, the most prominent of which is the concept of *horizontal equity*.[3] The horizontal equity standard suggests that individuals similarly situated (in terms of income, usually) should bear similar tax burdens. A tax that meets this criterion is termed *proportional* in that under such a scheme, taxes paid by low-income consumers represent the same percentage of income as those paid by high-income consumers. Taxes deviating from the horizontal equity standard are classified as either *regressive* or *progressive* accordingly as the tax bill rises proportionately slower or faster than income.

In this chapter we present evidence that taxes on tobacco products are regressive, that is, that excise taxes on cigarettes fall more heavily on low-income consumers. Our focus is on state excise taxes, but what we have to say applies equally to the federal excise tax as well as to state and local sales taxes on tobacco products. We first consider the appropriate income definition to be used in assessing tax equity. In particular, we discuss the effects of using measured income rather than permanent income as a base in calculating tax rates. Second, we summarize some existing evidence (Phares 1980) concerning effective tobacco tax rates by state. Third, we present more recent data that show cigarette taxes to be regressive in an overwhelming number of states. The methodology we employ consists of comparing the growth in real tobacco tax revenues with the growth in real personal income. Fourth, we report evidence from five European countries which suggests that taxes on tobacco products are regressive elsewhere.

The chapter is organized as follows. The following section contains a review of tax incidence theory and offers a discussion of the effects of tobacco taxes on consumers, tobacco product manufacturers, and tobacco farmers. We then discuss the income definition controversy and empirical evidence for the United States. Next we present the international data on tobacco taxes, and then offer our concluding remarks.

The Theory of Tax Incidence

The theoretical basis for assessing the incidence of a per unit or excise tax is well known. Although there are special cases in which such taxes will be either entirely shifted forward to consumers or entirely absorbed by producers, in general both groups will pay a portion of the total tax bill. The relative sizes of consumer and producer tax burdens depend upon the degree to which each group responds to a change in the price of the taxed good.[4] In particular, the relatively less responsive group will pay relatively more of the tax.

Consider the market for cigarettes depicted in figure 11–1. The downward-sloping demand schedule, D, shows the quantities of cigarettes consumers are willing and able to buy at each of the various possible prices per unit (package). Similarly, the supply schedule, S, indicates the amounts that

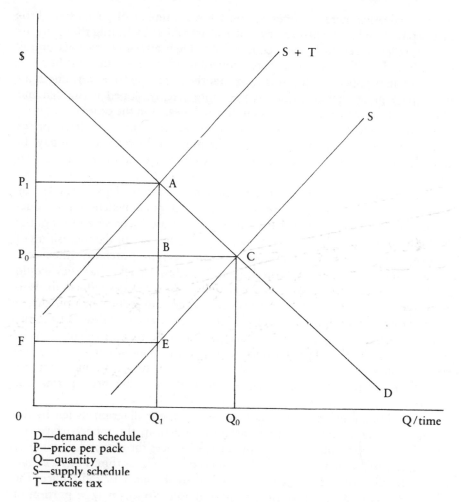

D—demand schedule
P—price per pack
Q—quantity
S—supply schedule
T—excise tax

Figure 11–1. Effects of Excise Tax on the Market for Cigarettes

producers are willing and able to offer for sale at each of the possible prices. In the absence of a tax, market equilibrium occurs at the point where the plans of producers and consumers dovetail. In the diagram, the market clears at C with Q_0 units bought and sold at a price of P_0 per pack.

Imposition of an excise tax, T, shifts the supply schedule upward by the amount of the tax, the distance AE in our example.[5] Market price rises to P_1, and the number of cigarette packages sold declines to Q_1. Government receives total tax revenues of Q_1 times AE, or the amount represented by the area of the rectangle P_1AEF. The proportion of the tax bill paid by consumers in the form of higher prices is given by the area of the rectangle P_1ABP_0, the tax-induced price increase times the now lower number of packs sold. Producers pay P_0BEF. The producers' share is arrived at by noting that prior to the tax, sellers received P_0 on each unit sold. Their after-tax price per unit is just F, however. The excise tax thus reduces producer revenue by P_0BEF.

Holding supply constant, it is clear that the less responsive consumers are to cigarette price changes (that is, the more steeply sloped is the demand schedule), the more of the tax burden they will bear. On the other hand, hold demand constant, the less sensitive producers are to a rise in cigarette prices (again, the steeper is the supply curve), the more of the tax they will pay. In general, then, the burden of the cigarette tax will be shared by consumers and producers.[6]

Excise taxes also impose a deadweight loss on society. This cost, given by the area of the triangle *ACE,* represents the monetary equivalent of the reduction in economic welfare borne by consumers and producers as a result of the tax-induced decline in cigarette output. That is, because of the imposition of the tax, consumers must economize on their cigarette purchases; their economic welfare is reduced because they now buy fewer packs than they would in the absence of the tax. Moreover, the fall in cigarette sales induces firms to cut back output and they therefore lay off workers and reduce their purchases of other inputs used in cigarette production. Resources are released from the cigarette industry and these inputs are forced to find employment in firms producing goods that at pretax relative prices consumers value less than cigarettes. Unlike the tax revenues, these deadweight costs are not merely transferred from the private sector to government. Rather, they are a permanent cost to society as a whole.

An additional effect of the tax (not shown in the diagram) is felt by the suppliers of the major input to cigarette production, the tobacco farmers. The fall in cigarette output caused by the tax reduces the demand on the part of tobacco product manufacturers for tobacco leaf. Other things being equal, this lowers the price of the product supplied by the farmers and reduces the value of the land devoted to tobacco production.[7] In this way, a portion of the cigarette producers' tax burden is shifted backward to tobacco farmers.

In sum, the effects of imposing an excise tax on cigarettes are felt by all of those directly participating in the market—consumers, producers, and tobacco farmers—as well as by society as a whole in the form of a deadweight welfare loss. In the following section, we consider the distributional impact of the tax on consumers of tobacco products.

Evidence on Tax Equity

An important issue in tax theory concerns how the burden of the tax is distributed across the individuals who must pay. Is the tax "fair" in some normative sense? That is, is the burden shared equally, or does the tax fall more heavily on certain taxpayers? In assessing the fairness of the cigarette tax, we adopt the concept of horizontal equity as our standard. Under this criterion, the cigarette tax can be considered equitable if similarly situated individuals pay similar taxes. More specifically, the horizontal equity standard suggests that tax payments should represent the same proportion of income for low-income consumers as for their high-income counterparts.

Our analysis implies, however, that the cigarette tax is not fair. In particular, we find substantial empirical evidence of regressivity in the tax. Smokers at low income levels pay proportionately more in taxes than do individuals at higher income levels.

The evidence we present for the United States falls into two categories. These are the effective tax rates on tobacco products calculated by Phares (1980), and more recent data on the relationship between real tobacco tax revenues and real personal income by state. Before presenting the results, however, we first consider the appropriate income definition to be used in assessing the equity of the cigarette tax. The usual approach is to calculate tax payments as a percentage of current income, but work by Friedman (1957) and others suggests that individuals base their consumption decisions on "permanent" income, a concept that takes account of the fact that in a given year some consumers will experience incomes that are transitorially higher or lower than normal. As we shall see, the degree to which a tax is considered fair may depend upon the income definition adopted.

Current v. Permanent Income

The standard approach to determining the fairness of a particular tax is conceptually quite simple. One first sorts individuals into income categories, and then calculates tax payments as a percentage of income. The tax is then classified as regressive, proportional, or progressive according to whether the proportion of income paid in taxes falls, remains the same, or rises as one goes up the income distribution. But what income definition is to be used as a base in these calculations? Most studies employ what can be termed measured or current income, the payments actually received by individuals over some time period, say a year, because such data are readily available. The permanent income hypothesis advanced by Friedman (1957), however, suggests that the appropriate income measure has two components.

According to Friedman, the *permanent income* component represents that income an individual expects to receive in a given year. This expected income level reflects a variety of factors, the most important of which are the value of the income-producing assets owned by the individual and his or her personal attributes, such as age, education, occupation, geographic location, and so forth. (Individuals receiving a college degree can expect to earn higher incomes than high school graduates, for example.) Second, income has a *transitory component* which, during a particular year, may cause current income to differ from permanent income. Unexpected events such as illness or layoff, the opportunity to work overtime, bonuses, and so on, result in incomes temporarily lower or higher than normal. Friedman's main point is that such transitory income changes will not cause people to alter their consumption patterns by as much as they would have had the change in income been viewed as permanent.

The permanent income hypothesis has important implications for studies of tax equity. If the theory is correct, when individuals are sorted into income categories on the basis of current income, some of those in the low-income groups will be individuals receiving measured incomes temporarily below normal. Similarly, some of those consumers included in the upper-income classes will have incomes that are unexpectedly high. Studies using current income as a base will therefore tend to overstate the degree of regressivity in the tax.

For example, smokers having current incomes below expected levels may not reduce their expenditures on cigarettes appreciably. Excise tax payments on these purchases will therefore remain relatively stable as measured income falls, biasing upwards the calculated tax burden. (The percentage of income going to taxes would be lower with permanent income as the base.) Alternatively, smokers experiencing temporarily high current incomes will not increase their cigarette purchases significantly under the Friedman hypothesis. Because tax payments remain roughly the same for these individuals, using measured income as the base will impart a downward bias to the burden calculations. In sum, equity studies that use the current income of consumers to assess the distributional burden of a tax tend to overstate the degree of regressivity in the tax.

Empirical work indeed confirms that alternative income definitions affect the conclusions reached concerning tax equity. For example, Davies (1960) found that the retail sales tax in Ohio during 1956 was regressive when he used measured income as a base, but progressive in terms of permanent income. Similar findings were obtained by Schaefer (1969) using data on New Jersey's sales tax for the years 1960 and 1961.

There is a practical difficulty with such studies, however. Being based on individuals' expected lifetime earnings, permanent income is not directly observable. In particular, "the most that can be observed are actual receipts and expenditures during some finite period, supplemented, perhaps, by some verbal statements about expectations for the future" (Friedman, 1957, p. 20). Friedman therefore recommends that permanent income levels be estimated by taking a weighted average of measured income levels over some period, say three years. (The implication is that the transitory components of income will even out over time.) Because of these additional data requirements, permanent income has failed to gain wide acceptance as an empirical construct.

An additional consideration mitigates against using permanent income in tax equity studies. As Musgrave and Musgrave (1976, p. 443) note, "taxes must be paid when they come due, and the more that has to be paid at any one time, the less is left for private use at that time." In other words, taxes such as those on tobacco products are no less burdensome just because an individual's measured income is temporarily below normal. The fact that tax payments cannot be deferred suggests that current income may be the appropriate base.

A resolution of the current–permanent income controversy is beyond the scope of this paper. However, we can shed some light on the extent to which the choice of an income base affects any conclusions reached concerning the incidence of taxes on tobacco products.

As of 1980, there were slightly fewer than 48 million Americans who regularly smoked cigarettes.[8] This figure represents about 30% of the total U.S population aged 17 years or older. Because Friedman's hypothesis suggests that permanent income levels depend upon personal attributes, in what follows we compare selected characteristics of smokers (age, income, and education level) with those of the general U.S. population.

Table 11–1 shows the distribution of regular cigarette smokers by age and (measured) income level for 1980. As one might expect, the incidence of smoking is lowest among the young (5% of smokers are 17–19 years of age) and the old (less than 8% are over 65). The largest percentage of smokers

Table 11–1
Number of Present Regular Smokers by Age and Family Income, and as a Percentage of Total Regular Smokers

Age Group	Income Class				
	< $7,000	$7–14,999	$15–24,999	$25,000+	Total
17–19	686,070 (1.4)	623,176 (1.3)	456,107 (1.0)	591,825 (1.2)	2,357,178 (4.9)
20–24	1,620,722 (3.4)	2,297,445 (4.8)	1,286,940 (2.7)	1,690,245 (3.5)	6,895,352 (14.4)
25–34	1,630,370 (3.4)	3,561,771 (7.4)	4,018,252 (8.4)	2,872,611 (6.0)	12,083,004 (25.2)
35–44	1,232,657 (2.6)	1,867,232 (3.9)	2,426,924 (5.1)	3,692,074 (7.7)	9,218,887 (19.2)
45–64	2,086,385 (4.4)	3,565,857 (7.4)	3,503,683 (7.3)	4,554,372 (9.5)	13,710,297 (28.6)
65+	1,394,020 (2.9)	1,375,431 (2.9)	436,731 (0.9)	427,728 (0.9)	3,633,910 (7.6)
Total	8,650,224 (18.1)	13,290,912 (27.7)	12,128,637 (25.3)	13,828,855 (28.9)	47,898,628 (100.0)

Source: Health Interview Survey (HIS), 1980.

Table 11-2
U.S. Population by Age and Family Income, and as a Percentage of Total
Population over 17 Years

Age Group	Income Class				Total
	< $7,000	$7–14,999	$15–24,999	$25,000+	
17–19	2,367,879 (1.6)	2,242,928 (1.5)	2,145,003 (1.4)	3,545,610 (2.4)	10,301,420 (6.9)
20–24	4,339,561 (2.9)	5,804,980 (3.9)	4,457,586 (3.0)	5,140,687 (3.5)	19,742,814 (13.3)
25–34	3,616,977 (2.4)	8,843,622 (5.9)	11,173,950 (7.5)	9,979,542 (6.7)	33,614,091 (22.6)
35–44	2,426,438 (1.6)	4,526,223 (3.0)	6,582,321 (4.4)	10,897,074 (7.3)	24,432,056 (16.4)
45–64	5,224,597 (3.5)	9,406,732 (6.3)	9,919,990 (6.7)	14,844,682 (10.0)	39,396,001 (26.5)
65+	8,251,944 (5.5)	7,654,082 (5.1)	2,966,711 (2.0)	2,365,020 (1.6)	21,237,757 (14.3)
Total	26,227,396 (17.6)	38,478,567 (25.9)	37,245,561 (25.0)	46,772,615 (31.4)	148,724,139 (100.0)

Source: HIS, 1980.

(28.6%) falls into the 45–64 age category. The current income levels of
smokers are relatively evenly distributed across the four income classes.
Eighteen percent of those regularly consuming cigarettes earn less than
$7,000 annually, while about 29% of smokers have yearly incomes exceed-
ing $25,000. How do these attributes compare with those for the general
population, which are given in table 11–2? A comparison of the two tables
suggest that smokers tend to have lower incomes, but that the distribution
across age categories is roughly the same as for the general population aged
17 years or more. For example, the data in table 11–2 show that 17.6% of all
individuals over 17 have incomes below $7,000, and 25.9% have incomes in
the $7,000–$14,999 range. The proportions observed for smokers in table
11–1, however, are 18.1% and 27.7%, respectively—figures which are significantly higher at the 1% level.[9] Moreover, although the proportion of
smokers in the $15,000–$24,999 interval is about the same as in the total
population (25.3% versus 25.0%), a significantly smaller fraction of cigarette consumers have incomes above $25,000 per year.

The row totals in the two tables allow us to compare the age distribution
of smokers with that of the general population. The comparisons here are less
clear-cut, with the proportion of smokers being less than expected only in the
17–19 and over-65 age categories. The average age of smokers in the over-17
sample was 40.1 years, while the population aged 17 or more was 41.9 years
old, on average.[10]

Similar comparisons based on educational attainment are given in tables 11–3 and 11–4.[11] On average, cigarette consumers completed 11.8 years of education; the average person in the over-17 population finished 12.1 years.[12] The principal sources of this difference are the proportions of smokers that are higher than expected in the 7–11 years-of-education category, and lower than expected in the 13 + class.

In sum, the evidence at hand suggests that individuals who regularly smoke cigarettes may be somewhat younger and have completed slightly less formal schooling than the general population. Both of these factors would tend to reduce the permanent incomes of smokers relative to consumers as a whole, an observation consistent with our finding that the former group has lower measured incomes. Any excise, sales, or per unit tax will therefore be more burdensome for smokers as a group (a larger fraction of their permanent incomes will go to taxes) than for the general population. This fact does not eliminate the bias associated with using current rather than permanent income as a base in cigarette tax equity studies, but it reduces the extent to which such studies may overstate the degree of regressivity in the tax.

Effective Tax Rates on Cigarettes

One method for evaluating the equity of taxes on tobacco products is to calculate the effective tax rates paid by individuals in various income classes.

Table 11–3
Number of Present Regular Smokers by Age and Education, and as a Percentage of Total Regular Smokers

Age Group	Education Level				Total
	< 7	7–11	12	13 +	
17–19	n.a.	1,407,391 (2.7)	932,961 (1.8)	196,117 (0.4)	2,536,475 (4.9)
20–24	21,330 (0.04)	2,275,938 (4.4)	3,573,360 (6.9)	1,529,731 (3.0)	7,400,359 (14.4)
25–34	221,138 (0.4)	2,514,928 (4.9)	5,350,987 (10.4)	4,746,323 (9.2)	12,833,376 (24.9)
35–44	298,458 (0.6)	2,300,116 (4.5)	3,848,400 (7.5)	3,198,983 (6.2)	9,645,957 (18.7)
45–64	1,198,706 (2.3)	4,710,893 (9.1)	5,800,893 (11.3)	3,308,202 (6.4)	15,018,694 (29.2)
65 +	572,354 (1.1)	1,594,880 (3.1)	1,132,577 (2.2)	774,389 (1.5)	4,074,200 (7.9)
Total	2,311,986 (4.5)	14,804,149 (28.7)	20,639,181 (40.1)	13,753,745 (26.7)	51,509,061 (100.0)

Source: HIS, 1980.

Note: n.a. denotes "not available."

Table 11–4
U.S. Population by Age and Education Level, and as a Percentage of Total
Population over 17 Years

Age Group	Education Level				Total
	< 7	7–11	12	13 +	
17–19	95,226 (0.06)	5,199,145 (3.2)	4,346,305 (2.7)	1,395,605 (0.9)	11,036,281 (6.9)
20–24	266,907 (0.2)	3,598,839 (2.3)	9,381,089 (5.9)	7,740,534 (4.8)	20,947,369 (13.1)
25–34	762,459 (0.5)	4,386,882 (2.7)	13,660,771 (8.5)	16,658,421 (10.4)	34,468,533 (21.6)
35–44	806,272 (0.5)	4,475,663 (2.8)	10,107,392 (6.3)	10,244,673 (6.4)	25,634,000 (16.0)
45–64	3,105,910 (1.9)	11,860,714 (7.4)	16,784,943 (10.5)	11,225,149 (7.0)	42,976,716 (26.9)
65 +	4,008,412 (2.5)	9,495,611 (5.9)	5,848,443 (3.7)	4,475,189 (2.8)	23,827,655 (14.9)
Total	9,045,186 (5.7)	39,016,854 (24.4)	60,128,943 (37.6)	51,739,571 (32.4)	159,930,554 (100.0)

Source: HIS, 1980.

Such a study was conducted by Phares (1980) using tobacco tax revenue and income data by state for 1976. In this section we summarize his results.

Phares resolved the income definition question in favor of an income base that included "money income," other labor income, imputed interest, imputed rent, food stamps, and capital gains (p. 51). His income measure, which was largely dictated by data availability considerations, resulted in a figure that was "slightly less than personal income for this period in dollar terms . . . but substantially different in composition and distribution" (p. 51).

State cigarette tax payments by individuals were calculated in the following way. Phares first assumed that the tobacco tax was paid entirely by consumers. He then obtained data from budget studies on tobacco product expenditures in each of 14 income categories, and allocated state tax revenues to the income groups on the basis of their expenditure shares. For example, if 10% of the total expenditures on tobacco in Wisconsin was made by individuals having incomes in the $7,000–$7,999 range, then these consumers were assumed to have paid 10% of the Wisconsin taxes. Phares further adjusted the tax allocations to take account of tax shifting between states (for example, a portion of Wisconsin's tobacco tax bill is paid by residents of other states, and Wisconsin residents pay some of the taxes in other jurisdictions) and any federal tax offset.

Phares's results are reproduced in table 11–5. Going up the income distribution, the national average tax rates drop steadily from 1.18% of income for those earning less than $3,000 per year to 0.14% in the over-$35,000 category. This pattern holds true across states, with the highest effective tax rates being paid by residents of New Hampshire, and the lowest by North Carolinians. Phares concluded that "the tax on tobacco is clearly regressive . . ." (p. 103). Moreover, Phares found the tax on cigarettes to be more regressive than another sumptuary tax—a tax the effect of which is thought desirable for moral reasons. In particular, the tax on alcoholic beverages turned out to be roughly proportional.

In sum, using a broad measure of current income, Phares produced strong evidence that taxes on cigarettes fall most heavily on those individuals at the lower end of the income distribution.

Elasticity Calculations

A second method for evaluating tax equity involves examining the growth in tax revenues in relation to the growth in income. In particular, a tax can be classified as regressive, proportional, or progressive according as revenues rise less rapidly, at the same rate, or more rapidly over time than income. Such a methodology has been applied in studies of sales tax incidence. Work by Davies (1962), Freidlaender et al. (1973), and Rafuse (1965) finds generally "that revenues and income increase at approximately the same rate, indicating probable proportionality when the sales tax is related to an income base" (Wagner, 1983, pp. 272–3). Given that the conventional wisdom on the sales tax is that it is regressive, the revenue–income relationship appears to be biased toward a finding of either proportionality or progressivity.

Tax revenue growth in relation to income can be estimated by calculating an elasticity, the percentage change in tax receipts divided by the percentage change in income. Tax equity will then be determined as follows.

Elasticity	Tax
>1	Progressive
=1	Proportional
<1	Regressive

For instance, if the calculated elasticity coefficient is greater than unity, the percentage change in tax revenues exceeds the percentage change in income. In other words, a 1% increase in income leads to a more than 1% increase in tax receipts, implying progressivity in the tax structure.

As another example, suppose that real income was growing by 5% per year on average in a particular state. Then if the cigarette excise tax was pro-

Table 11–5
Effective Tax Rates on Tobacco Products, 1976
(percent)

State	Under $3,000	$3,000– 3,999	$4,000– 4,999	$5,000– 5,999	$6,000– 6,999	$7,000– 7,999
Alabama	1.29	0.69	0.56	0.47	0.40	0.38
Alaska	0.77	0.44	0.39	0.35	0.31	0.26
Arizona	1.31	0.72	0.54	0.51	0.43	0.38
Arkansas	1.94	1.05	0.86	0.73	0.67	0.58
California	0.87	0.52	0.41	0.36	0.31	0.28
Colorado	0.96	0.55	0.43	0.38	0.35	0.30
Connecticut	1.25	0.82	0.68	0.63	0.56	0.57
Delaware	1.72	0.91	0.84	0.66	0.60	0.54
Florida	1.66	0.91	0.72	0.61	0.56	0.50
Georgia	1.38	0.70	0.60	0.52	0.46	0.42
Hawaii	0.67	0.40	0.37	0.32	0.28	0.26
Idaho	0.81	0.44	0.35	0.33	0.29	0.25
Illinois	0.94	0.59	0.50	0.44	0.39	0.36
Indiana	0.68	0.40	0.32	0.29	0.26	0.24
Iowa	1.05	0.61	0.55	0.43	0.41	0.38
Kansas	0.93	0.53	0.46	0.37	0.36	0.32
Kentucky	0.59	0.32	0.27	0.22	0.19	0.18
Louisiana	1.41	0.72	0.58	0.53	0.46	0.42
Maine	1.64	0.96	0.81	0.65	0.63	0.56
Maryland	1.13	0.62	0.51	0.41	0.37	0.33
Massachusetts	1.39	0.95	0.76	0.64	0.60	0.55
Michigan	1.00	0.60	0.48	0.41	0.37	0.36
Minnesota	1.42	0.87	0.66	0.60	0.54	0.53
Mississippi	1.34	0.74	0.57	0.49	0.42	0.40
Missouri	0.88	0.46	0.43	0.36	0.32	0.29
Montana	1.21	0.70	0.58	0.49	0.45	0.40
Nebraska	1.01	0.60	0.46	0.41	0.37	0.35
Nevada	1.12	0.68	0.55	0.47	0.44	0.39
New Hampshire	2.23	1.34	1.02	0.97	0.88	0.75
New Jersey	1.33	0.82	0.70	0.62	0.56	0.53
New Mexico	1.00	0.58	0.50	0.41	0.38	0.33
New York	1.22	0.69	0.55	0.48	0.45	0.41
North Carolina	0.38	0.20	0.17	0.13	0.12	0.11
North Dakota	1.04	0.58	0.49	0.42	0.38	0.35
Ohio	1.17	0.70	0.59	0.51	0.46	0.44
Oklahoma	1.75	0.87	0.71	0.63	0.56	0.49
Oregon	1.04	0.58	0.47	0.41	0.35	0.33
Pennsylvania	1.45	0.81	0.68	0.57	0.55	0.50
Rhode Island	1.81	0.97	0.92	0.77	0.66	0.62
South Carolina	0.79	0.44	0.35	0.31	0.27	0.25
South Dakota	1.01	0.57	0.49	0.43	0.39	0.35
Tennessee	1.37	0.77	0.62	0.55	0.47	0.43
Texas	1.91	1.05	0.83	0.74	0.64	0.57
Utah	0.56	0.31	0.24	0.20	0.20	0.17
Vermont	1.48	0.83	0.73	0.61	0.56	0.51
Virginia	0.33	0.16	0.14	0.12	0.10	0.09
Washington	1.29	0.72	0.56	0.48	0.42	0.40
West Virginia	1.43	0.78	0.60	0.50	0.45	0.41
Wisconsin	1.24	0.69	0.57	0.51	0.47	0.45
Wyoming	0.80	0.48	0.42	0.36	0.32	0.29
Average	1.18	0.67	0.55	0.48	0.43	0.39

Source: Phares (1980), p. 182.

$8,000– 8,999	$10,000– 11,999	$12,000– 14,999	$15,000– 19,999	$20,000– 24,999	$25,000– 29,000	$30,000– 34,999	Over $35,000
0.33	0.28	0.24	0.20	0.17	0.15	0.14	0.10
0.24	0.21	0.18	0.15	0.13	0.12	0.11	0.09
0.35	0.30	0.26	0.22	0.18	0.16	0.15	0.12
0.51	0.43	0.37	0.31	0.26	0.23	0.21	0.16
0.24	0.21	0.18	0.15	0.13	0.12	0.11	0.08
0.26	0.23	0.20	0.17	0.14	0.13	0.11	0.09
0.46	0.42	0.37	0.32	0.29	0.27	0.25	0.21
0.47	0.40	0.36	0.30	0.26	0.22	0.20	0.16
0.43	0.37	0.32	0.26	0.23	0.20	0.18	0.14
0.36	0.30	0.27	0.22	0.19	0.17	0.15	0.12
0.23	0.20	0.17	0.15	0.13	0.12	0.11	0.08
0.23	0.19	0.17	0.14	0.12	0.10	0.10	0.08
0.32	0.29	0.26	0.23	0.21	0.19	0.18	0.15
0.21	0.19	0.17	0.15	0.13	0.12	0.11	0.10
0.33	0.31	0.27	0.24	0.21	0.19	0.18	0.16
0.30	0.26	0.23	0.20	0.18	0.17	0.16	0.13
0.16	0.14	0.11	0.10	0.08	0.07	0.07	0.05
0.37	0.31	0.27	0.22	0.19	0.17	0.15	0.12
0.51	0.45	0.40	0.35	0.31	0.28	0.27	0.23
0.30	0.26	0.22	0.18	0.16	0.14	0.13	0.10
0.50	0.45	0.39	0.34	0.31	0.29	0.27	0.22
0.31	0.28	0.25	0.21	0.19	0.18	0.17	0.14
0.44	0.40	0.36	0.31	0.28	0.26	0.24	0.20
0.34	0.30	0.25	0.21	0.18	0.16	0.15	0.11
0.26	0.24	0.20	0.18	0.16	0.15	0.14	0.12
0.34	0.30	0.26	0.22	0.19	0.17	0.15	0.12
0.31	0.28	0.25	0.22	0.20	0.18	0.17	0.15
0.34	0.29	0.25	0.21	0.18	0.16	0.15	0.11
0.72	0.63	0.57	0.50	0.44	0.41	0.39	0.32
0.47	0.43	0.38	0.33	0.30	0.28	0.26	0.22
0.29	0.25	0.21	0.18	0.16	0.14	0.12	0.10
0.36	0.33	0.29	0.25	0.23	0.21	0.20	0.16
0.10	0.08	0.07	0.06	0.05	0.05	0.04	0.03
0.31	0.29	0.26	0.23	0.20	0.18	0.18	0.15
0.39	0.34	0.31	0.27	0.25	0.23	0.21	0.18
0.42	0.36	0.31	0.26	0.22	0.19	0.18	0.14
0.29	0.25	0.21	0.18	0.15	0.14	0.12	0.10
0.45	0.40	0.35	0.31	0.28	0.26	0.25	0.21
0.57	0.50	0.46	0.40	0.36	0.33	0.31	0.26
0.21	0.19	0.16	0.14	0.12	0.10	0.09	0.07
0.31	0.29	0.26	0.23	0.20	0.19	0.18	0.15
0.37	0.32	0.28	0.23	0.20	0.17	0.16	0.12
0.51	0.44	0.37	0.31	0.27	0.23	0.21	0.16
0.15	0.13	0.11	0.10	0.08	0.07	0.06	0.05
0.45	0.41	0.36	0.32	0.29	0.26	0.24	0.21
0.08	0.07	0.06	0.05	0.04	0.04	0.03	0.03
0.34	0.30	0.26	0.22	0.19	0.17	0.15	0.13
0.34	0.31	0.25	0.21	0.18	0.16	0.14	0.13
0.37	0.34	0.31	0.27	0.24	0.22	0.21	0.18
0.25	0.22	0.19	0.16	0.14	0.12	0.12	0.09
0.34	0.30	0.26	0.23	0.20	0.18	0.17	0.14

Table 11-6
Elasticity of Real Cigarette Tax Collections with Respect to Real Personal Income, by State, 1976–1981

State	1976–77	1977–78	1978–79	1979–80	1980–81	1976–81
Alabama	−0.9	−0.2	−1.7	10.2	7.8	−0.1
Alaska	−0.4	1.4	3.8	−3.1	0.0	−9.2
Arizona	−0.6	−0.4	−0.4	−0.8	−1.9	−0.5
Arkansas	−0.8	−0.3	−0.7	2.1	−2.0	−1.2
California	−0.9	−0.8	−1.3	−2.6	−1.5	−1.0
Colorado	−1.0	5.7	−3.0	−1.5	−0.4	−0.6
Connecticut	−0.5	−2.2	−1.0	−2.5	−3.4	−1.4
Delaware	—	−1.5	−3.6	—	−2.0	−3.2
District of Columbia	−4.7	−6.3	2.7	—	−4.3	6.0
Florida	−0.8	2.4	−0.5	−0.5	−0.6	−0.01
Georgia	−1.2	−0.7	−1.0	−4.6	−0.8	−0.9
Hawaii	0.3	0.0	−0.1	0.0	−0.8	−0.1
Idaho	—	−0.4	−1.3	—	−2.6	−1.3
Illinois	3.5	−1.0	−2.1	5.9	−7.0	−3.9
Indiana	−0.4	8.6	−3.4	3.6	8.3	1.1
Iowa	−3.4	−0.7	−3.6	3.0	—	−2.7
Kansas	−1.0	−1.1	−1.2	4.5	−2.2	−1.4
Kentucky	−1.3	−1.4	−4.2	12.7	−3.9	−2.3
Louisiana	−0.7	−0.5	−0.9	−1.0	−4.4	−0.6
Maine	—	−1.5	−1.6	−3.1	−3.7	−1.9
Maryland	−3.9	−3.0	−1.3	−6.9	10.9	−0.5
Massachusetts	−1.4	−1.5	−3.4	−3.4	−2.8	−1.9
Michigan	−1.6	−1.2	−2.5	2.9	−7.3	−3.4
Minnesota	−0.4	−1.5	−1.1	−14.4	−3.7	−1.1
Mississippi	−0.9	−0.5	−3.6	5.0	−2.6	−1.4
Missouri	−0.7	−1.2	−1.7	4.3	−2.5	−1.7
Montana	−0.8	−0.5	−3.4	—	−1.8	−1.2
Nebraska	−1.5	−2.9	−1.1	2.2	−1.6	−2.1
Nevada	−1.2	−0.3	−0.4	−1.3	0.0	−0.4
New Hampshire	−1.7	−0.9	−1.2	−4.0	−1.3	−1.1
New Jersey	−1.4	−2.0	−2.3	−3.8	−2.6	−1.9
New Mexico	−0.7	−1.0	−0.9	—	−1.0	−0.8
New York	6.3	−4.1	−5.2	−4.8	−2.3	−4.2
North Carolina	−2.3	−2.1	−2.9	−7.6	−2.3	−2.2
North Dakota	−0.5	−0.5	−2.8	−0.6	−0.6	−0.6
Ohio	−1.0	−1.0	−2.1	5.4	−7.9	−2.3
Oklahoma	−0.3	−0.7	−0.6	8.0	0.4	0.2
Oregon	−0.7	−0.6	−1.1	—	—	−1.2
Pennsylvania	−2.6	−1.8	−2.3	−40.0	−5.1	−2.9
Rhode Island	—	−1.7	−2.0	−3.1	−2.9	−2.2
South Carolina	−1.1	2.4	−2.8	−3.9	−1.0	−0.6
South Dakota	−0.4	−0.9	−2.6	−0.9	−2.1	−0.8
Tennessee	−1.3	−0.5	−1.2	—	−1.4	−1.1
Texas	−0.3	−0.4	−0.7	−0.6	−0.5	−0.4
Utah	−0.6	−0.2	−0.8	7.6	0.6	0.1
Vermont	—	−1.8	−1.7	—	−1.2	−2.0
Virginia	−0.8	−1.6	−1.7	−5.2	−1.3	−1.3
Washington	−0.8	−0.5	−0.5	−1.8	3.3	−0.3
West Virginia	−0.2	−2.9	2.5	6.5	5.5	−0.2
Wisconsin	−0.9	−1.8	−1.4	—	8.9	−2.2
Wyoming	−.03	−0.2	0.8	−1.2	0.0	−0.2
Weighted Average	−1.7	−1.0	−1.9	−3.4	−1.8	−1.9

Note: Column averages were weighted by the mean net real cigarette tax collections over each two-year interval. The cigarette tax collection data are from The Tobacco Institute (1984); the income data were taken from U.S. Department of Commerce (various years).

portional and if the individuals making the tax payments were distributed evenly across income categories, we would expect the state to collect an additional 5% in tax receipts each year, other things equal. If, however, a majority of the tax is paid by consumers whose incomes are growing by less than 5% per year, then tax receipts will rise less rapidly than the average growth rate in real income. An elasticity coefficient less than unity will thus provide evidence that the tax is regressive.

We calculated such elasticities by state for the period 1976 to 1981, employing personal income as our income definition and converting revenue and income figures to 1972 dollars.[13] The results are presented in table 11–6. Over the entire six-year interval, real cigarette tax revenues were income inelastic in all but four states. This effect is most dramatic in Alaska, where a 1% increase in real income resulted in a 9.2% drop in real tax receipts. Two other states meet the criterion for regressivity (an elasticity coefficient less than unity), so that in 49 out of 51 cases there is evidence that the tobacco tax fell most heavily on low-income consumers. Indeed, progressivity is evident only in the District of Columbia, while the tobacco tax appears approximately proportional in Illinois.

The weighted average elasticity across states is less than unity for every time interval considered. Moreover, coefficients exceeding unity in the table are coincident with increases in the excise tax rate in most instances. That is, the normal course of events is for revenues to be income elastic in the period that tax rates are boosted, but then to be income inelastic in subsequent periods. The bulk of the evidence thus clearly suggests that excise taxes on tobacco in the United States are regressive.

International Aspects of Tobacco Taxes

Western countries other than the United States rely heavily on consumption taxes as a source of revenue for the public sector. For example, taken as a group, consumption taxes—primarily the value-added tax (VAT) and excises levied on specific goods—account for about one-quarter of the revenues raised by the 24-member group of countries forming the Organization for Economic Cooperation and Development (OECD), making these the first or second most important revenue source in over half of the countries (OECD, 1981, p. 5).

How does the incidence of tobacco excise taxes paid by consumers in other countries compare with the distributional burden faced by American tobacco product buyers? Although it is not possible to draw firm conclusions on this score, the available evidence suggests that tobacco taxes levied elsewhere are also regressive. In particular, 1977 data for the United Kingdom show not only that the excise tax on tobacco there is regressive, but that it becomes more regressive as family size increases. Moreover, except in the case of two-person households, the tobacco tax is the most regressive of the U.K. consumption taxes. The data for four other European countries also imply regressivity, or at best proportionality, in the tobacco tax. We caution, however, that our conclusion for these countries is not based directly on information concerning taxes on tobacco alone. Rather, we are limited to data involving excise taxes taken as a group, and such observations combine taxes on a variety of commodities which might exhibit quite different distributional burdens if analyzed separately. (The Netherlands' data, for example, include that country's duties on wine, beer, spirits, sugar, tobacco, and soft drinks.) But, given that tobacco taxes are clearly regressive in the United States and the United Kingdom, and that U.K. excise taxes as a whole are roughly proportional, we suspect that disaggregation of the excise taxes in Belgium, Finland, the Netherlands, and Norway would reveal regressivity in the tobacco taxes levied by those countries as well.

Our data are taken from a recent study conducted by the OECD (1981), which examined the distributional impact of consumption taxes in seven European countries (Belgium, Finland, France, Germany, the Netherlands, Norway, and the United Kingdom). For all but two of the countries (France and Germany), the study reported excise tax rates by income category for two- and four-person households using gross annual income as the income definition. The income definition included earned and unearned income plus social transfers, but excluded the value of goods produced for home consumption (OECD, 1981, p. 13). The tax rates were calculated using the standard assumption that "the purchase price paid by the consumer includes the full amount of the tax" (p. 6). In what follows we summarize the results of the OECD study.

The Belgian data, taken from a survey of household budgets conducted in 1973–74, are the most sketchy. Excise tax burden calculations were made by the OECD for income quartiles within each of three household types classified by occupational status. These categories were blue-collar workers, white-collar workers, and "nonactive" households, that is, persons not participating in the labor force. For blue-collar households, the results showed an inverted U-shaped burden. Households in the first and fourth quartiles faced the same excise tax rate (3.9%), while the tax burden was slightly higher for the two middle-income groups (about 4.2%). In contrast, the excise tax appeared to be regressive for white-collar households. Going up the income quartiles for these families, the tax rates declined steadily from 4.1% to 3.5%. For nonactive households, the highest tax rate (3.5%) fell on families in the lowest quartile, but the lowest burden (2.9%) was experienced by households in the second quartile. Tax rates were lower for the third and fourth quartiles than for the first, however. Overall, the Belgian data suggest proportionality or a slight degree of regressivity in the excise tax.

More complete data are available for Finland, the Netherlands, Norway, and the United Kingdom. The OECD's tax burden calculations for these countries are reported in tables 11–7 and 11–8.

Table 11–7
Excise Tax Rates for Two-Person Households by
Disposable Income Class, The Netherlands, 1974

Disposable Income (florin)	Tax Rate (percent)
<16,000	2.7
16,000–19,000	2.4
19,000–21,000	2.3
21,000–24,000	2.2
24,000–30,000	2.0
30,000–37,000	2.0
37,000–44,000	1.9
>44,000	1.7
Total	2.0

Source: OECD (1981).

Excise tax rates for the Netherlands (table 11–7) are among the lowest in the OECD. Moreover, taxes on tobacco are of minor importance as a revenue source there. In 1977, for example, tobacco tax receipts represented just 5% of the Netherlands' total consumption taxes (OECD, p. 61). (Excise taxes on oil and imports generated larger shares of consumption tax revenue.) The Netherlands' excise tax nevertheless displays a uniformly regressive pattern. The tax rate for the lowest income class is nearly 59% higher than the tax rate paid by the upper-income households.

Finland and Norway (table 11–8) are similar to the Netherlands in their lack of reliance on tobacco taxes as a major revenue source. (Both countries collect higher excise tax receipts on alcohol, oil, and other goods.) For Finland, the two-person household data exhibit progressivity in the excise tax structure, but this is deceiving since most of the households in this sample are made up of retired persons (OECD, p. 28). On the other hand, the excise tax rates for four-person Finnish families are generally regressive, with the highest rate paid by households in the second income decile, and the lowest by families in the tenth decile. In contrast, excise taxes are regressive for two-person families, and proportional for four-person households in Norway.

No clear pattern emerges from the aggregated U.K. data presented in table 11–8. The overall structure of the excise tax there comes closest to proportionality, if anything, but some low-income households face quite high tax rates. (Among OECD members, the United Kingdom relies most heavily on excise taxes for revenue; in 1977, excise levies accounted for over 18% of consumption tax receipts (OECD, p. 61).)

More detailed information on the incidence of tobacco taxes in the United Kingdom is reported in the OECD study, however, in particular, the report gives separate excise tax elasticities for the duties on beer, gasoline, motor vehicles, spirits, tobacco, wines, and for the VAT for each of four

Table 11–8
Excise Tax Rates by Income Decile for Three Countries
(percent)

Gross Income	Finland (1976)		Norway (1975)		United Kingdom (1977)		
	Two-person Households	Four-person Households	Two-person Households	Four-person Households	Two-person Households	Four-person Households	All Households
First Decile	4.35	6.16	5.9	4.1	10.61	8.11	5.02
Second Decile	3.60	8.21	5.7	4.5	7.22	19.32	6.14
Third Decile	4.19	6.17	5.5	4.7	6.85	9.69	7.07
Fourth Decile	6.31	7.58	5.4	4.7	8.30	9.27	8.48
Fifth Decile	5.21	7.58	5.3	4.7	7.60	7.54	7.51
Sixth Decile	5.61	6.12	5.2	4.7	8.41	6.92	7.65
Seventh Decile	6.53	6.36	5.1	4.7	7.46	6.84	7.37
Eighth Decile	6.88	6.40	5.1	4.7	7.28	5.40	6.73
Ninth Decile	8.17	6.23	5.0	4.7	6.22	6.75	7.37
Tenth Decile	6.13	6.05	5.0	4.7	4.55	4.15	5.88
Total	5.96	6.60	n.a.	n.a.	6.90	6.42	6.94

Source: OECD (1981).

family sizes. (The calculations are reproduced in table 11–9.) The results show not only that the tax on tobacco in Great Britain is regressive, but that it becomes more regressive as household size increases. Moreover, except in the case of two-person households, the tobacco tax is the most regressive of the taxes studied.

Given that U.K. excise taxes taken as a group exhibit rough proportionality, the data in table 11–9 suggest that the results showing proportionality or slight regressivity in the excise taxes for Belgium, Finland, the Netherlands, and Norway mask important differences in the distributional burdens imposed by the various excise taxes. However, if expenditure patterns by households in these four countries are similar to those of families in the United Kingdom, an overall assessment of the data leads us to suspect that disaggregation of the excise taxes would reveal regressivity in the tobacco taxes levied by those countries as well.

The Growing Burden of Foreign Tobacco Taxes

Taxes on a variety of tobacco products have been increased in the last few years by federal and local governments in Australia, the Federal Republic of

Table 11–9
Elasticities of Excise Taxes with Respect to Disposable Income, Selected Goods, United Kingdom, 1977

Elasticity Coefficient	Household Size			
	One Adult	Two Adults	Two Adults One Child	Two Adults Two Children
>1.0	VAT	VAT	VAT Wines Spirits	VAT
0.75–1.0		Wine		Wines Spirits
0.50–1.0	Petrol Wines Beer Spirits	Spirits Petrol	VED Petrol	
0.25–0.50	VED Tobacco	Beer Tobacco	Beer	VED Petrol
0–0.25		VED	Tobacco	Beer Tobacco

Source: OECD (1981, p. 52).
Note: VAT is the value-added tax and VED is the motor vehicle excise duty. Taxes are classified as regressive, proportional, or progressive according as the elasticity coefficient is less than, equal to, or greater than unity.

Germany, France, and Great Britain. As a result of these events, the excise taxes and other levies imposed in the four countries now represent about 75% of the average retail price of cigarettes.

Excise tax rates for tobacco products in Australia were raised in 1978 and in 1982. The more recent hike was part of a general 20% increase in the existing duties levied on specific goods. The excise rate for cigarettes consequently rose to $A29.70 (US$30.32) per kilogram; the tax rate for manufactured tobacco rose to $A15.10 (US$15.42) per kilogram and the rate for cigars rose to $A25.34 (US$25.87). These higher duties led to an increase of between $A0.12 and $A0.15 (US$0.123–US$0.153) in the price of a 25-cigarette pack. Further increases in tobacco taxes are expected in the near future.[14]

In the case of the Federal Republic of Germany, tobacco taxes were most recently increased on June 1, 1982. As a result of the 39% boost in the cigarette excise enacted then, the retail price per pack rose to US$1.78 from the previous US$1.38. The tax on cigarettes has remained at this level into 1984, keeping German tax rates about 3 times higher than those imposed in neighboring countries.[15]

Although the Socialist government in France backed down on a proposal in 1983 to immediately raise the excise tax on cigarettes there by 25%, taxes were increased by lesser amounts in 1983 and again in early 1984. As a result, the average price of a 20-cigarette pack was 4.31 francs, or the equivalent of about US$0.54, of which taxes represented 3.27 francs (US$0.41). Further increases seem likely.[16]

Great Britain has been the most active of the four countries in imposing additional taxes on tobacco products. The excise tax on cigarettes was increased twice in 1981, once by 14 pence per pack and then by 3 pence; additional duties were enacted in the 1982 and 1983 budget years. Britain's 1984–1985 budget raises the cigarette excise by a further 10 pence per pack. This move is expected to increase the average retail price of cigarettes to 124 pence per pack (US$1.82); taxes now represent about 91 pence (US$1.34) of this retail price.[17]

Overall, the governments in these countries appear to be quite willing to add to the burden of an already regressive tax structure.

Concluding Remarks

Taxes on tobacco are not equitable. Using a standard that a fair tax structure is one in which individuals having similar incomes face similar tax bills, we find substantial empirical evidence that the share of income going to tobacco tax payments falls as income rises, that is, the tax is regressive. Our conclusion is based on three types of data. First, the effective tax rates on tobacco products calculated by Phares (1980) drop steadily as one goes up the income distribution in all 50 states. Second, over the period 1976–1981, we found that in 49 states tobacco tax revenues were income inelastic, indicating probable regressivity in the tax. Third, international data (OECD, 1981) strongly suggest that taxes on tobacco products are regressive in the United Kingdom, and probably so in four other European countries.

What implications do these findings have for U.S. tax policy? One conclusion is that a simple reduction in tobacco tax rates would not make the tax more equitable, even though such a change would lower the overall burden. (Indeed, the tax is regressive even in North Carolina, the state with the lowest tax rate.) Given that smokers as a group appear to have lower permanent incomes than the population as a whole, any per unit or excise tax on them will generally be regressive.

Notes

1. Tax and revenue data are from The Tobacco Institute (1984).

2. Crain et al. (1977) suggest, however, that an individual could approve an excise tax on a good that he or she consumes. Their argument is that the tax-induced price rise may lower the cost to consumers of exercising moral restraint. For example, when an excise tax on alcohol raises the price of liquor, it is cheaper at the margin to reduce drinking. This allows the individual to consume more of other commodities, including goods such as "safe driving." Alternatively, Buchanan and Flowers (1980, p. 427) contend that because taxes on smoking are discriminatory, it is unlikely that they could be enacted were it not for the nonrevenue aspects.

3. Other equity standards are of course possible. For example, taxes may be based on the *benefits-received* principle wherein the burden is heaviest on those individuals who stand to gain most from consumption of the good in question (highway tolls are one illustration). Similarly, the *ability-to-pay* principle suggests that individuals having greater financial resources should pay a larger proportion of the tax.

4. In economic terms, responsiveness to a price change is measured by an *elasticity*, calculated as the percentage change in quantity (demanded or supplied) divided by the percentage change in price.

5. We here assume that the tax is collected and paid by producers. Similar results would be obtained by assuming that consumers pay the tax directly to government. In that case, however, we would illustrate the effects of the tax by shifting the demand schedule downward by the amount of the tax.

6. Evidence that tobacco product manufacturers do indeed pay a portion of the cigarette excise tax is given by industry opposition to enactment of new taxes and support for repeal of existing taxes (Buchanan & Flowers, 1980, p. 439).

7. The impact of the tax on tobacco farmers is further complicated by the existence of an allotment program which restricts the acreage that can be devoted to production. By itself, this program would tend to raise tobacco land values and drive up the price of tobacco leaf, causing a reduction in the output of the final cigarette products. Balancing these effects against those caused by the excise tax, the overall impact

on tobacco prices and output is unclear. It is true, however, that with a cigarette output restriction already built into the allotment program, imposing a tax on the final product further distorts economic decision making by farmers and tobacco product manufacturers.

8. All data on smoking incidence are from the 1980 Health Interview Survey (HIS) conducted by the U.S. Department of Health and Human Services. There is some reason to believe that the information from such surveys tends to greatly underestimate actual cigarette consumption.

9. Based on chi-square tests for differences in sample proportions.

10. Calculated using the midpoints of the age intervals, and 70 years for the open-ended class.

11. The row totals in tables 11–3 and 11–4 do not agree with those in the earlier tables. We attribute the differences to sampling error.

12. Using sixteen years as the class mark for the 13 + category.

13. Dividing by the implicit GNP price deflator (1972 = 100).

14. *Tobacco Reporter,* May 1982, p. 32. In addition to the federal excise, each state in Australia, with the exception of Queensland, imposes a tax on cigarettes which ranges between 10% and 12.5% of the wholesale price.

15. *Tobacco Reporter,* January 1982, p. 12; *Wall Street Journal,* May 12, 1982; *Economist,* March 17, 1984, p. 52.

16. *Tobacco Reporter,* June 1983, p. 100; *Economist,* March 17, 1984.

17. *Tobacco Reporter,* December 1981, p. 10, March 1982, p. 8, May 1982, p. 21, June 1983, p. 100; *Economist,* March 27, 1982, p. 46, March 17, 1984, pp. 51–52.

References

Buchanan, J.M. & Flowers, M.R. 1980. *The public finances, An introductory textbook.* 5th ed. Homewood, Ill.: Irwin.

Crain, W.M., Deaton, T., Holcombe, R. & Tollison, R. 1977. Rational choice and the taxation of sin. *Journal of Public Economics* 8, 239–245.

Davies, D.G. 1960. Progressiveness of a sales tax in relation to various income bases. *American Economic Review* 50, 987–995.

———. 1962. The sensitivity of consumption taxes to fluctuations in income. *National Tax Journal* 15, 281–290.

Friedlaender, A.F., Swanson, G.J. & Due, J.F. 1973. Estimating sales tax revenue changes in response to changes in personal income and sales tax rates. *National Tax Journal* 26 103–110.

Friedman, M. 1957. *A theory of the consumption function.* Princeton: Princeton University Press.

Musgrave, R.A. & Musgrave, P.B. 1976. *Public finance in theory and practice.* 2nd ed. New York: McGraw-Hill.

Organization for Economic Cooperation and Development, Committee on Fiscal Affairs. 1981. *The impact of consumption taxes at different income levels.* Paris: OECD.

Phares, D. 1980. *Who pays state and local taxes?* Cambridge, Mass.: Oelgeschlager, Gunn and Hain.

Rafuse, R. 1965. Cyclical behavior of state-local finances. In R.A. Musgrave (ed.), *Essays in fiscal federalism.* Washington, D.C.: Brookings Institution, pp. 63–121.

Schaefer, J.M. 1969. Sales tax regressivity under alternative tax bases and income concepts. *National Tax Journal* 22, 510–527.

The Tobacco Institute. 1984. *The tax burden on tobacco, historical compilation 1983.* Washington, D.C.: The Tobacco Institute.

U.S. Department of Commerce, Bureau of the Census. 1982. *Statistical Abstract of the U.S. 1982–83.* Washington, D.C.: USGPO.

Wagner, R.E. 1983. *Public finance: Revenues and expenditures in a democratic society.* Boston: Little, Brown.

12
Tobacco Advertising in a Free Society

J.J. Boddewyn

C itizens and governments may ban or severely restrict tobacco advertising because the people and the State are in principle sovereign. But
should they do so in free—or at least relatively free—societies outside of totalitarian regimes where governments exercise practically unlimited
control over what individuals and organizations may do, say, hear and see?

In response to the above questions, this essay argues that restrictions on
tobacco advertising should not exceed those reasonably applying to other
products and services because (1) the socioeconomic role of advertising is often
misunderstood and exaggerated; (2) there are constitutional or other legal
limits to government regulatory powers, and (3) there is a dangerous ongoing
crusade against advertising, which is threatening to engulf many products and
services—not just tobacco.

This analysis focuses on the U.S. situation but refers to various foreign
developments. In any case, the U.S. experience is generally relevant in terms
of identifying major issues and in outlining alternative answers to them.

The Role of Advertising is Misunderstood
and Exaggerated[1]

People favoring tobacco-advertising bans or severe restrictions work on the
assumption that advertising significantly increases tobacco sales and consumption. This is an incorrect assumption due largely to both advertising
practitioners and critics tending to exaggerate its influence—the former
because they have to justify expenditures, and the latter because they fear its
impact on consumers.

The truth is more sobering: *advertising is only one of many variables affecting consumer choice and competitive behavior, and its role is limited.* So,
how does it work, and under what conditions?

Advertising Is Only One Factor Affecting Consumer Decisions

Obviously, consumers will not look and ask for goods of which they are not *aware*. Their *interest*—as related to their needs—must also be tapped or generated. The message must then be *evaluated*: is it credible and worth pursuing (that is, to go out and examine the product)? Such *trial* (simple or complex) must take place before the *decisions* to buy and consume are made as well as to repurchase the product if satisfaction followed.[2]

In this context, advertising usually plays a very important role at the awareness and interest stages—at least in developed economies where the public is exposed to many advertisements. But even here, people also learn of products from relatives, friends and acquaintances; and they discover them through observing them as used by other people and in stores, offices, homes, publications, films, lectures, and so forth. Thinking of the recently introduced videocassette recorders, it is obvious that people came to know of them and became curious about them on account of many sources of information—not just advertising. Even without advertising, people could be aware and interested—as with unadvertised marijuana or relatively unadvertised Rolls Royces. The large volume of hard-liquor sales, even without television advertising, also supports this argument.

At the later stages of evaluation, trial, and decision, the influence of advertising decreases drastically because many other factors intervene: the advice of others, the ready availability and actual "feel" of the product in the store as well as its price, competitive offerings, the persuasion of salesmen, one's financial resources, state of mind, immediate needs, and so on. It is practically impossible to extricate the impact of any one of these variables even in relatively simple situations such as direct-mail or television invitations to "order it now." *In short, advertising cannot make anyone do anything but can only inform or influence choice:* people do not buy a Ford Capri simply or mainly because they saw an advertisement for it.

Consumers Are Quite Rational

If advertising's role is largely limited to the awareness and interest stages, does it use unfair manipulative methods, compared to other sources of information? (This question assumes that the advertisement is not false, misleading or otherwise illegal—a subject discussed in the second part of this chapter.) The specter of the "hidden persuader" playing on subconscious motives is regularly resurrected. Others fear that emotional appeals (such as those which tap the fear of aging) and crass ones (appealing to our desire for status or to our envy, lust, gluttony, and so forth) impede rational comparison and choice on the part of consumers relatively deprived of "hard information" about products and services.

Psychologists and sociologists argue that such an overly rational view of consumers is unrealistic. People do have emotions, and they are affected by other people as well as by general societal values. Most decisions—including the crucial voting for the presidency of the United States—are influenced by a variety of factors, including, but not limited to, hard facts.

Economists, who tend to take a more rational view of consumer behavior, have concluded that the power to manipulate people has been vastly overrated since most consumers make aware choices when real economic risk is involved.[3] Thus, in advertising-intensive markets, consumers respond more readily to copy that incorporates tangible selling propositions than they do to purely persuasive advertising. This suggests that factual and informative advertising content is welcomed in consumer markets, although its influence is not necessarily predominant in consumer decisions.[4]

In any case, there is no reliable evidence to support a statement such as: "Advertising is one way in which the choices we make are influenced so that the concept of free choice is violated." First, no one is totally "free" because of various genetic, personality, and environmental factors. Second, advertising ranks relatively low among these influences.

Businessmen define "information" as any data or argument that truthfully puts forth the attractiveness of a product in the context of a consumer's own buying criteria, wherever these come from: society, his/her past, immediate environment, current situation, or anything else, whether rational or emotional.[5] However, in the case of tobacco, companies are often prevented from providing this kind of information by (1) bans or severe restrictions on comparative advertising in many countries, (2) limitations on the claims they can make (for example, "Our cigarettes taste good"), and (3) bans on the use of various media.[6] On the other hand, the mandatory disclosure of tar and nicotine yields based on official tests helps provide information that potential buyers appear to desire.

In this context, advertising largely reflects prevailing values, attitudes, and social relations, and it cannot be too far behind or ahead of them.[7] It is extremely difficult to make people believe things they are not inclined to believe. All the commercials in the world could hardly interest many people in wearing hairshirts or chastity belts. Those who do certainly did not learn of them from advertising. Unless aimed at removing prejudices or misinformation, industry-wide campaigns aimed at increasing the consumption of well established products such as milk or butter can hardly succeed. The same would apply to tobacco products, although no such campaigns have been run.

Smoking had been accepted by many individuals as a satisfying activity for a long time before mass promotion. Tobacco advertising is a consequence, not a cause, of that acceptance (see the chapter by Sherwin Feinhandler on the social functions of smoking in this volume).[8]

Advertising Is Crucial for the Market System

Denying product information to consumers effectively limits competition and adversely affects the functioning of the market system since it depends on rivalry. This is definitely evidenced by the greater price competition and more attractive offerings resulting from the recent relaxation of U.S. bans on the advertising of eyeglasses and simple legal services. Conversely, centrally planned economies where advertising is minimal are notorious for the limited availability, variety, and quality of their goods and services. Further, without an avenue to promote their inventions, innovators have a reduced incentive to come up with new products appealing to consumers. One may well invent a better mousetrap, but how many people will beat a path to one's door if they do not know of the invention and where it is available? Consumers everywhere require such information to help them judge one offer versus another. It is their guarantee of genuine freedom of choice. Bans, on the other hand, cut the lines of communication upon which the market system and the customers it serves depend.[9]

Where information is denied by bans or severe restrictions, changes in brand selection would be far less likely. Any such action would tend to freeze the market-share situation in favor of existing products and dominant brands, thus slowing down the rate of innovation and preserving monopolistic or oligopolistic positions (see the chapter by Stephen Littlechild in this volume). Conversely, a manufacturer who is free to advertise will be more energized by the possibility of winning a greater market share by developing new, more acceptable product types and by adjusting products more accurately to current tastes, preferences, and income levels.[10]

Therefore, bans and severe restrictions bring about serious economic and social penalties. Many people would still continue to smoke and so manufacturers would continue to produce cigarettes, but they would be discouraged from bringing out product innovations (such as new flavors, lengths, filters, yields). In addition, competition would be significantly reduced, consumers would be denied information on which to base their purchases, and the media would be starved of advertising revenue. Such economic losses can hardly be justified in the pursuit of "good" goals through ineffective means.

On the other hand, one could argue that banning or severely curtailing advertising results in lower demand on account of less consumer awareness, lower competition, and so forth. Lower competition, in turn, would result in higher prices which discourage purchases—as happened with war toys which are not much advertised any more.[11] Applied to cigarette advertising, this implies that bans or severe restrictions would make this product less well known and more expensive, and thereby decrease sales. However, this case illustrates that the demand for products like war toys is affected by broad social factors such as revulsion against the Vietnam war and atomic warfare, for example—with advertising playing a much more modest role in creating or maintaining demand for such products. Advertising in such a case only reflects existing values but does not fundamentally create them.

Advertising Is Hard to Link to Overall Demand

The limited power of advertising is also evidenced by the coming and going of entire product lines as well as of major brands. If advertising could directly, singlehandedly, and significantly affect aggregate purchases, horse carriages would still be with us. Besides, if it were true that advertising expenditures determine consumer purchases, poor countries would merely have to increase advertising levels in order to become richer.[12] M.J. Waterson adds:

> If advertising were as powerful as its critics claim, heavily advertised product groups could be expected over time to capture an ever increasing share of total consumers' expenditures at the expense of less heavily promoted products. Yet, despite huge differences in the amounts of money spent on advertising relative to sales in different product areas (the U.K. Advertising Association Statistical Yearbook shows advertising/sales ratios across product groups varying from 0.003% up to over 50%), such trends cannot be identified.[13]

Even antismoking advertisements have had limited success: they can attract attention to their arguments, but no substantial effect can be expected from a "stop smoking" advertising campaign.

In fact, economists ascribe only a minor role to advertising in determining overall buyer expenditures. Thus, J.J. Lambin concluded on the basis of extensive research that advertising—while an effective marketing instrument—has only limited power to increase the sales or market share of a particular company.[14] Only rarely can it be credited with stimulating primary demand for a product, since this happens only in rapidly growing markets where demand seems to expand almost spontaneously under the influence of general socioeconomic factors, as with marijuana and videocassette recorders. Clearly, cigarettes are not a "new" product for which demand is fast growing in most countries. Even in less-developed nations, other factors are at play, such as urbanization, growing income, and the copying of Western lifestyles.[15]

More specifically, a number of econometric studies dealing exclusively with the relationship between cigarette advertising and sales have revealed that total advertising expenditures in a mature competitive market—such as the cigarette market in such countries as the United Kingdom and the United States—do not tend to expand the total market for that product. Thus, a 1979 Metra Consulting Group study covering a 25-year period concluded that no evidence had been found of a significant association between the total level of

U.K. media advertising and total U.K. cigarette sales.[16] Similarly, Chiplin, Sturgess, and Dunning have stated that:

> The causal relationship between advertising and aggregate demand is still a matter of considerable controversy, but the latest careful research using sophisticated estimation procedures does tend to suggest that any causal effect is rather weak. Thus, it seems to remain unproven that advertising has led to any marked increase in aggregate demand in general, or in the demand for either tobacco or alcoholic products.[17]

In the same vein, Waterson mentions U.K. market forecasts—that employ advanced econometric methods and are widely relied upon by food and drink companies—which never use advertising as an independent variable because it does not appear to affect the market for some fifty main product categories, including tea, butter, wine, biscuits, and bread.[18]

Advertising Is Mostly about Brands

But then why do tobacco companies advertise if advertising does not expand the total market for cigarettes? Are they wasting their own and the consumer's money? The answer to these questions lies in recognizing that cigarette advertising is essentially centered on brands. *Companies advertise in order to obtain a larger market share for their existing branded products or to obtain one for a new brand among existing smokers*—not to enlarge the total market, which remains static in most developed countries. There are no campaigns advocating that people "smoke" or "smoke more," only campaigns urging people to smoke "my" cigarettes rather than "theirs."

It is the competitive process of striving for market share that is at the heart of the market system. Whatever the size of the total market—stable, growing or declining, tobacco companies and brand managers want a bigger slice of it because profitability is often linked to larger market shares for particular brands. Even here, advertising is no guarantee that a particular brand will succeed, since the rate of failure among new ones is high.

Does this result only in mindless shifting of consumer preferences among fairly identical products? An affirmative answer to this question ignores the fact that brand advertising is usually linked with the dissemination of information about the availability of new products or product features such as filters, lower tar and nicotine yields, and lighter or novel flavors. While consumers may consider some of these new features to be desirable in themselves, these decisions often reflect changing tastes in society at large. Thus in the United States, there has been a marked shift to "lighter" products such as "light beer," "light white wine," and "white" spirits such as vodka—and this is true also for milder cigarettes. Tobacco companies emphasize such features in order to capitalize on changing preferences which result from a variety of social factors.

Advertising Bans Do Not Work—And May Be Harmful

The above arguments are buttressed by several studies of the impact of tobacco-advertising bans in a number of countries. Waterson found in the 16 nations he studied that: (1) cigarette-advertising bans (total or near total) have generally *not* been followed by a decrease in per capita tobacco consumption; and (2) banning countries have a much higher proportion of smokers who smoke nonfilter and high-tar brands than countries where cigarette advertising is allowed (see tables 12–1 and 12–2).[19]

While any such study does not provide absolutely conclusive "proof," the mass of evidence points only in one direction: *bans are not followed by the intended effect of curtailing consumption, but have often impeded the spread of information about the availability of new products or product features which consumers may desire.* There can be no doubt that shifts toward filtered and low-tar brands (which some public-health officials view as desirable) of these magnitudes in countries where advertising is allowed could not have occurred within such a short timespan without advertising support.

Some nations have experienced a decline in total or per capita consumption following advertising bans, but it has been a mere continuation of decreases which had been in evidence throughout preban years. If advertising were a significant contributory factor to the incidence of smoking and overall tobacco consumption, one would expect to see some signs of a decline among the youngest age groups because of their nonexposure to advertising while they grew from children to adults.

The Norwegian experience provides no evidence that the youngest age group has decreased its consumption more than other age groups. Altogether,

Table 12–1

Sales of Filter Cigarettes in Countries with and without Advertising Bans

(percentage of total cigarette sales)

Countries with Advertising Bans	Filter Sales 1982	Countries without Advertising Bans	Filter Sales 1982
Finland	97	Japan	99
Italy	92	Australia	98
Singapore	89	Canada	97
Norway	85	Switzerland	95
Czechoslovakia	70	United Kingdom	94
East Germany	70	Hong Kong	94
Hungary	70	United States	93
Poland	44	West Germany	90
USSR	30	Sweden	90

Source: Lehman Brothers Kuhn Research (New York), *Maxwell Estimates*. Cited in M.J. Waterson, *Advertising and Cigarette Consumption* (London: The Advertising Association), pp. 7–8.

Table 12–2
Penetration of Low Tar (0–15mgs tar) Cigarettes in Countries with and without Advertising Bans
(percentage of total sales)

Countries with Advertising Bans	Low-Tar Sales	Countries without Advertising Bans	Low-Tar Sales
Finland	32	West Germany	88
Norway	22	Switzerland	74
Italy	20	United States	65
Singapore	1	United Kingdom (0-16 mgs)	53
		Sweden	48
		France	47
		Hong Kong	25

Source: Lehman Brothers Kuhn Research (New York), *Maxwell Estimates*. Cited in M.J. Waterson, *Advertising and Cigarette Consumption* (London: The Advertising Association), pp. 7–8.

tobacco consumption in Norway has remained roughly constant since the ban was imposed in July, 1975.[20] This compares with a 25% decline in cigarette consumption in the United Kingdom over the same period. There are no restrictions on the volume of U.K. advertising for cigarettes, although there has been no cigarette advertising on British television since 1965. Consequently, "All the available data point to one conclusion, and one conclusion only. Imposing a ban on cigarette advertising—irrespective of the media forms to which it applies and irrespective of the time when it comes into force—is not an effective way of slowing down the rise in cigarette consumption, still less a means of producing a decline in consumption."[21]

Other studies have revealed that, compared to other factors, television cigarette commercials do not significantly influence smoking behavior.[22] Similarly, smoking by women is affected much more by socioeconomic factors such as social emancipation, greater income, and work participation than by advertising. (Other chapters in this volume address themselves to some of the factors affecting smoking behavior.)

Altogether, the available evidence that cigarette advertising by itself generates "new" smokers is weak. Whether "old smokers" keep smoking or smoke more on account of it is an equally tenuous proposition since many other variables are involved. Even smoker loyalty to a particular brand is fragile as market shares keep shifting among brands.

Evidence that relatively little is known about the behavioral aspects of smoking is provided by a recent $1.4 million grant to Harvard's Institute for the Study of Smoking Behavior and Policy. Behavioral research of that kind is only a small fraction of the estimated 33,000 existing studies of smoking and its possible effects.[23] It would thus seem premature to blame advertising and penalize tobacco advertising when so little is known about what affects smoking behavior.

If critics really wish to see cigarettes with lower tar and nicotine yields, they must acknowledge that: (1) the sales of brands with such features have grown faster in countries which allow advertising than in those which do not, and (2) advertising plays a crucial role in making such brands known and attractive to smokers. This is an example of the responsiveness of competitive industry to shifts in consumer taste—a responsiveness which depends on the freedom to advertise and inform people about product innovations.

It may be added that tobacco-advertising bans or severe restrictions are more likely to hurt advertising agencies and media than the tobacco industry itself since per capita tobacco consumption is not significantly affected by advertising. This has clear implications for the existence of nonsubsidized media since most publications and broadcast stations depend on advertising revenues. Clearly, brand advertising does not increase total sales and consumption even though people who do not smoke believe that advertising has more influence on smokers than smokers believe it does.

Government Regulatory Powers Are Limited

Advertising's impact on overall cigarette consumption is limited and, as such, does not warrant too much interest from an economic viewpoint. But even if it did, the government's right to interfere with the truthful advertising of a legal product in a free society is or should be curtailed.

Reaction against Overregulation

May governments concern themselves with every single problem or issue, whether real or imaginary? Considering the broad mandate assumed by or imposed on modern governments, there is no denying that they have in fact come to concern themselves with a long list of tasks ranging well beyond the general provision of "law and order." Pressure groups coming from all directions want to obtain government support through regulation, subsidies, and other programs designed to further their causes. Bureaucrats themselves have an inherent interest in maintaining and expanding such activities, in addition to any personal zeal they may feel about certain causes.

Fortunately, there are limits to such increasing state intervention in personal, economic, and social life. International declarations of human rights, constitutions (written or unwritten), and general laws set boundaries which a variety of courts do enforce to some degree in most free countries (see the chapter by Douglas Den Uyl in this volume). Yet there are times when the judiciary is more lax in interpreting them and in protecting fundamental freedoms.

The lack of financial and human resources also restrains governments, which hesitate to assume new responsibilities and/or can hardly fulfill existing ones. Still, it is not unusual to have regulations enacted just to prove that the government cares, irrespective of any enforcement intention or resources; or to have something to fall back on when the need arises to go after some particularly recalcitrant individual, organization, or group.

Finally, there are broad public-opinion movements that express dissatisfaction over the state's encroachment through taxation, regulation, and other forms of intervention. The recent "deregulation" movement reflects such a popular revulsion after several decades of growing governmental zeal and meddling. Politicians, judges, and bureaucrats sense such reactions and, when regulation is out of favor, usually limit its reach.

Smoking and the advertising of tobacco products are issues to which public policy has increasingly addressed itself in most countries and in various international forums such as the Council of Europe. Considering the interest and even passion generated by these issues, their seriousness in terms of health issues, and the magnitude of the groups involved—male adults are often split in half between those who smoke and those who do not—it would be futile to argue that governments have no business dealing with them. But just how far can the State go in coping with them, without harming those fundamental liberties that distinguish free societies from totalitarian ones? This discussion will only address tobacco *advertising,* and will not deal with the production, distribution, and consumption of tobacco products.

Economic and Political Freedoms Are Linked

There is a fundamental relationship between economic and political liberties. Without alternative centers of power based on the freedoms to have property, to associate, and to express economic preferences, there is little to check the expansion of the State's authority.[24] After all, speaking up or seeking redress costs money, and exercising these rights should not have to depend on the government's largesse or discretion. Conversely, the elaboration and use of political rights to equality, justice, participation, individual sovereignty, and the like cannot be overly dependent on economic rights which may "buy" too much power in the system and unduly infringe on others' equal rights.

In this context, advertising is particularly linked to freedom of information—both to give it and to receive it—because its lack hinders effective economic choices, both personal and social. Thus the Council of Europe has issued a declaration on Freedom of Expression and Information, which stresses it as a "fundamental element of the principles of democracy" and as necessary for the social, economic, cultural, and political development of every human being. Article 10 of the European Convention on Human Rights states that: "Everyone has the right to freedom of expression . . . and to hold opinions and to receive and impart information and ideas without interference by public authority and regardless of frontiers," even if the information or ideas offend, shock, or disturb the State or any sector of the population, according to the European Court of Human Rights.[25]

U.S. Constitutional Protection of Advertising

Advertising has always been recognized as an instrument of commerce and as an acceptable business practice—subject, of course, to controls consistent with the U.S. free-enterprise system. In fact, the free flow of information is considered indispensable for the proper allocations of resources in a free-enterprise system;[26] and there is a clear relationship between commercial speech in "the marketplace of products and services" and free expression in the "marketplace of ideas," which is proper to a free society.

The power of the U.S. Congress to regulate advertising springs exclusively from the Interstate Commerce Clause of the U.S. Constitution, which gives it power to regulate commerce among the states.[27] This congressional power, however, is restricted by protection granted under the Constitution's First Amendment: "Congress shall make no law . . . abridging the freedom of speech, or of the press." To what extent, then, can advertising carried in interstate commerce be regulated?

Two main bodies of law are particularly relevent here: *sales law* (contract law, including the caveat emptor principle) and *communications law* (based on the First Amendment).[28] At first, advertising regulation was only related to the attachment of liability to the use of language in connection with a sales transaction and contract. As H.J. Rotfeld explains:

> A contract can be seen as an arrangement for certain goods to be delivered in accordance with a description provided by the seller; advertising can be seen as a "mass offer" (in legal terms, an express warranty) to deliver certain goods as described. Accordingly, the history of advertising regulation consisted of rules for interpreting the language of advertising . . . and liabilities to make sure advertisers were delivering what they promised.[29]

The prohibition of false, misleading and deceptive advertising through a variety of statutes (including the 1914 Federal Trade Commission Act and its subsequent amendments) rests on this notion that business must deliver what it promised.[30] In this context, any tobacco advertising that is false, misleading, or makes or implies certain claims which cannot be substantiated might elicit regulatory attention. Since the 1930s, a number of FTC proceedings, proposals, and guides about cigarette advertising have involved these issues.[31]

The application of First Amendment protection to advertising is more recent. Such abuses of free speech as slander, libel, and obscenity have traditionally not been protected. However, even "commercial speech" was excluded until U.S. Supreme Court decisions starting in 1976.[32]

Particularly significant is the fact that the eventual application of the First Amendment to commercial speech began with the "birth of a right to receive information" as a part of the freedom of speech and press. U.S. courts came to recognize that advertising is the predominant institution for the dissemination of marketing information to consumers.[33] The courts thus concluded that it was essential that consumers be able to receive the information they needed to make purchasing decisions: "So long as we preserve a predominantly free enterprise economy, the allocation of our resources in large measure will be made through numerous private economic decisions. It is a matter of public interest that those decisions, in the aggregate, be intelligent and well informed. To this end, the free flow of commercial information is indispensable.[34]

Hence, the Supreme Court has come to conclude that "commercial speech" is protected by the First Amendment although to a somewhat lesser extent than "non-commercial" speech, which is considered more valuable and vulnerable.[35] Therefore, *total bans on truthful commercial advertising conveying information of value to a diverse audience are now untenable in the United States,* although the precise limits of government regulation are still being cautiously redefined.

What are these present limits? A four-part test of the constitutionality of restrictions imposed on "commercial-speech" advertising[36] was articulated by the Supreme Court in 1980:

> At the outset, we must determine whether the expression is protected by the First Amendment. For commercial speech to come within the provision, it at least must concern lawful activity and not be misleading. Next, we ask whether the asserted governmental interest is substantial. We must determine whether the regulation directly advances the governmental interest asserted, and whether it is not more extensive than necessary to service that interest.[37]

The first test ("lawful activity and not misleading") presents no particular problem for tobacco advertising since such a requirement is desirable to protect the quality of commercial information and to maintain general respect for the law. In fact, it constitutes a plus since tobacco marketing, being a legal activity, derives from it the right to advertise what is legal ("Legal to make and sell, legal to advertise"). Besides, there can be no serious suggestion that current cigarette advertising is misleading since health warnings are now required. It has been alleged that cigarette advertising was misleading—that is, omitted important information—prior to the time that health warnings were required. Such allegations, however, ignore the fact that claims regarding the possible adverse health effects of tobacco have been well known for hundreds of years (see the chapter by Sherwin Feinhandler in this volume).

So much for "bad" advertising that is false, misleading or contrary to public order. What about restrictions on *truthful* advertising? The government's right to control "the time, manner and place of advertising" is not particularly burdensome if fairly applied and if alternative means of reaching consumers are available. A special problem arises here on account of the special treatment of radio and television broadcasting under U.S. law.[38] In view of the originally limited number of stations and of their ability to reach vast undifferentiated audiences, the courts have usually accepted that stricter restrictions could apply to broadcasting media, although this view has been challenged.[39]

However, the multiplication of broadcasting sources—particularly, the advent of limited-access cable television—is changing the situation. Looser restrictions apply to the latter, and the British government has even ventured the notion that if someone wanted to watch cigarette commercials on Teletel (an information network available only on request), this right should not be denied. Besides, extending the present U.S. ban of cigarette commercials on off-the-air (that is, via antenna reception) radio and television to other media would conflict with the Supreme Court requirement that alternative means of communication remain available.[40]

Regarding another part of the Supreme Court test, the notion of what constitutes "governmental interest" is open to many changing and possibly arbitrary interpretations. For example, it can be readily agreed that governments have a legitimate and compelling interest in regulating health matters.[41] When, however, will the government have sufficient evidence that a significant health controversy exists and warrants commercial-speech restrictions when the law does not and cannot demand conclusive proof?[42] The notions of "unsophisticated audiences" and "vulnerable groups" exposed to cigarette advertising is elastic, and there have been many waverings on the part of the Federal Trade Commission, the Federal Communications Commission, and the courts regarding such concepts. The only safeguard here is the Supreme Court's insistence that restrictions be precisely tailored to accomplish their purpose and that the least burdensome means be used: "no greater than is essential to the furtherance of an important or substantial governmental interest."[43]

The U.S. situation can thus be interpreted to mean that "restrictions on particular speakers or modes of speech are legitimate so long as they do not interfere with reception of the information and ideas in question from other speakers or via other modes of speech."[44] This clearly precludes total bans on tobacco advertising. It must also be realized that overly drastic remedies can prompt advertisers to forego providing customers with relevant data and switch instead to puffery and emotional appeals. There is also the possibility of promotion being shifted to less controllable media and techniques or even uncontrollable ones (such as word-of-mouth recommendations).

In conclusion, one can agree with Lee Loevinger, a Federal Communications Commission member during the 1960s, that "In 40 years, advertising has advanced from a commercial practice that could be regulated or suppressed virtually at will by any state, city, village, township or hamlet, to a constitutionally protected right which is recognized as having real social value."[45] Permissible restraints on commercial speech have been limited to measures designed to protect consumers from fraudulent, misleading, or coercive sales techniques. Those designed to deprive consumers of information about products or services that are legally offered for sale have been increasingly invalidated.[46] Restrictions, whether effective or not, may be permissible, but it appears that no ban on cigarette advertising would be supported by U.S. courts nowadays.

The Limits of the "Unfairness" Concept

While it is a murky concept, the issue of "unfairness" has often been raised in connection with advertising to "unsophisticated audiences" and "vulnerable groups" such as the young.[47] Thus, the U.S. Federal Trade Commission (FTC) tried to impose mandatory warnings on packages and in cigarette advertisements on the ground that the lack of disclosure that smoking may be dangerous to health would be deceptive and, as such, constitutes an unfair practice.[48] In this context, three brief comments are in order.

First, as was mentioned before, claims regarding the possible adverse health effects of tobacco have been well known for hundreds of years (see the Feinhandler chapter in this volume), and they have been crystalized in the message: "Warning: The Surgeon General has determined that cigarette smoking is dangerous to your health" (other versions have recently been mandated). It is thus difficult to argue that cigarette advertising is operating "unfairly" in an informational vacuum where no countervailing data or opinions are available to audiences, sophisticated or not, young or old.

Second, if emotional or subjective messages (such as the association of "having a good time" with smoking) are considered "unfair," what about the current use of fear in antismoking messages?[49] It would appear that a double standard is being applied here.

Third, most discussions about "vulnerable groups" appear to be misinformed according to a study commissioned and published by the British Government's Office of Fair Trading:

> There is also no evidence whatever from the research that groups of people who could be hypothesized to be susceptible to advertising to their detriment (for example, because they are relatively poor, young or old, infirm, less well educated, have children, etc., or live in relatively deprived types of area) react to advertising differently from the rest. All comments in these subgroups agreed closely with the overall pattern of comments. The same applies to people holding attitudes which could relate to psychological vulnerability (e.g., who say they find it difficult to make ends meet, are prepared to buy on credit or worry about what others think of them).[50]

Finally, there is no constitutional protection for "false, inaccurate, misleading or deceptive" speech, but recent U.S. Supreme Court decisions in this area do *not* refer to "unfair" speech which happens to be true and nondeceptive.[51] Such decisions cast doubt on the power of the FTC to use the nebulous concept of "unfairness" in broad rulemaking against such products as cigarettes.

Overzealous Crusaders Endanger a Free Society

Cigarette smoking and advertising are controversial issues. That individuals and organizations care about them, get excited about them, and militate against them is to be expected in free societies. However, such action endangers freedom when it is uninformed in fact and antidemocratic in nature, besides being overtrusting in governmental solutions.

Available Information Is Ignored or Dismissed

As the two previous sections have demonstrated, there are serious misconceptions about the role and effectiveness of advertising in promoting cigarette purchase and consumption as well as about a growing body of U.S. constitutional limitations on the restriction and banning of the truthful advertising of cigarettes. A cursory reading of the antitobacco literature evidences little or no awareness or acceptance of this evidence.[52] Most of it largely details increasing governmental controls as a valid exercise of state police power and as something worth emulating in other countries, without any substantial discussion of constitutional and other legal limitations. While ignorance may well be bliss to crusaders, a free society requires a more rational discourse. Unfortunately, "Don't confuse me with facts or relevant contrary principles" often seems to be the crusaders' guiding rule.

Antidemocratic Tendencies

While enjoying the right of speaking up freely about their cause, antitobacco proponents act antidemocratically when they pretend that the debate is closed—as if all the evidence was in and the other side did not have the right to speak up as well through advertising and other means. While few people embrace total censorship of expression, a strange distinction is made between truthful expression in advertising and other forms of expression such as books, articles, editorials, speeches, and programs. The "marketplace of ideas" (that is, political speech) is often more fraudulent than the "marketplace of products and services," but a strange double standard applies here. One can say practically anything—false, misleading, unfair—in a book, article, and so forth about a political party or opponent. But even the truthful advertiser (such as that Firm A has a particular brand with such and such characteristics) has to be wary of running afoul of the law or is denied access to certain media.

The merest possibility that advertising *can* err (as it does at times, of course) is considered grounds for severe restriction if not prohibition: again, an antidemocratic notion that would justify practically any shackling of expression. It is appropriate to forbid the advertising of an illegal product but not of one freely produceable and saleable. Similarly, the argument that "In discussing the effect of cigarette promotion, it is worth noting that it is time for the onus of proof to be shifted from anti-smoking organizations to the tobacco industry"[53] is hardly a proliberty one in societies where people are presumed innocent until proven guilty (see the Den Uyl chapter on "Smoking, Human Rights and Civil Liberties").

Even public opinion is a treacherous guide in this matter. If one asked people today whether the rights of communists and homosexuals should be abridged, and whether there should be restrictions on the advertising of tobacco, alcohol, and other "guilty pleasures," one may very well obtain a majority of positive answers.[54] Such a majority opinion, however, is susceptible to varying moods (as in the case of the U.S. Prohibition Amendment), so that one cannot definitely say that it is a sound or permanent judgment. When translated into law, it imposes burdens on everyone (see the chapter by James Buchanan in this volume).

Hypocrisy

The regulatory distinction between the production, marketing (including advertising), and consumption of cigarettes is certainly tenuous and hypocritical. Statements to the effect that consumption cannot be prohibited but there is no reason, "now that the risks are so well known, for allowing the continuation of promotion"[55] are objectionable. If "the risks are so well known," why does the government not forbid cigarette production, distribution, and consumption too?

The reasons seem fairly obvious: tobacco growers, cigarette manufacturers and distributors and their employees, and cigarette smokers (up to one-half of the adult population in some countries) would be antagonized; government tax revenues would be significantly curtailed; and "underground economy" (as in the case of hard drugs) would develop, possibly making smoking as fashionable as drinking during the Prohibition Era; and—last but not least—the smoking and health controversy is not as settled as antitobacco groups argue (see the chapter by Hans Eysenck in this volume).

So, one falls back on the argument that although "the evidence of the effects of [cigarette] promotion is difficult to quantify [and] promotion [is] only one factor, it is . . . one that is *controllable*."[56] Obviously, advertising is being made into the scapegoat, and its restriction turns out to be the token evidence of government concern. But is this a strong legal, as opposed to political, argument for shackling it?

In fact, the zeal of tobacco opponents may have played in favor of the industry and to the detriment of other business sectors and of the public. Thus, the U.S. ban on radio and television commercials hurt the broadcasting industry and favored other media while leaving the industry free to advertise elsewhere. It also removed from the air many antitobacco messages that had been mandated on account of the "fairness doctrine" to counter cigarette advertising.[57]

Arrogance and Paternalism

Australian scholars have pointed to the "arrogance and paternalism" of consumer advocates who wish to replace "the rhetoric of democracy" with their own value systems or who ignore "the danger of bureaucratically imposed value judgments arising out of an assumption that consumers have to be protected against themselves and which thus impinges upon our democratic notions of freedom of expression."[58] There is always the danger that moral crusaders will think they are "above the law" because "in the right." Thus, Waterson reports that an Australian "crusader-type" session at the 1983 Fifth World Conference on Smoking and Health was the only one to be repeated by popular demand: "The purpose of BUGA-UP [Billboard-Utilizing Graffitists Against Unhealthy Promotions] is to convert the one-way DICTATORSHIP of the billboard false advertising [of cigarettes and other products] to a two-way communication, which is inherent in the origin and current meaning of the word [quoting a BUGA-UP statement]."[59]

To applaud such "graffitizing" of billboards does not evidence much respect for advertising or for contrary views, but does indicate much in the way of moral superiority. As S.B. Foote and R.H. Mnookin state, "Crusaders have not historically valued diversity of opinion; they are typically undeterred by the lack of consensus. Rather, they take disagreement as an opportunity to proselytize, and if necessary, use coercion to force conversions."[60]

A number of people do not like our modern societies, their values and behaviors. While advertising, by and large, only reflects these values and behaviors, they pick on this "bearer of bad news" or accuse it of creating "false values."[61] Once more, this amounts to attacking the symptom rather than the condition, and presents a serious danger to freedom of communication.

Conspiracy or Convergence?

It is difficult if not impossible to prove that some conspiracy against advertising actually exists. Too many disparate individuals and organizations oppose it to support such an argument. Yet so many oppositions parallel and build up on each other that they warrant the fear that they do or will amount to an additive attack against advertising's role and existence (see also Peter Berger's chapter in this volume).

It is true that the opponents of cigarette advertising are not always those who argue against alcohol advertising, because the relevant factors and interests are not consistently identical.[62] Still, they often rejoice in each other's victories and support each other's endeavors. Thus, Waterson reported on the 1983 Fifth World Conference on Smoking and Health as follows:

> A second characteristic was the obvious anti-advertising (as opposed to anti-tobacco) bias of many speakers. Speaker after speaker referred to other areas of "concern," and hostility was expressed to the advertising of alcohol, drugs, pesticides, infant foods, etc. . . . The links between anti-smoking groups and other non-tobacco oriented "activist" groups so often decried (in the United Kingdom) as being a figment of our imagination, became very visible . . . Several delegates urged the building of closer links with groups operating in other areas.[63]

There is no end to "objectionable" products and services which so far have not been banned: alcohol, tea, coffee, salt, butter, sweets, snack foods, junk foods, pharmaceuticals, even aspirin.[64] Each one has enlisted ardent adversaries who usually envision an advertising ban or severe restriction as a remedy. Cumulatively, these separate attacks and proposals would eliminate a major part of advertising. Therefore, there is logic to opposing any one of them on the ground that "freedom is indivisible:"

> Many health-educationalists have, for several years, been offering deals in Europe to the effect: "Give us tobacco advertising and we won't touch anything else." This is a very seductive idea in many quarters—particularly, of course, in the drink and chocolate industries . . . It is after all, often stated that tobacco is a pretty dirty business; and if we could just give that away, maybe all our other problems will go away. It won't happen. . . . Exactly the same arguments [will be] applied to confectionary, drink, fats, drugs and so on. The critics all believe that more is bad and less is good for all products in the firing line.[65]

In other words, advertising is vulnerable to the "salami approach": "I don't want your salami—just a slice of it, now another one, and so on," until one is left with the string.

Over-reliance on Government and Regulation

Two analysts of a FTC attempt to ban advertising to children have commented that: "One characteristic of our age is the impulse to identify something as a 'social problem' and then look to government for a solution . . . There is nothing wrong with this impulse, so long as it is recognized that not all 'problems' as seen by reformers can be 'solved' by government, at least without unacceptable social cost."[66] These comments are echoed by R.E. Oliver of the Canadian Advertising Standards Council, who has pointed out that:

> We now walk with unsure feet through the troubled waters of social and ethical concern. Perhaps that higher state of awareness represents a stepping-stone to progress. But beneath that same stone, a dangerous viper lurks. In our country, many politicians and social reformers propose to resolve complex social problems by regulating or removing advertising—whether the problem be excessive or unwise use of credit, the use or misuse of drugs, undue dependence on tobacco or alcohol, or a cloudy set of personal values.
>
> Oh, if Life were only that simple! The truth is there are no easy solutions to the behavior problems of individuals and society. Further, there are very few such problems that advertising can cause and not too many it can cure. But the fallacy persists.[67]

Critics often speak as if any government pronouncement (such as "Smoking is dangerous to your health") ends any debate or advocacy, and as if governments had never erred in relaying information and adopting policies which were later corrected or reversed (at great pain, usually). Thus, bans on cigarette advertising are sometimes justified on the grounds that they convey the idea that smoking does not have official approval, and that such bans "provide evidence of government concern."[68] Arguments of this sort hardly foster healthy skepticism about the wisdom of governmental action which, as we know, varies widely in time and place.

Furthermore, pointing to government action as evidence that a legitimate problem exists ignores the "symbolic" use of regulation.[69] As mentioned above, it is not unusual for governments to enact regulation just to prove that they "care" and to placate pressure groups—often without any intention of providing the necessary means to insure implementation and compliance.

Similarly, pressure groups are often satisfied with ineffective legislation as they are "trying to maximize such subgoals as rectitude and status . . . recognition, visibility and expansion of organizational activity . . . [so that] the health groups, too, clearly gained from the controversy and from the regulation [of cigarette advertising]."[70] Such masquerading is hardly justification for denying freedom of commercial speech.

Even when granting that cigarette brands with lower tar and nicotine yields should be publicized, some tobacco-advertising critics argue that "the responsibility for publicizing new low-tar brands, together with their advantages and disadvantages, should lie with governments and health authorities instead of with the tobacco industry."[71] Such trust in and reliance on government could be used to justify a ban on *all* advertising for any product since so little faith is put in advertisers and consumers.

Furthermore, to what extent is it the government's task "to help make smoking socially unacceptable and to help create a non-smoking environment?"[72] Some would argue that governments should provide information but stop short of "propaganda" and of attempts to change behavior. This is certainly a difficult issue, if only because the line between "information" and "propaganda" is tenuous. Still, allowing governments to decide that it is not appropriate to "[convey] the idea that smoking is a civilized pleasure worth preserving"[73] raises a significant question about whether this kind of state intervention in private life is dangerous and should be resisted in a free society.

Even opposing what antitobacco groups assert is the association of smoking with "youth, sex, virility, femininity, courage, or glamour"[74] through image or mood advertising is debatable since it amounts to imposing a single view of what government thinks is "good."[75] It would seem that any pressure group would abhor such a single-minded position on the part of the State, but crusaders apparently have no such fears.

Altogether, the ignorance of advertising's true economic effects on cigarette consumption and of constitutional limits to restrictions on commercial speech are often combined with an antidemocratic spirit of intolerance and overreliance on regulatory solutions. Such a combination is dangerous to free societies and deserves a "warning" of its own in all discussions of tobacco advertising.

Notes

1. For more analysis, see J.M. Ferguson, *Advertising and Competition: Theory, Measurement, Fact* (Cambridge, MA: Ballinger, 1974), pp. 535–565; and M.J. Waterson, *Advertising, Brands and Markets* (London: Advertising Association, 1984). This section discusses a number of economic issues connected with advertising but there are many more which will not be handled here: advertising as a source of monopolistic power and its impact on prices, employment and government revenues, among others.

2. "Buying" and "consuming" are not the same things, although the word "consumer" is often incorrectly applied to denote both the purchaser and the user of a good. In fact, both may be distinct as when someone buys something for somebody else (such as baby food for a child).

3. Ferguson, *Advertising and Competition*, p. 539.

4. J.J. Lambin, "What Is the Real Impact of Advertising?" *Harvard Business Review* (May–June 1975), pp. 139–147, and *Advertising, Competition and Market Conduct; A Statistical Investigation in Western European Countries* (New York: American Elsevier, 1975).

5. Ferguson, *Advertising and Competition*, p. 541.

6. J. J. Boddewyn and K. Marton, *Comparison Advertising: A Worldwide Study* (New York: Hastings House, 1978). In France, cigarette advertisements can only show the package, and no specific claims can be made.

7. For a recent elaboration of this view (applied to cigarettes in Chapter 6) see Michael Schudson, *Advertising, the Uneasy Persuasion; Its Dubious Impact on American Society* (New York: Basic Books, 1984).

8. International Advertising Association (IAA), *Tobacco and Advertising: Five Arguments Against Censorship* (New York, 1983), p. 3.

9. Ibid., pp. 1–2.

10. Ibid., p. 21.

11. R.L. Steiner, "Does Advertising Lower Consumer Prices?" *Journal of Marketing* 37 (October 1973), pp. 19–26; and Waterson, *Advertising, Brands and Markets*.

12. M.J. Waterson, *Advertising and Cigarette Consumption* (London: The Advertising Association, 1983), p. 11.

13. M.J. Waterson, "Advertising and Health; Presentation to the Council of Europe's Health Division" (29 September 1983), p. 4.

14. Lambin, "Real Impact" and *Advertising, Competition and Market Conduct*.

15. Relatively little is known about cigarette consumption in less-developed countries. See Bo Wickström, *Cigarette Marketing in the Third World, A Study of Four Countries* (Gothenburg, Sweden: University of Gothenburg, Department of Business Administration, Marketing Section, 1979).

16. Patrick Sinnott, *The Relationship Between Total Cigarette Advertising and Total Cigarette Consumption in the United Kingdom* (London: Metra Consulting Group, 1979).

17. Brian Chiplin, Brian Sturgess and J.H. Dunning, *Economics of Advertising* (New York: Holt, Rinehart & Winston, 1981), p. 97.

18. Waterson, "Advertising and Health," pp. 4–5.

19. Waterson, *Advertising and Cigarette Consumption*; and International Advertising Association, *Tobacco Advertising Bans and Consumption in 16 Countries* (New York, 1983). See also Lynne Schneider et al., "Governmental Regulation of Cigarette Health Information," *Journal of Law and Economics* 24, 3 (December 1981), p. 610.

20. Waterson, *Advertising and Cigarette Consumption*, p. 24. See also S.J. Teel et al., "Lessons Learned From the Broadcast Cigarette Advertising Ban," *Journal of Marketing* 43 (January 1979), pp. 45–50, about the U.S. ban experience, which has not been particularly successful.

21. Rheinhold Bergler, *Advertising and Cigarette Smoking—A Psychological Study* (Bern-Stuttgart-Vienna: Hans Huber, 1981). For additional evidence, see IAA, *Tobacco and Advertising*, pp. 11–13.

22. E.E. Levitt, "The Cigarette Ad Ban: Unexpected Fallout," *World Smoking and Health* 2, 2 (Autumn 1977), p. 5; and J.L. Hamilton, "The Demand for Cigarettes: Advertising, the Health Scare, and the Cigarette Advertising Ban," *Review of Economics and Statistics*, 54, 4 (November 1972), pp. 401–411.

23. "Why People Smoke Is the Burning Issue in a Harvard Study," *Wall Street Journal* (10 May 1984), p. 12.

24. L.M. Wright, "A Survey of Economic Freedoms," *Freedom at Issue* 64 (January–February 1982), p. 15. See also B.M. Owen, *Economics and Freedom of Expression; Media Structure and the First Amendment* (Cambridge, MA: Ballinger, 1975), p. 5ff.

25. Adopted by the Committee of Ministers on 29 April 1982 (Strasbourg, France). The European Convention on Human Rights also provides some protection to commercial speech. See J.W. Thompson, "Human Rights in a Commercial Context," *Consumer Affairs* 65 (September–October 1983), pp. 13–14; and Anthony Lester and David Pannick, *Advertising and Freedom of Expression in Europe; The Scope and Effect of the European Convention on Human Rights* (Paris: International Chamber of Commerce, Marketing Commission, 1984).

26. Dorothy Cohen, "Advertising and the First Amendment," *Journal of Marketing* 42 (July 1978), pp. 59–68.

27. G.E. Rosden and P.E. Rosden, *The Law of Advertising*, vol. 1 (New York: Matthew Bender, 1982), pp. 4–1. U.S. courts have tended to give a very liberal interpretation of what constitutes "interstate" vs. "intrastate" commerce, so that many state regulations and intrastate economic activities are vulnerable to federal challenge. In any case, intrastate commerce will not be discussed here.

28. H.J. Rotfeld, "The Compatibility of Advertising Regulation and the First Amendment—Another View," *Journal of Public Policy and Marketing* 1 (1982), pp. 139–146.

29. Ibid., p. 141.

30. "Unfair" advertising is also regulated but will be discussed separately in connection with the issue of advertising to "vulnerable groups" such as children.

31. 29 Fed. Reg. Rep. (2 July 1961), p. 8, 324ff. ("Unfair or Deceptive Advertising and Labeling of Cigarettes in Relation to the Health Hazards of Smoking"—Proposed FTC Trade Regulation Rule). See also K.N. Friedman, *Public Policy and the Smoking-Health Controversy* (Lexington, MA: Lexington Books, 1975).

32. There is a voluminous legal literature on advertising and the First Amendment, but only selected court cases and analyses will be quoted here. For recent reviews, see B.S. Roberts, "Toward a General Theory of Commercial Speech and the First Amendment," *Ohio State Law Journal* 40, 115 (1979), pp. 115–152; Jonathan Weinberg, "Constitutional Protection of Commercial Speech," *Columbia Law Journal* 82, 4 (May 1982), pp. 720–750; P.C. DeVore and R.D. Sack, "Advertising and Commercial Speech, *"Legal Notes and Viewpoints Quarterly* 3 (May 1983), pp. 21–73; and J.D. Healy, "Commercial Speech: An Update," *Advertising Compliance Service* 4, 7 (2 April 1984), pp. 3–8.

33. Rotfeld, "Compatibility," pp. 142–143.

34. *Virginia State Board of Pharmacy* v. *Virginia Citizens Consumer Council*, 425 U.S. (1976), p. 765.

35. Roberts, "Toward a General Theory," p. 130. See also Michael Schein, "Commercial Speech and the Limits of Legal Advertising," *Oregon Law Review* 58, 2 (1979), p. 207; and Weinberg, "Constitutional Protection," pp. 747–748.

36. "Opinion" advertising is fully protected and free—as when the R.J. Reynolds Tobacco Company uses paid advertisements to state its position regarding the smoking and health controversy. See "Health Groups Assail Cigarette Ads" *New York Times* (17 February 1984), p. A17, and Margaret Loeb, "Reynolds Takes Major Risks in Ads Defending Cigarettes," *Wall Street Journal* (16 February 1984), p. 37.

37. *Central Hudson Gas and Electric Corporation* v. *Public Service Commission,* 447 U.S. 557 (1980).

38. "After January 1, 1971, it shall be unlawful to advertise cigarettes [and little cigars] in any medium of electronic communication subject to the jurisdiction of the Federal Communications Commission." Section 6 of Public Law 91–222 (Public Health Cigarette Smoking Act) of 1 April 1970. For arguments against restricting broadcast advertising, see Rosden and Rosden, Law of Advertising, section 7, pp. 74–75.

39. Owen, *Economics.* See also G.T. Wuliger, "The Constitutional Rights of Puffery: Commercial Speech and the Cigarette Broadcast Advertising Ban," *Federal Communications Law Journal* 36, 1 (1983), pp. 1–25.

40. Cohen, "First Amendment," p. 67.

41. *Banzhaf* v. *FCC*, 405 F. 2d 1082 (D.C. Cir. 1968), p. 1097: "The power to protect the public health lies at the heart of the states' police power."

42. Ibid., p. 1098.

43. *United States* v. *O'Brien*, 391 U.S. 367 (1968), p. 377.

44. Weinberg, "Constitutional Protection," p. 747. See also Wuliger, "Puffery."

45. Lee Loevinger, "Free Speech in Advertising" (a paper presented at the 7th Annual Law and Public Affairs Conference of the American Advertising Federation; Washington, D.C., 8 December 1983), p. 16.

46. Ibid., p. 12 (quoting Justices Blackmun and Brennan in the *Hudson Gas & Electric* v. *Public Service Commission* case, 447 U.S. 557, 1980).

47. Dorothy Cohen, "Unfairness in Advertising Revisited," *Journal of Marketing*, 46 (Winter 1982), pp. 73–80. See also S.B. Foote and R.H. Mnookin, "The KidVid Crusade," *The Public Interest* 61 (Fall 1980), pp. 90–105, for a discussion of unfairness in connection with advertising to children.

48. 29 Fed. Reg. Rep. (2 July 1964), p. 8357. In fact, this trade regulation rule never went into effect because Congress enacted the Cigarette Labeling and Advertising Act of 1965.

49. S.A. Greyser, "Advertising: Attacks and Counters," *Harvard Business Review* (March–April 1972), p. 140.

50. *Assessment of Advertisements: Report on Stage Two of a Research Project Prepared for the Office of Fair Trading by the British Market Research Bureau Limited*, BMRB/CMD/87113 (London: September 1978), p. vi.

51. Foote and Mnookin, "KidVid Crusade," p. 98. See Cohen's "Unfairness in Advertising," p. 76, for a less restrictive interpretation of FTC power in the matter of unfairness, although she acknowledges its uncertain character at this time.

52. See, for example: Ruth Roemer, *Legislative Action to Combat the World Smoking Epidemic* (Geneva: World Health Organization, 1982); and Nigel Gray and Michael Daube, eds., *Guidelines for Smoking Control* (Geneva: International Union Against Cancer, 1980).

53. Gray and Daube, *Guidelines*, p. 113.

54. Ronnie Kirkwood, "Tobacco Advertising," in J.J.D. Bullmore and M.J. Waterson, eds., *The [U.K.] Advertising Association Handbook* (London-New York: Holt, Rinehart & Winston, 1983), pp. 309–315.

55. Gray and Daube, *Guidelines*, p. 107.

56. Ibid., pp. 109–111, emphasis added.

57. R.H. Miles, *Coffin Nails and Corporate Strategies* (Englewood Cliffs, N.J.:

Prentice-Hall, 1982), p. 85. A similar conclusion can be found in Jules Stuyck, "Tobacco Advertising Regulation in Belgium," *Journal of Consumer Policy* 6, 2 (1983), pp. 225–230, and in Wuliger, "Puffery," pp. 21–22.

58. Michael Blakeney and Shenagh Barnes, "Advertising Regulation in Australia: An Evaluation," *Adelaide Law Review* 8 (February 1982), pp. 30 and 40.

59. M.J. Waterson, "Report on Fifth World Conference on Smoking and Health; Winnipeg, Canada, 10–15 July 1983" (London: Advertising Information Group, 1983, AIG/83/35), p. 1.

60. Foote and Mnookin, "KidVid Crusade," p. 104, discussing advertising to children.

61. Roemer, *Legislative Action*, p. 24.

62. Gray and Daube, *Guidelines*, p. 117.

63. Waterson, "Conference on Smoking and Health," pp. 1–2.

64. Gray and Daube, *Guidelines*, p. 101. See Loevinger's fears expressed in WCBS TV, 9 FCC 2d, 921 (1967), p. 954.

65. M.J. Waterson, "The Crystal Ball: Advertising Under Attack in the 80s" (mimeograph; speech presented before the Australian Federation of Advertising, AFA Convention 1983), p. 31.

66. Foote and Mnookin, "KidVid Crusade," p. 104.

67. International Advertising Association, *Progress in Effective Advertising Self-Regulation* (New York, 1976), p. 31.

68. Roemer, *Legislative Action*, p. 34; Gray and Daube, *Guidelines*, p. 115.

69. Murray Edelman, *The Symbolic Uses of Politics* (Urbana, IL: University of Illinois Press, 1967).

70. Gideon Doron, "Administrative Regulation of an Industry: The Cigarette Case," *Public Administration Review* 39, 2 (March–April 1979), p. 168. See also Friedman, *Public Policy,* p. 161.

71. Roemer, *Legislative Action*, p. 26.

72. Ibid., p. 24. The U.S. Surgeon General, backed up by the Coalition on Smoking and Health, has recently issued a call for a "smoking-free society by the Year 2000" through education, boycotts, and lobbying for further restrictions on cigarette advertising. See "A 'Stop-smoking' Coalition Formed," *New York Times* (30 May 1984), p. C4.

73. Roemer, *Legislative Action*, p. 25.

74. Ibid.

75. For similar qualms about the regulation of advertising to children, see Foote and Mnookin, "KidVid Crusade."

Part V
Final Perspective

13
Politics and Meddlesome Preferences

James M. Buchanan

Each of us has a preferred pattern of behavior for others, whether they be members of our family, our neighbors, our professional peers, or our fellow citizens. I prefer that my neighbors control their children's noise making and disposal of their tricycles; I prefer that these neighbors refrain from rock music altogether, and that, if such "music" is to be played, the decibel level be kept low. I prefer that their backyard parties be arranged when I am out of town. I also prefer that my neighbors plant and maintain shrubs that flower in May for my own as well as their enjoyment.

I do not, however, exert much effort to enforce my own preferences on my neighbors' behavior. I trust largely to their own sense of fair play, common decency, and mutual respect. I do this because I know that my neighbors, also, have their own preferences about my behavior. They prefer that I control the barking of my dogs, and that, if dogs must bark, that this be allowed only in normal hours. The neighbors also prefer that I refrain from operating my chain saw or power mower early on Sunday mornings.

There is an implicit recognition by all parties here that, although each may have preferences over the others' behavior, any attempt to *impose* one person's preferences on the behavior of another must be predicted to set off reciprocal attempts to have one's own behavior constrained in a like fashion. An attitude of "live and let live," or mutual tolerance and mutual respect, may be better for all of us, despite the occasional deviance from ordinary standards of common decency.

Such an attitude would seem to be that of anyone who claimed to hold to democratic and individualistic values, in which each person's preferences are held to count equally with those of others. By contrast, the genuine elitist, who somehow thinks that his or her own preferences are "superior to," "better than" or "more correct," than those of others, will, of course, try to control the behavior of everyone else, while holding fast to his or her own liberty to do as he or she pleases.

Private Spaces

I commenced this chapter with reference to my own personal relationships with my neighbors. Each person could fill in his or her own bill of particulars that would be descriptive of his or her own set of "social interdependencies." The general point to be emphasized is that such "social interdependencies" are necessary elements of life in civil society and that such interdependencies cannot be eliminated even in the most idealized allocation and assignment of "individual rights" among separate persons. A somewhat different way of putting this point is to say that there are no self-evident "natural boundaries" that define the "private spaces" within which individuals may be allowed to behave as they wish without affecting the utility or satisfaction of other persons, whether negatively or positively. Robinson Crusoe on the island before Friday arrives is useful as an expository device precisely because such a setting of total social isolation can *never* be experienced by an individual in a society.

To say that social interdependencies must always be present is not to argue that the assignment of property rights to persons cannot be of great value in reducing the potential for conflict among persons. As Thomas Hobbes recognized, the definition of what is "mine and thine," combined with the coercive power of the state to enforce the boundary lines so drawn, allows individuals to get on with producing their own goods rather than fighting over goods that belong to no one. The point is that no matter how carefully drawn and detailed is the assignment of rights, there must remain some potential for conflict. The fact that my preferences extend to your behavior over activities that are well within your defined rights, and vice versa, insures that my satisfaction is influenced by the way that you behave and that your satisfaction is also affected by my behavior.

The extent, range, scope, intensity, and importance of the social interdependencies among persons depend on the characteristics of the setting. The hermit in the forest may approach the Crusoe extreme. The frontiersman who ventures to the trading post only once a year remains largely independent, behaviorally and socially. By contrast, the suburbanite who lives in the townhouse must affect and be affected by the behavior of neighbors, fellow commuters, fellow consumers in the shops, those from whom he or she purchases goods and services, fellow workers, and numerous other separate interacting groups. So long as his or her allowable activities are well-defined and enforced, the suburbanite coexists with others in the urbanized society without undue potential for overt conflict, retaining his or her preferences over the behavior of other persons in many of the roles that he or she confronts. But the suburbanite also proceeds to behave within his or her own well-defined and legally protected sphere of behavior on the presupposition that this sphere will be respected by others, that the set of rights he or she possesses will not be subject to invasion, either by other persons or by the collectivity as a unit. Civil order is described by each person "doing his own thing" within the limits of his assigned "private space," even when each person recognizes that some elements in his or her behavior will affect the satisfaction of other persons, and that, reciprocally, the behavior of others, again within their own "private spaces" will influence his or her own well-being.

The Emergence of Potential Conflict

A potential for conflict may emerge from any one of several sources. The social juxtaposition of persons from totally divergent cultures may destroy the behavioral reciprocity that normally characterizes stable civil order. (For example, the alleged behavior of Asian political refugees in eating dogs created major social tensions in long-established communities.) The explicit violation of established patterns of behavior for the sheer purpose of attracting attention may create antagonisms that were not previously recognized. (For example, the flaunting of manners, hairstyle, and dress in the 1960s, primarily by the young, opened up the generational conflict that remained present in the 1980s.) An increase in moral fervor accompanied by conversion to life-styles that are dictated by a "new religion" may make tolerance for contrasting life-styles more difficult to accept.

My concern here is not with these, or other, possible sources of potential conflict among persons, families, and communities in the areas of social interdependencies. From the fact that we do have preferences about the behavior patterns of others, there is always a latent potential for conflict. And, as with other preferences, the attempted expression of these will depend on the relative prices required for their satisfaction. I shall suggest later that the relative prices of satisfying our preferences over the behavior of others are dramatically reduced, in an apparent sense, by the overt *politicization* of social interdependency. Before exploring this process more fully, it will be useful to examine nonpolitical means of adjusting to potential conflicts in areas of social interdependence.

Conflict Resolution Through Voluntary Adjustment

Because each of us has preferences over the behavior of others in many separate social interdependencies, there remains always a potential for conflict. There is no guarantee that tolerable levels of mutual adjustment in behavior will be acceptable to all parties in an interaction. It may well be necessary to initiate or to undertake actions aimed at a voluntary resolution of the potential conflict. I may feel intensely negative toward the life-style of my neighbor, a life-style that does not allow me to invoke the laws of nuisance. If my preferences about his or her behavior patterns are so important to me as to suggest initiation of action on my part, there are several avenues open. I may make some effort to bribe or compensate my neighbor to modify his or her behavior in ways more pleasing to me. (To economists, this would be the avenue suggested by the Coase theorem. To noneconomists, this would perhaps seem one of the least plausible approaches to the problem.[1]) Or I may take actions that will reduce the spillover harms that the behavior exerts on me: I may install sound barriers, for example, to keep out the sound of rock music. As an ultimate step, I may consider shifting my location to a new set of neighbors, and, indeed, this potential for residential, locational, occupational, professional, purchasing, selling mobility is one of the most attractive features of the American society by comparison with those of other more rigid structures. The mere existence of effective alternatives, even if I never choose to exercise the exit option, insures that there are relevant thresholds of spillover effects that cannot readily be crossed. These thresholds are important for each of us, and their existence surely helps make life in society tolerable.

The point to be emphasized about each and every one of these voluntary adjustments to potential conflict among interacting persons and groups is that the satisfaction of preferences over others' behavior within their legal rights is *costly*. That is to say, if my neighbor does not act in accordance with my preferences, I can either compensate him or her, build protection against the damage, or move. Each of these activities involves costs to me, and this cost will insure that my interest in my neighbor's behavior is important enough to make the outlay worthwhile. There is a great difference between being merely irritated at the behavior patterns of my slovenly neighbor and actually paying him or her to "clean up his act." My "meddlesome preferences," to use Amartya Sen's expression, can be satisfied only at a positive opportunity cost.[2]

Conflict Resolution Through Politics

There is no such rough matching of costs and benefits when the resolution of conflicts in social interdependence is approached through political mechanisms. If my neighbor's behavior irritates me, but not sufficiently to make it worthwhile to seek voluntary resolution, I may still be quite pleased if the town council will pass a regulation outlawing the behavior in question. It will cost me little or nothing to vote for the prospective councilman who will promise to outlaw leaf burning on the lawn; I may gain perhaps a few cents worth of utility on one or two autumn afternoons by imposing, through politics, my preferences on the actions of my neighbor. The costly steps that might be required in the absence of political institutions seem to be avoided. It seems that I can impose my own preferences on others at relatively low prices.

The cost saving here is only apparent, however. If I can resort to politics to impose my own preferences on the behavior of others, even if these preferences are not highly valued intrinsically, then it would seem that other persons, in working democratic process, can do the same to me. I may find that the political process is double-edged. If it can be used to my advantage in imposing my personal preferences over the behavior of other persons, it can be used to my disadvantage in imposing the preferences of others on my own behavior. I may gain a few pennies worth of utility by the regulation against leaf burning, but find that possessing a handgun in my house is politically prohibited. And it may happen that I very strongly value the liberty to possess a handgun. The political process, which is allegedly open equally to all citizens, is evenhanded here. It generates a few pennies worth of utility to me in restricting my neighbor's leaf burning; it generates a few pennies worth of utility to my neighbor by outlawing the possession of handguns. But, in so doing, it imposes many dollars worth of loss on me through preventing my possession of a handgun, and imposes many dollars' worth of damage on my neighbor who highly values the liberty of burning his or her own autumn leaves.[3]

The Partitioning of Political Issues

The central thrust of my argument should be clear. The majoritarian institutions of modern democratic politics are exceedingly dangerous weapons to call upon in any attempts to reduce conflicts in areas of social interdependence. They are dangerous precisely because the institutions are democratic and open to all citizens on equal terms: what is sauce for the goose is sauce for the gander. Unless the person who calls upon politics can insure that he or she retains some monopoly of political power, his or her own preferences are as likely to be imposed upon as imposed.

This danger inherent in democratic institutions tends to be overlooked because political decisions are partitioned so that each potential conflict is handled separately and one at a time. The interdependencies among the separated political decisions tend to be obscured and overlooked, with the result that it is quite possible that *all* persons will be placed in positions less desired than those which would be present in the total absence of politicization.

This central point may be illustrated by concrete examples, all of which have been at least partially politicized at one level of government or another in recent years in the United States or in other Western countries. Consider the following politically orchestrated regulations:

1. Prohibition on private leaf burning.
2. Prohibition of the possession of handguns.

3. Prohibition of the sale or use of alcoholic beverages.

4. Prohibition of smoking in public places or places of business.

5. Prohibition on driving or riding in an automobile without fastening seat belts.

6. Prohibition on driving or riding on a motorcycle without wearing crash helmets.

The listing here could be expanded greatly if we should add activities that some persons or groups have advanced as candidates for politicization. The six activities listed are, however, sufficient for my purposes here, and these are all familiar examples.

It seems quite possible that, at least in some political jurisdictions, a majority of voters might be found to support each and every one of the six activities listed. As noted earlier, however, the critical weakness in ordinary majoritarian procedures is that the intensities of preference are not taken into account. A bare majority of voters may support the prohibition on handgun possession, but a small minority may value highly the liberty to own handguns. The same result may hold for each of these activities. Yet, because the issues can be isolated and considered one at a time for political action, all of the regulations listed might secure majority support. But the handgun owners may find their loss of liberty much more valuable than the very mild feelings of benefits they secure from having the other activities prohibited. The same thing may hold for those who value intensely the liberty of drinking or smoking. The political process may well work so as to make each and every person in the relevant community worse off with enactment and enforcement of all of the prohibitions listed than he or she would be if none of the prohibitions were enacted.

There is a message in my argument here. Let those who would use the political process to impose their preferences on the behavior of others be wary of the threat to their own liberties, as described in the possible components of their own behavior that may also be subjected to control and regulation. The apparent costlessness of restricting the liberties of others through politics is deceptive. The liberties of some cannot readily be restricted without limiting the liberties of all.

The "Scientistic" Mentality

Critics of my argument here can charge that I have discussed the dangers of using the political process to impose one set of private and personal preferences over the behavior of others as if these preferences were mere whims, analogous to my dislike of the hairstyles of the youth of the 1960s. These critics might suggest, with respect to the set of activities listed above, and others, that the sumptuary prohibitions or regulations need not reflect purely private preferences. These prohibitions and regulations, existing or proposed, may be based on "scientific grounds." These critics might allege that leaf burning releases dangerous elements in the atmosphere; that handguns kill people; that alcohol is addictive and a causal factor in disease; that smoking is dangerous to health; and that seat belts and crash helmets save lives.

These arguments are highly deceiving in that they attempt to introduce, under the varying guises of "science," an objective value standard, one that "should" be imposed on all persons. Strictly interpreted, of course, almost any activity each of us undertakes is, in some way or another, a possible risk to our health. Once this is recognized, the question is one of drawing lines, and there is no well-defined set of activities that fall into one category or the other.

Towards a Sumptuary Constitution

We have been caught up in a wave of politicization for several decades. As a result, the set of activities that have been subjected to governmental-bureaucratic prohibition, regulation, and control has been expanded dramatically. Once politics was discovered as the apparent low-cost means of imposing preferences on behavior, a Pandora's box was opened that shows no signs of closing itself.

In these as in other aspects of the relationship between the citizens and the government, the dangers of excessive politicization cannot be avoided merely by a change in the makeup of political parties or by a change of politicians. In democracy, politicians respond to the electorates, and electoral majorities may, in a piecemeal fashion, close off one liberty after another. Prediction of such a prospect suggests that genuine reform can come only by *constitutional* rules that will prevent ordinary democratic majorities, in the electorates or in legislative assemblies, from entering too readily into the sumptuary areas of activities. Until and unless we recognize that politics, too, must operate within constitutional limits, each of our liberties, whether valued highly or slightly, is up for grabs.

Notes

1. See R.H. Coase, "The Problem of Social Cost," *Journal of Law and Economics* (October 1960), 1–44. Briefly stated, the Coase theorem is that efficient outcomes of interactions will emerge so long as persons are free to enter into voluntary contractual agreement. In the example, if I place a higher negative value on silence than the positive value that my neighbor places on rock music, I can successfully bribe

342 · *Smoking and Society*

him or her. Perhaps only to economists would this explicit approach to mutual adjustment seem plausibly meaningful. Indirect exchanges, in behavioral rather than monetary dimensions, would be normal in many settings.

2. See Amartya K. Sen, "The Impossibility of a Paretian Liberal," *Journal of Political Economy* 78 (1970), 152–157.

3. For a more technical discussion of the potential externalities of political process, see my paper, "Politics, Policy, and the Pigovian Margins," *Economica* 29 (February 1962), 17–28.

14
Concluding Remarks

Robert D. Tollison

A conclusion is a place for reckoning. After reading the separate chapters, the reader will have some judgment about the whole versus the sum of the parts. As editor, I naturally incline to the view that the whole is greater than the sum of the parts and that the volume has this impact because tobacco smoking, particularly cigarettes, is not an isolated issue that is somehow different from the other issues that swirl around us in these modern times. The lessons that we can learn from the study of the smoking issue carry over to the broad social and scientific plane in which we live. I shall return to this theme after enunciating some of the more prominent lessons to be drawn from the preceding chapters. Through restraint I have held my list to ten.

1. The scientific case with respect to the causes and effects of smoking is *not* established. Far from it. Rather, much work remains to be done to understand why people smoke and the possible effects of smoking on those who choose to smoke (Eysenck, Spielberger).

2. Although environmental tobacco smoke may be annoying to some nonsmokers, there is no substantial scientific evidence to support the view that it presents a significant health hazard to nonsmokers. Indeed, it is conceivable that reported adverse reactions to environmental tobacco smoke are psychosocial in origin (Aviado).

3. Smoking produces certain benefits in a social setting which are historically conditioned and ill-understood. The relationship between smoking and productivity on the job, for example, cannot be dismissed lightly (Feinhandler).

4. Smoking behavior poses intriguing questions of social interaction. When analyzed from the perspective of philosophy and basic rights, the smoking issue yields to the result that there is not much of a case for restraints on public smoking, properly practiced, with courtesy (Den Uyl).

5. The antismoking movement has spawned interest groups, both in and out of government, to push its cause. As with all interest groups, self-interest is never very far from the surface in animating their activities (Berger, Shughart and Tollison).

6. In the jargon of modern economics, smoking does not represent a market failure. Rather, there are ample incentives among actors in the private marketplace to evolve institutions that make the peaceful and profitable coexistence of smokers and nonsmokers possible. There is no case for further government intervention in this area (Littlechild).

7. The contribution of the tobacco industry in terms of jobs, income, and taxes to economies around the world is substantial. Moreover, the employment of resources in the tobacco sector is revealed to be preferred by consumers to alternative uses of these resources. Tobacco products are what consumers want, and to further restrict production in this area is to make an economy worse off (Gray and Walter).

8. Taxation of tobacco products is one of the most regressive and unfair means of raising revenue by a government. These taxes are primarily paid by low-income consumers, and they retard employment and production in the tobacco industry and impose sizable efficiency loss on the economy (Savarese and Shughart).

9. The advertising of tobacco products is mostly about the competition of tobacco companies for the business of *existing* smokers. There is no hard, quantitative evidence that advertising alters the total amount of cigarettes sold (Boddewyn).

10. Everyone finds certain activities of others bothersome. If we regulated all the things that anyone found bothersome, the world would be full of regulations, and we would all be worse off as a result (Buchanan).

My list represents the more specific implications that flow from the analyses in this book. I could have easily come up with a larger list, and I stop here only for the sake of brevity. Returning to my earlier theme, however, there are some additional general implications of this work which should not go unnoted.

If the whole of the volume is greater than the sum of its parts, it is for this reason: we carry forth from the opposite side of a complicated and controversial issue. If we have done our job well, the reader will no doubt pause to reflect that the world is no longer as simple as the other side would have it. Why should we acquiesce to more taxation, more regulation, more control over our lives, more politicized science, more abuse of a productive sector of our economies, and so on, without a careful consideration of the consequences? It is time to stop, look, and listen, and to see if, through reason and science we can come to grips with saner and more polite attitudes and policies toward the role of smoking in society.

More than this, suppose a hypothetical case: suppose that the antismoking forces carry the day. Suppose that smoking is abolished from the face of the earth. What then? Does anyone really think that these people will stop there? The menu of behavior that they could attack is large, and the prospect of their attack is real and frightening. Our freedom to act and do as we please so long as others do not pay for any of the consequences of our behavior is clearly at stake in this debate. Smoking is but the tip of the iceberg; many other crusades wait in the wings. Down this road lies not an overregulated society, but a totally regulated society.

Thus, both smokers and nonsmokers should be alert to what the antismoking crusade represents: nothing more and nothing less than an assault on individual liberty. It is time to draw the line somewhere; we draw it at smoking and urge others to see the reason in our defense.

Author Index

Italic numbers refer to pages of reference entries.

Abrams, M., 25, *71*
Abramson, J.H., 25, 26, *70*
Abran, N., 144, 160 n.31
Abse, D.W., 55, 57, *70*
Ader, R., 64, 68, *70, 72, 73*
Adesso, V.J., 168, *186*
Albano, W., 52, *80*
Albert, S., 51, *71*
Allen, R.G., *74*
Allen, R.J., 144, 159 n.27
Almond, J.W., 67, *71*
Altmann, H., 144, 159 n.23
Anderson, A.E., 31, *85*
Anderson, D.E., 51, *71*
Anderson, G., 142, 158 n.5
Anerbach, O., 31, *87*
Angerer, J., 144, 160 n.37
Anisman, H., 62, 63, 66, 67, *84*
Antognoni, G., 163 n.87
Aranson, P.H., 213 n.28
Armitage, A.K., 92, *128*
Arnet, D.B., 151, 162 n.84
Aronow, W.S., 142, 145–146, 159 n.18,
    160 nn.43, 44, 163 n.90
Asher, J.J., 63, *71*
Astrup, P., 142, 158 n.9
Atkinson, A.B., 280, *284*
Aviado, D.M., 7–8, 163 n.101, 164 n.104,
    165 n.128, 279, 343, *347*
Avis, N., 96, *130*

Baars, A., 163 n.92
Badre, R., 144, 160 n.31
Bahnson, C.B., 54, 59–60, 63, *71*
Bahnson, M.B., 54, 59–60, 63, *71*
Baker, A., 17, *84*
Balckwelder, W.C., 45, *82*
Ballard, G.P., 17, *84*
Ballenger, J.C., 66, *82*
Bammer, K., 62, 63, *71*
Banks, M.H., 96, *129*
Barchas, J.D., 67, *71*
Barclay, W., 175
Barefoot, J.C., 61, *71, 86*
Barnes, S., 332 n.58
Barrahee, E.C., 61, *80*
Bastiaans, J., 58, 59, 69, *76*
Bauer, F.W., 26, 27, *71*

Bauman, J., 66, *86*
Beadenkopf, W.G., 25, *71*
Beardsmore, C.S., 161 n.69
Beaucent, C., 144, 159 n.22
Beck, G.J., 149, 162 nn.74, 85
Beck, I., 30, *83*
Becker, C.G., 147, 161 nn.54, 55, 56
Becker, V., 77
Beckford, V., 66, *78*
Belcher, J.R., 35, *71*
Belsky, J., 45, *80*
Bendien, J., 61, *71*
Berch, V., 89
Berger, B., 239 n.3
Berger, P.L., 9–10, 239 n.3, 344, *347*
Bergler, R., 329 n.21
Berkson, J., 18, *71*
Berndt, H., 55, 56, *71*
Best, J.A., 112, 113, *129*, 168, *186*
Betoret, J.L.D., 162 n.72
Bewley, B.R., 96, *129*
Bishop, M.M., 150, 162 n.79
Black, L., 52, *80*
Blackmore, M., *81*
Blakeney, M., 332 n.58
Bland, J.M., 96, *129*
Bloch, S., 99, 100, *129*
Block, W., 213 n.29
Blöhmke, M., 57, *71*
Bloom, B.L., 63, *71*
Blumberg, E.M., 57, *71*
Blumenthal, J.A., 61, *71*
Boddewyn, J.J., 13, 329 n.6, 344, *347*
Bohnke, H., 142, 158 n.7
Bohus, B., 65, *72*
Bolin, J.F., 142, 159 n.17
Bolles, R.C., 68, *72*
Bonami, M., 61, *83*
Borland, B.L., 96, *129*
Borysenko, J., 62, *72*
Borysenko, U., 62, *72*
Bosse, R., 95, *129*
Bouhuys, A., 149, 162 nn.74, 85
Bourdin, M., 144, 160 n.31
Bovbjerg, D., 64, *72, 73*
Boyer, B., 149, 162 n.77
Boyko, E.P., 168, *186*
Brackenridge, C.J., 99, 100, *129*

Brady, J.P., 67, *81*
Brebner, J., *85*
Breidenbach, S.T., 165 n.124
Breier, C., 67, *72*
Breslow, N., 35, *84*
Briggs, R.L., 25, *72*
Bristow, O.V., *73*
Britton, D.R., 65, *72*
Britton, K.T., 65, *72*
Britton, M., 25, 26, *72*
Broadhurst, P.L., 67, *76*
Broll, T., 62, *74*
Brown, E., 142, 148, 159 n.16
Brown, F., *55*, *72*
Brown, R.S., *55*, 57, *70*
Brownlee, K.A., 24, *72*
Brygoo-Butor, F., 144, 159 n.22
Buchanan, J.M., 13, 285, 305 nn.2, 6,
    306, 324, 344, 347
Bullmore, J.J.D., 331 n.54
Burch, H., 24
Burch, P.R.J., 18, 23–25, 29–33, 35, 36,
    38, 39, 42–44, 47, 48, 51, *72*, *73*
Burg, W.R., 144, 160 n.33
Burke, M.H., 31, *86*
Burrows, B., 149, 162 n.77
Butler, J., *73*
Buxton, M., 66, *74*
Buxton, W.D., *55*, 57, *70*
Bylin, G., 163 n.96

Cabana, E., 25, 26, *70*
Cairns, J., 52, *73*
Califano, J., 18–19, 237
Camacho, E.J., 162 n.72
Cameron, H.M., 25–26, *73*
Cameron, M., 26–27, *73*
Cameron, P., 148, 161 n.60
Carpenter, T.B., 64, *83*
Castle, R.C., *55*, 57, *70*
Cederlof, R., 31, 45, 51, 52, *73*, *78*
Chan, W.C., 35, *73*, 164 n.113
Chapman, V.D., 31, *78*
Chappell, S.B., 144, 159 nn.21, 28
Charles, E., 63, *78*
Chenery, H.B., 268 n.18
Cherry, N., 102, *129*
Chesher, G.B., 67, *73*
Chesney, M., 61, *83*
Chiarelli, B., 52, *74*
Child, M., 51, *71*
Chiplin, B., 314, 329 n.17
Cho, D., 66, *86*
Choi, N.W., 20, *73*
Christie, M.J., 67, *73*
Cinader, B., 51, *73*
Ciofetta, G., 163 n.87

Cirscione, S., 163 n.87
Clark, R., 168, *186*
Clarke, C.M., 64, *83*
Clarke, J., 25–26, *73*
Clausen, J.A., 96, *129*
Cleary, P.D., 90, 96, *130*, 182, *186*
Coan, R.W., 95, *129*
Coase, R.H., 277, *284*, 338, 341 n.1
Cobb, S., 61, *80*
Coburn, R.F., 144, 159 n.24
Cocorozis, T., 162 n.73
Cohen, B.H., 51, 60–61, *73*, *85*
Cohen, D., 330 n.26, 331 n.47
Cohen, J.B., 45, *80*
Cohen, N., 64, 68, *70*, *72*, *73*
Cohen, S., *73*
Colbourne, M.J., 35, *73*
Cole, P.V., 142, 148, 159 n.16
Collaron, T., *82*
Collector, M.I., 67, *80*
Colley, J.R.T., 149, 161 nn.61, 66, 67
Collins, R., 163 n.98
Colomer, P.R., 162 n.72
Colvell, L., 25, 41–42, *83*
Commins, B.T., 142, 158 n.8
Concannon, J.T., 65, *73*
Conteno, F., 52, *74*
Convertino, Fra., 175
Cooper, C.L., 62, *74*
Coppen, A., 56, *74*
Corkhill, R., 149, 161 nn.66, 67
Cornet, A., 144, *159*
Correa, P., 154, 164 n.116
Corti, E.C., 175, *186*
Costa, P.T., 62, *84*, 95, 99, *129*
Courts, F.A., 96, *130*
Coyne, L., *55*, 57, *74*
Crabbe, J.C., *74*
Crain, W.M., 305 n.2, *306*
Crane, R.S., 89, 96, 103, *131*
Creswell, W.H., 96, *130*
Cuddebach, J.E., 144, 160 n.33
Curtis, G.C., 66, *74*

Dackis, C.A., 67, *74*
da Costa, J., 35, *80*
Dahl, C.J., 35, *84*
Dahlstrom, W.B., 61, *71*
Dahms, T.E., 142, 159 n.17
Dales, L.G., 40, *76*
Dalhamm, T., 142, 158 n.5
Dallman, M.F., 66, *82*
Daoud, A., 25, *71*
Dattore, P.J., *55*, 57, *74*
Daube, M., 331 nn.52, 53, 55, 56, 332 n. 64
Davies, D.G., 290, 295, *306*
Davis, N., 62, *76*

Day, N.E., 35, *80*
Day, S.B., 62, *85*
Dean, J.R., 96, *129*
Deaton, T., 305 n.2, *306*
DeChambre, R.F., 62, *74*
de Cupertino, D., *175*
de Jong, U.W., *84*
dc Jong, W., 35, 66, *74*
de Kloet, E.R., *65, 72*
Demars, J.P., 55, 57, *70*
Dencker, S.J., 52, *76*
Den Uyl, D.J., 8–9, 317, 324, 343, 348
Deser, 29
DeVore, P.C., 330 n.32
de Wied, D., *65*, 66, *74*
Diamond, E.L., 51, *73*
Dickson, S.A., 170, 175, *186*
Dijl, H., *74*
Dimich, H., 164 n.107
Dluhy, R.G., 66, *85*
Dodge, R., 149, 162 n.77
Doering, C.R., 17, *80*
Dohrenwend, B.P., 62, *74*
Dohrenwend, B.S., 62, *74*
Dolgoff, S., 17, *84*
Doll, R., 18, 31, 36, 37, 47–48, *74, 81*
Donovan, J.R., 144, 160 n.33
Dorman, N., 182, *186*
Doron, G., 332 n.70
Douglas, M., 178, *186*
Downham, M.A.P.S., 161 n.64
Drugan, R.C., 67, *80*
Dubin, T., 147, 161 nn.54, 55, 56
Dublin, W.B., 144, 159 n.25
Duckitt, J., 62, *74*
Dudek, B.C., 67, *78, 84*
Due, J.F., *306*
Duffy, C.P., 162 n.81
Dumas, C., 144, 160 n.31
Dunbar, F., 61, *74*
Dunning, J.H., 314, 329
Duszynski, K.R., 60, *85*
Dyck, D.G., 66, *76*

Edelman, M., 332 n.69
Effenberger, E., 138, 142, 158 n.2
Ekwo, E.E., 149, 161 n.62
Eleftherliow, B.E., *86*
Eliot, R.S., 62, *74*
Ellis, C., 149, 162 n.77
Ellis, F.W., 57, *71*
Elveback, L., 18, *71*
Englehardt, B., 57, *71*
Enstrom, J.E., 42, *75*
Eppinger, H., 61, *75*
Eriksson, A., *65, 81*
Ernster, V.L., 63, *75*

Erotokristow, A., *82*
Evans, K.A., 51, *84*
Evans, R.I., 89, 90, 97, *129*
Eyer, J., 62, *85*
Eysenck, H.J., 6, 7, 21, 25, 37, 40, 43,
  49, 52, 53, 55, 56, 57, 59–65, 67, *75,*
  79, 89–92, 96, 99, 100–102, 111, 127,
  129, 130, 279, 324, 343, 348
Eysenck, M.W., 53, 57, *75*
Eysenck, S.B.G., 99, 100, 111, *129, 130*

Fain, P.R., 52, *80*
Faine, D., 51, *75*
Fanger, O., 162 n.80
Fanselow, M.S., 68, *72*
Fehm, H.L., 66, *75*
Feinberg, J., 193, 194, 205, 211 n.3, 213 n.21
Feingold, J., 51, *75*
Feinhandler, S.J., 8, 89–90, 157, 164 n.123,
  168, 172, 181, 182, *186,* 320, 322,
  343, 348
Feinstein, A.R., 27–29, *75, 87*
Fendt, R., Jr., 251, 268 n.19
Ferguson, J.M., 328 nn.1, 3
Ferris, B.G., Jr., 162 n.81
Ferris, G., 150, 162 n.79
Fetherstone, P., 277–278, *284*
Fields, H.L., 66, *84*
First, M.W., 152, 163 n.93
Fischer, T., 144, 160 nn.32, 38, 39
Fisher, R.A., 18, 25, 37, 49, 52, *75, 76*
Fitsmaurice, M.A., 62, *83*
Flannery, G.R., 64, *86*
Floderus, B., 61, *76*, 99
Flowers, M.R., 285, 305 nn.2, 6, *306*
Fonthain, E., 154, 164 n.116
Foote, S.B., 325, 331 nn.47, 51, 332 nn.60,
  66, *75*
Forster, R.E., 144, 159 n.24
Fortmarker, S.L., 163 n.86
Fountain, L.H., 163 n.103
Fox, B.H., 62, 63, 65, *76*
Fox, S., 60, *82*
Frahm, B., 163 n.92
Frankenhaeuser, M., 62, *76*
Franklin, R.V., 67, *76*
Frederickson, M., *81*
Freedman, A., 153, 163 n.102
Freis, E.D., 26, *77*
Frentzel-Beyme, R., *77*
Friberg, L., 31, 45, 51, 52, *73, 76, 78*
Friedlaender, A.F., 295, *306*
Friedman, G.D., 40, *76*
Friedman, M., 289–290, *306*
Frith, C.D., 111–114, 116, *130*
Froeb, H.F., 144, 153, *160,* 204, 213 n.17
Frye, R.L., 48, *86*

Fulker, D.W., 52, 61, 75, 76
Fung, S.C., 35, 73, 164 n.113

Gafforio Van Ree, J.M., 66, 74
Galabmos, E., 162 n.71
Galen, 53
Galgoczy, G., 162 n.71
Galuskinova, V., 163 n.91
Gantte, N.D., 74
Garcia, J., 64, 76
Gardner, J.W., 42, 80
Gardner, P.S., 161 n.64
Garfinkel, L., 47, 77, 154, 164 n.115
Gaston, L.P., 156
Geostl, B., 31, 87
Gerhardt, P.R., 17, 79
Gertler, M.G., 51, 76
Giammona, S.T., 96, 132
Gillham, B., 66, 78
Ginorio, A.B., 168, 172, 187
Glad, W., 168, 186
Gleich, G.J., 148, 161 n.58
Godber, G., 237
Gold, M.S., 67, 74
Goldstein, H., 17, 79
Gono, E., 142, 159 n.14
Gordon, T., 45, 78
Goulis, K., 82
Graham, E.A., 17, 87
Grandjean, E., 144, 160 n.32
Graves, C.G., 51, 73
Gray, H.P., 10–11, 344, 348–349
Gray, J., 62, 76
Gray, N., 331 nn.52, 53, 55, 56, 332 n.64
Green, D., 93–96, 109, 110, 112, 113, 130
Green, N., 64, 73
Greenberg, A.H., 66, 76
Greene, W.A., 63, 76
Greenstein, B.D., 66, 78
Greenstreet, R.L., 60, 85
Greer, S., 56, 57, 76, 81
Gregory, P.R., 268 n.9
Greyser, S.A., 331 n.49
Grimmer, G., 142, 158 n.7
Groen, J., 61, 71
Grossarth-Maticek, R., 58, 59, 66, 69, 76, 77
Grossen, N.E., 68, 77
Grotoerton, A., 82
Grown, B.S., 142, 158 n.10
Grünewald, A., 144, 159 n.22
Gruver, R.H., 26, 77
Grylls, D.G., 100, 131
Guberan, E., 48–49, 77
Guillerm, R., 144, 160 n.31
Gullen, W.H., 20, 73
Gunther, H., 55, 71

Gupta, A.K., 100, 130
Gupta, S.C., 100, 130
Gurpegui, M., 67, 74
Guyton, R.S., 142, 158 n.10

Haenszel, W., 154, 164 n.116
Hager, J.L., 68, 84
Hagnell, O., 56, 77
Hakstian, A.R., 112, 113, 129, 168, 186
Halberstam, M., 164 n.122
Hall, G.N., 92, 128
Hallowell, C., 162 n.80
Hamilton, P.J.S., 25, 41–42, 83
Hammond, E.C., 18, 20, 47, 48, 77
Hamtoft, H., 52, 77
Hankins, W.G., 64, 76
Harford, T.C., 182, 186
Harke, H.P., 142–144, 158 n.7, 159 nn.15, 20, 160 n.37, 163 n.92
Harmsen, H., 138, 142, 158 n.2
Harris, C.C., 51–52, 77
Harris, D.H., 145–146, 160 n.42
Hartveit, F., 26, 27, 77
Harvald, B., 51, 52, 77
Hauge, M., 51, 52, 77
Hawkins, L., 142, 158 n.9
Hayashi, T., 45, 82, 85
Haynes, L., 162 n.73
Healy, J.D., 330 n.32
Heasman, M.A., 26, 27, 78
Heathcote, J., 67, 78
Heller, W.D., 164 n.112
Hemistra, N.W., 165 n.124
Henderson, A.H., 35, 89, 90, 97, 129
Herrera, L., 18, 80
Herrold, 36
Hertz, M., 144, 159 n.26
Heston, 52
Higgenbottam, 37
Higginson, 18
Hill, A.B., 18, 47, 74
Hill, P.C., 89, 90, 97, 129
Hinde, 68
Hinds, W.C., 152, 163 n.93
Hirayama, T., 21, 153–155, 164 nn.108, 110
Hjermann, 41
Ho, H.C., 35, 73
Ho, J.H.C., 155, 164 n.119
Hobbes, T., 189, 336
Hoffman, D.T., 168, 186
Holcombe, R., 305 n.2, 306
Holland, W.W., 149, 161 nn.66, 67
Holma, B., 162 n.70
Holme, M.C., 66, 78
Hoogeveen-Scroot, H.C.A., 149, 162 n.75
Hor, M.B., 164 n.120

Horn, D.H., 18, 77, 93–96, 109, 110, 112, 113, *130*
Horne, R.L., 53, 63, *78*
Horrabin, D.F., 21, *84*
Horwitz, G.P., 67, *78*
Houston, J.P., 100, *130, 131*
Hrubec, Z., 45, 51, 73, *78*
Huffman, W., 96, *130*
Hugdahl, K., 65, *81*
Hugod, C., 142, 158 n.9
Hui, S.L., 149, 162 nn.74, 85
Huntley, W.H., 149, 161 n.62
Hurshman, L.G., 142, 158 n.10
Hyson, R.L., 67, *80*

Ikard, F.F., 92–96, 109, 110, 112, 113, 121, *130*
Iker, H.D., 66, *87*
Ill, T.K., 48, *86*
Imparato, B., 145–146, 160 n.42
Imperato, C., 163 n.87
Insel, T.R., 66, *78*
Irwig, L.M., 149, 161 n.66
Isbell, M.W., 145–146, 160 nn.42, 43

Jackson, L.G., 52, *78*
Jacobs, F.H., 163 n.86
Jacobs, G.A., 89, 96, 100, 101, 103, *131*
Jacobs, M.A., 99, *130*
Jacobs, T.J., 63, *78*
Jacquet, Y.F., 65, *78*
James, B., 66, *86*
James I of England, 156, 173, 175, 176
Jamison, R.N., 99, 100, *130*
Jarvis, M., 31, *85*
Jefferson, T., 191, 192, 198
Jemmott, J.B., 66, *78*
Jensen, J., 62, *79*
Jolles, J., 65, *74*
Jones, J.C., 31, *78*
Jones, M.T., 66, *78*
Jones, R., *81*
Joneson, E., 52, *76*
Joseph, M.S., 66, *82*

Kabat, G.C., 154–155, 164 n.177
Kagan, A., 27, 45, *78, 80, 82, 85, 87*
Kahn, H.A., 20, *78*
Kain, H., 67, *72*
Kalandidi, A., 154, 164 nn.109, 111
Kalin, N.H., 66, *78*
Kanasir, D.T., 58, 59, 69, *76, 77*
Kane, P.B., 144, 159 n.24
Karaiossefidis, K., *82*
Karl, V.C., 20, *81*
Kasl, S.V., 62, *78*
Kato, H., 45, *80, 85, 87*

Katsuki, S., 27, *78*
Katz, L., 18, *78*
Kay, L., 52, *76*
Kearns, W., 89
Keehn, R., 45, *85*
Kelepouris, M., 60, *82*
Kelley, M.J., 68, *77*
Kellner, M., 239 n.3
Kelly, M., 65
Kern, W.H., 31, *78*
Kerpe, S., 30, *83*
Kerrebijn, K.F., 149, 162 n.75
Kessler, I.I., 21, *78*
Keys, A., 46, *78*
Kiernan, K.E., 102, *129*
Kilduff, M., 212 n.15
Kirchoff, H., 29, *82*
Kirkwood, R., 331 n.54
Kirschner, L.G., 55, 57, *70*
Kissen, D.M., 54–57, 59, 60, *79*
Klein, E., 66, *75*
Klein Walker, D., 163 n.86
Klosterkötter, W., 142, 159 n.14
Knudson, A.G., 52, *79*
Knudson, R., 151, 162 n.84
Kobayashi, D.M., 164 n.107
Koch, 37
Koeppe, P., 38, *79*
Kohl, F., 52, *79*
Kolin, E.K., *132*
Kollar, K., 162 n.71
Kong, Y., 61, *71*
Konzett, H., 67, *72*
Koo, L.C., 155, 164 n.119
Koob, G.F., 65, *72*
Kopp, M.S., *79*
Koranyi, L., *79*
Kossova, D., 162 n.73
Kouri, R.E., *79*
Kreiss, O., 51, *73*
Kroumal, R.A., 48, *86*

Lachenbruch, P.A., 149, 161 n.62
Lambin, J.J., 313, 328 n.4, 329 n.14
Landers, A., 137
Laoye, J.A., 96, *130*
Laufer, B., 175, *186*
Law, C.H., 35, *80*
Lawlis, G.F., *73*
Lawther, J., 142, 158 n.8
Lebovitz, B.Z., 61, *81*
Lebowitz, M.D., 151, 153, 162 n.84, 163 n.103
Lee, J.R., 195–196, 212 n.7
Lee, K., 45, *85*
Leeder, S.R., 149, 161 nn.66, 67
Lehrer, S.B., 161 n.59

Leijonhufvud, A., 268 n.10
Lenfant, C., 153, 163 n.100
Leontief, W., 268 n.12
LeShan, L.C., 54, 63, 79
Lester, A., 330 n.25
Letai, A.D., 149, 162 nn.74, 85
Letz, R., 162 n.81
Leu, R.E., 274, 280, *284*
Leventhal, H., 90, 96, *130*, 182, *186*
Levi, R.N., 60, 79
Levin, M.I., 17, 79
Levitt, E.E., 329 n.22
Levy, D.A., 51, 73
Lichtenstein, E., 182, *186*
Lilienfeld, A.M., 51, *85*
Lin, Y., 154, 164 n.116
Lindhardt, M., 52, 77
Linn, B.S., 62, 79
Linn, M.W., 62, 79
Lippman, D., 66, 74
Lipworth, L., 26, 27, 78
Littlechild, S.C., 11–12, 272, *284*, 344, 349
Litwin, S.D., 52, 79
Liu, B.M., 153, 163 n.100
Locke, J., 191, 198
Locke, S.E., 62, 66, *78, 79*
Loeb, M., 330 n.36
Loevinger, L., 321–322, 331 n.45
LoLordo, V.M., 68, 79
Lombard, H.I., 17, *80*
Lombard, H.L., 63, *80*
Lowrey, A.H., 164 n.118
Luckman, T., 239 n.3
Lundman, T., 31, 51, 52, *73, 80*
Lynch, H.T., 51, *52, 80*
Lynch, J., *52, 80*
Lyon, J.L., 42, *80*

McCall, J., 59, *82*
McCarthy, E.G., 31, *80*
McCrae, R.R., *95*, 99, 100, *129*
McDougall, J.C., 148, 161 n.58
McGoogan, E., 25–27, *73*
Machan, T.R., 212 nn.9, 12, 213 n.27
McKelvey, J., *65, 73*
McKennell, A.C., *95*, 109, 110, 112, 113, *130*
Mackintosh, N.J., 68, *80*
MacLennan, J.A., 67, *80*
MacLennan, R., 35, *80, 84*
MacMahon, B., 96, *131*, 164 n.109
McManus, I.C., 99, 100, *130*
Macri, F., 163 n.87
Mahler, H., 215
Maier, S.F., 67, *80*
Mainland, D., 18, *80*
Maloney, R., *65, 73*

Mandi, A., 162 n.71
Margenau, H., 267 n.2
Markle, G.E., 167, *186*
Marks, D.A., *52, 80*
Marks, R.U., 25, *71*
Marmot, M.G., 45, *80, 85*
Martinez, F., 163 n.87
Marton, K., 329 n.6
Mason, J.I., *52, 85*
Matarazzo, J.D., 90, 98, 99, *130*
Matarazzo, R.G., 90, 99, *130*
Mausner, B., 168, *186*
Meade, J.E., 268 n.16
Meade, T.W., 168, *186*, 280, *284*
Menkes, H.A., 51, *73*
Merki, E.J., 96, *130*
Metcalfe, M., 56, *74*
Mettlin, C., 168, *186*
Mile, S.H.H.,*80*
Miles, H.H., 61
Miles, R.H., 331–332 n.57
Miller, S.M., *62, 80*
Mills, C.A., 17, *80*
Mintz, M., 160 n.45
Mitchell, R.S., 31, *85*
Mnookin, R.H., 325, 331 nn.47, 51, 332 n.60, 66, 75
Monitor, S., 21, *80*
Monjan, A.A., 67, *80*
Monson, R.R., 21, *83*
Moore, J.E., *81*
Morfopoulous, J., 162 n.73
Morris, T., 56, 57, *76, 81*
Moschandreas, D., 162 n.80
Muller, F.H., 17, *81*
Mulvihill, J.J., *52, 81*
Munoz, A., 151, 162 n.83
Muramatsu, M., 152, 163 n.94
Murray, I.D., 24, *81*
Musgrave, P.B., 269 n.29, 291, *306*
Musgrave, R.A., 269 n.29, 291, *306*
Myrtek, M., 61, *81*

Naber, D., 66, *82*
Nakashima, T., 45, *85*
Nefzger, M.D., 20, *81*
Nesse, R., 66, *74*
Newberry, B.H., *62*, 65, *71, 76*
Newell, D.Z., *81*
Newman, M.S., 96, *130*
Ng, Y.K., 35, *80*
Norman, R., *86*
Nuehring, E., 167, *186*
Nylander, L.R., 144, 160 n.35

O'Brien, C.P., 67, *81*
O'Brien, T.J., 67, *81*

Oechsli, F., 102, 103, *131*
Oeser, H., 18, 38, *79, 81*
Ohman, A., 65, *81*
Okada, T., 152, 163 n.94
O'Leary, C., 182, *186*
Oliver, M.F., 41, *81*
Oliver, R.E., 327
Olofsson, C., 65, *81*
Omaskey, S., 51, *73*
Osler, W., 61, *81*
Ost, L., 65, *81*
Ostfeld, A.M., 61, *81*
Owen, S., 62, 76, 331 n.39

Padover, S.K., 211 n.1
Palmer, A.B., 96, *131*
Pannick, D., 330 n.25
Parker, R.J., 144, 159 nn.21, 28
Pashigian, B.P., 213 n.32
Passey, R.D., 36, *81*
Patel, U.A., 95, 109–114, 116, 121, *131*
Paul, O., 61, *81*
Payne, R., 62, *74*
Pearl, R., 24, *81*
Pepys, S., 176
Permutt, S., 51, *73*
Perria, G.U., 55, *81*
Perry, J., 160 n.36
Peters, H., 163 n.92
Peterson, C., 160 n.46
Peterson, Y., 142, 144, 158 n.1
Peto, J., 95, 109–114, 116, 121, *131*
Peto, R., 18, 31, 37, *74*
Petrakis, N.L., 63, *75*
Pettingale, K.W., 57, *81*
Pevnick, J., 66, *86*
Phares, D., 286, 289, 294–296, 304, *307*
Philbert, M., 144, 159 n.22
Picard, R.S., 53, 63, *78*
Pickar, D., 66, *78, 82*
Pickle, L.W., 154, 164 n.116
Pierce, I.R., 55, *81*
Pigou, A.C., 276, *284*
Pike, M.C., 36, *81*
Pimm, P., 142, 144, 159 nn.12, 29
Platt, E.S., 168, *186*
Pleszewski, Z., 61, *82*
Polak, E., 142, 159 n.11
Pollard, V., 96, *129*
Porter, M.Y., 17, *80*
Portheine, F., 144, 159 n.19
Post, R.M., 66, *82*
Pottash, A.L.C., 67, *74*
Potter, E.A., 63, *80*
Powell, A., 53, *83*
Powell, G.E., 53, 100, *131*
Pratt, P., 31, *85*

Price, L., *132*
Price, V.A., 61, *82*
Pullman, P.T., 67, *82*
Puska, P., 41, *82*
Putnam, H., 17, *82*

Quadsfasel, F.A., 20, *81*

Rach, K., 38, *79*
Rae, G., 59, *82*, 99, *131*
Rafuse, R., 295, *307*
Raines, B.E., 89, 90, 97, *129*
Rapaport, W., 67, *82*
Rassidakis, N.C., 60, *82*
Regelson, W., *73*
Reich, T.B., 64, *83*
Reid, D.D., 31, *82*
Reif, A.E., *82*
Reker, D., 66, *86*
Repace, J.L., 164 n.118
Restrepo, G., 31, *85*
Reus, V.I., 66, *82*
Rhoads, G.G., 45, *78, 82, 85, 87*
Riccio, D.C., 65, 67, *73, 86*
Richter, O., 144, 159 n.23
Rigdon, R.H., 29, *82*
Riley, A.L., 64, *83*
Riley, V., 62, *83*
Rime, B., 61, *83*
Rimmo, P., *81*
River, J., 65, *72*
Robbins, S.L., 26, 27, *71*
Roberts, B.S., 330 nn.32, 35
Roemer, R., 214 n., 331 n.52, 332 nn.61, 71, 72, 73
Rogers, M.P., 64, *83*
Rohte, G., 55, *71*
Rokaw, S.N., 145–146, 160 n.42
Ronchetti, R., 163 n.87
Rosden, G.E., 330 n.27, 331 n.38
Rosden, P.E., 330 n.27, 331 n.38
Rose, G.A., 25, 31, 41–42, 51, *82, 83*
Rosellini, R.A., 67, *84*
Rosenblatt, M.B., 30, *83*
Rosenman, R.H., 61, *83*
Rosner, B., 148, 151, 161 nn.65, 68, 162 n.83
Rotfeld, H.J., 319, 330 nn.28, 29, 33
Rothman, K.J., 21, *83*
Rowe, L.G., 55, *79*
Royce, J.R., 53, *83*
Rubinow, D.R., 66, *82*
Ruch-Ross, H., 163 n.86
Ruckphaopunt, K., 35, *84*
Rudiger, H.W., 52, *79*
Rudolph, J.P., 96, *129*
Ruma, T., 52, *80*

Rummel, R., *164*
Rusiniak, K.W., 64, *76*
Russell, M.A.H., *95*, 109–114, 116, 121, *131*, 142, 148, 159 n.16
Russell, S.F., 89, 96, 103, *131*
Ryan, S.F., 31, *85*
Rylander, R., 142, 144, 158 n.1, 160 n.48

Sack, R.D., 330 n.32
Sacks, S.T., 45, 63, *75, 87*
Sacks, U.I., 25, 26, *70*
Salber, E.J., *96, 131*
Saloney, J., 41, *82*
Salvaggio, J.E., 161 n.59
Samet, J.M., 149, 161 n.63
Sandler, L.S., 66, *76*
Saslow, G., 90, 98, 99, *130*
Savarese, J.M., *9, 12–13*, 344, 349
Saw, D., 155, 164 n.119
Schaefer, J.M., 290, *307*
Schairer, E., 17, *83*
Scheelings, P., 35, *84*
Schein, M., 330 n.35
Schenker, M.B., 149, 161 n.63
Schievelbein, H., 164 nn.105, 106
Schiffman, J.C., 45, *78*
Schilling, R.S.F., 149, 162 nn.74, 85
Schmidt, C.F., 165 n.128
Schmidt, P., 59, 69, *76, 77*
Schneider, N.G., 100, *130, 131*
Schneider, N.R., 52, *83*
Schoenberg, J.B., 149, 162 nn.74, 85
Schoeniger, E., 17, *83*
Schonfield, J., *83*
Schrek, R., 17, *84*
Schroeder, D.H., 62, *84*
Schudson, M., 329 n.7
Schuld, D., 57, *86*
Schultz, G., 163 n.92
Schumann, L.M., 20, *73*
Schumpeter, J., 210
Sebben, J., 144, 159 n.29
Seely, S., 21, *84*
Segall, J., *84*
Sehrt, E., 29, *84*
Selfman, N.A., *87*
Seligman, M.E.P., 68, *84*
Sellers, C.M., 92, *128*
Seltzer, C.C., 40, 44–48, *76, 84*, 102, 103, *131*
Selvin, S., 63, *75*
Selye, M., 62, *85*
Sen, A.K., 342 n.2
Seow, S.S.W., 67, *82*
Seppänen, A., 142, 144, 158 n.6, 160 n.30
Seth, A.K., 48, *86*
Sethi, B.B., 100, *130*

Shabalala, F., 162 n.73
Shanmugaratnam, K., *35, 80*, 164 n.114
Shapiro, N.R., 67, *84*
Shautz, F.C., *55*, 57, *74*
Shekelle, R.B., 61, *81, 86*
Shelton, S.E., 66, *78*
Shephard, R.J., 142, 144, 159 nn.12, 29, 163 nn.97, 98
Shettleworth, S.J., 68, *84*
Shields, J., 52, *84*
Shipley, M.J., 25, 41–42, *83*
Shoba, F., 162 n.73
Shor, M.B., 157, 165 n.27
Shor, R.E., 157, 164 n.120, 165 nn.125, 126, 127
Shouka, M., 52, *80*
Shughart II, W.F., *9, 12–13*, 282, 344, 349
Siegan, B.H., 198, 212 n.10
Siegelaub, A.B., 40, *76*
Siegrist, J., *77*
Silverman, F., 142, 159 n.12, 163 n.98
Silverman, M., 161 n.69
Simarak, S., *35, 84*
Sims, D.G., 161 n.94
Singer, G., 64, *86*
Sinnott, P., 329 n.16
Sklar, L.S., 62, 63, 66, 67, *84*
Slack, J., 51, *84*
Slavin, R.G., 142, 144, 159 nn.17, 26
Smith, G.M., 99, *131*
Smithers, D.W., 30, *84*
Smock, T., 66, *84*
Snella, M.C., 142, 144, 158 n.1
Solomon, E.S., *96, 130*
Spackman, D.H., 62, *83*
Sparros, L., 154, 164 nn.109, 111
Speer, F., 147, 160 n.51
Speizer, F.E., 148–151, 161 nn.63, 65, 68, 162 nn.79, 83
Spence, J.T., 64, *84*
Spence, K.W., 64, *84*
Spengler, J.D., 150, 162 nn.79, 80, 81
Spielberger, C.D., 6–7, 89, 96, 100, 101, 103, *131, 133,* 343, 349
Spilken, A.Z., 99, *130*
Srch, M., 138, 158 n.3
Stack, J., *74*
Stanaway, R.G., *95*, 111–113, *131*
Stebbings, J.H., 31, *84*
Stedman, R.L., 148, 161 n.57
Steer, A., 45, *85*
Stehlik, G., 144, 159 n.23
Steiner, R.L., 329 n.11
Stelzer, D., 57, *71*
Stemmermann, G.A., 45, *82, 85*
Steptoe, A., 61, *85*
Sterling, P., 62, *85*

Sterling, T.D., 18, *85*, 164 n.107
Sternley, N., 27, *78*
Stevenson-Hinde, 68
Stewart, R.A., 100, *131*
Stone, D.B., 96, *130*
Stone, J.D., 165 n.124
Strom, T.B., 64, *83*
Strong, L.C., 52, *85*
Stuart, R.C., 268 n.9
Sturgess, B., 314, *329*
Stuyck, J., 332 n.57
Sullivan, S., 67, *71*
Suppe, F., 17, *85*
Swanson, G.J., *306*
Swisher, S.N., 63, *76*
Syme, S.L., 45, *80, 85, 87*
Szabo, M., 162 n.71
Szadkowski, D., 144, 160 n.37

Tache, D., 62, *85*
Tager, I.B., 148, 151, 161 nn.65, 68, 162 n.83
Tahle, I., 152, 163 n.95
Takuhata, G.K., *85*
Tate, C.F., 151–152, 163 n.89
Taylor, G., 148, 161 n.53
Taylor, J.A., 100, *131*, 161 n.59
Taylor, K.B., 67, *78*
Taylor, R.M., 96, *130*
Taylor, T., 66, *85*
Tenb, P.K., 30, *83*
Testa, T., 67, *81*
Thomas, C.B., 60–61, *85*, 100, *131*
Thomas, C.G., 44, 51, 60, 61, *85*
Thompson, J.W., 330 n.25
Thompson, L.W., 61, *71*
Thompson, M., 226, 232, 238, 239 n.1, 240 n.4
Thurlbeck, W.M., 31, *85*
Tibbitts, T.W., 162 n.81
Tibbling, L., 152, 163 n.95
Tiggeman, M., 67, *85*
Tinbergen, J., 267 n.1
Tockman, M.S., 51, *73*
Todd, G.F., 52, *85*
Tokuhata, G.K., 51, *85*
Tollison, R.D., 9, 282, 305 n.2, *306*, 344, 351
Tomita, H., 152, 163 n.94
Tomkins, S.S., 7, 90, 92–95, 110, 127, *130, 131*
Townsend, J.I., 280, *284*
Tramutoli, G.M., 163 n.87
Trichopoulos, D., 154, 164 nn.109, 111
Trisdikoon, P., 67, *73*
Tristani, F.E., 48, *86*
Troyer, R.J., 167, *186*

Tryon, W.W., 168, 172, *187*
Tullock, G., 224 n.3
Tuomilehito, J., 41, *82*

Umemura, S., 152, 163 n.94
Uusitalo, A.J., 144, 160 n.30

Vale, W., 65, *72*
Validou, M., *82*
Van De Wal, M.C., 149, 162 n.75
Van Dijl, 61, *86*
Vanecek, R., 27, *78*
Van Ree, J.M., 66
Vaughter, R.M., 168, 172, *187*
Veldhuis, H.D., 65, *72*
Vesterlund, J., 160 n.48
Veter, H., 77
Vetter, H., 59, 69, *76, 77*
Vickerstaff, L., 26, *86*
Vincent, T., 31, *85*
Vlieststra, R.E., 48, *86*
Voight, K.H., 66, *75*
Volavka, J., 66, *86*

Wadden, R.A., 144, 159 n.27
Wagner, R.E., 295, *307*
Waingrow, S., 113, *130*
Wald, N.J., 168, *186*
Waldron, H.A., 26, *86*
Waldvogel, S., 61, *80*
Walter, I., 10–11, 344, 349–350
Walter, T.A., 67, *86*
Wang, Y.C., 161 n.69
Warbrick-Smith, D., *81*
Warburton, D.M., 184, *187*
Waterson, M.J., 313–316, 325, 326, 328 n.1, 329 nn.12, 13, 18, 19, 20, 331 n.54, 332 nn.59, 65
Watson, C.G., 57, *86*
Watson, D.W., 95, 112–113, *131*
Watson, F.E., 67, *82*
Watson, M., 57, *81*
Waxman, S., 60, *79*
Wayner, E.A., 64, *86*
Webb, J.K.G., 161 n.94
Weber, A., 142, 144, 159 n.13, 160 nn.32, 38, 39, 40
Weber, M., 226, 240 n.5
Weeks, S.J., 99, 100, *130*
Weightman, D., 161 n.64
Weiler, S.J., 66, *78*
Weinberg, J., 330 nn.32, 35, 331 n.44
Weinberger, M.M., 149, 161 n.62
Weiss, S.T., 148, 151, 161 nn.65, 68, 162 n.83
Wells, B., 67, *81*
Wells, C.K., 27–29, *75*

Wells, H.G., 25, *86*
Werko, L., 44, *86*
Wesnes, K., 184, *187*
West, D.W., 42, *80*
West, P.M., 57, *71*
Westlund, K., 21, *86*
White, J.R., 144, 153, *160*, 204, 213 n.17
White, P.D., 51, 76
White, S.W., 63, *71*
Wichert, P., 52, 79
Wickström, B., 329 n.15
Widmer, G.W., 31, *80*
Wiedemann, H.P., 147, 161 n.54, 163 n.99
Wilkins, M.M., 55, 57, *70*
Williams, B.R., 61, *71*
Williams, C.B., 164 n.120
Williams, D.C., 157, 165 nn.125, 126, 127
Williams, G.H., 66, *85*
Williams, R.B., 61, 62, *71*, *86*
Willis, R.A., 25, 29, *86*
Wilson, B.A., 25–26, *73*
Wilson, E.B., 31, *86*
Wimer, R.E., *86*

Winding, O., 162 n.70
Winfefield, A.H., *85*
Winkelstein, W., 45, *87*
Wiseman, J., 272, *284*
Wohlford, P., 96, *132*
Woodfield, A.E., 280, *284*
Woolf, P.D., 66, *87*
Worden, T., 89
Worth, R.M., 45, *87*
Wright, J., 66, *74*
Wright, L.M., 330 n. 24
Wuliger, G.T., 331 nn.39, 44
Wynder, E.L., 17, *87*, 154–155, 164 n.117

Xaba, M., *162*

Yerevanian, B.I., 66, *87*
Yerushalmy, J., 18, 23, *87*, 102, *132*
Yesner, R., 31, *87*
Young, A.K., *74*

Zoob, I., *132*
Zuckerman, M., *132*

Subject Index

Ability-to-pay principle, 305 n.3
Acceptability, social, 114–127, 156
Accommodation as market incentive, 209–210
Acetaldehyde, 152
Acrolein, 152
ACTH, 65–68, 87
Acute stress, 63–64
Addiction, 93, 110, 211 n.6
Adjustment, voluntary, 337–338
Adrenocorticotrophic hormone (ACTH), 65–68, 87
Adult respiratory diseases, 151–155
Advertising, 309–332; bans or severe restrictions on, 312–313, 315–317; brand, 314; constitutional protection of, 319–322; consumers and, 310–311; crusades against, 323–328; demand and, 313–314; economic freedom–political freedom link and, 318–319; effect of, 104–109; government regulation and, 317–323; issues in, 13; market system and, 312–313; misleading, 275, 320; "opinion", 330 n.36; socioeconomic role of, 309–317; truthful, 320–321; unfairness issue in, 322–323
Affect control model, 92–95
Age, coronary heart disease and, 46
Airspace, violation of, 206–209
Allergens from smoke, 147–148
Allergy. See Passive smoking
Allotment program, 305 n.7
Alternatives, providing, principle of, 205–206
Anger, 120–127
Angina pectoris, 45
Animal models, 23
Antismoking movement, 225–240; bifurcation of, 230–232; bureaucratic component of, 10, 230–231; class-specificity of, 233, 239; consumer movement and, 235; defensive character of, 234; environmentalism and, 235; health cult and, 234–236; ideology of, 234–237; internationalization of, 232–233; politics of, 9–10, 230–233; self-interest and, 221–223; social costs notion and, 237; state legislations and, 217–220;

stigmatization strategy of, 236–237; targets of, 220–221; Third World ideology and, 232–233; WHO and, 214–216, 237–239. See also Rights; San Francisco Ordinance
Anxiety, 60–61, 120–127, 180. See also Personality
Argentina, tobacco industry in, 261
Arrogance, paternalism and, 325
Asocializing forces, 109
Assessment, 3–14
Association, statistical, 17–18, 21. See also Cancer–smoking association
Assortative mating, 87
Asthmatics, 151–153
Attention, focusing, 184
Australia, 256–258, 304
Automatic/habitual smoking factor, 110, 114–127
Autopsies, 26–27, 30–31, 87
Avoidability, reasonable, 205–206

Balance of interests approach, 204–208
Balance-of-payments, 249–250
Bans on advertising, 312–313, 315–317
Bars, passive smoking in, 144–145. See also Property rights
Behavior therapy, 69
Belgium, 256, 258, 300
Benefits-received principle, 305 n.3
Benzo(a)pyrene, 152
Bias, detection, 27–29, 53, 87
Bill of Rights, 191
Boredom, as reason for smoking, 91, 104–109
Boundary context, 177–178
Boundary maintenance, 183
Boundary mediation, 183
Brand advertising, 314
Brazil, 250, 251
Bronchial carcinoma, 35
Bureaucracy, antismoking, 10, 230–231

Canada, tobacco industry in, 258
Cancer–smoking association, 17–43; arguments for, 18–23; autopsies and, 26–27, 30–31; causation vs. statistical association and, 17–18, 21; coherence of,

Cancer–smoking association: (*continued*)
39–43; consistency of, 32–33, 35; death
certificate data and, 25–27; detection
bias and, 27–29, 53, 87; mortality and,
31, 33, 35, 38; passive smoking, 153–
155; personality and, 52–62, 66–69;
reliability of data on, 23–32; rise in lung
cancer and, 29–30; self-selection and,
25, 40; sex-ratio and, 35; specificity of,
37–38; strength of, 33–37; stress and,
62–69; temporal relationship of, 38–39.
See also Constitutional hypothesis
Capacity-utilization, 246
Capital formation, 249
Carbon monoxide: early research on, 138–
139; health effects of, 146; as index of
smoke exposure, 140–146
Carboxyhemoglobin levels, 142–143
Cattell 16PF scale, 87
Causality: epidemiological criteria for,
32–43; statistical association and,
17–18, 21
Chain of repercussions, 247
Childhood respiratory diseases, 148–151
Children: lung function in, 151; stigmatiza-
tion strategy and, 236–237
Chronic stress, 63–64
Circulatory system, passive smoking and,
140–146
Civil liberties, 198–199. *See also* Rights
Class, antismoking movement and, 233, 239
Clean Indoor Air Acts, 189
Coase theorem, 223, 341 n.1
Commercial speech, 319–320
Commonsense, 13
Conditioning, Pavlovian, 64, 88
Conference rooms, passive smoking and,
143–144. *See also* Property rights
Conflict: of interest, irreconcilable, 208;
potential for, 337; resolution, avenues
of, 337–339
Connecticut law on smoking, 217, 218
Constitutional factors, 87
Constitutional hypothesis, 49–70; adumbra-
tion, 6, 50–51; coronary heart disease
and, 45–46, 48; dose-response phenomenon and, 35–37, 46, 87; genetic transpositions, 52; mechanism of, 25; mortality ratios across races and, 33–35;
personality and, 52–62, 66–69; rise in
cancer and, 29; stress and, 62–70. *See
also* Psychological determinants
Consumers: advertising and decisions of, 310;
advocates, 4–5, 235, 325; government
protection of, 4; rationality of, 310–311
Contagion, concept of, 176–177
Contract, sales transaction and, 319

Contraction, industrial, 246–247
Converse causal hypothesis, 24
Coronary heart disease: carbon monoxide
levels and, 145–146; constitutional
hypothesis and, 45–46, 48; death certificate data on, 27; epidemiology and,
43–49; ex-smokers and, 47; inhalation
and, 46–47; intervention programs for,
40; mortality rates and, 40, 47–49;
passive smoking and, 145–146; personality and, 60–62; stress and, 69–70.
See also Constitutional hypothesis
Cortical arousal, 111
Cost(s): -benefit analysis, 4–5, 207; deadweight, 288; social, 237, 264
Counter-Blaste to Tobacco (James I), 156
Cult, health, 234–236
Curiosity, 101–102, 104–109, 114–127
Current income, 289–293

Deadweight costs, 288
Death certificate data, 25–27
Declaration of Independence, 190–191
Demand, advertising and, 313–314
Demerit goods, 261
Denmark, 256, 258
Depression, ACTH oversecretion in, 66
Detection bias, 27–29, 53, 87
Developing countries, economic contribu-
tion in, 249–251
Diagnosis, false-positive, 30
Diagnostic techniques, cancer incidence
and, 29–30
Diathesis-stress model, 91–92
Dominance, gene, 87
Dose-response phenomenon, 35–37, 46, 87
Dysphoria, 180
DZ twins, 87

Economic contributions of tobacco in-
dustry, 243–269; analysis and measure-
ment of, 245–252; in Argentina, 261; in
Australia, 256–258; in Canada, 258;
fiscal, 251, 261–266; in Malaysia,
258–260; nature of, 243–245; in U.S.,
252–254; in Western Europe, 254–256;
in Zimbabwe, 260
Economic freedom, 198–199, 318–319
Economic growth, 11
Ego-defense mechanisms, 54
Elasticity, 295–299, 305 n.4
Elizabethans, 170, 173–174
Emotional determinants, 6–7. *See also*
Psychological determinants
Employers, state laws applied to, 218–220
Employment, 246, 247
Endogenous opiates, 67

Endorphins, 65–66
Engineering, social, 215–216
Enjoyment, as reason for smoking, 104–109
Environment, initiation of smoking and, 95–96
Environmental Protection Agency (EPA), 137
Environmental tobacco smoke. *See* Passive smoking
Environmentalism, antismoking movement and, 235
EPA, 137
EPI, 99, 112
Epidemiology, 23–30, 87; animal models for, 23; of childhood respiratory diseases, 149–150; of coronary heart disease, 43–49; criteria for causality in, 32–43; death certificate data in, 25–27; detection bias in, 27–29; hypotheses untested in, 24–25; rise in lung cancer and, 29–30; self-selection and, 25
EPQ, 99–101
Equity, horizontal, 12, 285–286, 289
Ethnicity, 172
European Convention on Human Rights, 318
Event marking, 184
Evil-good opposition, 178
Exchange: foreign, 249–250; freedom of, 210; function of, 183
Excise tax. *See* Tax(es)
Expenditures, induced, 248
Experimental smoking, 89
Exports, 247
Ex-smokers: coronary heart disease and, 47; curiosity and, 101–102
Externalities, 273–274, 276–279
Extraversion, 53–57, 59, 61, 91–92, 99–100. *See also* Personality
Eysenck Personality Inventory (EPI), 99, 112
Eysenck Personality Questionnaire (EPQ), 99–101, 121–127

Failure, market. *See* Market failure
False-positive diagnoses of cancer, 30
Family smoking habits, 95–98
Fear, incubation of, 65
Federal Republic of Germany, 256, 258, 304
Females: cross-cultural regularities among, 171–172; increase in smoking among, 89; nonsmoking wives, 153–154
Feminism, 238–239
Finnish tobacco taxes, 301, 302
First Amendment, 319–320
Fiscal contributions, 251, 261–266

Foreign exchange, 249–250
Framingham heart study, 46–47
France, 256, 258
Freedom: economic, 198–199, 318–319; of exchange, 210; political, 209–211, 318–319; WHO's definition of, 215
Freedom of Expression and Information, 318
French tobacco taxes, 304
Functions of tobacco use, 181–184

Gender, social role of smoking and, 171–172
Genetic factors, 25, 87, 88
Genetic transpositions, 52
Germany, Federal Republic of, 256, 258, 304
Good-evil opposition, 178
Goods, demerit, 261
Government: advertising and, 317–323; antismoking bureaucracy in, 10, 230–231; consumer protection and, 4; limiting power of, 200–202, 209–211; market processes and, 203; objective function of, 266; over-reliance on, 326–328. *See also* Economic contributions of tobacco industry; Market failure; Rights
Greece, 256, 258
Group definition, 183

Habit, 93–95, 110, 114–127, 211 n.6
Hallways, San Francisco Ordinance on, 204–206
Harms, rights and, 194–196
Harvard's Institute for the Study of Smoking Behavior and Policy, 316
Healing, symbolic value of, 180
Health cult, 234–236
Health issue. *See* Cancer–smoking association; Coronary heart disease
Horizontal equity, 12, 285–286, 289
Hormones, 67
Horn–Waingrow Smoker Survey, 94
Hostility, 61
Human rights. *See* Rights
Hypocortisolism, 67

Ideas, vested interests and, 228–229
Ideology: of antismoking movement, 234–237; definition of, 229; Third World, 232–233
Immune reaction, conditioning of, 64–68
Immunology, 87
Immunosuppression, 66–67
Imports, 247
Income, current vs. permanent, 289–293
Incubation, 88

Indirect taxation, 261–266
Induced expenditures, 248
Indulgent smoking factor, 110
Industrialized countries, economic contribution in, 246–249
Industry, contraction in, 246–247
Information: businessmen's definition of, 311; imperfect, 273, 274–276; provision of, 275–276
Infrastructure, 250–251
Inhalation: coronary heart disease and, 46–47; mortality ratios and degree of, 37
Innocent bystander notion, 236, 237
Inoculation hypothesis, 63–64
Input–Output table, 247–249
Intellectual stimulation/curiosity factor, 114–127
Interactional transition, 183
Interdependency, social, 335–342
Interests: balance of, 204–206, 207–208; conflicts of, 208; self-, 221–223; vested, ideas and, 228–229
Internationalization of antismoking movement, 232–233
Intraversion, 61, 64. *See also* Personality
Ireland, 256, 258
Italy, 256, 258

Japan, lung cancer risks in, 34

Knowledge: class, 233; sociology of, 227–230

Labor-force augmentation, 250
Legal paternalism: arrogance and, 325; property and, 203; rights approach vs., 8–9, 192–194; in WHO political philosophy, 214–215
Legislation, 217–220; as last resort, 209–211; redistributive effect of, 222–223; self-interest and, 221–223
Less developed countries, economic contribution in, 251–252
Leukemia, 63
Liberties: civil, 198–199; personal, 8–9. *See also* Freedom; Rights
Lobbies, San Francisco Ordinance on, 204–206
Logical positivism, 17
Lounges, San Francisco Ordinance on, 204–206
Lung cancer. *See* Cancer–smoking association
Lung function in children, 151
Luxembourg, 256, 258

Maintenance of smoking, family influence on, 98
Malaysia, tobacco industry in, 258–260

Manners, good, 211
Market, free: advertising and, 312–313; incentives, 209–210; political liberty and, 209–211; state intervention in, 203
Market failure, 271–284; concept of, 11–12; correction of, 272–274; externalities and, 273–274, 276–279; imperfect information, and 273, 274–276; issues in, 271–272; medical expenses and, 279–280; nuisance issue and, 280–282
Mating, assortative, 87
Meddlesome preferences, 335–342
Mediation, boundary, 183
Medical expenses, 176–177, 279–280
Medical model of smoking, 167–169
Metastasis, 88
Mexico, 171
Minnesota law on smoking, 219
Minnesota Multiphasic Personality Inventory (MMPI), 88
Misleading advertising, 275, 320
Monopoly, 273
Montana law on smoking, 218
Moral issue, 175
Moral perspective on rights, 192, 211 n.2
Mormons, 42
Mortality: from coronary heart disease, 40, 47–49; decline in, 40–42; overall, 31, 38; ratios, 19–21, 33–35, 37
Motivational determinants, 6–7. *See also* Psychological determinants
Multiple Risk Factor Intervention Trial Research Group, 40–41
Multiplier effect, 247

Naloxone, 66
National Heart, Lung, and Blood Institute, 150
National Institute of Education, 98
Natural rights. *See* Rights
Nebraska law on smoking, 218
Negative affect management, 93–95, 110–111, 114–127, 183
Nervous irritation smoking, 111
Netherlands, 256, 258, 301
Neuropeptides, 65–68
Neuroticism, 53, 55–56, 63, 64–66, 91–92, 99, 100. *See* Personality
New World, 169–170, 176
Nicotine: atmospheric levels, 152; diathesis-stress model and, 92
Nightclubs, passive smoking in, 144–145
Norms, 228
North Jarelia project, 41
Norway, 301, 302, 315–316
Nuisance, 209, 280–282

Objective function of government, 266
Offense concept, 209, 280–282
Offices, passive smoking and, 143–144. *See also* San Francisco Ordinance
Opiates, endogenous, 67
Opinion advertising, 330 n.36
Order, restoration of, 180–181
Ordering functions, 8, 182, 184
Overregulation, reaction against, 317–318

Pacing, 184
Parental smoking: childhood respiratory disease and, 148–151; influence on children's smoking, 90, 97
Passive smoking, 137–165; asthma and, 151–153; cancer and, 153–155; carbon monoxide levels and, 140–146; carboxyhemoglobin levels and, 142; circulatory system and, 140–146; coronary heart disease and, 145–146; historical context, 176–177; lack of specific disease associated with, 139; lung cancer and, 153–155; in offices and conference rooms, 143–144; psychosocial basis of claims about, 7–8, 155–158; public property and, 203–204; respiratory system and, 147–155; in restaurants, bars, taverns, and nightclubs, 144–145; social cost of, 9; stigmatization strategy and, 236–237; symptom complex, 138–140, 155–158; vasomotor rhinitis and, 147–148
Paternalism: arrogance and, 325; property and, 203; rights approach vs., 8–9, 192–194; in WHO political philosophy, 214–215
Pavlovian conditioning, 64, 88
Payments, balance of, 249–250
Peer-group pressure, 90, 104–109
Peptides, 65–68, 88
Permanent income, 289–293
Personal functions, 8, 182, 183
Personal liberties, 8–9
Personal space, 178–179, 336–337
Personality, 98–103; of American college students, 100–102; cancer–smoking association and, 52–62, 66–69; coronary heart disease and, 60–62; diathesis-stress model and, 91–92; extravert, 53–57, 59, 61, 91–92, 99–100; neurotic, 53, 55–56, 63, 64–66, 91–92, 99, 100; prospective studies of, 102–103; psychotic, 53, 54, 59–60, 63, 92, 100; stress and, 62
Philosophy, political, of WHO, 214–216
Phobias, 65
Pituitary hormones, 67

Plausibility structure, 227–228
Political freedom, 209–211, 318–319
Politics: of antismoking movement, 230–233; conflict resolution through, 338–339; issue-partitioning in, 339–340; meddlesome preferences and, 335–342
Pollution: cultural relativity of, 179; privatization and, 207; –purity opposition, 179–181, 185; rights approach and, 206–209; technological, 185; tobacco as symbol of, 173. *See also* Passive smoking
Portugal, 256, 258
Positive affect smoking, 93–95, 111, 183
Positivism, logical, 17
Preferences, meddlesome, 335–342
Presentation of self, 183
Pressure, peer-group, 90, 104–109
Price stability, 246
Private property, 200–202, 220–221, 336–337
Private spaces, 178–179, 336–337
Privatization, pollution and, 207
Progressive tax, 286
Property: private, 200–202, 220–221, 336–337; public, 200–209, 218–220
Property rights, 196–203; centrality of, 191; conflict reduction and, 336; externalities and, 277; liberty and, 198–200; nuisance issue and, 281–282; protection of, 199–200; smoker/nonsmoker conflict and, 8–9, 217–220
Proportional tax, 285–286
Proposition P. *See* San Francisco Ordinance
Psychological determinants, 89–134; affect control model, 92–95; diathesis stress model, 91–92; from EPQ scales, 121–127; family smoking habits, 95–98; models of, 90–95; motivation and emotion, 6–7, 103–127; personality, 98–103; situational determinants and, 109–113, 168; from Smoking Motivation Questionnaire, 115–127; State-Trait Personality Inventory and, 100–101, 113–114, 124–127
Psychosocial smoking, 95, 110
Psychoticism, 53, 54, 59–60, 63, 92, 100. *See also* Personality
Public policy. *See* Government; Legislation
Public property, 200–209; balance of interests approach to, 204–206; harm concept and, 203–204; offense behavior, 204–206; passive smoking and, 203–204; paternalism and, 203; private property vs., 200–202; rights approach to, 206–209; state laws on, 218–220
Public smoking. *See* Passive smoking
Purity–pollution opposition, 179–181, 185

Randomization, 25
Rational expectation framework, 195–196, 212 n.8
Rationality, consumer, 310–311
Read's Weekly, 174
Reasonable avoidability, standard of, 205–206
Reasons for smoking, 104–109
Rebellion, as reason for smoking, 104–109
Received view of theories, 6, 17. *See also* Cancer–smoking association
Recessive genes, 88
Regressive tax, 286
Regulators, 5
Relative risk ratios for lung cancer mortality, 33, 35
Relaxation smoking, 111, 114–127
Religion, 174–175, 239, 240
Repercussions, chain of, 247
Respiratory diseases: adult, 151–155; childhood, 148–151
Restaurants, passive smoking in, 144–145. *See also* Private property
Restrictions on advertising, 312–313, 315–317
Rhinitis, vasomotor, 147–148
Rights, 189–213; civil liberties, 198–199; Declaration of Independence on, 190–191; free market and, 209–211; harms and, 194–196; legal paternalism and, 8–9, 192–194; limiting government power and, 200–202, 209–211; moral perspective on, 192, 211 n.2; pollution and, 206–209; property, 8–9, 191, 196–203, 217–220, 277, 281–282, 336; public property and, 203–209; regulation-protection issue and, 199–200
Risk-benefit analysis, 4–5, 207
Ritual use. *See* Social role of smoking
Royal College of Physicians, 17, 18
Rule-switching, concept of, 216

Sales, reduction in, 247–248
Sales transaction: contract and, 319
San Francisco Chronicle, 202
San Francisco Ordinance, 217; on hallways, lobbies and lounges, 204–206; nature of, 196–198; private alternatives to, 202–203; public property–private property distinction and, 200–202
SBQ, 96–98
Schizophrenia, 60
Scientistic mentality, 340–341
Sedative smoking, 93–95, 110–111, 114–127, 183
Self-interest, 221–223
Self-presentation, 183

Self-selection, 25, 40
Sensitivity to smoke. *See* Passive smoking
Sensorimotor smoking factor, 110
Sensory stimulation factor, 114–127
Seventh Day Adventists, 42
Sex-ratio of bronchial carcinoma, 35
Sibling influence on smoking, 97–98
Situational determinants, 109–113, 168. *See also* Social role of smoking
Smoking Behavior Questionnaire (SBQ), 96–98
Smoking Motivation Questionnaire (SMQ), 115–127, 133–134
Smoking Pollution Control Ordinance. *See* San Francisco Ordinance
Snuffing, 171
Social acceptability, 114–127, 156
Social confidence factor, 95
Social costs, 237, 264
Social engineering implicit in WHO's political philosophy, 215–216
Social functions, 8, 182, 183
Social influence variables, 90
Social interdependency, 335–342; politicization of, 337, 338–341; potential for conflict from, 337; voluntary adjustments and, 337–338
Social role of smoking, 167–187; boundary context of, 177–178; ethnicity and, 172; functions of tobacco use, 181–184; gender and, 171–172; history of, 169–178; medical model and, 167–169; medicine and, 176–177; opposition structures of, 178–181; positive and negative aspects of, 173–174; religion and, 174–175
Social Systems Analysts, Inc., 171
Sociological perspective, 8–10, 225–240; ideas–vested interest relationship and, 228–229; plausibility structure and, 227–228; sociology of knowledge, 227–230; value-free concept and, 226
South America, 171
Space, personal, 178–179, 336–337
Spain, 256, 258
Spaniards in the New World, 169–170, 176
Spectator, 174
Speech, commercial, 319–320
Stability, price, 246
State laws restricting smoking, 217–220. *See also* Government; Legislation
State-Trait Personality Inventory (STPI), 100–101, 113–114, 124–127
Statistical association, 17–18, 21
Stigmatization strategy, 236–237
Stimulation, as reason for smoking, 104–109, 110

Stress, 62–70; acute and chronic, 63–64; cancer–smoking association and, 62–69; coronary heart disease and, 69–70; defined, 88; diathesis model of, 91–92; personality and, 62; psychosocial views of disease and, 54

Structure, plausibility, 227–228

Students: personality of, 100–102; reasons for smoking, 103–109

Surgeon General of the U.S., 17, 18. *See also* Cancer–smoking association

Surgeon General's report (1979), 167

Switzerland, cardiovascular mortalities in, 48–49

Symbolic role. *See* Social role of smoking

Sympatheticotomia vs. Vagotomia theory, 61

Task Force on Alcohol and Tobacco Tax Indexation, 265

Taverns, passive smoking in, 144–145. *See also* Property rights

Tax(es), 285–307; differential impact of, 11, 12–13; effective rates, 293–295, 296–297; elasticity calculations and, 295–299, 305 n.4; horizontal equity and, 12, 285–286, 289; incidence, theory of, 286–288; income definition and, 289–293; indirect, 261–266; international aspects of, 299–304; progressive, 286; proportional, 285–286; regressive, 286; social costs of increasing, 264; value-added, 299

Technological pollution, 185

Technology augmentation, 250

Teenage smokers, 102–103

Tension, 104–109, 180

They–we opposition, 178–179

Thinking, facilitation of, 104–109

Third World ideology, 232–233

Time filling, 184

Time out, 184

Tobacco industry: analysis and measurement of economic contributions of, 10–11, 245–252, in Argentina, 261; in Australia, 256–258; in Canada, 258; fiscal contributions of, 251, 261–266; in Malaysia, 258–260; nature of economic contributions of, 243–245; as symbol of multinational corporation's evil, 235; in

U.S., 252–254; vested interests of, 230; in Western Europe, 254–256; in Zimbabwe, 260

Transaction, contract and, 319

Transpositions, genetic, 52

Truthful advertising, 320–321

Twins, 52, 63, 87

Type A behavior, 61–62

Unalienable rights. *See* Rights

United Kingdom: relative risks of lung cancer in, 34; tobacco taxes in, 256, 258, 299–300, 301–303

United Nations, 232

United States, tobacco industry in, 252–254

Universality, standard of, 205

Utah law on smoking, 219

Utilitarianism in WHO's political philosophy, 216

Vagotomia vs. Sympatheticotomia theory, 61

Value-added tax (VAT), 299

Value-free concept, 226

Variance, 88

Vasomotor rhinitis, 147–148

VAT, 299

Victorians, 171, 173–174

Vienna School, 17

Western Europe, tobacco industry in, 254–256

We–they opposition, 178–179

Wives, nonsmoking, 153–154

Women. *See* Females

Workplace, legislation affecting, 217–220, 222–223. *See also* San Francisco Ordinance

World Conference on Smoking and Health, 10, 151, 152, 237–239

World Health Organization European Trial, 41

World Health Organization (WHO): antismoking movement and, 214–216, 237–239; definition of freedom, 215; political philosophy of, 214–216; Third World ideology and, 232–233

Zimbabwe, tobacco industry in, 260

About the Contributors

Domingo M. Aviado, M.D., is the founder and president of Atmospheric Health Sciences, Inc., a research consulting firm for governmental agencies, educational institutions, and private industry in the United States, Europe, and Asia. Dr. Aviado obtained his M.D. at the University of Pennsylvania School of Medicine in 1948. He remained on the faculty of that University for thirty years, with a terminal appointment of Professor of Pharmacology. He has authored a textbook of pharmacology, two medical dictionaries, eight monographs and over two hundred and fifty scientific articles on the subject of inhalational toxicology and treatment of diseases associated with inhaled substances.

Peter L. Berger is a distinguished sociologist who is presently University Professor at Boston University. He is a fellow of the American Academy of Arts and Letters, and has published several major works, including most recently *The War Over the Family* (with Brigitte Berger).

J.J. Boddewyn is professor of marketing and international business, and coordinator of international business programs at the Baruch College of the City University of New York. He holds a commercial engineer degree from the University of Louvain (Belgium), a MBA from the University of Oregon, and a Ph.D. in business administration from the University of Washington (Seattle). He is a fellow of the Academy of International Business, the Academy of Management, and the International Academy of Management. Among many other publications, he is the author of a series of international surveys of the regulation and self-regulation of advertising around the world.

James M. Buchanan is University Distinguished Professor and general director of the Center for Study of Public Choice at George Mason University in Fairfax, Virginia. He is normally regarded as a founder of the public choice movement, and has had a high impact on the scope and direction of modern economics. Among his better known works are *The Calculus of Consent* (with Gordon Tullock), *Public Finance in Democratic Process,* and *The Power to Tax* (with Geoffrey Brennan).

Douglas J. Den Uyl is assistant professor of philosophy at Bellarmine College, Louisville, Kentucky. He received his M.A. in political science from the University of Chicago and his Ph.D. in philosophy from Marquette University. His areas of specialty include ethics and political philosophy and he has published books and articles in these areas.

Hans J. Eysenck was born in Berlin in 1916, but left Germany for political reasons in 1934. He studied in Dijon, France, for a while before coming to London where he obtained the degree of Ph.D. in psychology from the University of London in 1940. During the war he worked at the Mill Hill Emergency Hospital as research psychologist, and was later appointed reader and then professor of psychology at the newly founded Institute of Psychiatry, which is part of the University of London and associated with the Maudsley and the Bethlem Royal Hospitals. He was appointed psychologist to the joint hospitals, and was director of the psychological laboratories at the Institute. He recently retired as professor emeritus, but is continuing research at the Institute. He has published some 40 books and some 800 articles, has been visiting professor at the Universities of Philadelphia and California (at Berkeley), and is currently president of the International Society for the Study of Individual Differences.

Sherwin J. Feinhandler, Ph.D., is president of Social Systems Analysts, Inc., a social and behavioral research and consulting firm in Watertown, Massachusetts. Dr. Feinhandler is trained as a cultural anthropologist with degrees from the Departments of Sociology at Northwestern University, Anthropology at Syracuse University, and Social Relations at Harvard University. He has been an assistant professor in the Department of Psychiatry and the Department of Anthropology at Boston University. More recently, he was a lecturer in anthropology in the Department of Psychiatry at Harvard Medical School. His research activities have included a focus on social and cultural processes in everyday life, communities, and organizations. He has published articles, presented papers, and delivered testimony on various topics related to these areas.

H. Peter Gray is professor of economics and finance at Rutgers University, New Brunswick, New Jersey. A postwar degree from Cambridge University and seven years' business experience preceded his entry into the graduate program at the University of California at Berkeley. Since earning the Ph.D. degree in 1963, he has been professor of economics at Wayne State University in Detroit, visiting scholar at the Brookings Institution, and visiting professor at Thammasat University in Bangkok, Thailand, and Jilin University, China. At Rutgers, he has been chairman of economics at Douglass College and acting director of the undergraduate business program in addition to teaching in the Economics Department. He is currently associate dean of the Faculty of Professional Studies and chairman of the Department of Finance in the newly formed School of Business. The author of six books, he has published in many scholarly journals in Europe, Asia, and the United States.

Stephen C. Littlechild is professor of commerce and head of the Department of Industrial Economics and Business Studies, University of Birmingham, England. He has contributed extensively to the literature of professional economics, including the well known *The Fallacy of the Mixed Economy* published by the Institute of Economic Affairs, and recently was appointed to the Monopolies Commission in England.

James M. Savarese is President of James M. Savarese and Associates, a consulting firm in Washington, D.C. He was formerly the executive director of the American Federation of State, Local, and Municipal Employees.

William F. Shughart II is associate professor of economics at George Mason University, Fairfax, Virginia. He formerly served as a staff economist with the Federal Trade Commission and as special assistant to the director of the FTC's Bureau of Economics. A graduate of Texas A & M University, he has taught at the University of Arizona, Clemson University, and has published numerous articles in professional journals on the economics of antitrust, regulation, and public choice.

Charles D. Spielberger is professor of psychology and director of the Center for Research in Community Psychology at the University of South Florida, Tampa, Florida. From 1972 to 1977 he served as professor of psychology and director of the school's Doctoral Program in Clinical and Community Psychology. He previously taught at Duke University, Vanderbilt University, and at the National Institute of Mental Health in Bethesda, Maryland. He received his Ph.D. in psychology in 1954 from the University of Iowa. Dr. Spielberger's principal areas of research include stress, anxiety and anger, coronary-prone behavior, and personality. He has published many papers in various professional journals and has several editorial appointments. He has authored, edited, and contributed chapters to more than fifty books.

Ingo Walter is professor of economics and finance and chairman of the Department of International Business at the Graduate School of Business Administration of New York University. From 1971 to 1976 he served as the school's associate dean of academic affairs. He previously taught at the University of Missouri, St. Louis, where he was chairman of the Department of Economics from 1967 to 1970. He received his A.B. and M.S. degrees from Lehigh University and his Ph.D. degree in 1966 from New York University. Dr. Walter's principal areas of research include international trade policy, international banking, environmental economics, and economics of multinational corporate operations. He has published papers in various professional journals in these fields and is the author or editor of a dozen books, including a widely used textbook. One of his recent books is *Handbook of International Business,* published by John Wiley in 1982.

About the Editor

Robert D. Tollison is professor of economics and director of the Center for Study of Public Choice at George Mason University, Fairfax, Virginia. He is formerly director of the Bureau of Economics at the Federal Trade Commission. He has written extensively on economics and public policy, and recently published *The Theory of Public Choice—II* with James M. Buchanan.